The Complete Book of
Wood Mouldings

The Center Lumber Collection

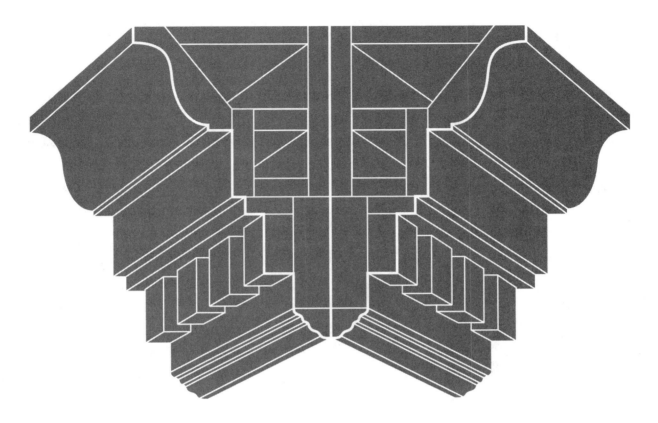

The Complete Book of
Wood Mouldings

*1,850 profiles for builders, decorators,
architects, and homeowners*

Nalla Wollen

Fox
Chapel Publishing

CAMBIUM PRESS

The Complete Book of Wood Mouldings

ISBN-13: 978–1–892836–25–0
ISBN-10: 1–892836–25–4

First printing: July 2006

A Cambium Press Title
John Kelsey, Editor

Cambium Press books are published by
Fox Chapel Publishing
1970 Broad Street
East Petersburg PA 17520
www.FoxChapelPublishing.com

Publisher's Cataloging-in-Publication Data

Wollen, Nalla.
  The complete book of wood mouldings : 1,850 profiles for builders, decorators, architects, and homeowners / Nalla Wollen. -- East Petersburg, PA : Cambium Press, c2006.

    p. ; cm.

    ISBN-13: 978-1-892836-25-0
    ISBN-10: 1-892836-25-4
    "The Center Lumber collection."--Cover.
    Includes index.

    1. Moldings--Patterns. 2. Interior decoration. 3. Woodwork.
  I. Title.

TH2553 .W65 2006
747--dc22   0607

Printed in the United States of America
10 9 8 7 6 5 4 3 2 1

CONTENTS

INTRODUCTION

The 1,850 wood mouldings in this selection are drawn from more than 4,000 custom-ground moulding knives accumulated over the past years here at Center Lumber Company (CLC) in Paterson, NJ. Center Lumber was established in 1896 by my family. Today we are a major producer of mouldings in the New York area, and one of the oldest producers in the United States.

Were it not for our Center Lumber customers, this book would not exist. Twenty five years ago we had one little room with two grinding wheels at which we hand-ground all our knives. Where space permitted, the room was packed with cubbyholes and drawers labeled with repeat customer's names. Since then, we've grown a new grinding room with more and more storage. The profiles carry numbers now, but we still have some of the same customers.

Over the years, our customers have ordered new shapes or asked us to copy existing samples. Further, there are many ways our existing profiles can be combined or modified, as can be seen on the following pages.

The selection here was made based on economy to manufacture, current popularity/taste, beauty to us, the selectors, and, in some cases, downright extravagance.

In the pages that follow, we grouped the mouldings by their function starting at the ceiling and ending at the floor. At the beginning of each grouping there is a three-dimensional drawing to help visualize how a moulding will look when installed. The drawings are full-size unless otherwise noted. Each moulding is accompanied by its Center Lumber catalog number and, importantly, by the dimensions of the finished moulding. This information is a source for architects, builders and woodworkers who wish to incorporate Center Lumber mouldings in their work. There is a comprehensive index allowing the user to quickly find any moulding in the book.

The moulding profiles in this book are also available on a CD containing PDF files of the pages themselves, plus a complete set of drawings in both DWG and EPS formats. The DWG files, in Autocad format, are meant for architects and builders who are preparing working drawings and presentation renderings. They may be directly imported into most professional drafting programs, and placed where needed. The EPS files, in Adobe Illustrator format, may be directly viewed and placed in most drawing and illustration programs. To obtain a copy of the mouldings CD, please contact the author directly at the address below.

For us at Center Lumber, this is a story book! We see certain profiles and they trigger memories of entire jobs and the customers who brought them to us. Manufacturing a beautiful product has brought us much satisfaction -- and this is a twenty-five year album of a tiny niche in the local economy which has fed us in many ways.

We hope you enjoy this book and put it to good use.

--Nalla Wollen, April 2006

Center Lumber Co.
85 Fulton Street
Paterson NJ 07509
201-742-8300

The mouldings in this collection have been selected and arranged by Nalla Wollen, the president of Center Lumber in Paterson, NJ. The drawings were prepared by Rob Chi of San Francisco, CA, and the page layouts by John Kelsey of Ridgefield, CT.

WHAT ARE MOULDINGS?

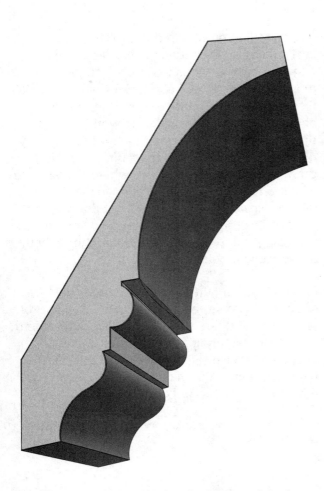

Mouldings create attractive bands of light and shadow, adding life and interest. CLC-1270, page 35.

Mouldings are lengths of wood whose surfaces have been machined to create attractive bands of light and shadow. Some have sharp edges and flats, some consist of soft, gentle curves, some combine both flats and curves in a pleasing composition. Most simple mouldings can be combined to create complex and beautiful effects.

We nail mouldings where walls meet floor or ceiling, and around door and window openings, for three fundamental and interrelated purposes:

Mouldings look good. They add variety and interest to a living space. They define areas and accentuate openings. They call attention to the proportions of the room and lead the eye from one feature to the next. They contribute a sense of finish and completion, a visual richness, to the interior environment. That's their aesthetic function.

Mouldings cover gaps. There's usually a gap or a ragged edge where different materials and surfaces connect or intersect. It's just about impossible to make a neat transition between drywall or wall paneling and a door jamb or a hardwood floor, but it doesn't matter because the door casing and the baseboard will cover the gaps. The door and window casings help seal out the weather, and firm up the connection of the jambs and frames to the structure of the building. Mouldings also protect delicate wall surfaces from cleaning equipment, bumping furniture, muddy boots, and dirty fingers. That's their technical function.

Mouldings add value. Elegant mouldings more than pay for themselves, not only in gracious living while you own the real estate, but also in the price appreciation you may expect when you sell it. Mouldings made from hardwoods add exceptional value to a property. That's their economic function.

The variety of mouldings you can buy is enormous, and may seem complicated at first glance. Actually, most mouldings are made up of a small number of very simple shapes, combined in infinitely various ways.

The pine mouldings at the home center are manufactured in large quantities, there aren't many shapes, the pieces are thin and the profiles lack crispness. Yet for low budget jobs pine is the right choice.

For complex shapes, period authenticity, and rich quality, builders go to custom quality manufacturers who archive thousands of moulding patterns -- Center Lumber Company in Paterson, NJ, has a collection of more than 4,000 knives, and daily grinds new knives.

Most stock and custom mouldings are made of poplar, a clear, stable hardwood that machines cleanly and paints well. Like their plaster ancestors, poplar mouldings are meant to be painted. Poplar also takes stain, so it can be finished to imitate more expensive hardwoods, or faux-finished to resemble marble or granite.

Manufacturers will also run stock or custom profiles in virtually any hardwood, for all types of finishing. It is worth noting that the more richly figured the wood, the less visible the contours of the moulding.

The price of a moulding depends on the size of the wood blank needed to manufacture it. Thickness of a moulding tends to drive the cost more than the width as it has the greater impact on the total volume, or board footage, of wood needed.

The diagram shows yields from standard thicknesses of rough lumber from which mouldings are made. Be sure when ordering mouldings that you add extra for miter joints, waste, and mistakes. If you measure the actual footage needed and add 10% to 15%, that should be sufficient.

4/4 (1 inch) rough lumber   yields $^{13}/_{16}$ inch thick profiles, maximum

5/4 (1¼ inch) rough lumber   yields   1$^{1}/_{16}$ inch thick profiles, maximum, requiring 25% more material than profiles from 4/4 lumber.

6/4 (1½ inch) rough lumber   yields   1$^{5}/_{16}$ inch thick profiles, maximum, requiring 50% more material than profiles from 4/4 lumber.

8/4 (2 inch) rough lumber   yields   1³/₄ inch thick profiles, maximum, requiring twice as much material as profiles from 4/4 lumber.

WHAT ARE MOULDINGS

WHERE MOULDINGS GO

The drawing below relates common mouldings to features of a room. For the purposes of this book, the mouldings have been organized into groupings from ceiling to floor and with four tab placements from top to bottom of the page edge to reflect the moulding's location.

1. Ceiling related -- Crowns, crown accessories, picture mouldings.

2. Wall, related to casing function -- Back band, casing, plinth, stool, door stop.

3. Wall, related to paneling -- Chair rail, paneling cap, panel moulding, tongue-and-groove paneling.

3. Miscellaneous -- Hand rail, bar rail, sill/drip cap, water table, oddities.

4. Floor related -- Base cap, baseboard, shoe.

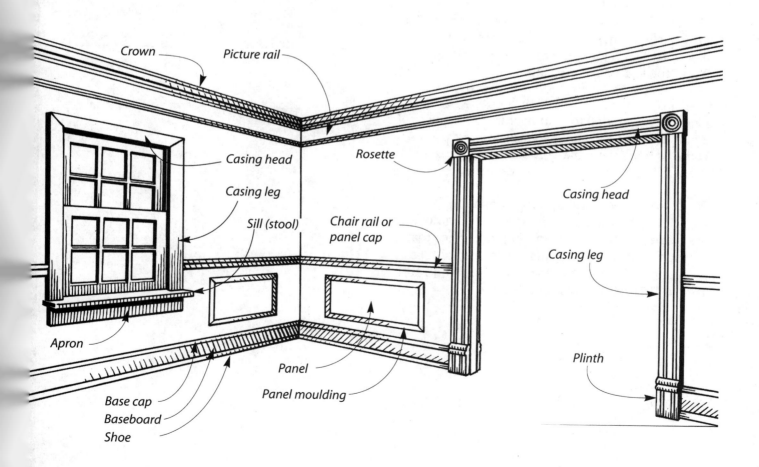

CEILING RELATED MOULDINGS

Crowns

Crown mouldings crown the room or trim the roofs of buildings. Which is the top of the crown?.is a frequent question. A guide to knowing is to relate the moulding to a royal crown, where the denser decoration can be imagined around the headband, and the part that springs from the head is less ornate, and then the top edge may have some lesser detail. However, folks freely reverse these profiles. If you have the opportunity to experiment with samples first, you will be able to see which way you like them.

Crowns are generally two types: Springback and solid. Springback crowns connect the ceiling with the wall, leaving a triangular-shaped void behind them. Solid crowns have a square back and would fit solidly into the wall-ceiling connection, but usually they are not used that way — it would waste material and be expensive to make. Solid crowns are generally used where the flat top stands free as wall decoration, or as pilaster capital, or is rabbeted to support a springback crown. Solid crowns, because of machine limitations, occur in the smaller sizes. However, when a large solid crown is required, often a casing can be used instead. Likewise some solid crowns can function as dramatic and unusual casings. Crowns are beautiful creations, and show off their shapes exceptionally well when mitered around an outside corner, say at a chimney bump-out above a mantel.

Crown, <2"   Small crowns can function variously as base caps, window stool trim, springboards for larger crowns, or brick moulds. If they are not the springback type they can be modified in many ways — thicker/thinner, with rabbets, grooves, or tongues.

Crown, 2"   Some smaller solid crowns can function nicely as casings and brick moulds. There are some beautiful and unusual pilaster caps in this selection also.

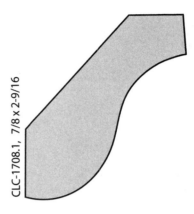

CLC-1708.1, 7/8 x 2-9/16

Springback crowns bridge ceiling and wall.

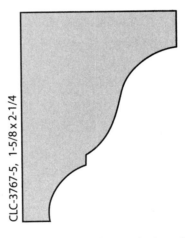

CLC-3767-5, 1-5/8 x 2-1/4

Solid crowns can be used when the top is visible.

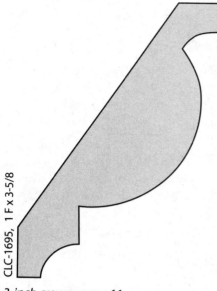

CLC-1695, 1 F x 3-5/8

3-inch crown, page 11

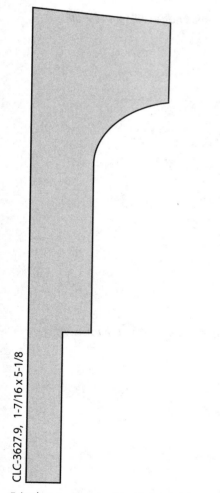

CLC-3627.9, 1-7/16 x 5-1/8

5-inch exterior trim band, page 22

Crown, 3"   Some of the shapes, alone, or with a cover piece at the top or a band of wood at the bottom, make dramatic capitals for columns and pilasters as well as room crowns.

Crown, 4"   Dentil crowns begin appearing in this section. They have a rabbet, in the face parallel to wall and ceiling, into which a strip of dentil moulding or other decorative trim, such as egg-and-dart, can be installed. Dentil mouldings come in various forms, sizes, proportions — the word itself comes from the French, dentille, a little tooth. Examples of profiles which may be cross-cut to make individual dentils can be found in crown accessories, page 110.

Crown, 5"   In the first pages there are two solid crowns. These were used on the exterior of a building but not as crowns at the eaves or beneath the soffit, but as a belt course. These, or something similar, also could be used in the traditional way at the eaves and soffits, which would avoid installing two pieces of crown plus fascia, but it would probably be the more expensive choice.

Crown, 6"   Along about 6-inch crown, one begins to see a variety in thickness of crown from 4/4 (1 inch) to 10/4 ($2^{1}/_2$ inch), that is, the thickness of lumber stock the crown is made from. The thicker a crown, the more expensive at a given width. Where a big crown is desired, and the budget is tight, one may look for a thinner one that might satisfy both constraints.

Crown, 7"   We have so many profiles...here is an example why. A very old profile from 25 years ago, CLC-805 (page 66) has a rabbet at the top that casts a shadow line. A customer came along who did not like the shadow, so we modified the profile, using the same cutters to come up with CLC-805.1. Later came another customer who liked the shadow, but wanted the crown to install more vertically and to change the beads. That required a new knife, CLC-1367.1M (page 65).

Crown, 8"   Some of the larger crowns are designed to replace two or more smaller pieces, and. so may be a cost saver. There are even a few made from 5/4 lumber, such as CLC-3346 and CLC 1265, (page 78).

Crown, 9"   Another way to suggest a large span of ceiling trim is to place a separate piece on the ceiling, see page 28, CLC-3916.5, with CLC-3916.6, or take the standard crown you select and place your baseboard at the top or on the wall at the back of your crown. The small piece added to crown CLC-3820.11 (page 85) is very effective. In tight spaces, such as a vestibule ceiling or in coffer boxes, it can create the illusion of ceiling panelling.

Crown, 10+"   Super large crowns or cornice can be made from more than one piece, see pages 102 to 104.

Crown, plasterlike   Over the years customers have brought us designs that emulate plaster mouldings, and turn out to be a lot less expensive. They will look particularly beautiful if you have an outside corner to trim.

Crown accessories   Crown accessories, or embellishments, aid the transformation of a single crown into a cornice. In this section you will find profiles that will imitate soffit, others that can be cross-cut to make dentils (modillions) and also platform shapes upon which crowns can be installed.

Picture Rail   Picture rails are sometimes called picture-hanging mouldings. Some serve only as decorative bands that might not be strong enough to support heavy hangings. CLC-985 (page 113) is a good example of a strong one. It would also make an interesting casing with back shadowing along the outside or heel.

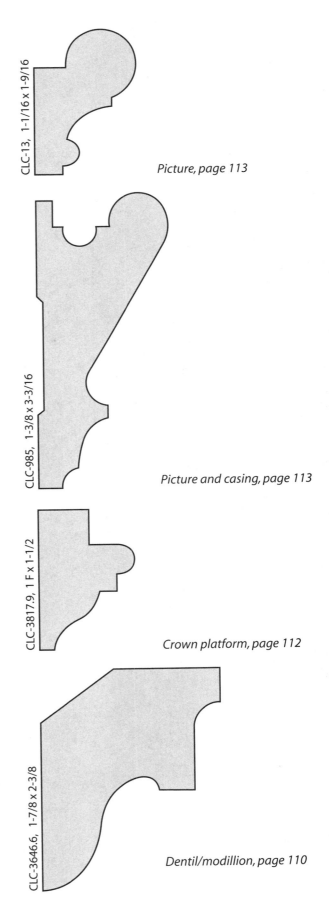

CLC-13, 1-1/16 x 1-9/16

Picture, page 113

CLC-985, 1-3/8 x 3-3/16

Picture and casing, page 113

CLC-3817.9, 1 F x 1-1/2

Crown platform, page 112

CLC-3646.6, 1-7/8 x 2-3/8

Dentil/modillion, page 110

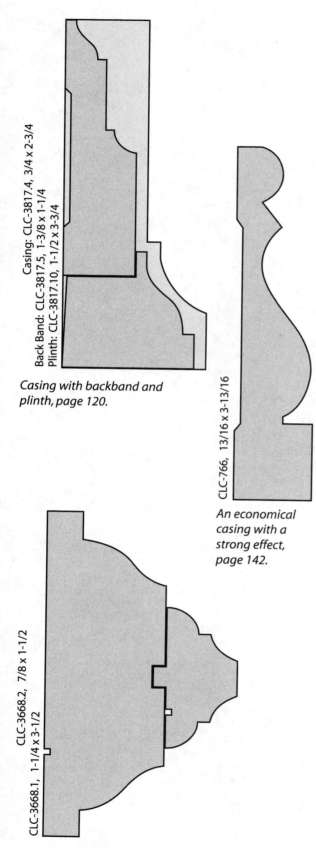

Casing: CLC-3817.4, 3/4 x 2-3/4
Back Band: CLC-3817.5, 1-3/8 x 1-1/4
Plinth: CLC-3817.10, 1-1/2 x 3-3/4

Casing with backband and plinth, page 120.

CLC-766, 13/16 x 3-13/16

An economical casing with a strong effect, page 142.

CLC-3668.2, 7/8 x 1-1/2
CLC-3668.1, 1-1/4 x 3-1/2

A lavish two-piece chair rail, page 145.

WALL RELATED

Casings

Casings encase door and window openings. They cover gaps between the opening frame and the wall surface. Casings usually start thin at one edge and end up as thick as the material they are made from will allow at the other edge. Sometimes, the thin edge is called toe and the thick, heel. Routinely the toe is placed on the frame/jamb of the opening, set back $1/4$ inch or so from the exposed face of the jamb. This setback is called a reveal. The vertical pieces of the opening trim are called legs or side-casings and the horizontal, top piece is called a head.

There are two basic styles of casing installation: Legs and head all the same profile are mitered at the top corners, or legs are one profile and the head is another, with the legs butt-joined into the head. The head may be very ornate and may include a pediment. The same is true for windows if a stool (window sill) is used. If there is an apron beneath the stool, it's likely to be the same profile as the legs. If there is no stool, then four pieces of the same profile are used, mitered at all four corners and called picture framing. Door legs may end at the floor or upon a plinth block. When no plinth is used, be sure that the outside edge of the casing is thicker than the baseboard so no end grain will show.

Back band   Back bands appear to be used for a number of reasons: To make a standard house casing more impressive; to ease installation where casing size needs to vary; to appear older in style as in times when mouldings were hand-planed and made up of small pieces.

Chair rail   Chair rails provide a visual break in broad expanses of wall, they offer an attractive means of capping wall paneling or wainscoting, and they continue to serve their traditional function of keeping chair backs from damaging the wall surface. Big voluptuous chair rails are called bolection mouldings. They may be used as casings, chair rails and mantel surrounds.

Plinth   Plinth is a block, often with a special

profile to complement the casing, located on the floor at the intersection of the casing and baseboard. People install plinth for the look of it and the way the casing looks butting into it. It prevents carpeting from obscuring the casing's shape. It also enables base parts to butt into something without exposed endgrain {which the casing may not be thick enough to accomplish). Casing running straight to the floor is also a good look, and it is less expensive: one less trim to setup and run, plus less detailed installation.

Stool Stool is interior window sill material. A brief sampling is shown. Many of the examples are simply one of many small moulding profiles modified wider. Stool is supported partially by the apron installed beneath it. Apron may be the same as the casing, or a piece of less detailed design, or in some situations a composite of several pieces including a bracket type to support a super-wide stool. Usually apron and stool are mitered and returned to the wall.

Stop Door stop is applied to all three pieces of the door jamb at the point where it can stop the door from swinging any farther than a position perpendicular to the jamb.

Paneling related Here are included various parts to make up wall paneling, excluding stile and rail flat stock pieces and sheet goods. However, chair rail may stand alone, as may panel moulding, applied directly to the wall. Chair rail may also be used as casing.

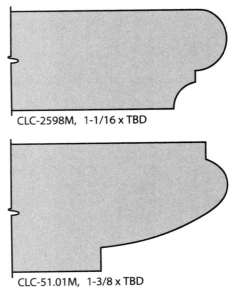

CLC-2598M, 1-1/16 x TBD

CLC-51.01M, 1-3/8 x TBD

A standard and not-so-standard stool, page 199.

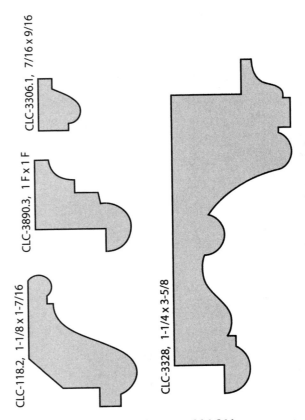

CLC-3306.1, 7/16 x 9/16

CLC-3890.3, 1 F x 1 F

CLC-118.2, 1-1/8 x 1-7/16

CLC-3328, 1-1/4 x 3-5/8

A variety of panel moulds, pages 206-211.

FLOOR RELATED

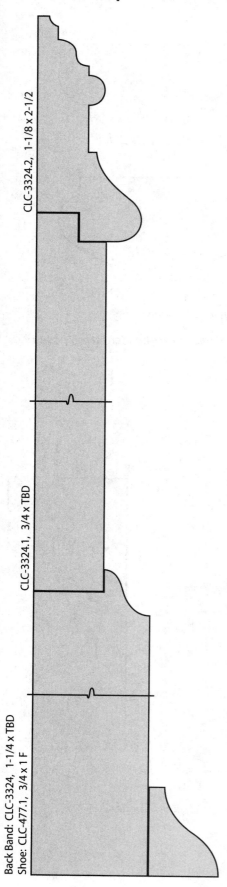

CLC-3324.2, 1-1/8 x 2-1/2

CLC-3324.1, 3/4 x TBD

Back Band: CLC-3324, 1-1/4 x TBD
Shoe: CLC-477.1, 3/4 x 1 F

FLOOR RELATED

Baseboard

Baseboard hides the junction of floor and wall. It may be one or several pieces. Electrical outlets can be located in the base if desired. One-piece base is usually less expensive to manufacture and install than two-piece. Many people prefer to make base in two or more pieces for ease of installation.

Shoe   Shoe mould hides the gap between the base and the floor. The flooring is installed first, then the shoe is nailed to the base to cover gaps.

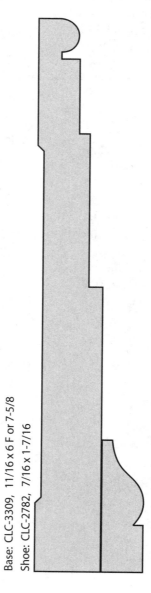

Base: CLC-3309, 11/16 x 6 F or 7-5/8
Shoe: CLC-2782, 7/16 x 1-7/16

Composite baseboards, pages 250 and 254.

PROFILE MODIFICATION

Modifyng an existing profile is easy and can save
the cost of grinding new knives.

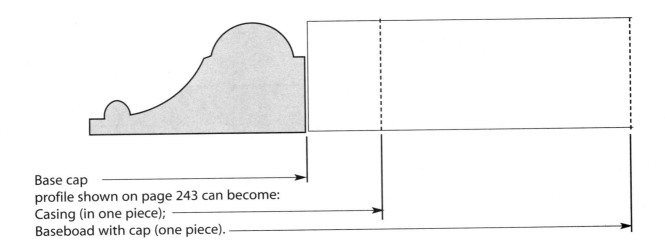

Base cap
profile shown on page 243 can become:
Casing (in one piece);
Baseboad with cap (one piece).

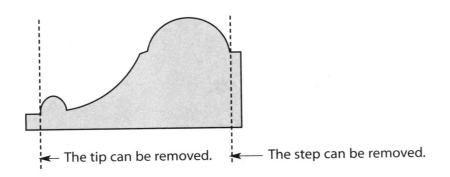

←— The tip can be removed.   ←— The step can be removed.

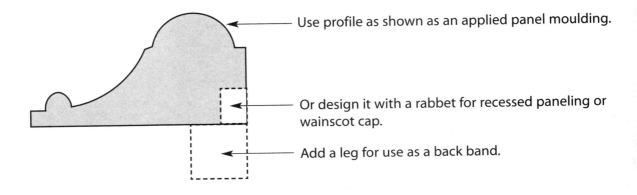

—— Use profile as shown as an applied panel moulding.

—— Or design it with a rabbet for recessed paneling or
wainscot cap.

—— Add a leg for use as a back band.

A FEW BASIC TERMS

All mouldings are made up of a few basic shapes, as shown at right. Some definitions:

Rabbet: a right-angle cut into the material.

Tongue: a U-shaped or 3-sided rectangular protrusion milled from the material, usually designed to fit into a corresponding groove.

Groove: A U-shaped or 3-sided rectangular shape milled into the material.

Plow: a wide groove as in the underside of a hand rail.

Incidentally, on the back of symmetrical mouldings and near-symmetrical mouldings we mill a tiny groove to facilitate installation.

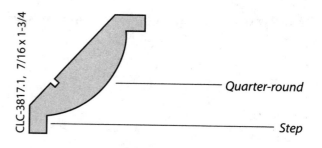

Quarter-round

Step

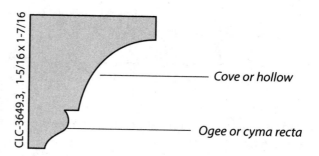

Cove or hollow

Ogee or cyma recta

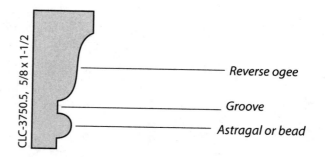

Reverse ogee

Groove

Astragal or bead

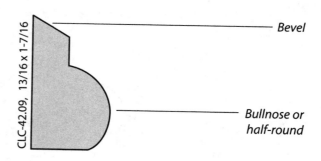

Bevel

Bullnose or half-round

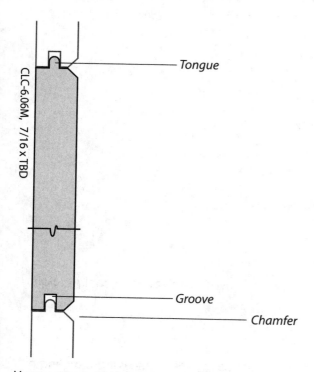

Tongue

Groove

Chamfer

V-groove tongue-and-groove paneling. The "V" is created by joining two pieces of moulding that each have chamfered edges.

Complex mouldings consist of a few simple shapes arranged in harmonious ways.

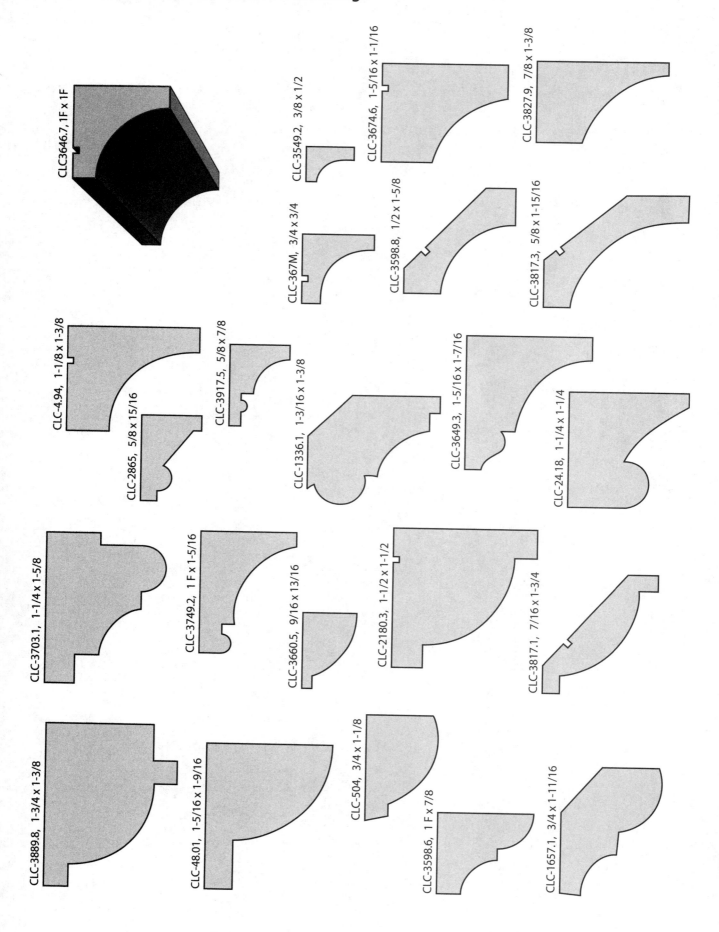

CLC3646.7, 1F x 1F

CLC-3549.2, 3/8 x 1/2

CLC-3674.6, 1-5/16 x 1-1/16

CLC-3827.9, 7/8 x 1-3/8

CLC-367M, 3/4 x 3/4

CLC-3598.8, 1/2 x 1-5/8

CLC-3817.3, 5/8 x 1-15/16

CLC-4.94, 1-1/8 x 1-3/8

CLC-2865, 5/8 x 15/16

CLC-3917.5, 5/8 x 7/8

CLC-1336.1, 1-3/16 x 1-3/8

CLC-3649.3, 1-5/16 x 1-7/16

CLC-24.18, 1-1/4 x 1-1/4

CLC-3703.1, 1-1/4 x 1-5/8

CLC-3749.2, 1 F x 1-5/16

CLC-3660.5, 9/16 x 13/16

CLC-2180.3, 1-1/2 x 1-1/2

CLC-3817.1, 7/16 x 1-3/4

CLC-3889.8, 1-3/4 x 1-3/8

CLC-48.01, 1-5/16 x 1-9/16

CLC-504, 3/4 x 1-1/8

CLC-3598.6, 1 F x 7/8

CLC-1657.1, 3/4 x 1-11/16

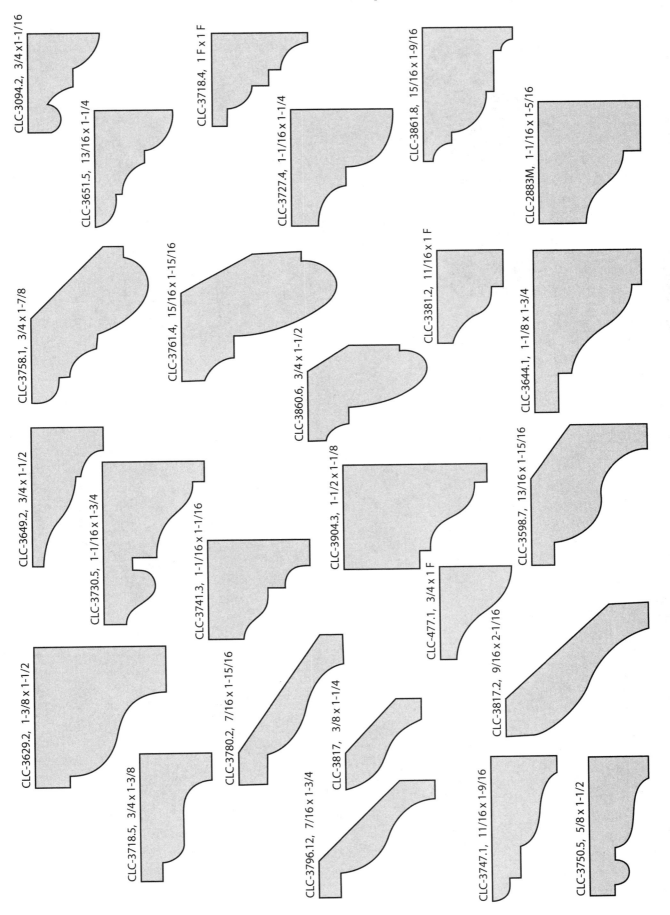

CLC-3094.2, 3/4 x1-1/16

CLC-3651.5, 13/16 x 1-1/4

CLC-3718.4, 1 F x 1 F

CLC-3727.4, 1-1/16 x 1-1/4

CLC-3861.8, 15/16 x 1-9/16

CLC-2883M, 1-1/16 x 1-5/16

CLC-3758.1, 3/4 x 1-7/8

CLC-3761.4, 15/16 x 1-15/16

CLC-3860.6, 3/4 x 1-1/2

CLC-3381.2, 11/16 x 1 F

CLC-3644.1, 1-1/8 x 1-3/4

CLC-3649.2, 3/4 x 1-1/2

CLC-3730.5, 1-1/16 x 1-3/4

CLC-3741.3, 1-1/16 x 1-1/16

CLC-3904.3, 1-1/2 x 1-1/8

CLC-477.1, 3/4 x 1 F

CLC-3598.7, 13/16 x 1-15/16

CLC-3629.2, 1-3/8 x 1-1/2

CLC-3780.2, 7/16 x 1-15/16

CLC-3718.5, 3/4 x 1-3/8

CLC-3817, 3/8 x 1-1/4

CLC-3796.12, 7/16 x 1-3/4

CLC-3817.2, 9/16 x 2-1/16

CLC-3747.1, 11/16 x 1-9/16

CLC-3750.5, 5/8 x 1-1/2

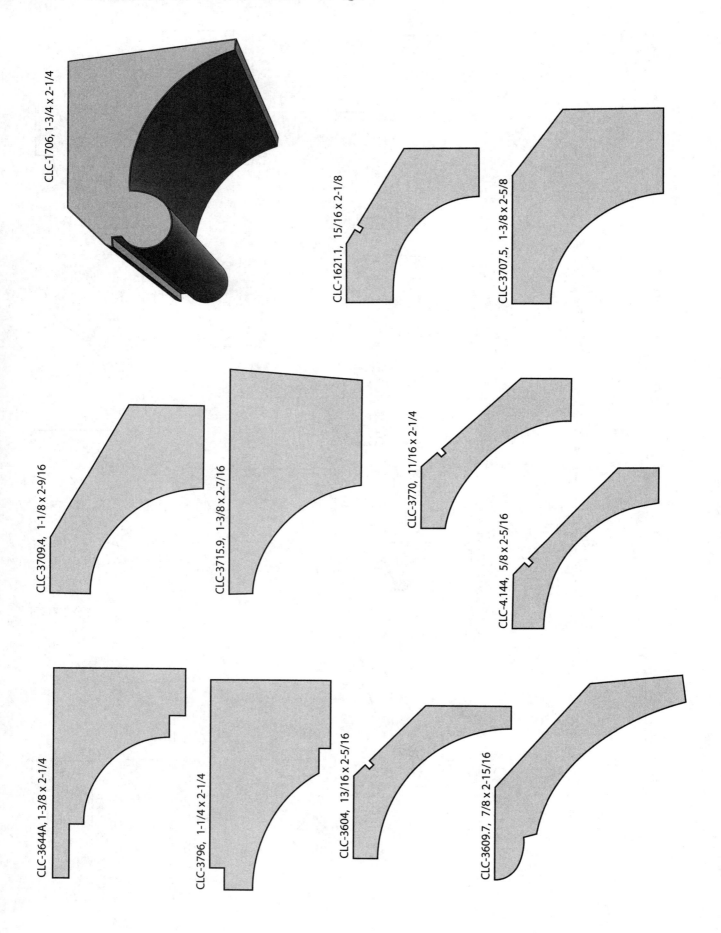

CLC-1706, 1-3/4 x 2-1/4

CLC-1621.1, 15/16 x 2-1/8

CLC-3707.5, 1-3/8 x 2-5/8

CLC-3709.4, 1-1/8 x 2-9/16

CLC-3715.9, 1-3/8 x 2-7/16

CLC-3770, 11/16 x 2-1/4

CLC-4.144, 5/8 x 2-5/16

CLC-3644A, 1-3/8 x 2-1/4

CLC-3796, 1-1/4 x 2-1/4

CLC-3604, 13/16 x 2-5/16

CLC-3609.7, 7/8 x 2-15/16

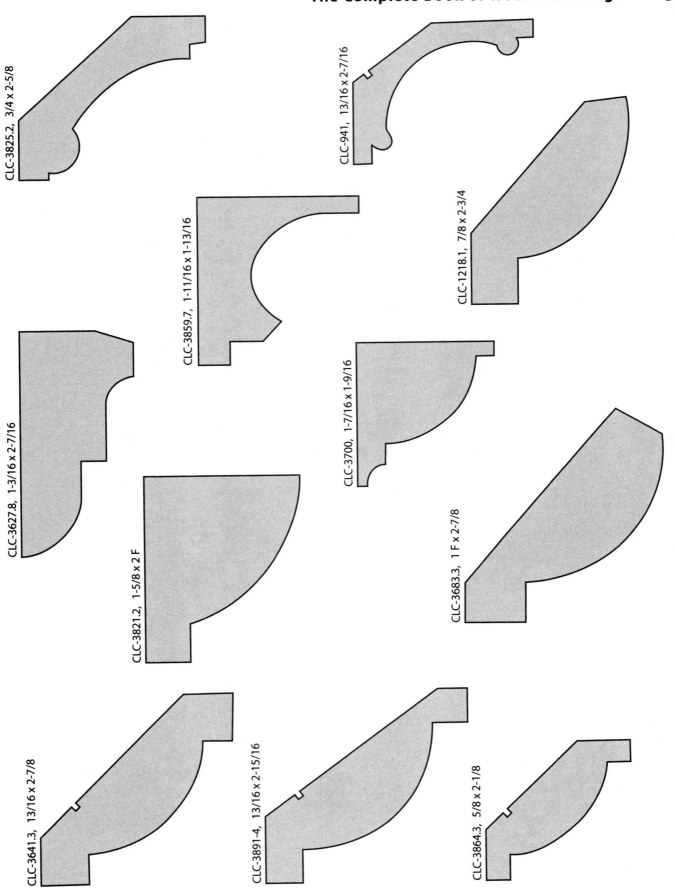

CLC-3825.2, 3/4 x 2-5/8

CLC-941, 13/16 x 2-7/16

CLC-1218.1, 7/8 x 2-3/4

CLC-3859.7, 1-11/16 x 1-13/16

CLC-3627.8, 1-3/16 x 2-7/16

CLC-3700, 1-7/16 x 1-9/16

CLC-3821.2, 1-5/8 x 2 F

CLC-3683.3, 1 F x 2-7/8

CLC-3641.3, 13/16 x 2-7/8

CLC-3891-4, 13/16 x 2-15/16

CLC-3864.3, 5/8 x 2-1/8

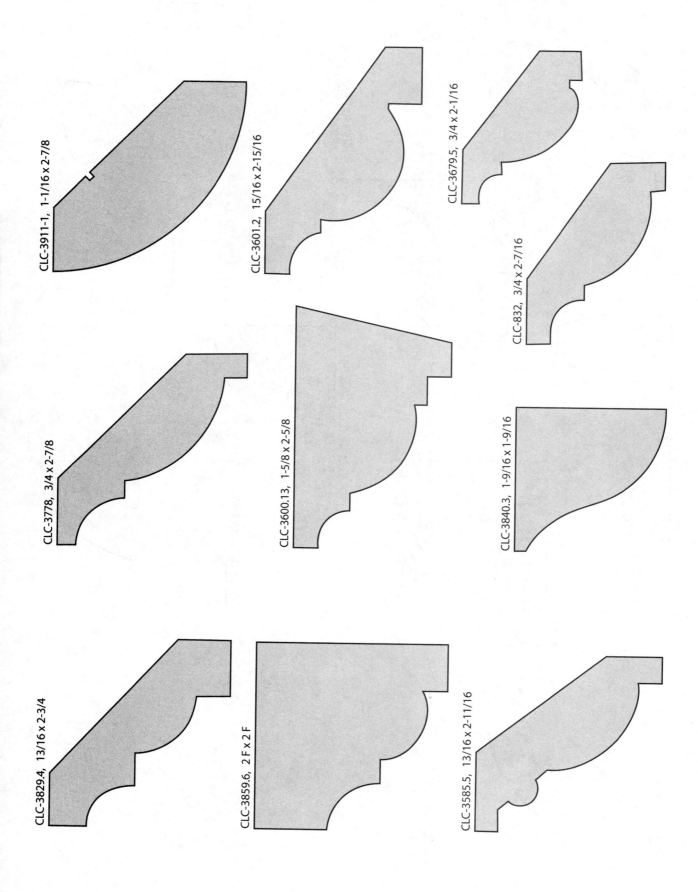

CLC-3911-1, 1-1/16 x 2-7/8

CLC-3601.2, 15/16 x 2-15/16

CLC-3679.5, 3/4 x 2-1/16

CLC-832, 3/4 x 2-7/16

CLC-3778, 3/4 x 2-7/8

CLC-3600.13, 1-5/8 x 2-5/8

CLC-3840.3, 1-9/16 x 1-9/16

CLC-3829.4, 13/16 x 2-3/4

CLC-3859.6, 2 F x 2 F

CLC-3585.5, 13/16 x 2-11/16

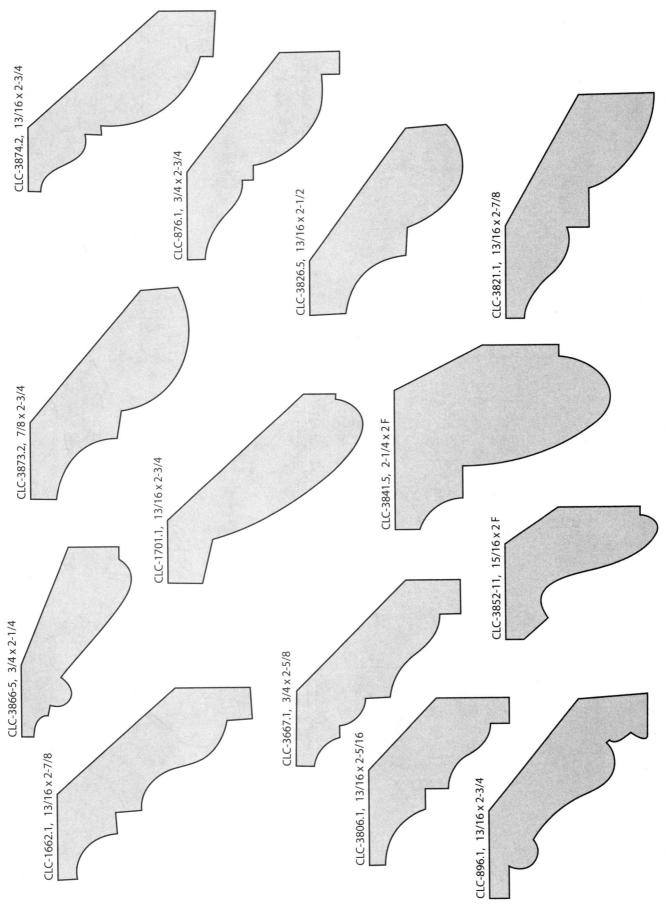

CLC-3874.2, 13/16 x 2-3/4

CLC-876.1, 3/4 x 2-3/4

CLC-3826.5, 13/16 x 2-1/2

CLC-3821.1, 13/16 x 2-7/8

CLC-3873.2, 7/8 x 2-3/4

CLC-1701.1, 13/16 x 2-3/4

CLC-3841.5, 2-1/4 x 2 F

CLC-3852-11, 15/16 x 2 F

CLC-3866-5, 3/4 x 2-1/4

CLC-1662.1, 13/16 x 2-7/8

CLC-3667.1, 3/4 x 2-5/8

CLC-3806.1, 13/16 x 2-5/16

CLC-896.1, 13/16 x 2-3/4

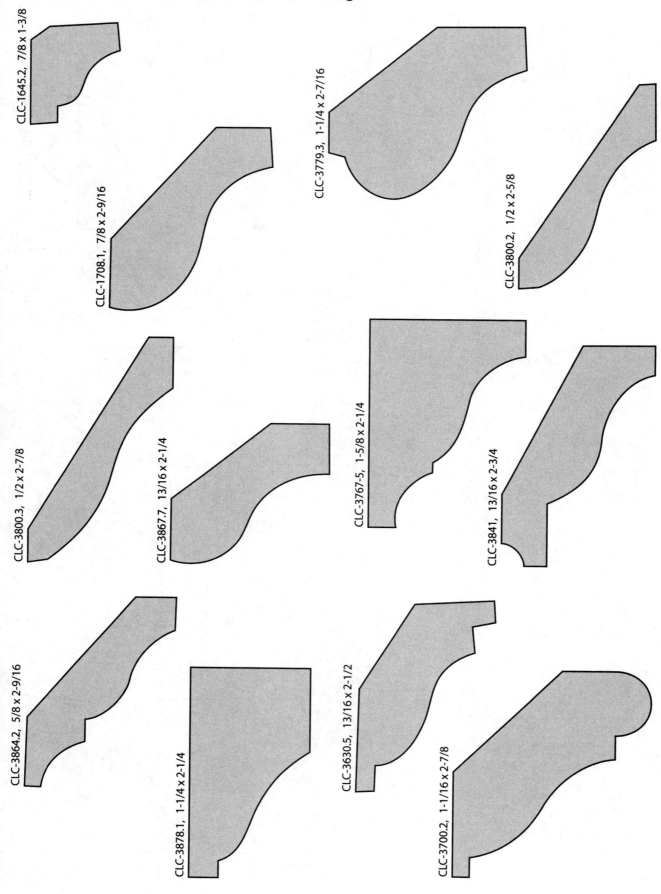

CLC-1645.2, 7/8 x 1-3/8

CLC-1708.1, 7/8 x 2-9/16

CLC-3779.3, 1-1/4 x 2-7/16

CLC-3800.2, 1/2 x 2-5/8

CLC-3800.3, 1/2 x 2-7/8

CLC-3867.7, 13/16 x 2-1/4

CLC-3767-5, 1-5/8 x 2-1/4

CLC-3841, 13/16 x 2-3/4

CLC-3864.2, 5/8 x 2-9/16

CLC-3878.1, 1-1/4 x 2-1/4

CLC-3630.5, 13/16 x 2-1/2

CLC-3700.2, 1-1/16 x 2-7/8

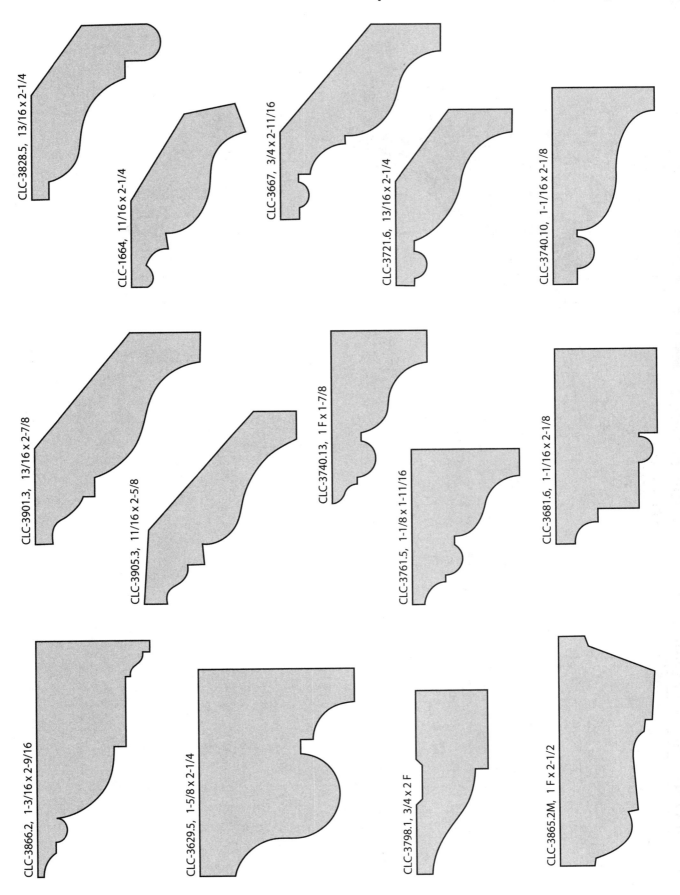

CLC-3828.5, 13/16 x 2-1/4

CLC-1664, 11/16 x 2-1/4

CLC-3667, 3/4 x 2-11/16

CLC-3721.6, 13/16 x 2-1/4

CLC-3740.10, 1-1/16 x 2-1/8

CLC-3901.3, 13/16 x 2-7/8

CLC-3905.3, 11/16 x 2-5/8

CLC-3740.13, 1 F x 1-7/8

CLC-3761.5, 1-1/8 x 1-11/16

CLC-3681.6, 1-1/16 x 2-1/8

CLC-3866.2, 1-3/16 x 2-9/16

CLC-3629.5, 1-5/8 x 2-1/4

CLC-3798.1, 3/4 x 2 F

CLC-3865.2M, 1 F x 2-1/2

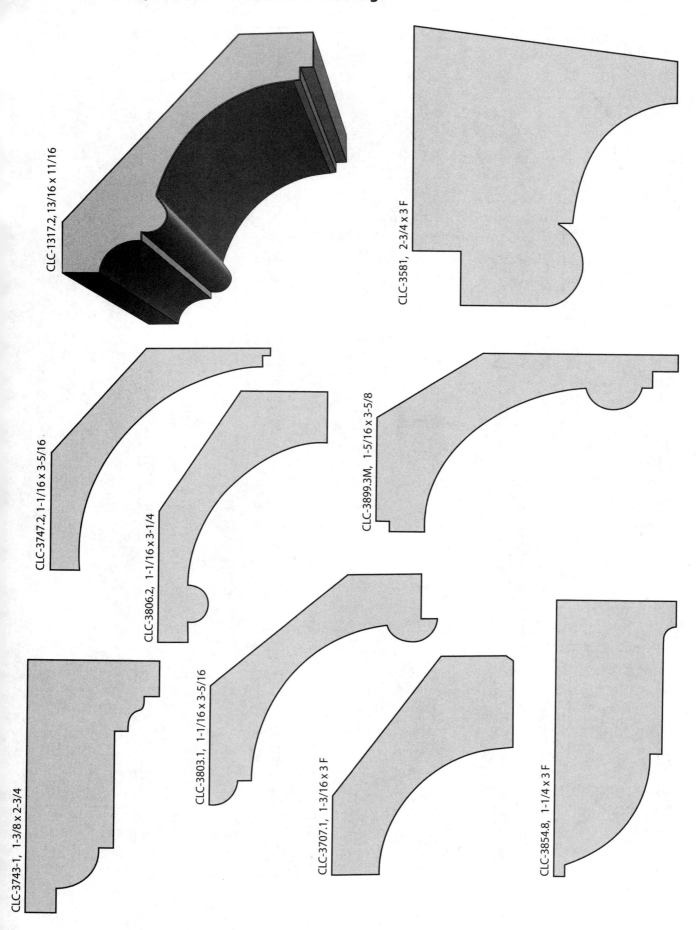

CLC-1317.2, 13/16 x 11/16

CLC-3581, 2-3/4 x 3 F

CLC-3747.2, 1-1/16 x 3-5/16

CLC-3806.2, 1-1/16 x 3-1/4

CLC-3899.3M, 1-5/16 x 3-5/8

CLC-3743-1, 1-3/8 x 2-3/4

CLC-3803.1, 1-1/16 x 3-5/16

CLC-3707.1, 1-3/16 x 3 F

CLC-3854.8, 1-1/4 x 3 F

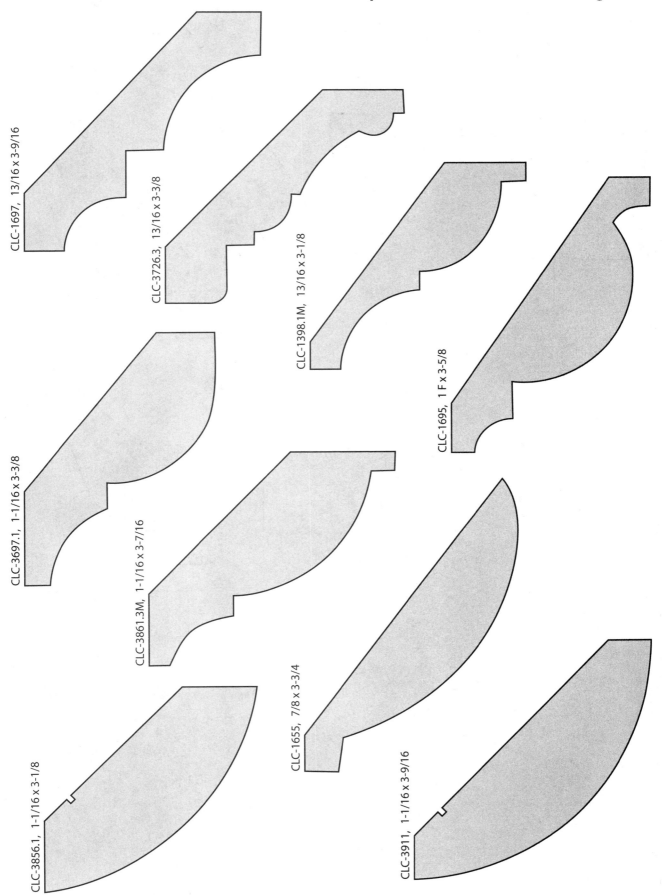

CLC-1697, 13/16 x 3-9/16

CLC-3726.3, 13/16 x 3-3/8

CLC-1398.1M, 13/16 x 3-1/8

CLC-1695, 1 F x 3-5/8

CLC-3697.1, 1-1/16 x 3-3/8

CLC-3861.3M, 1-1/16 x 3-7/16

CLC-3856.1, 1-1/16 x 3-1/8

CLC-1655, 7/8 x 3-3/4

CLC-3911, 1-1/16 x 3-9/16

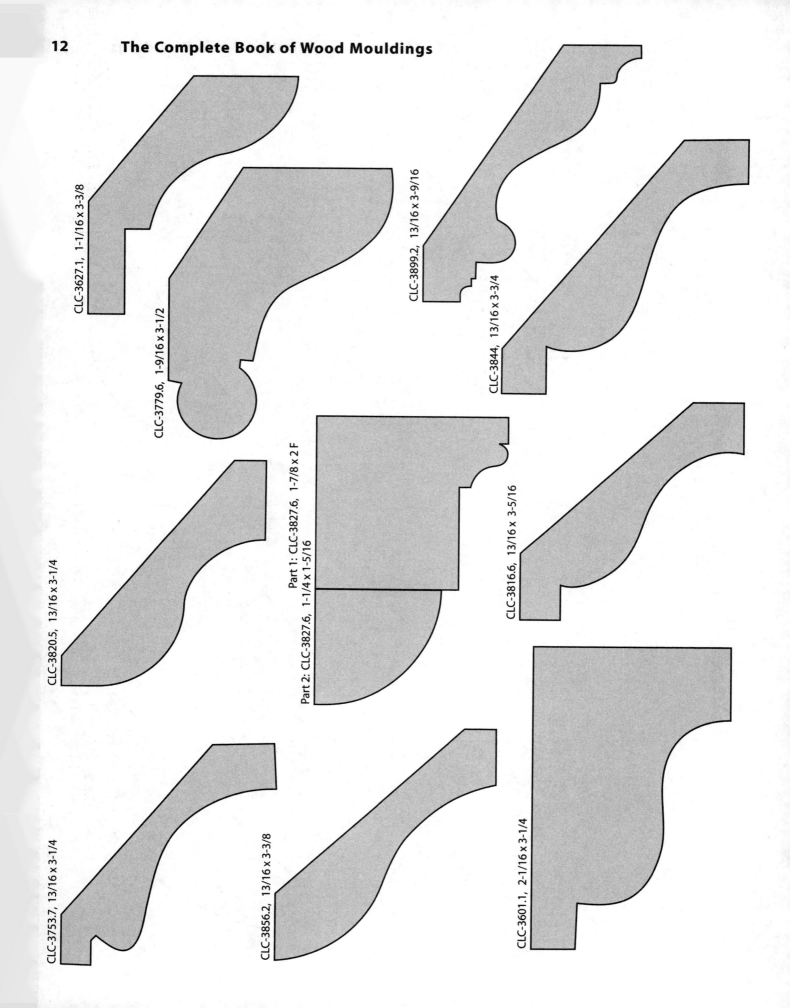

CLC-3627.1, 1-1/16 x 3-3/8

CLC-3779.6, 1-9/16 x 3-1/2

CLC-3899.2, 13/16 x 3-9/16

CLC-3844, 13/16 x 3-3/4

CLC-3820.5, 13/16 x 3-1/4

Part 1: CLC-3827.6, 1-7/8 x 2 F

Part 2: CLC-3827.6, 1-1/4 x 1-5/16

CLC-3816.6, 13/16 x 3-5/16

CLC-3753.7, 13/16 x 3-1/4

CLC-3856.2, 13/16 x 3-3/8

CLC-3601.1, 2-1/16 x 3-1/4

CLC-1656.2, 13/16 x 3-1/4

CLC-1664.1, 13/16 x 3-1/2

CLC-1708, 1-1/16 x 3 F

CLC-3743.8, 1/2 x 3-1/8

CLC-3602, 1-13/16 x 2-13/16

CLC-1638.1M, 1-1/8 x 3 F

CLC-3748-10, 13/16 x 3-3/8

CLC-3749, 1-1/16 x 3-1/16

CLC-879.1, 3/4 x 3-5/8

CLC-3646.6, 1-7/8 x 2-3/8

CLC-3668.4, 13/16 x 3-3/4

CLC-3700.7, 13/16 x 3-7/16

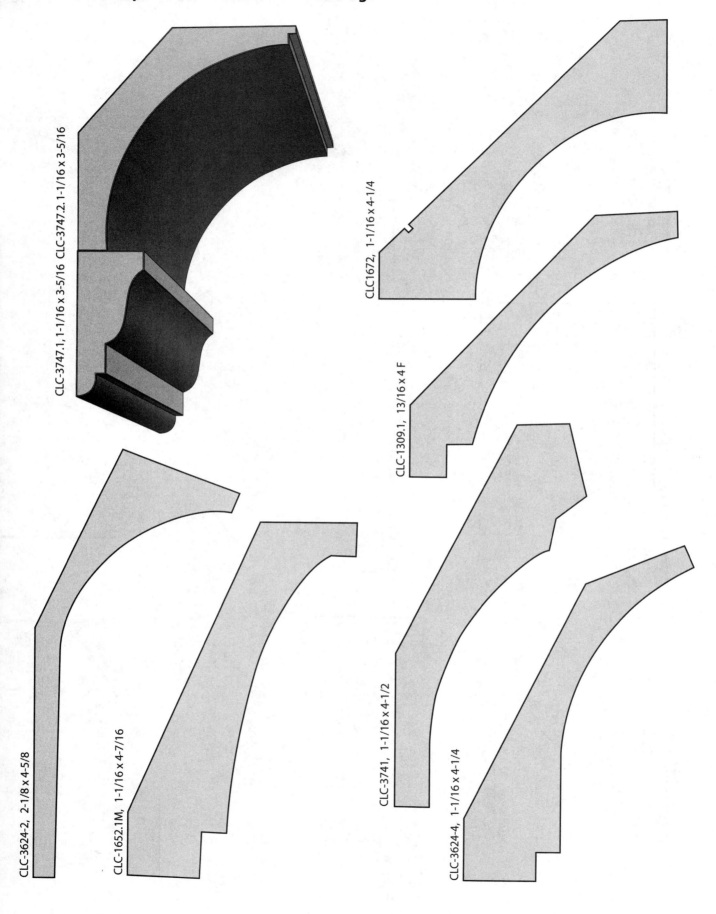

CLC-3747.1, 1-1/16 x 3-5/16 CLC-3747.2, 1-1/16 x 3-5/16

CLC1672, 1-1/16 x 4-1/4

CLC-1309.1, 13/16 x 4 F

CLC-3624-2, 2-1/8 x 4-5/8

CLC-1652.1M, 1-1/16 x 4-7/16

CLC-3741, 1-1/16 x 4-1/2

CLC-3624-4, 1-1/16 x 4-1/4

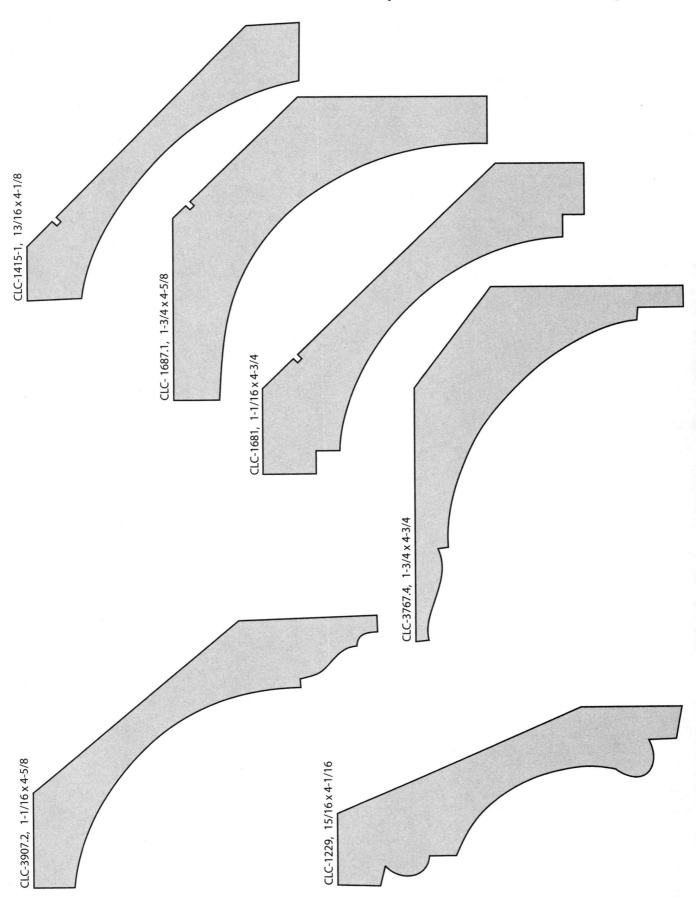

CLC-1415-1, 13/16 x 4-1/8

CLC-1687.1, 1-3/4 x 4-5/8

CLC-1681, 1-1/16 x 4-3/4

CLC-3767.4, 1-3/4 x 4-3/4

CLC-3907.2, 1-1/16 x 4-5/8

CLC-1229, 15/16 x 4-1/16

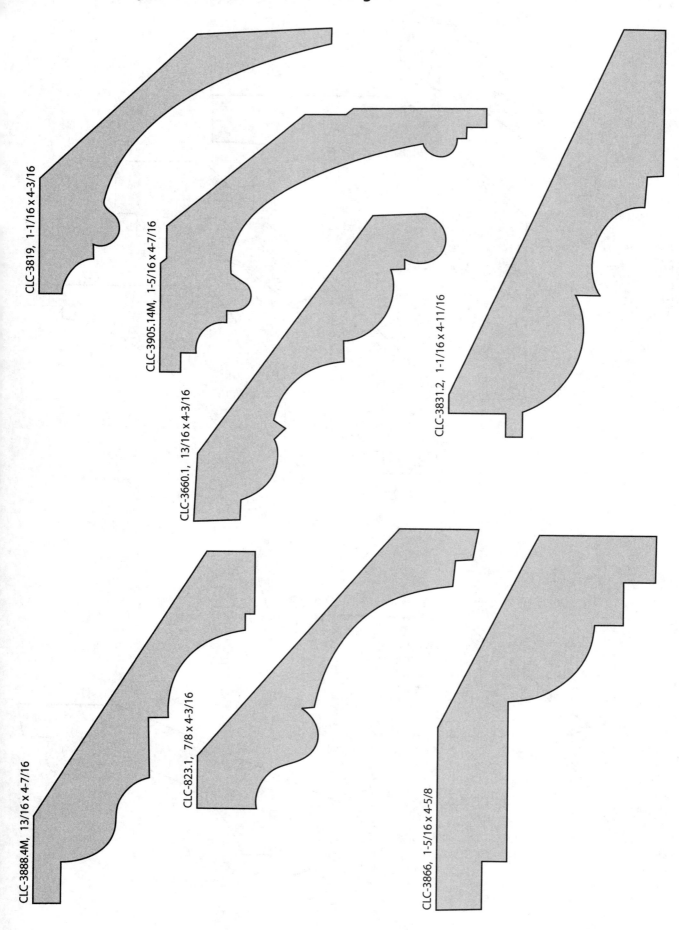

CLC-3819, 1-1/16 x 4-3/16

CLC-3905.14M, 1-5/16 x 4-7/16

CLC-3660.1, 13/16 x 4-3/16

CLC-3831.2, 1-1/16 x 4-11/16

CLC-3888.4M, 13/16 x 4-7/16

CLC-823.1, 7/8 x 4-3/16

CLC-3866, 1-5/16 x 4-5/8

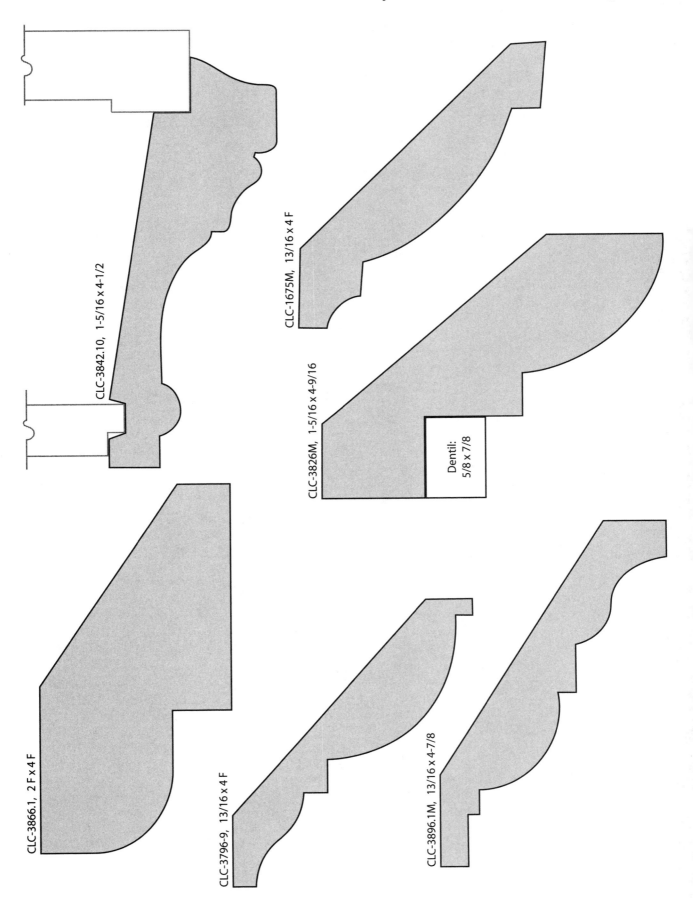

CLC-3842.10, 1-5/16 x 4-1/2

CLC-1675M, 13/16 x 4 F

CLC-3826M, 1-5/16 x 4-9/16

Dentil:
5/8 x 7/8

CLC-3866.1, 2 F x 4 F

CLC-3796-9, 13/16 x 4 F

CLC-3896.1M, 13/16 x 4-7/8

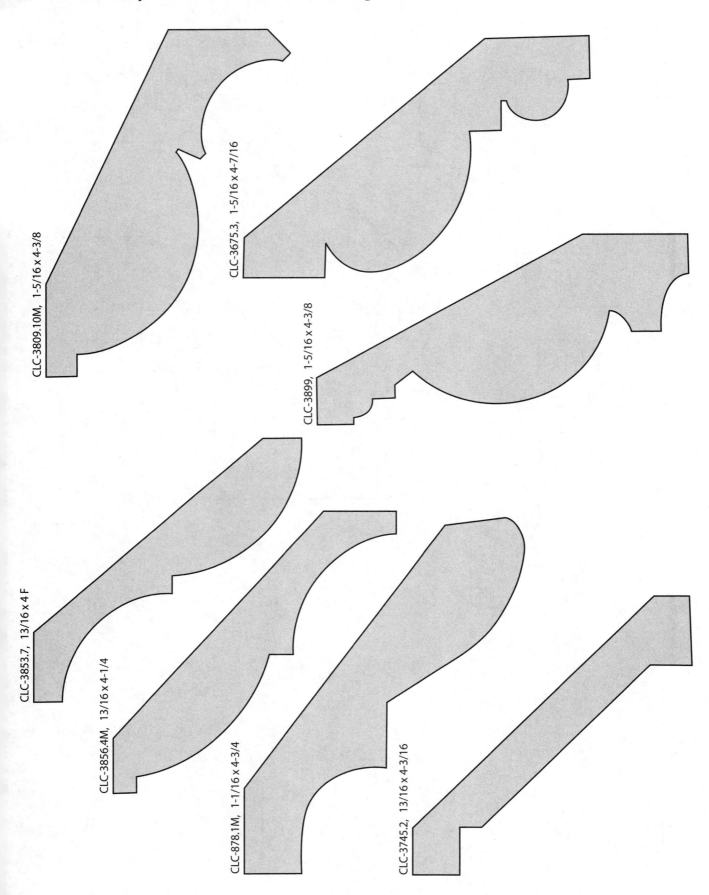

CLC-3809.10M, 1-5/16 x 4-3/8

CLC-3675.3, 1-5/16 x 4-7/16

CLC-3899, 1-5/16 x 4-3/8

CLC-3853.7, 13/16 x 4 F

CLC-3856.4M, 13/16 x 4-1/4

CLC-878.1M, 1-1/16 x 4-3/4

CLC-3745.2, 13/16 x 4-3/16

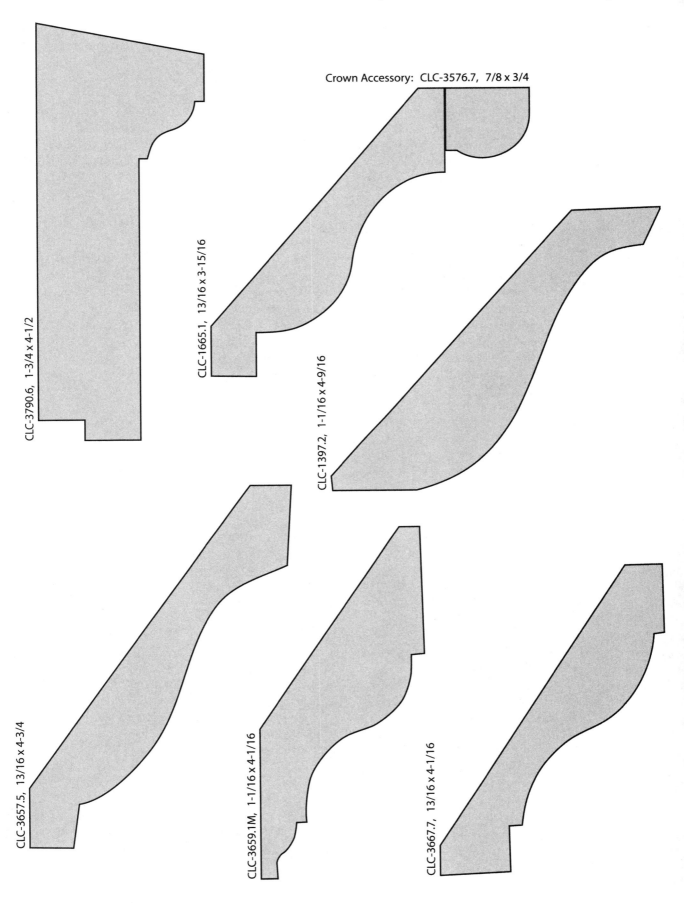

CLC-3790.6, 1-3/4 x 4-1/2

Crown Accessory: CLC-3576.7, 7/8 x 3/4

CLC-1665.1, 13/16 x 3-15/16

CLC-1397.2, 1-1/16 x 4-9/16

CLC-3657.5, 13/16 x 4-3/4

CLC-3659.1M, 1-1/16 x 4-1/16

CLC-3667.7, 13/16 x 4-1/16

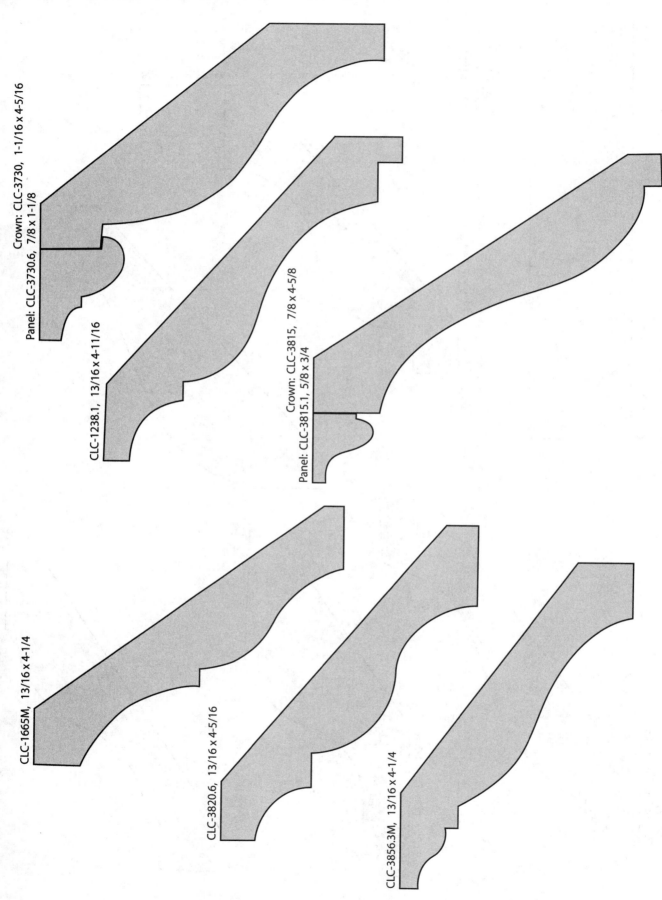

Crown: CLC-3730, 1-1/16 x 4-5/16

Panel: CLC-3730.6, 7/8 x 1-1/8

CLC-1238.1, 13/16 x 4-11/16

Crown: CLC-3815, 7/8 x 4-5/8

Panel: CLC-3815.1, 5/8 x 3/4

CLC-1665M, 13/16 x 4-1/4

CLC-3820.6, 13/16 x 4-5/16

CLC-3856.3M, 13/16 x 4-1/4

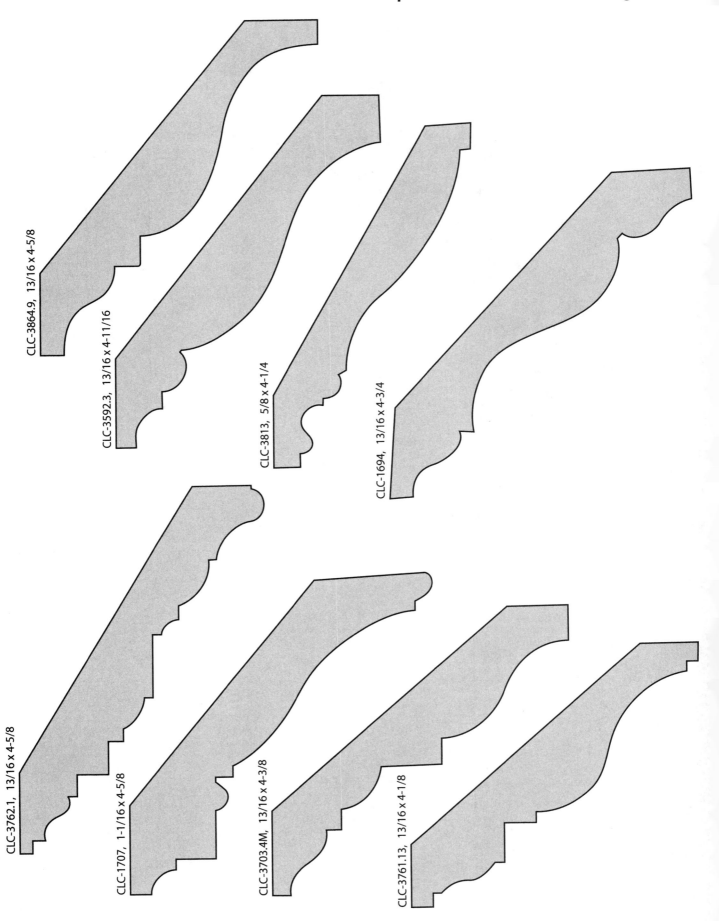

CLC-3864.9, 13/16 x 4-5/8

CLC-3592.3, 13/16 x 4-11/16

CLC-3813, 5/8 x 4-1/4

CLC-1694, 13/16 x 4-3/4

CLC-3762.1, 13/16 x 4-5/8

CLC-1707, 1-1/16 x 4-5/8

CLC-3703.4M, 13/16 x 4-3/8

CLC-3761.13, 13/16 x 4-1/8

CROWN 5"

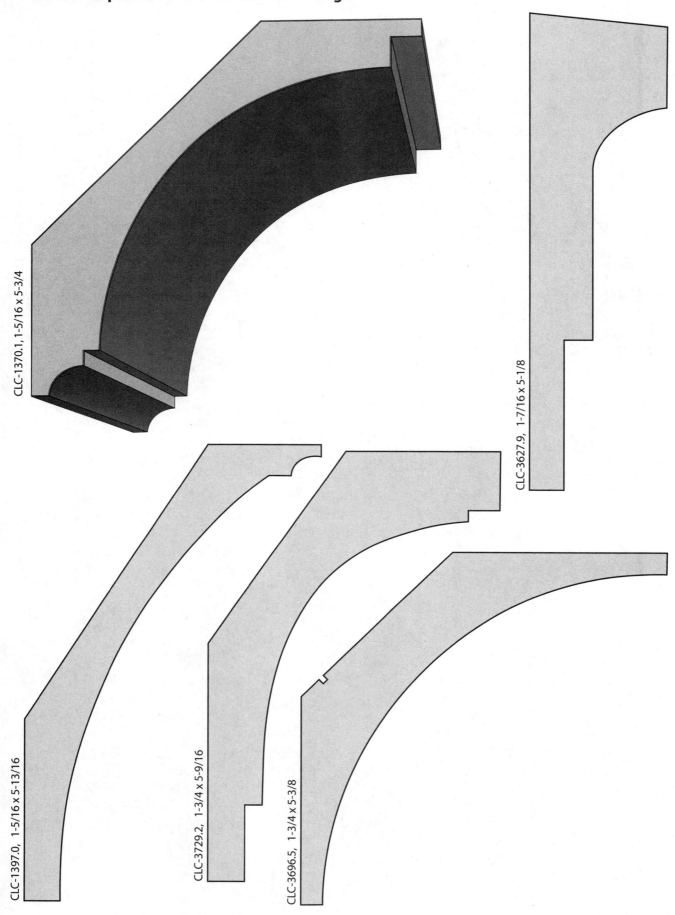

CLC-1370.1, 1-5/16 x 5-3/4

CLC-1397.0, 1-5/16 x 5-13/16

CLC-3729.2, 1-3/4 x 5-9/16

CLC-3696.5, 1-3/4 x 5-3/8

CLC-3627.9, 1-7/16 x 5-1/8

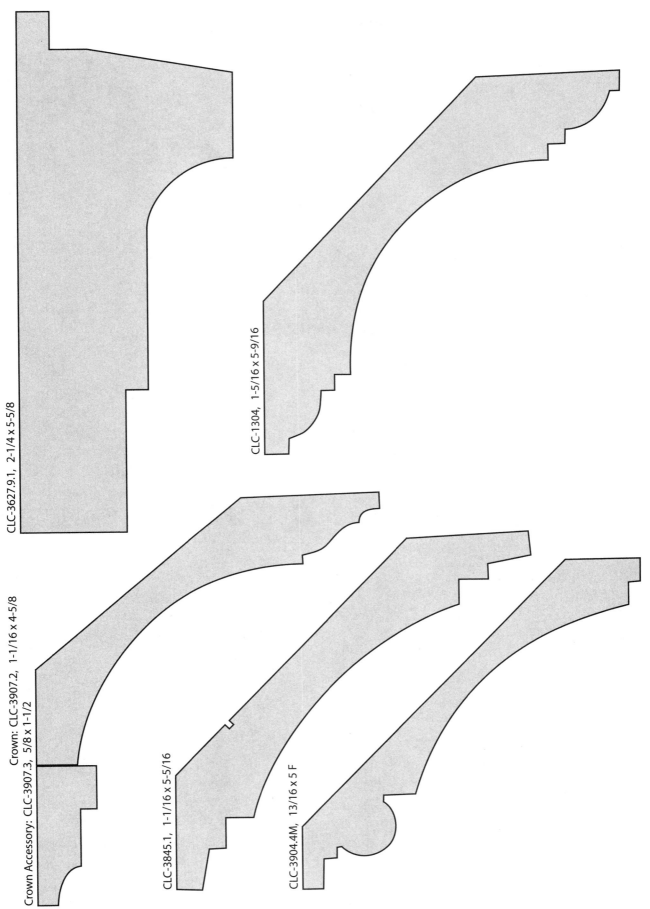

CLC-3627.9.1, 2-1/4 x 5-5/8

CLC-1304, 1-5/16 x 5-9/16

Crown: CLC-3907.2, 1-1/16 x 4-5/8

Crown Accessory: CLC-3907.3, 5/8 x 1-1/2

CLC-3845.1, 1-1/16 x 5-5/16

CLC-3904.4M, 13/16 x 5 F

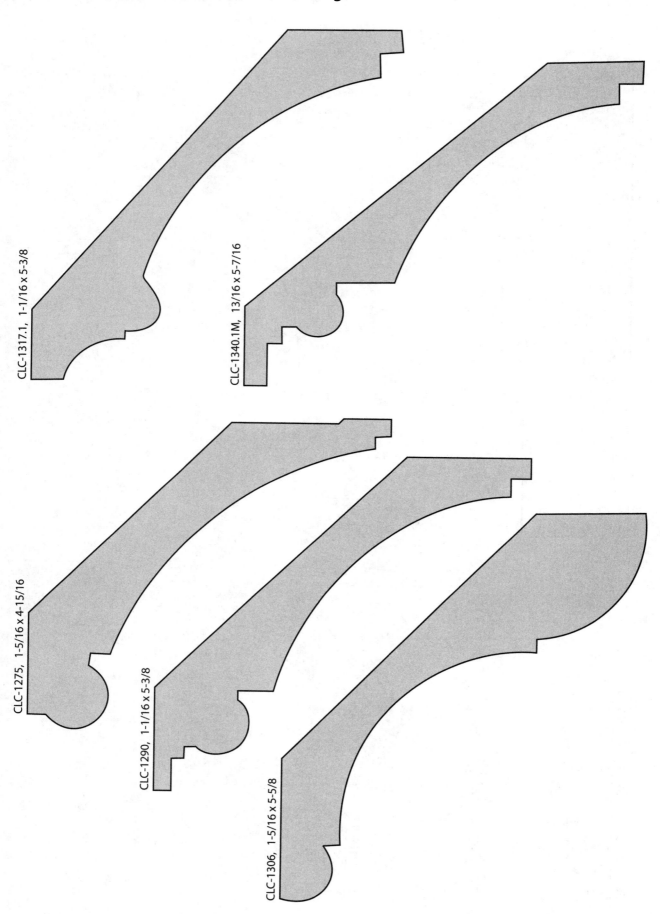

CLC-1317.1, 1-1/16 x 5-3/8

CLC-1340.1M, 13/16 x 5-7/16

CLC-1275, 1-5/16 x 4-15/16

CLC-1290, 1-1/16 x 5-3/8

CLC-1306, 1-5/16 x 5-5/8

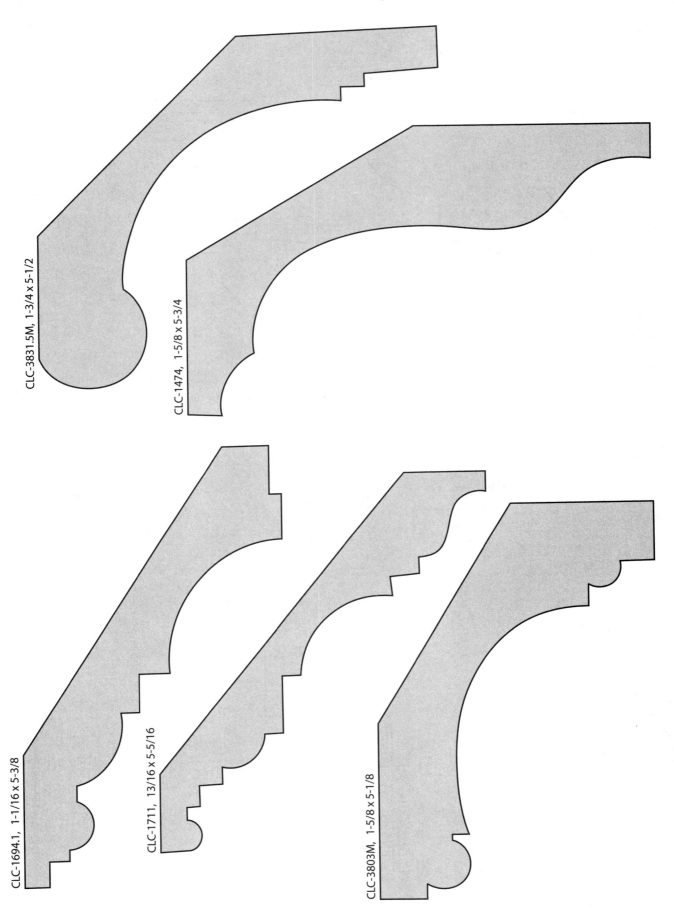

CLC-3831.5M, 1-3/4 x 5-1/2

CLC-1474, 1-5/8 x 5-3/4

CLC-1694.1, 1-1/16 x 5-3/8

CLC-1711, 13/16 x 5-5/16

CLC-3803M, 1-5/8 x 5-1/8

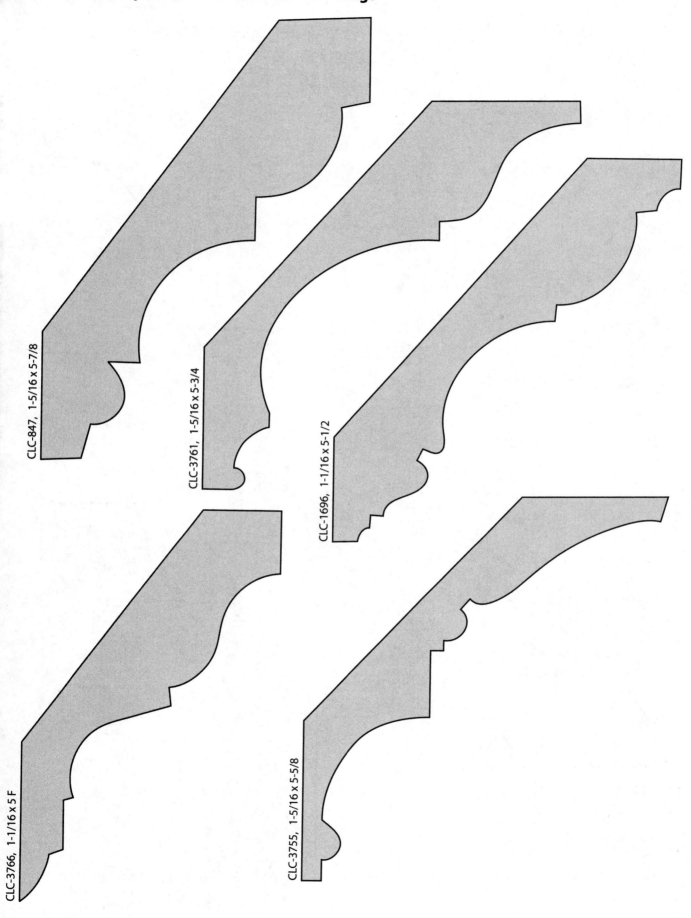

CLC-847, 1-5/16 x 5-7/8

CLC-3761, 1-5/16 x 5-3/4

CLC-1696, 1-1/16 x 5-1/2

CLC-3766, 1-1/16 x 5 F

CLC-3755, 1-5/16 x 5-5/8

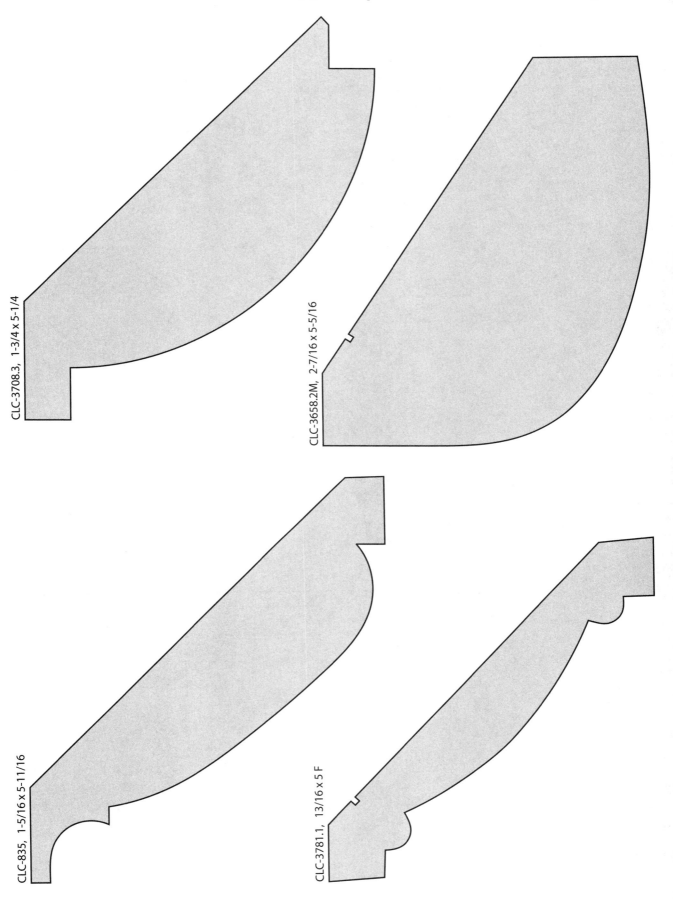

CLC-3708.3, 1-3/4 x 5-1/4

CLC-3658.2M, 2-7/16 x 5-5/16

CLC-835, 1-5/16 x 5-11/16

CLC-3781.1, 13/16 x 5 F

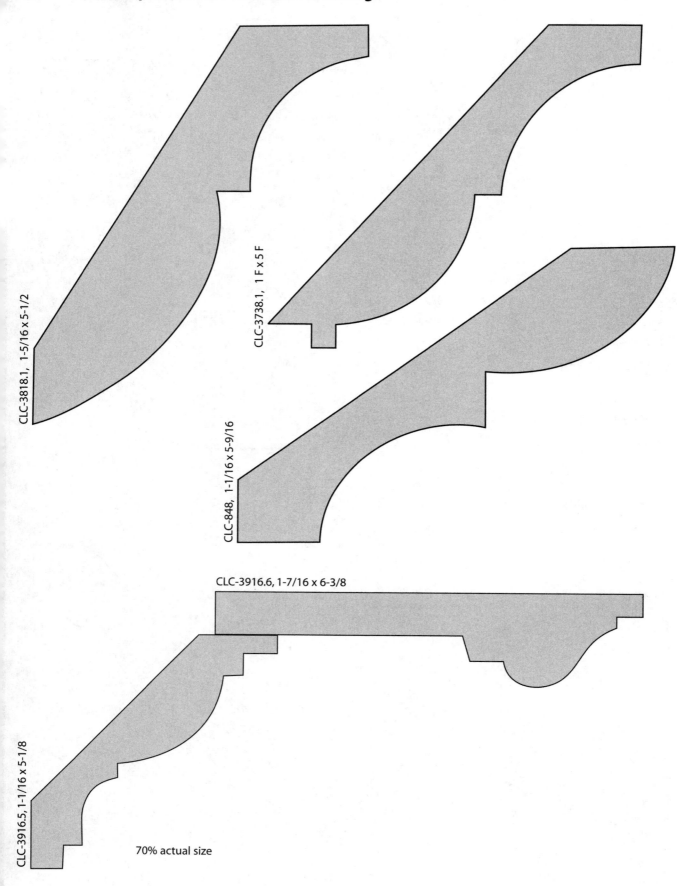

CLC-3818.1, 1-5/16 x 5-1/2

CLC-3738.1, 1 F x 5 F

CLC-848, 1-1/16 x 5-9/16

CLC-3916.6, 1-7/16 x 6-3/8

CLC-3916.5, 1-1/16 x 5-1/8

70% actual size

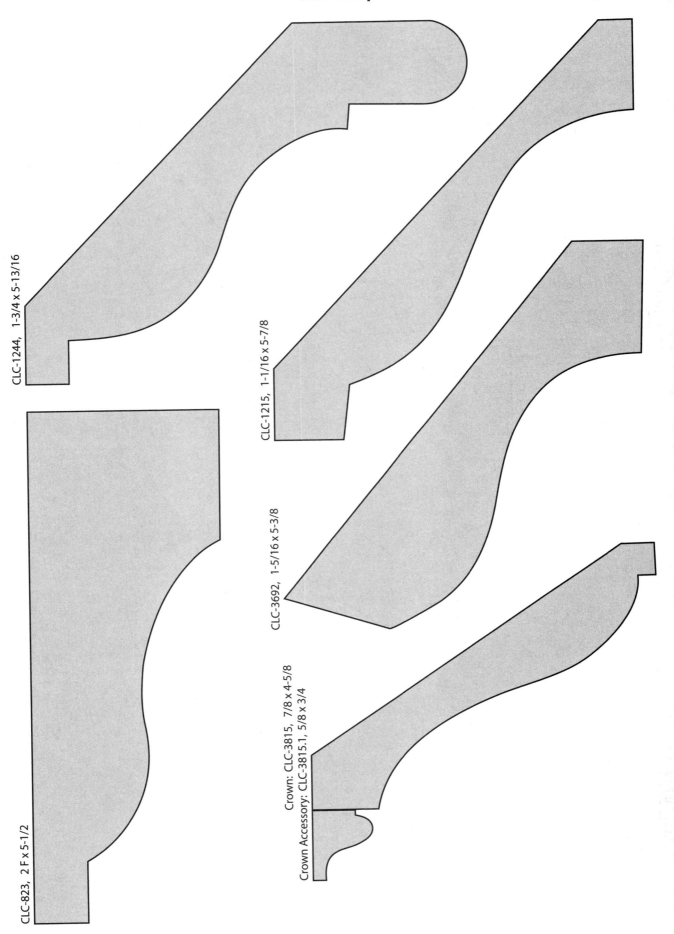

CLC-1244, 1-3/4 x 5-13/16

CLC-1215, 1-1/16 x 5-7/8

CLC-823, 2 F x 5-1/2

CLC-3692, 1-5/16 x 5-3/8

Crown: CLC-3815, 7/8 x 4-5/8
Crown Accessory: CLC-3815.1, 5/8 x 3/4

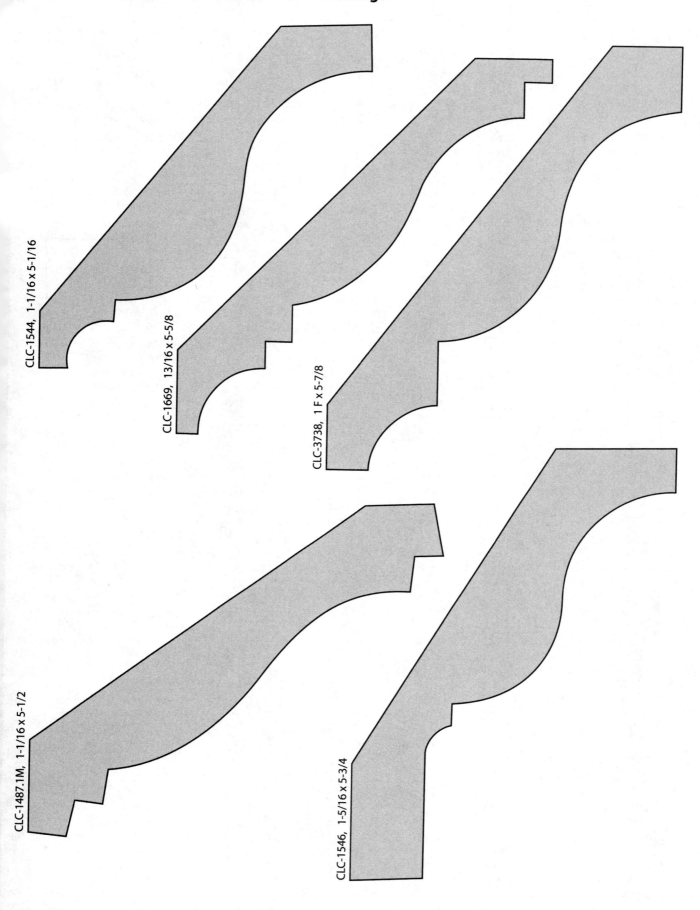

CLC-1544, 1-1/16 x 5-1/16

CLC-1669, 13/16 x 5-5/8

CLC-3738, 1 F x 5-7/8

CLC-1487.1M, 1-1/16 x 5-1/2

CLC-1546, 1-5/16 x 5-3/4

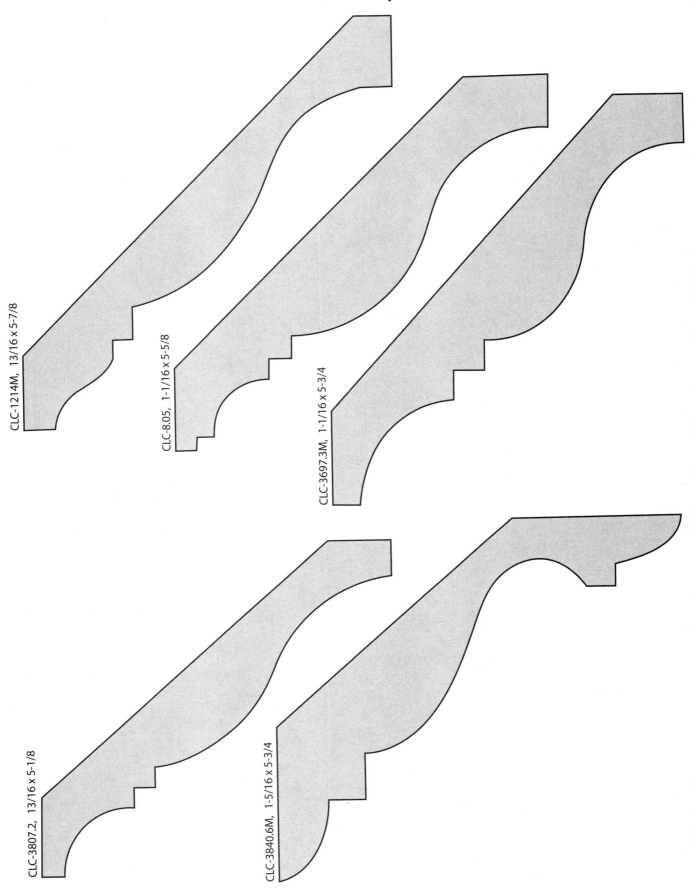

CLC-1214M, 13/16 x 5-7/8

CLC-8.05, 1-1/16 x 5-5/8

CLC-3697.3M, 1-1/16 x 5-3/4

CLC-3807.2, 13/16 x 5-1/8

CLC-3840.6M, 1-5/16 x 5-3/4

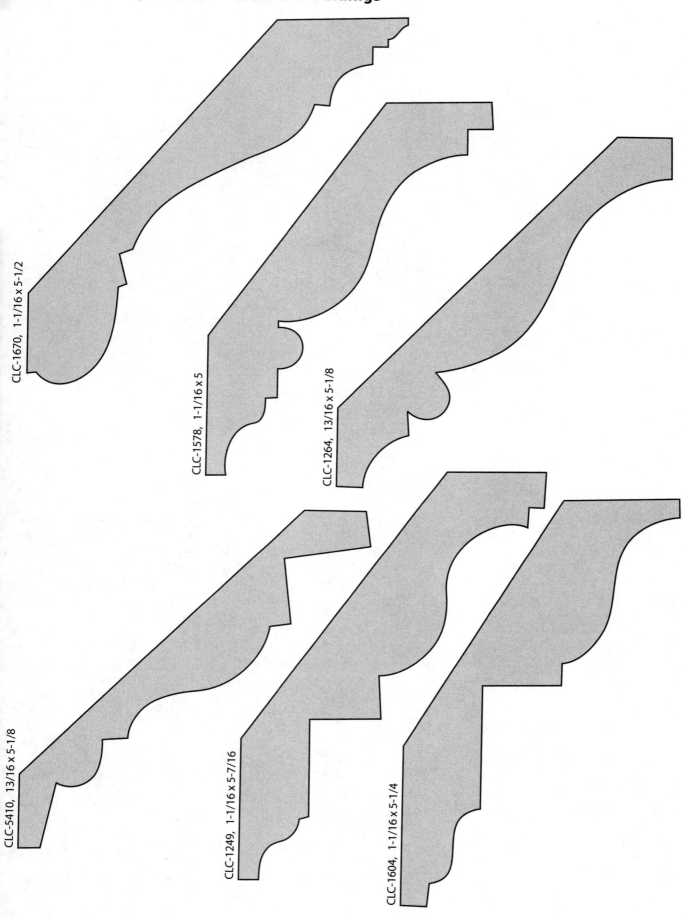

CLC-1670, 1-1/16 x 5-1/2

CLC-1578, 1-1/16 x 5

CLC-1264, 13/16 x 5-1/8

CLC-5410, 13/16 x 5-1/8

CLC-1249, 1-1/16 x 5-7/16

CLC-1604, 1-1/16 x 5-1/4

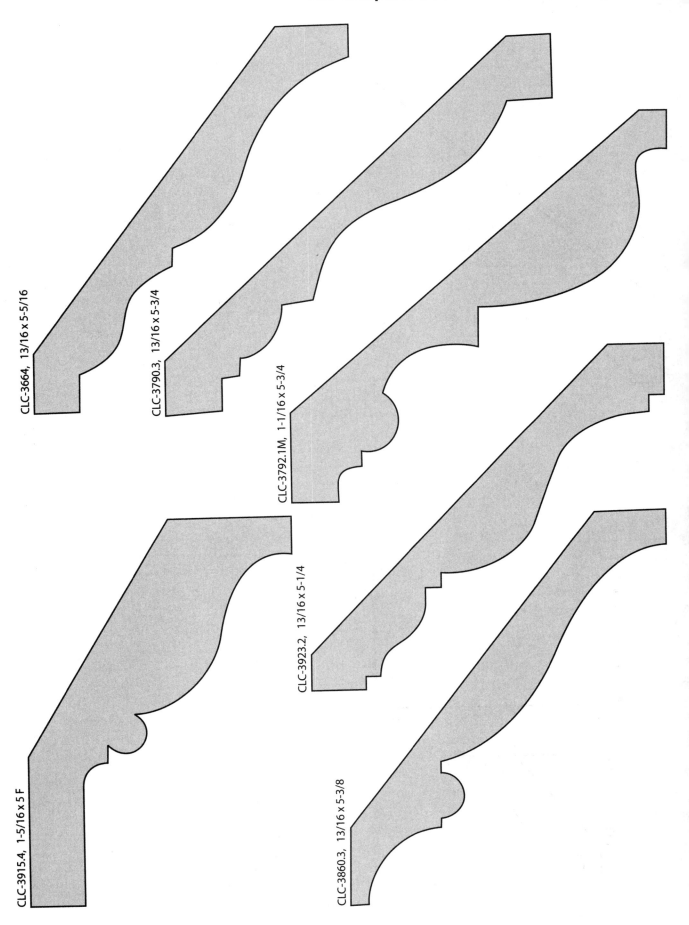

CLC-3664, 13/16 x 5-5/16

CLC-3790.3, 13/16 x 5-3/4

CLC-3792.1M, 1-1/16 x 5-3/4

CLC-3915.4, 1-5/16 x 5 F

CLC-3923.2, 13/16 x 5-1/4

CLC-3860.3, 13/16 x 5-3/8

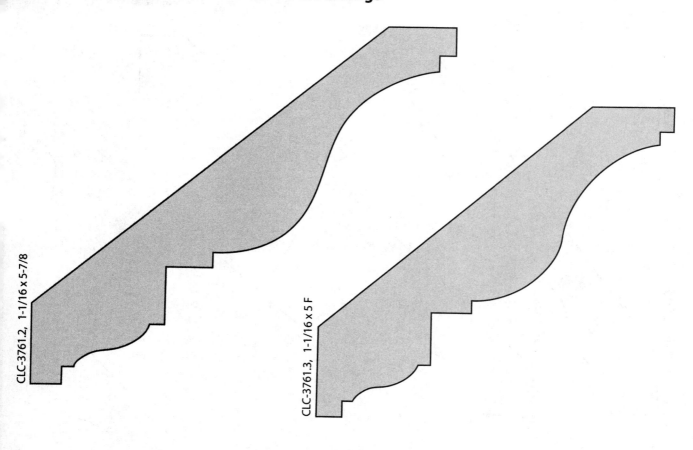

CLC-3761.2, 1-1/16 x 5-7/8

CLC-3761.3, 1-1/16 x 5 F

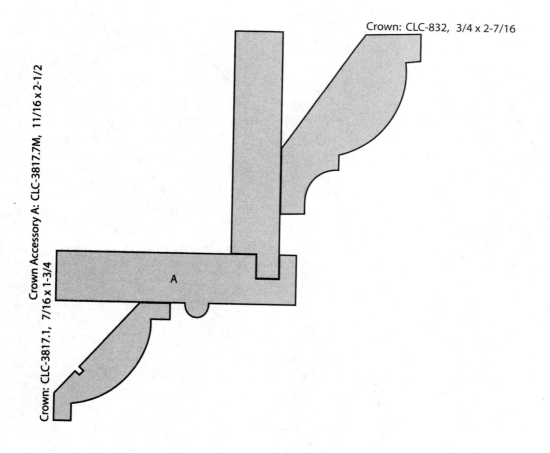

Crown: CLC-832, 3/4 x 2-7/16

Crown Accessory A: CLC-3817.7M, 11/16 x 2-1/2

A

Crown: CLC-3817.1, 7/16 x 1-3/4

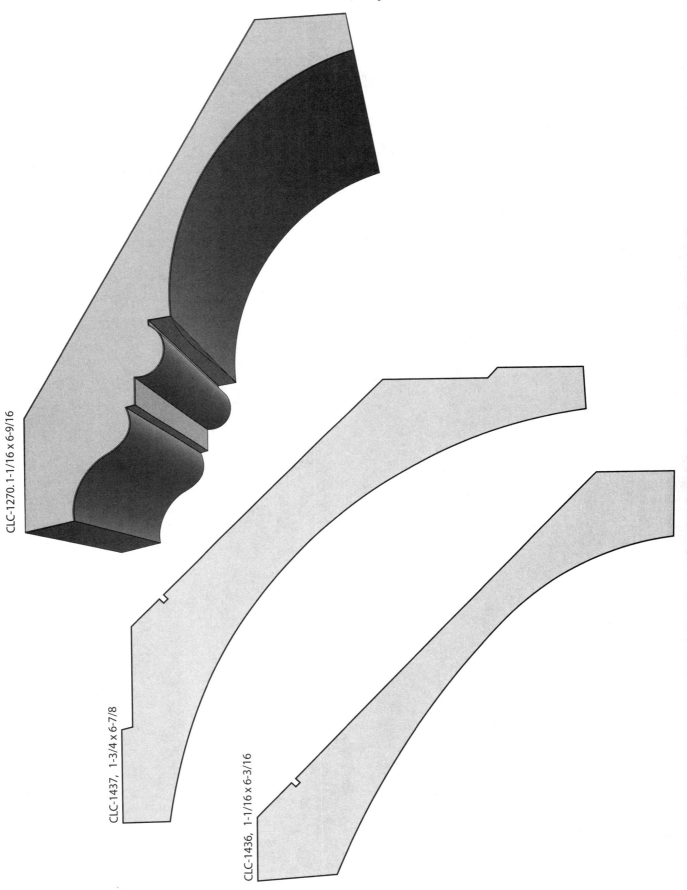

CLC-1270. 1-1/16 x 6-9/16

CLC-1437, 1-3/4 x 6-7/8

CLC-1436, 1-1/16 x 6-3/16

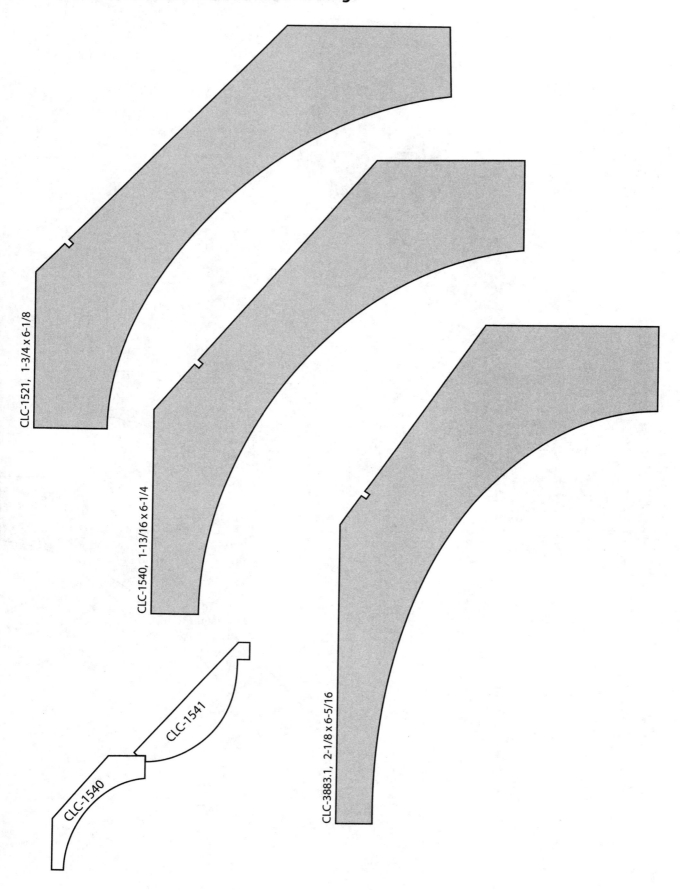

CLC-1521, 1-3/4 x 6-1/8

CLC-1540, 1-13/16 x 6-1/4

CLC-3883.1, 2-1/8 x 6-5/16

CLC-1541

CLC-1540

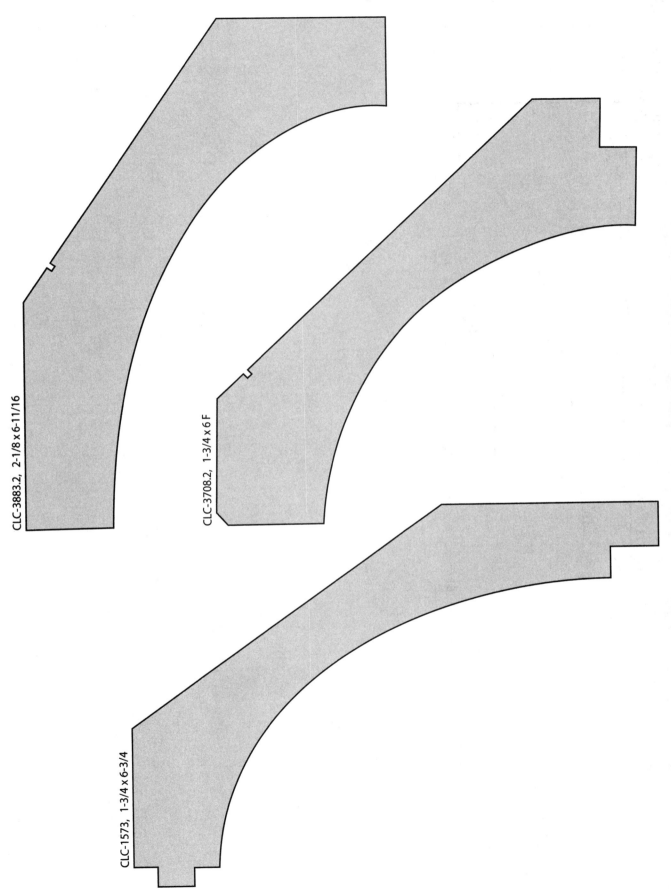

CLC-3883.2, 2-1/8 x 6-11/16

CLC-3708.2, 1-3/4 x 6 F

CLC-1573, 1-3/4 x 6-3/4

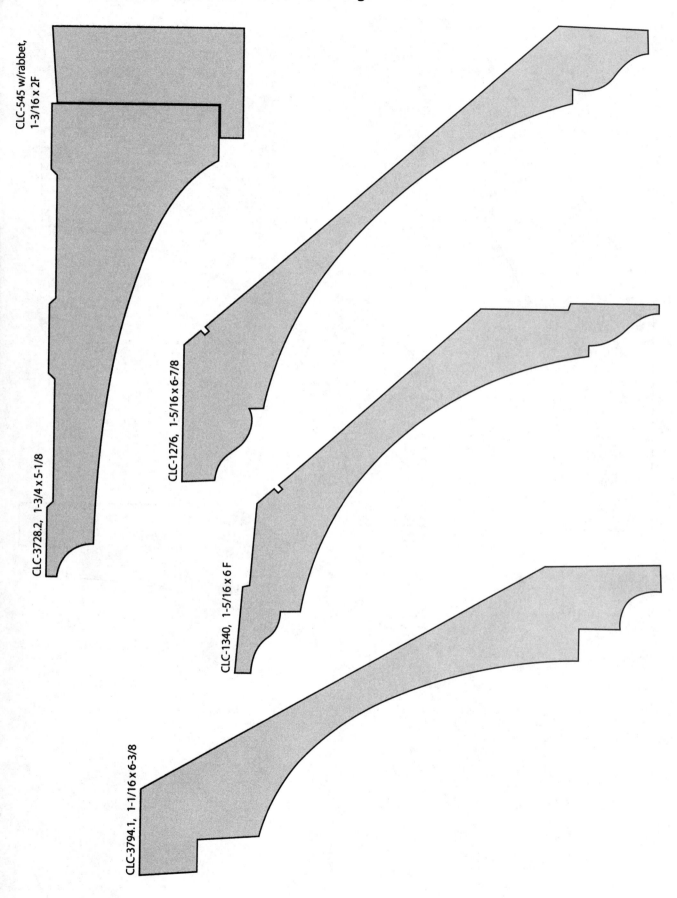

CLC-545 w/rabbet,
1-3/16 x 2F

CLC-3728.2, 1-3/4 x 5-1/8

CLC-1276, 1-5/16 x 6-7/8

CLC-1340, 1-5/16 x 6 F

CLC-3794.1, 1-1/16 x 6-3/8

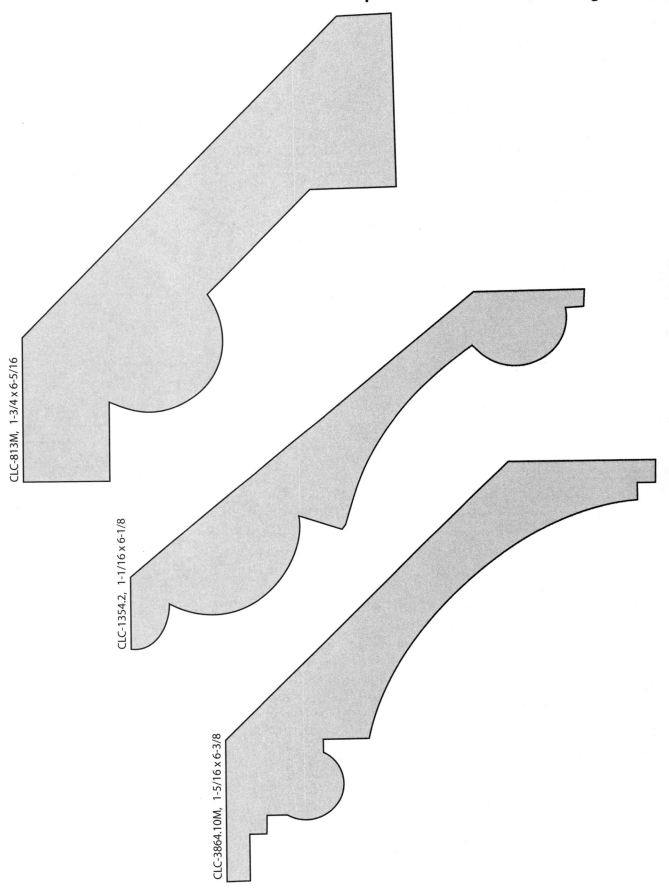

CLC-813M, 1-3/4 x 6-5/16

CLC-1354.2, 1-1/16 x 6-1/8

CLC-3864.10M, 1-5/16 x 6-3/8

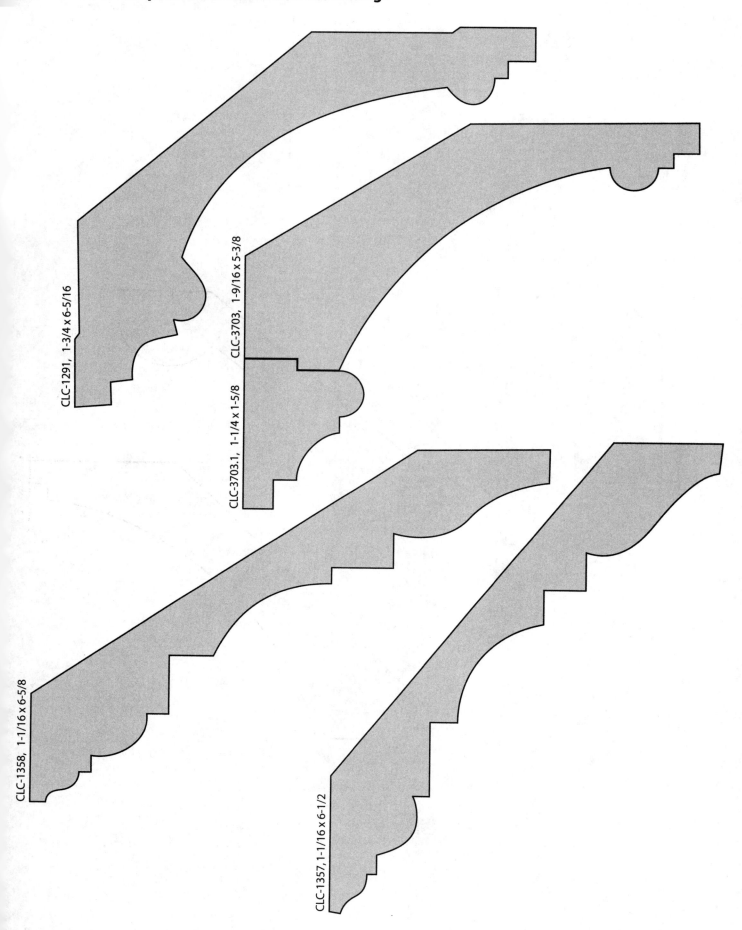

CLC-1291, 1-3/4 x 6-5/16

CLC-3703, 1-9/16 x 5-3/8

CLC-3703.1, 1-1/4 x 1-5/8

CLC-1358, 1-1/16 x 6-5/8

CLC-1357, 1-1/16 x 6-1/2

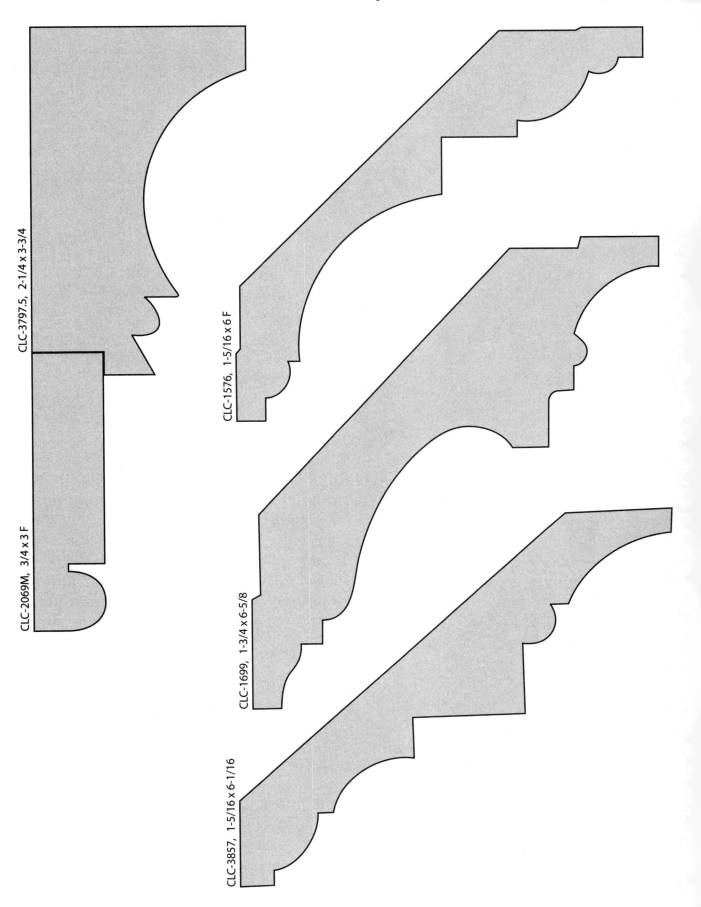

CLC-3797.5, 2-1/4 x 3-3/4

CLC-2069M, 3/4 x 3 F

CLC-1576, 1-5/16 x 6 F

CLC-1699, 1-3/4 x 6-5/8

CLC-3857, 1-5/16 x 6-1/16

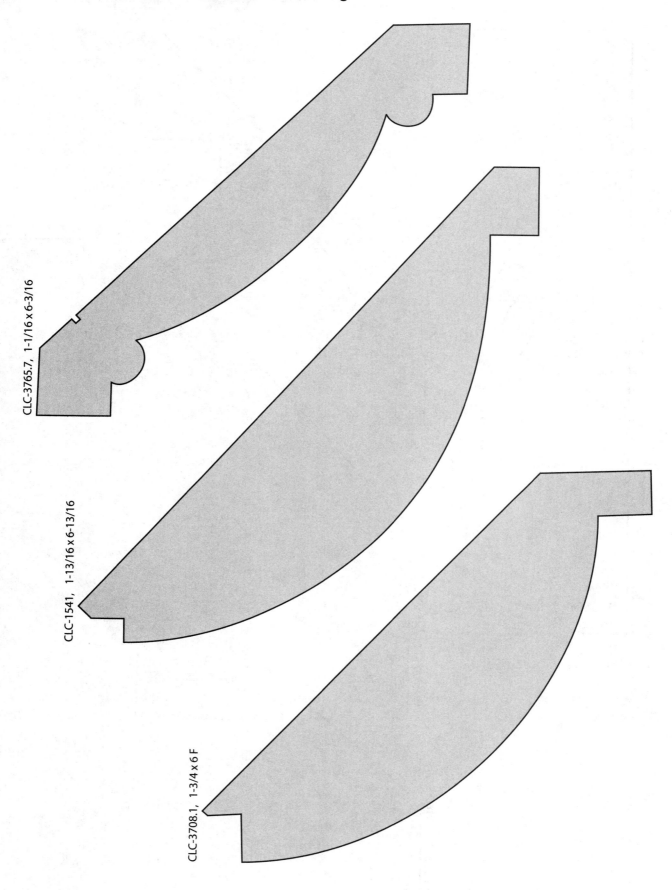

CLC-3765.7, 1-1/16 x 6-3/16

CLC-1541, 1-13/16 x 6-13/16

CLC-3708.1, 1-3/4 x 6 F

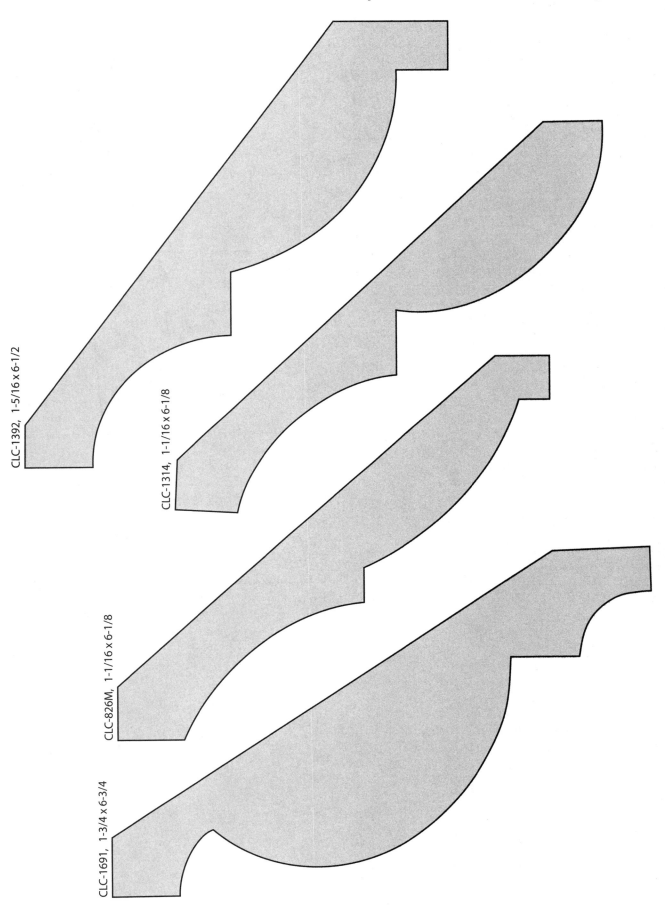

CLC-1392, 1-5/16 x 6-1/2

CLC-1314, 1-1/16 x 6-1/8

CLC-826M, 1-1/16 x 6-1/8

CLC-1691, 1-3/4 x 6-3/4

CLC 60.07, 1-5/8 x 6-5/8

CLC-3823.3, 1-1/16 x 6-5/8

CLC/D-52.10, 1-5/16 x 6-3/8

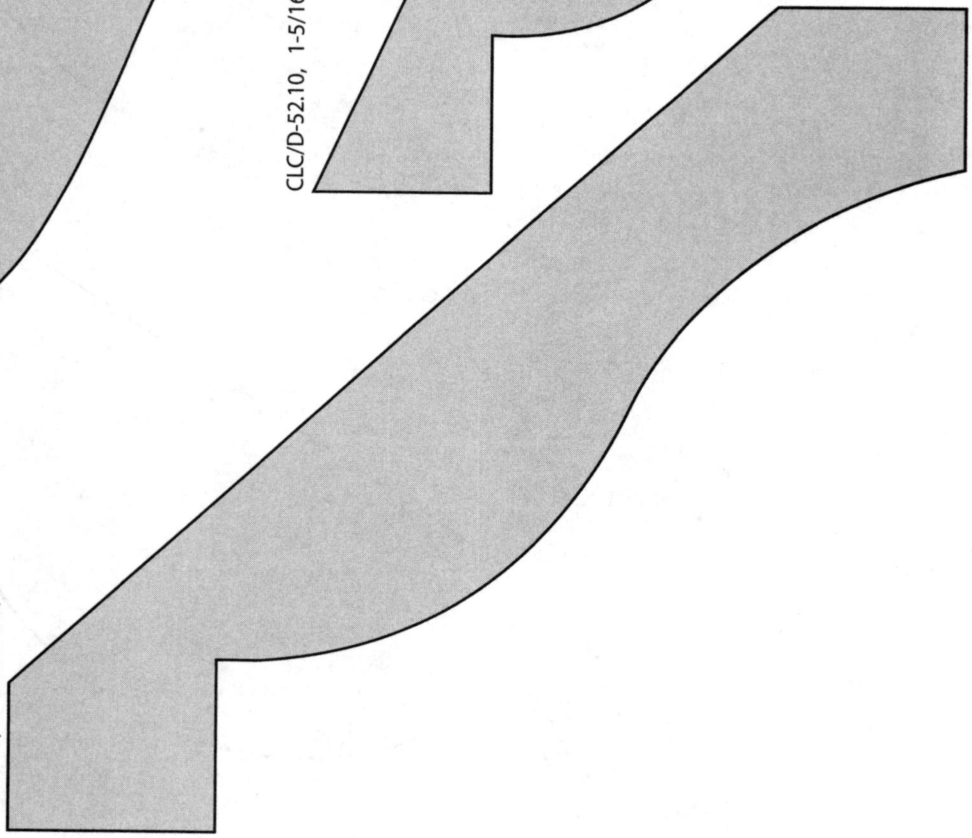

CLC-1235, 1-5/16 x 6-3/4

CLC-57.01, 1-5/16 x 6-3/4

CLC-1656.1, 1-1/8 x 6 F

CLC-1208, 13/16 x 6 F

CLC-3793.7M, 1-1/16 x 6-13/16

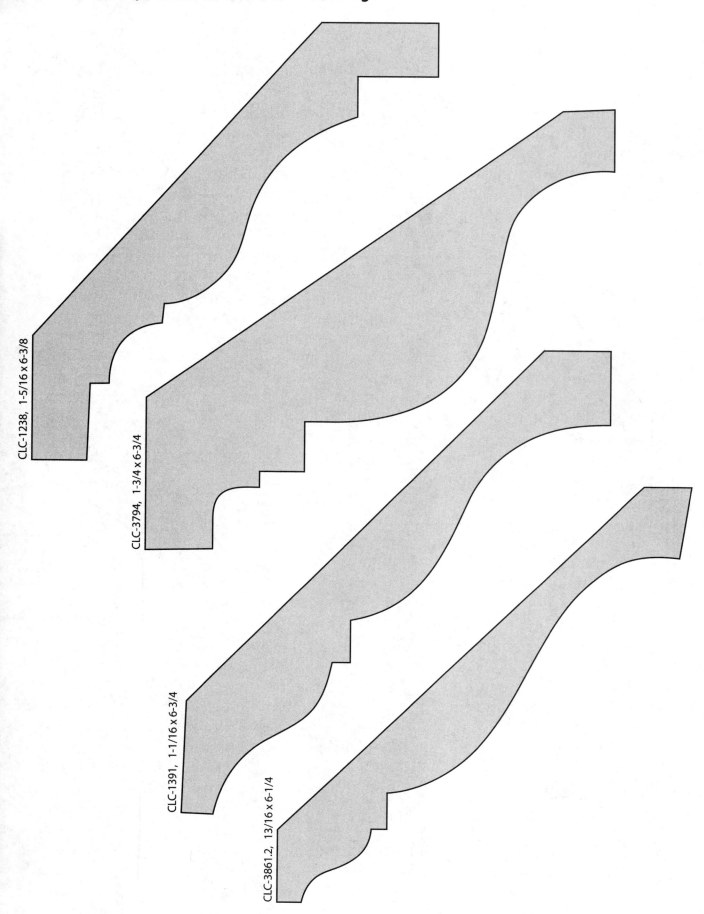

CLC-1238, 1-5/16 x 6-3/8

CLC-3794, 1-3/4 x 6-3/4

CLC-1391, 1-1/16 x 6-3/4

CLC-3861.2, 13/16 x 6-1/4

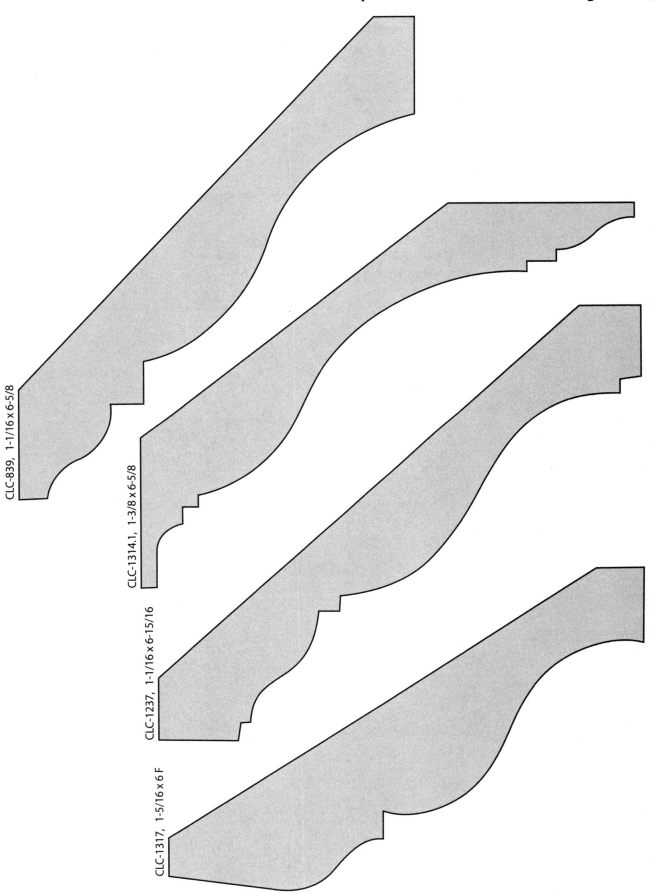

CLC-839, 1-1/16 x 6-5/8

CLC-1314.1, 1-3/8 x 6-5/8

CLC-1237, 1-1/16 x 6-15/16

CLC-1317, 1-5/16 x 6 F

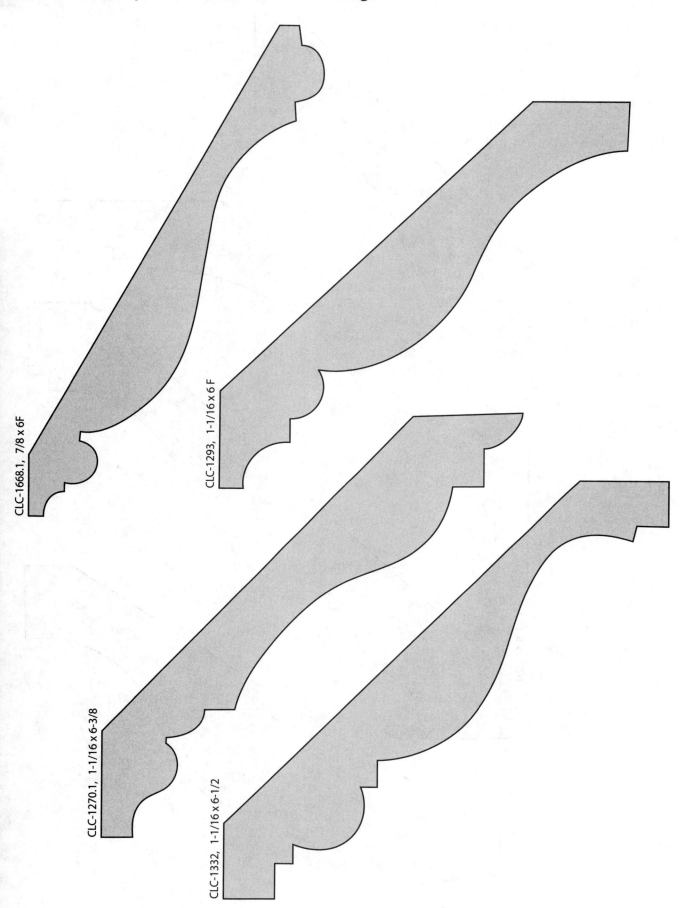

CLC-1668.1, 7/8 x 6F

CLC-1293, 1-1/16 x 6 F

CLC-1270.1, 1-1/16 x 6-3/8

CLC-1332, 1-1/16 x 6-1/2

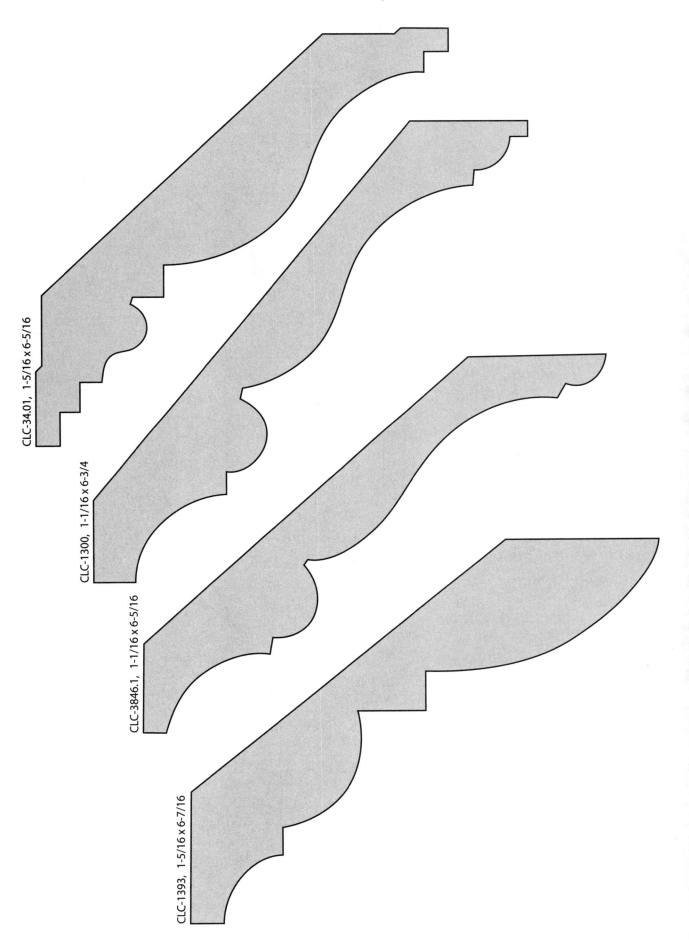

CLC-34.01, 1-5/16 x 6-5/16

CLC-1300, 1-1/16 x 6-3/4

CLC-3846.1, 1-1/16 x 6-5/16

CLC-1393, 1-5/16 x 6-7/16

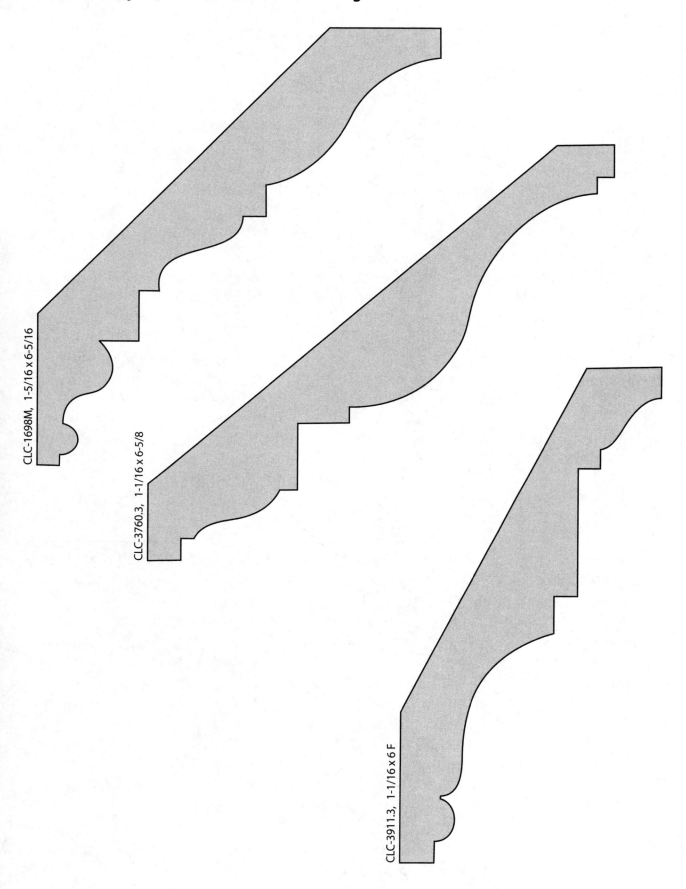

CLC-1698M, 1-5/16 x 6-5/16

CLC-3760.3, 1-1/16 x 6-5/8

CLC-3911.3, 1-1/16 x 6 F

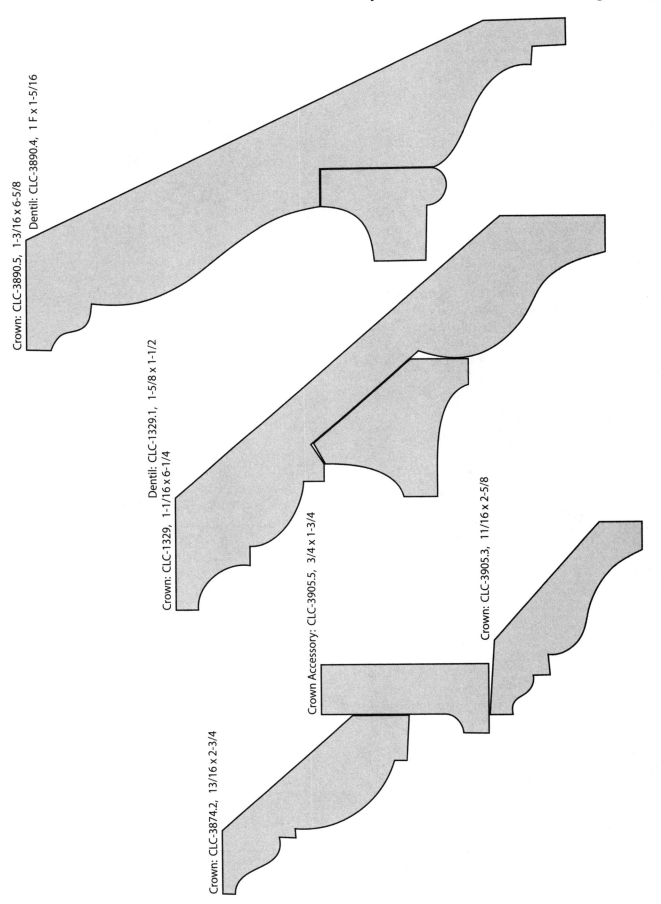

Crown: CLC-3890.5, 1-3/16 x 6-5/8

Dentil: CLC-3890.4, 1 F x 1-5/16

Dentil: CLC-1329.1, 1-5/8 x 1-1/2

Crown: CLC-1329, 1-1/16 x 6-1/4

Crown Accessory: CLC-3905.5, 3/4 x 1-3/4

Crown: CLC-3905.3, 11/16 x 2-5/8

Crown: CLC-3874.2, 13/16 x 2-3/4

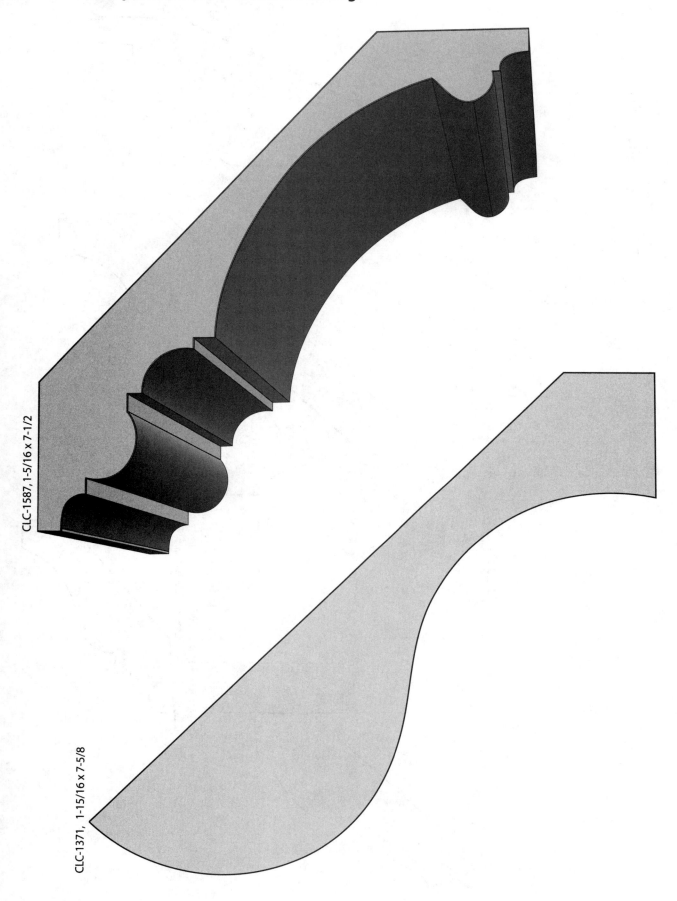

CLC-1587, 1-5/16 x 7-1/2

CLC-1371, 1-15/16 x 7-5/8

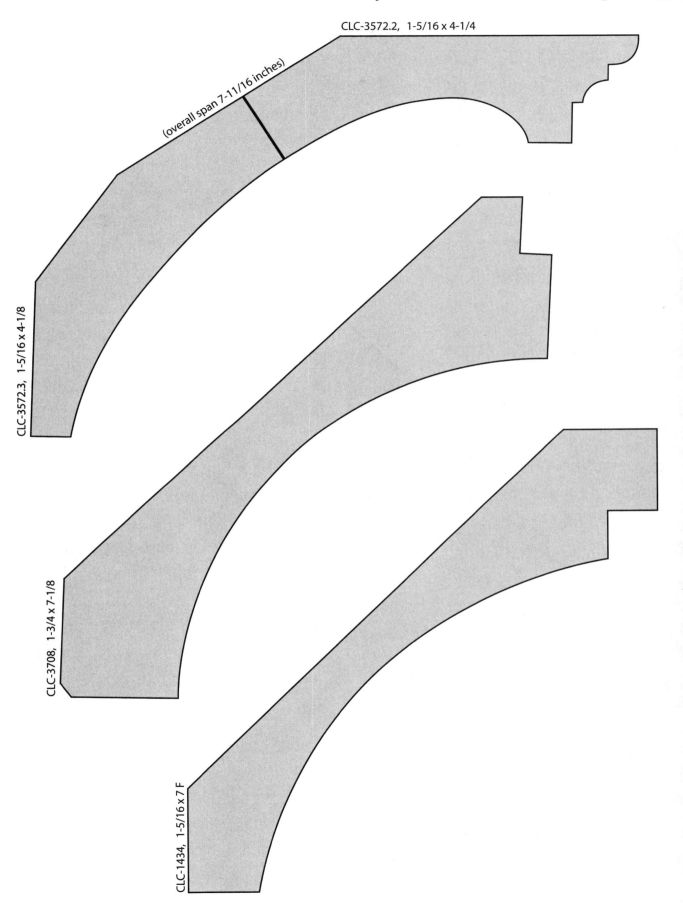

CLC-3572.2, 1-5/16 x 4-1/4

(overall span 7-11/16 inches)

CLC-3572.3, 1-5/16 x 4-1/8

CLC-3708, 1-3/4 x 7-1/8

CLC-1434, 1-5/16 x 7 F

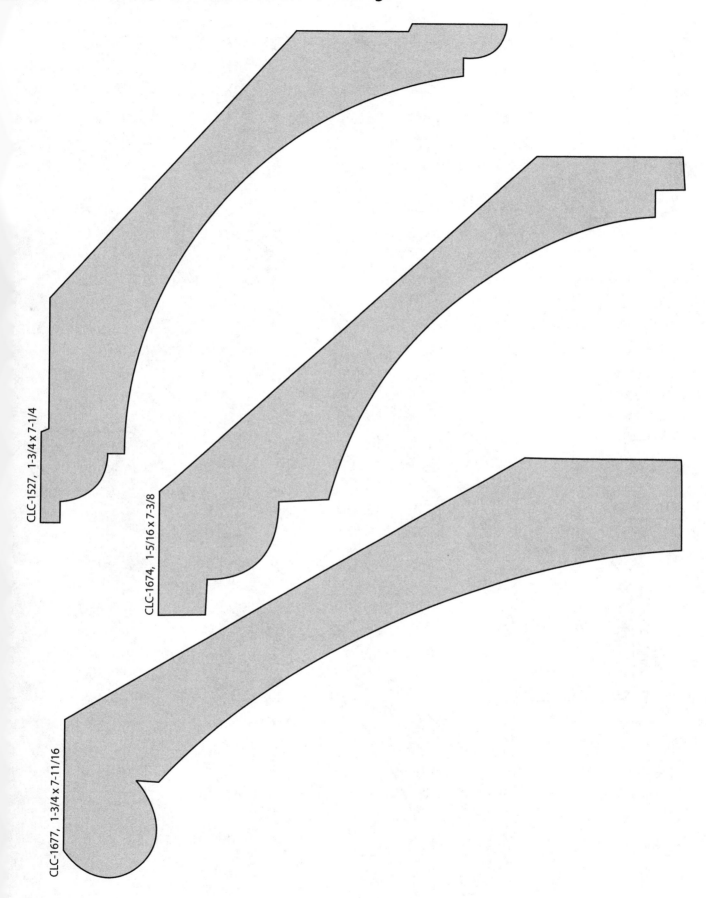

CLC-1527, 1-3/4 x 7-1/4

CLC-1674, 1-5/16 x 7-3/8

CLC-1677, 1-3/4 x 7-11/16

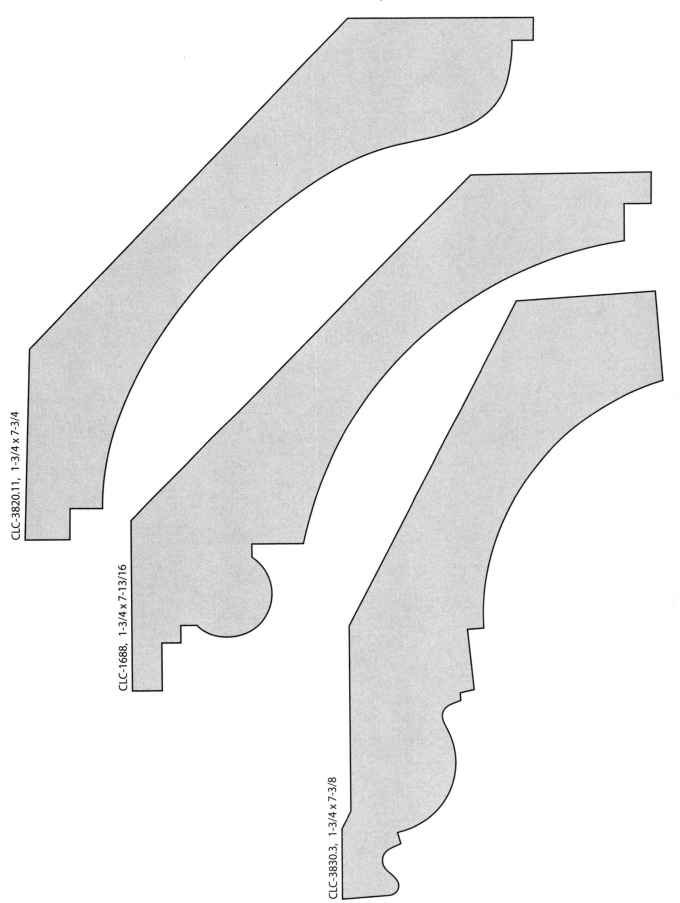

CLC-3820.11, 1-3/4 x 7-3/4

CLC-1688, 1-3/4 x 7-13/16

CLC-3830.3, 1-3/4 x 7-3/8

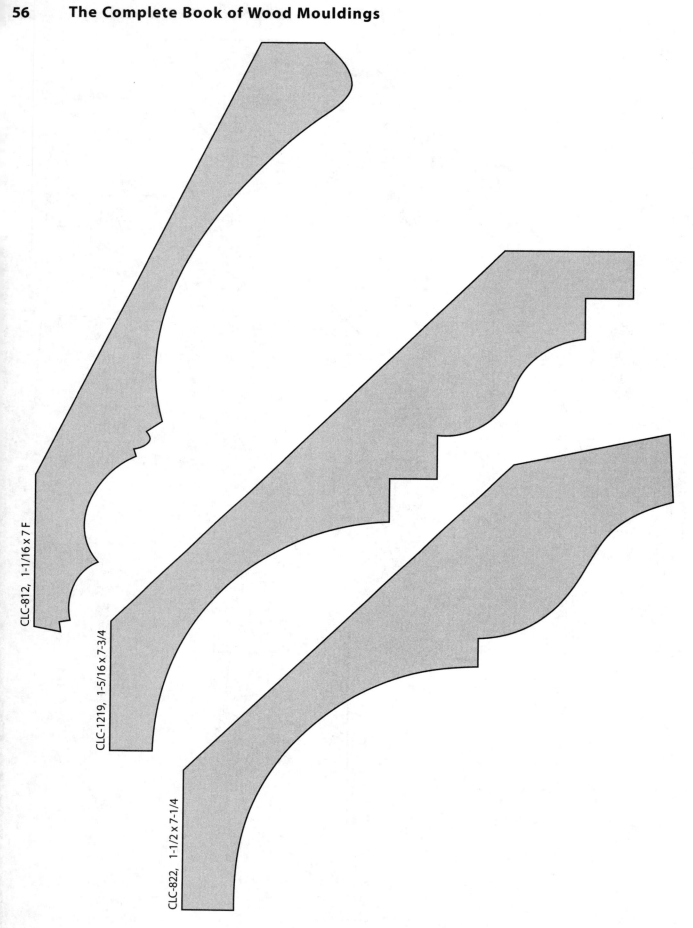

CLC-812, 1-1/16 x 7 F

CLC-1219, 1-5/16 x 7-3/4

CLC-822, 1-1/2 x 7-1/4

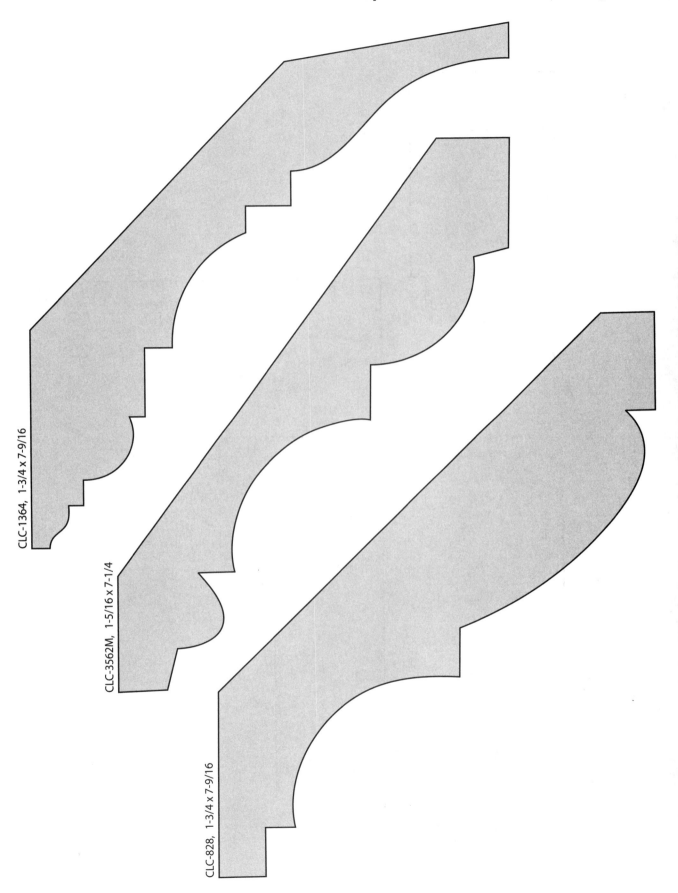

CLC-1364, 1-3/4 x 7-9/16

CLC-3562M, 1-5/16 x 7-1/4

CLC-828, 1-3/4 x 7-9/16

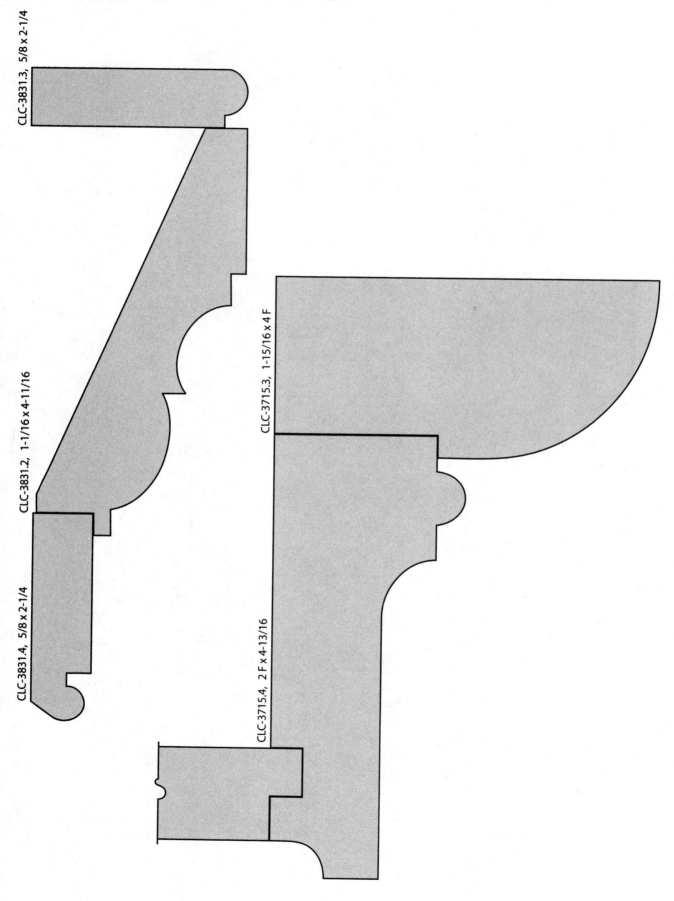

CLC-3831.3, 5/8 x 2-1/4

CLC-3831.2, 1-1/16 x 4-11/16

CLC-3831.4, 5/8 x 2-1/4

CLC-3715.3, 1-15/16 x 4 F

CLC-3715.4, 2 F x 4-13/16

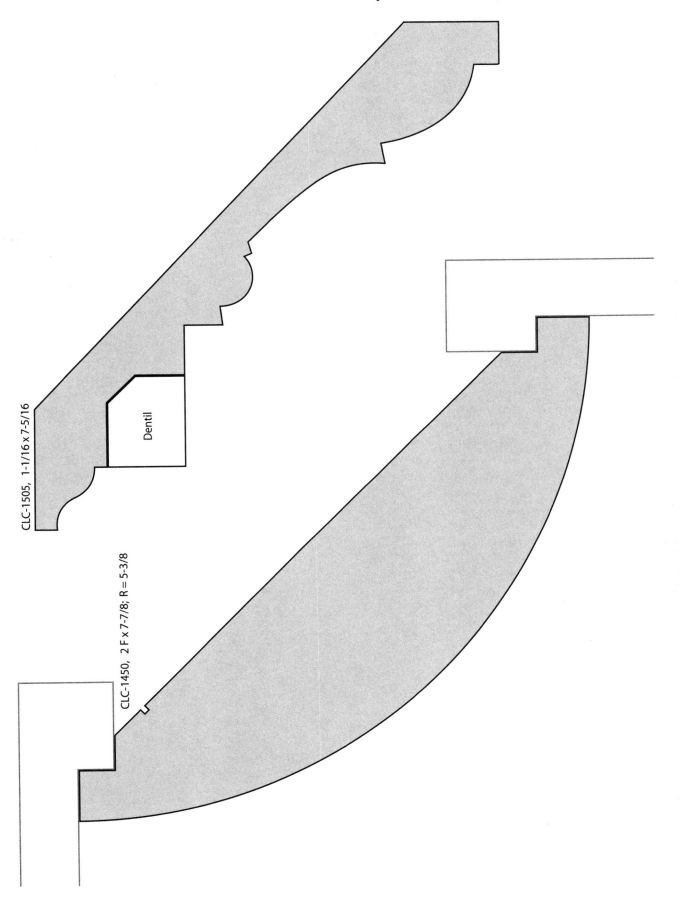

CLC-1505, 1-1/16 x 7-5/16

Dentil

CLC-1450, 2 F x 7-7/8; R = 5-3/8

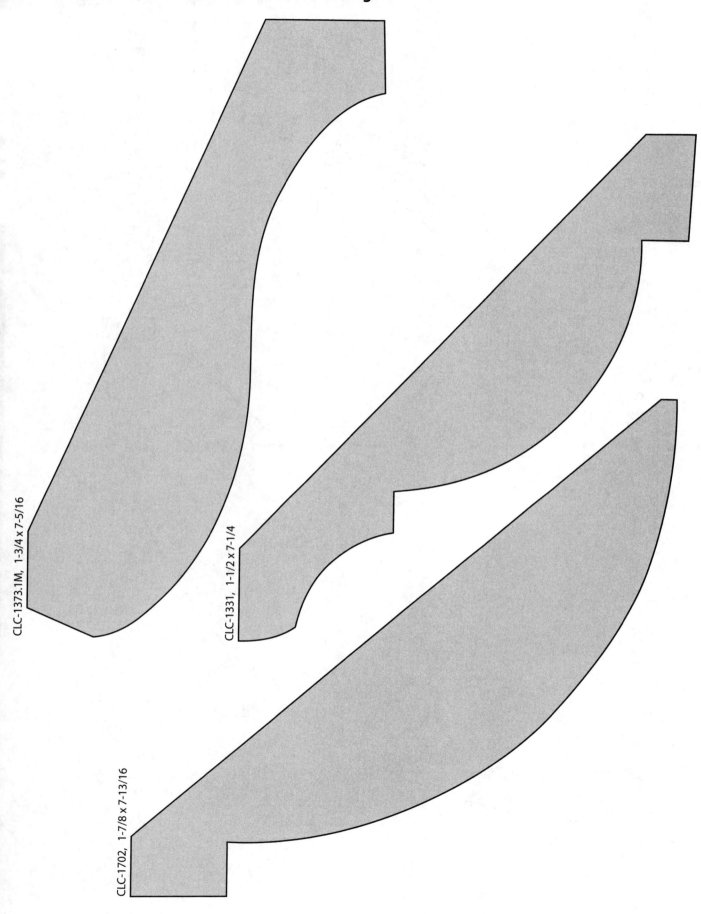

CLC-1373.1M, 1-3/4 x 7-5/16

CLC-1331, 1-1/2 x 7-1/4

CLC-1702, 1-7/8 x 7-13/16

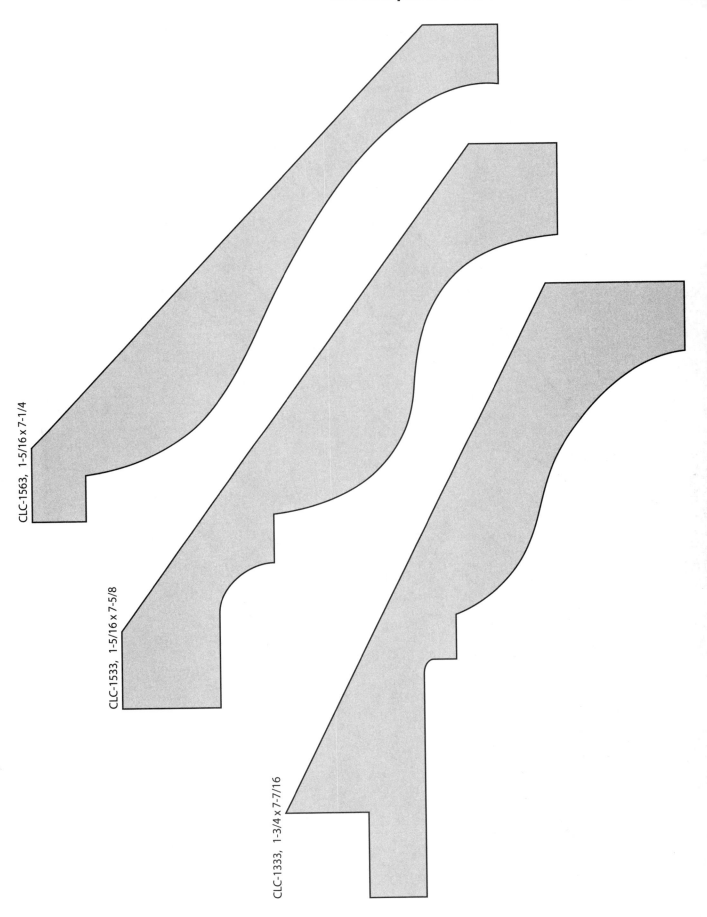

CLC-1563, 1-5/16 x 7-1/4

CLC-1533, 1-5/16 x 7-5/8

CLC-1333, 1-3/4 x 7-7/16

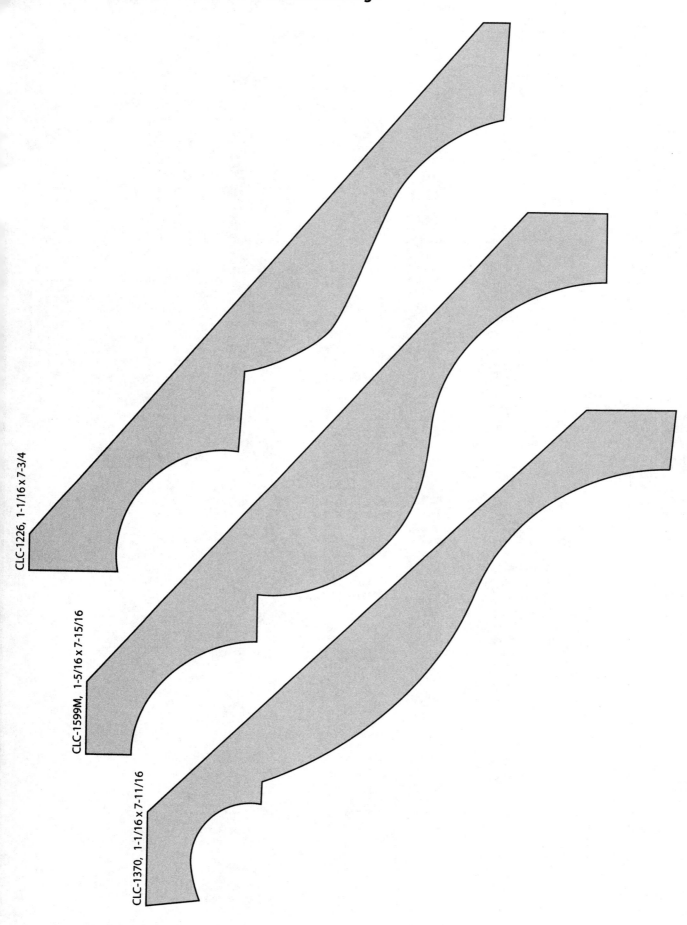

CLC-1226, 1-1/16 x 7-3/4

CLC-1599M, 1-5/16 x 7-15/16

CLC-1370, 1-1/16 x 7-11/16

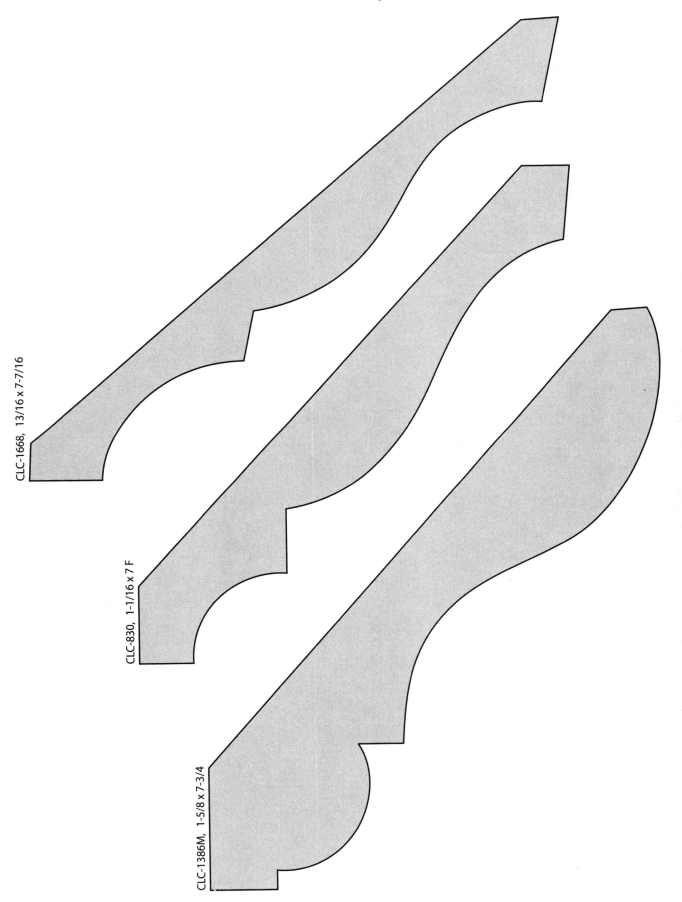

CLC-1668, 13/16 x 7-7/16

CLC-830, 1-1/16 x 7 F

CLC-1386M, 1-5/8 x 7-3/4

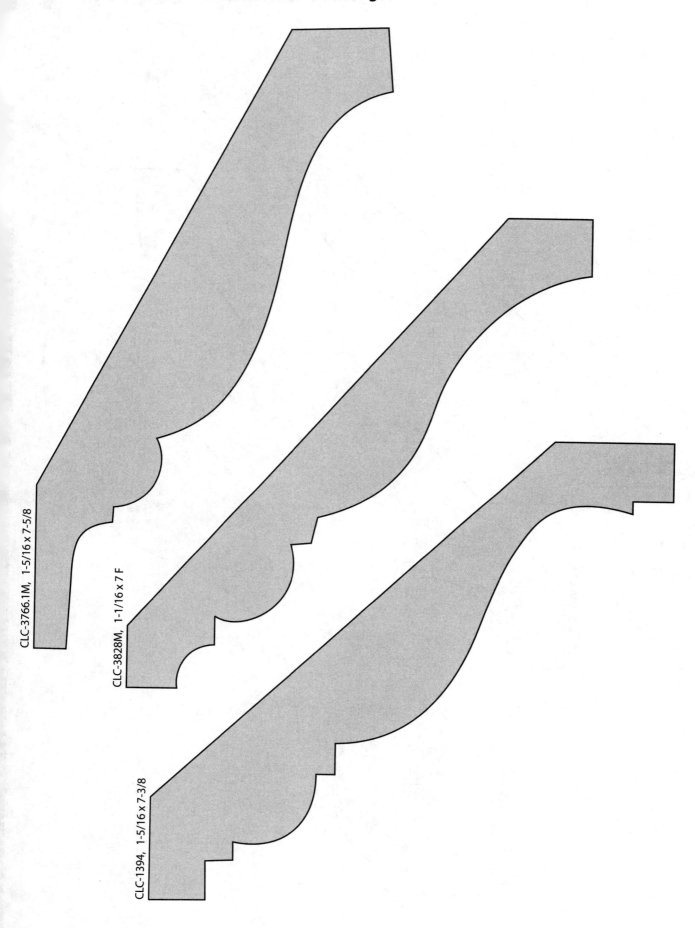

CLC-3766.1M, 1-5/16 x 7-5/8

CLC-3828M, 1-1/16 x 7 F

CLC-1394, 1-5/16 x 7-3/8

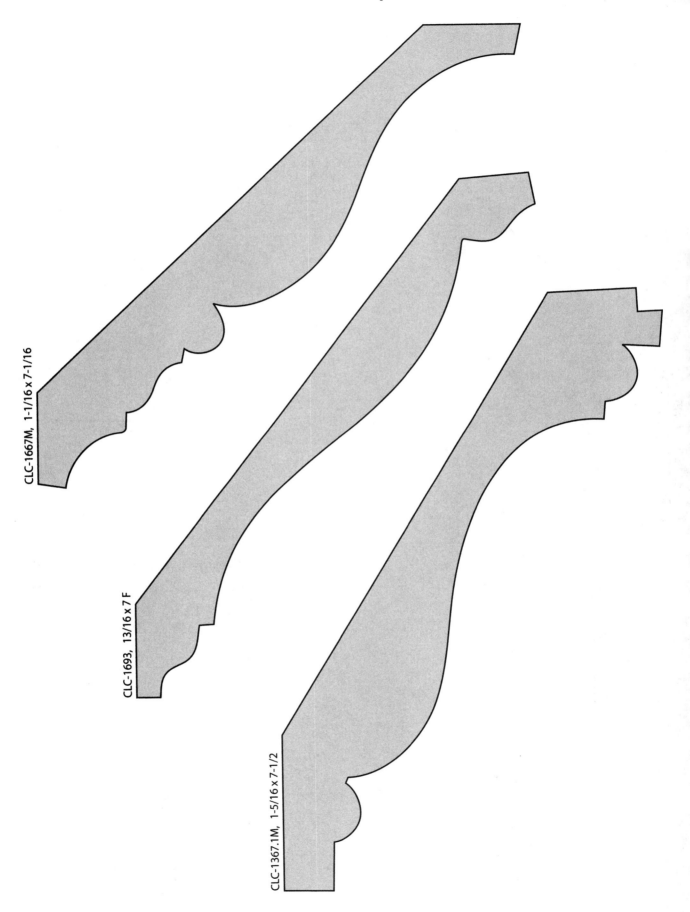

CLC-1667M, 1-1/16 x 7-1/16

CLC-1693, 13/16 x 7 F

CLC-1367.1M, 1-5/16 x 7-1/2

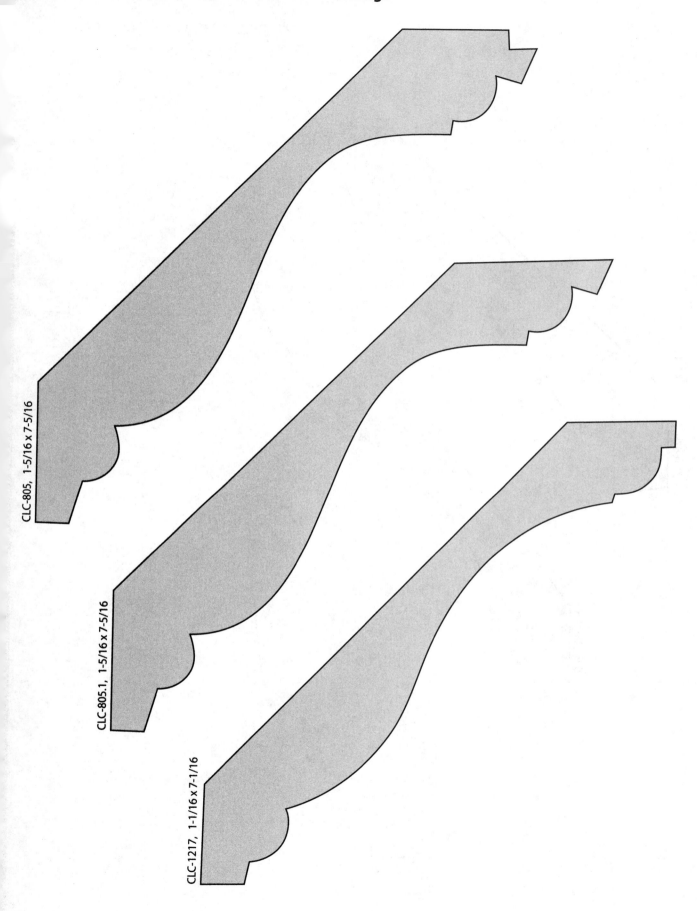

CLC-805, 1-5/16 x 7-5/16

CLC-805.1, 1-5/16 x 7-5/16

CLC-1217, 1-1/16 x 7-1/16

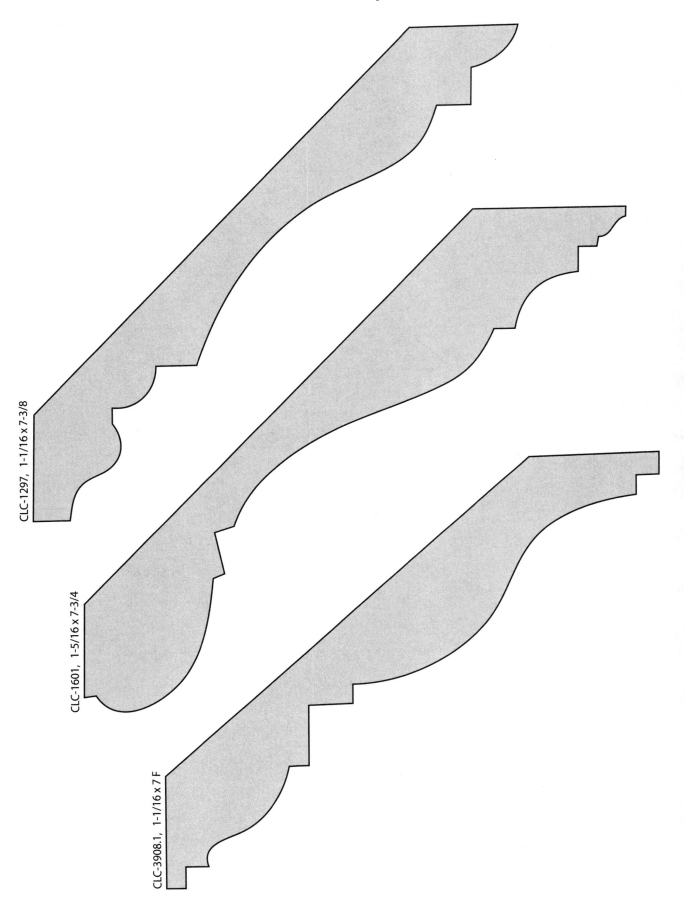

CLC-1297, 1-1/16 x 7-3/8

CLC-1601, 1-5/16 x 7-3/4

CLC-3908.1, 1-1/16 x 7 F

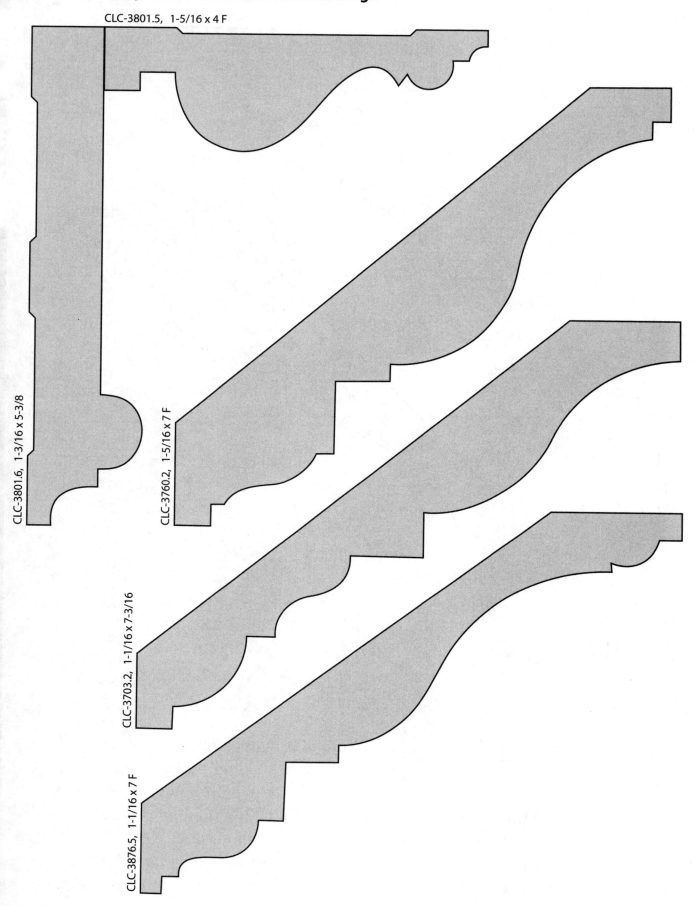

CLC-3801.5, 1-5/16 x 4 F

CLC-3801.6, 1-3/16 x 5-3/8

CLC-3760.2, 1-5/16 x 7 F

CLC-3703.2, 1-1/16 x 7-3/16

CLC-3876.5, 1-1/16 x 7 F

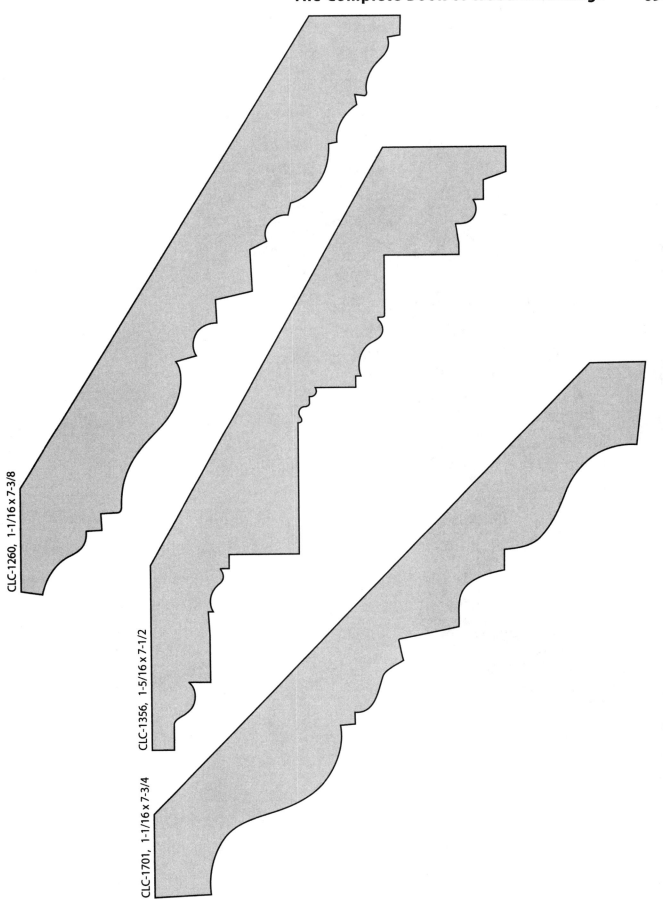

CLC-1260, 1-1/16 x 7-3/8

CLC-1356, 1-5/16 x 7-1/2

CLC-1701, 1-1/16 x 7-3/4

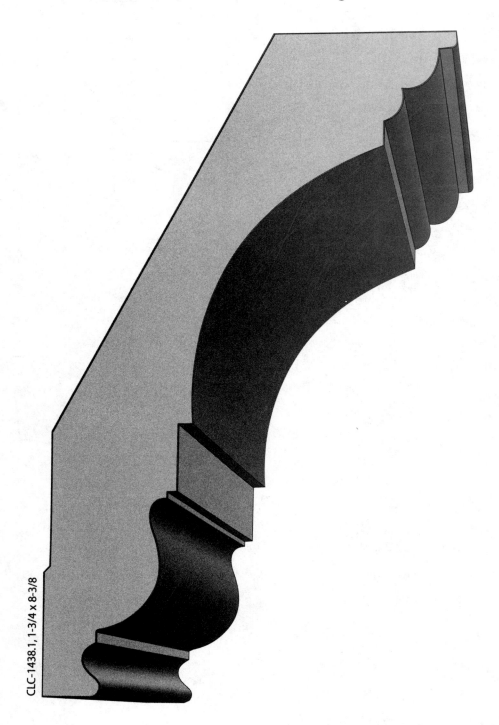

CLC-1438.1, 1-3/4 x 8-3/8

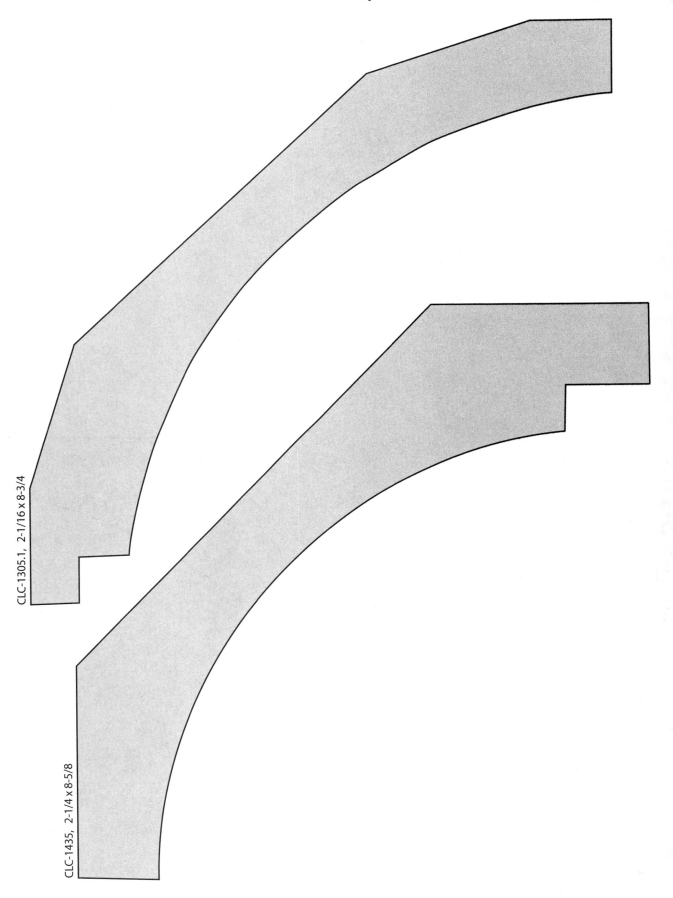

CLC-1305.1, 2-1/16 x 8-3/4

CLC-1435, 2-1/4 x 8-5/8

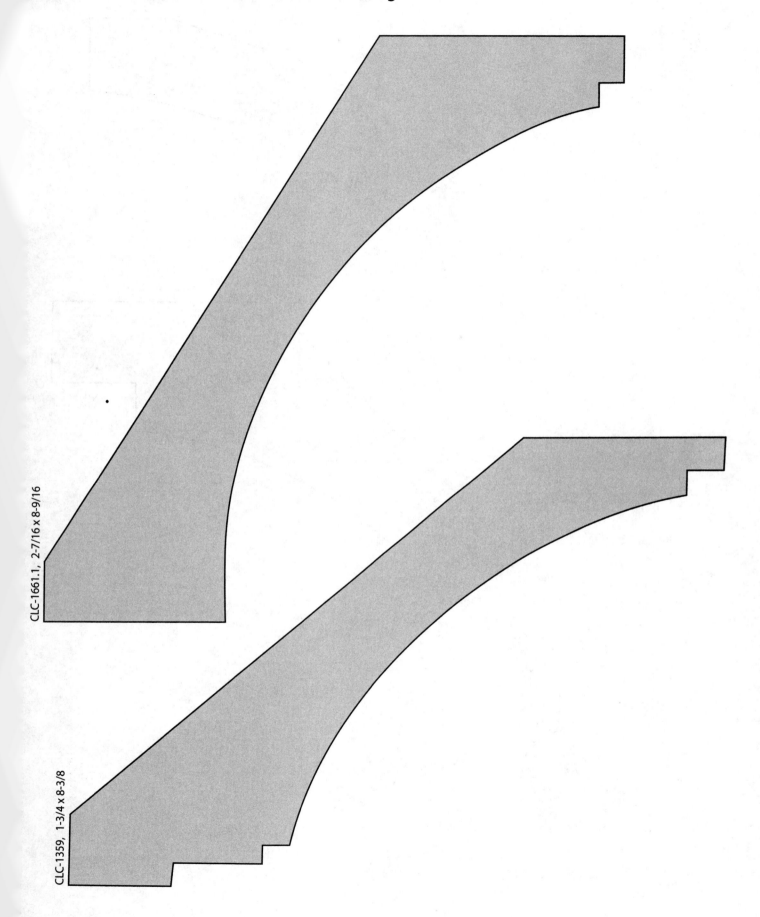

CLC-1661.1, 2-7/16 x 8-9/16

CLC-1359, 1-3/4 x 8-3/8

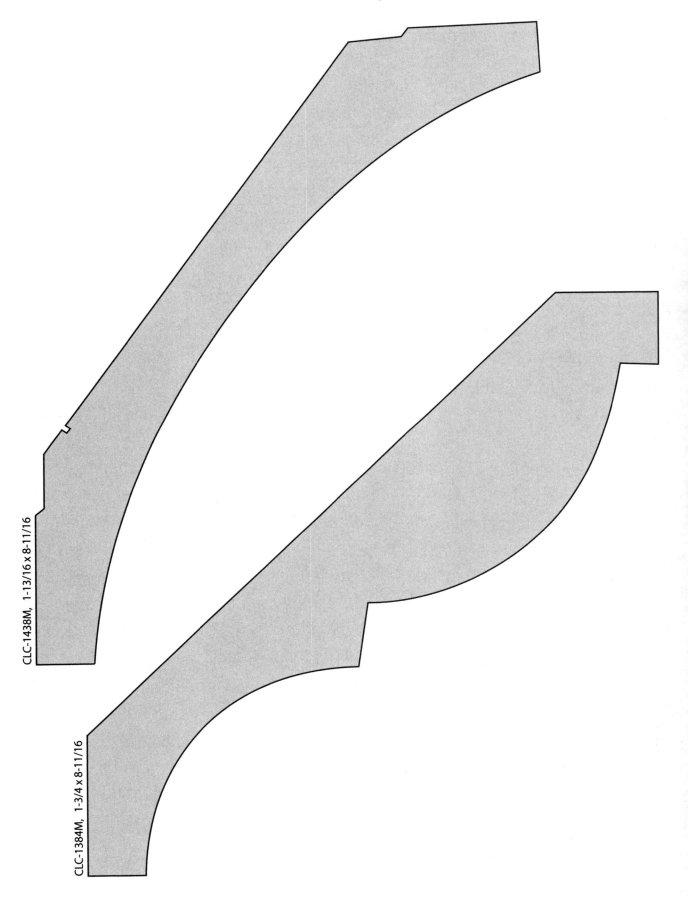

CLC-1438M, 1-13/16 x 8-11/16

CLC-1384M, 1-3/4 x 8-11/16

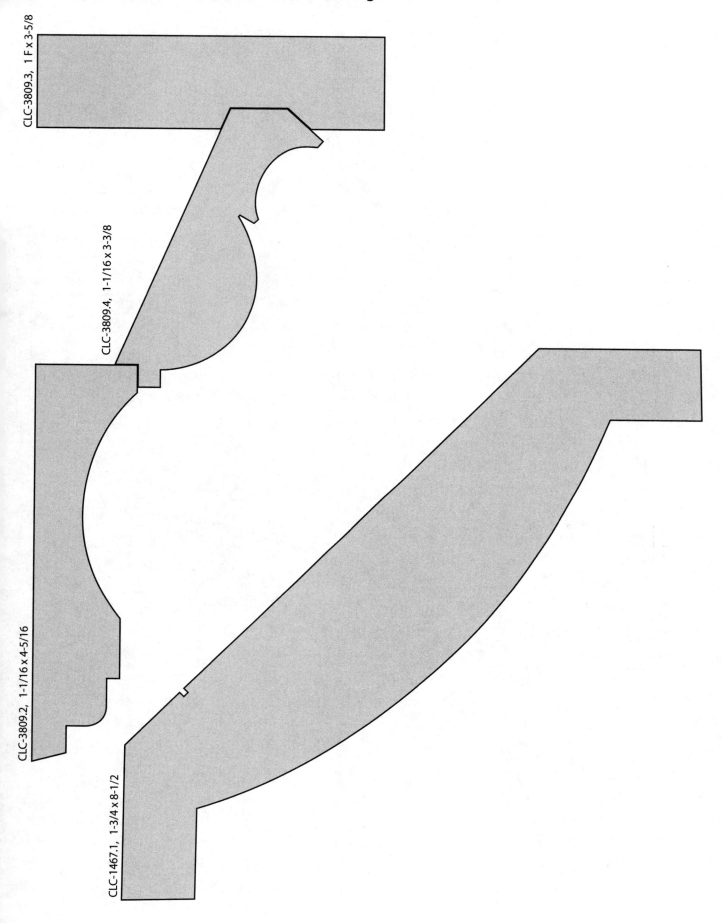

CLC-3809.3, 1 F x 3-5/8

CLC-3809.4, 1-1/16 x 3-3/8

CLC-3809.2, 1-1/16 x 4-5/16

CLC-1467.1, 1-3/4 x 8-1/2

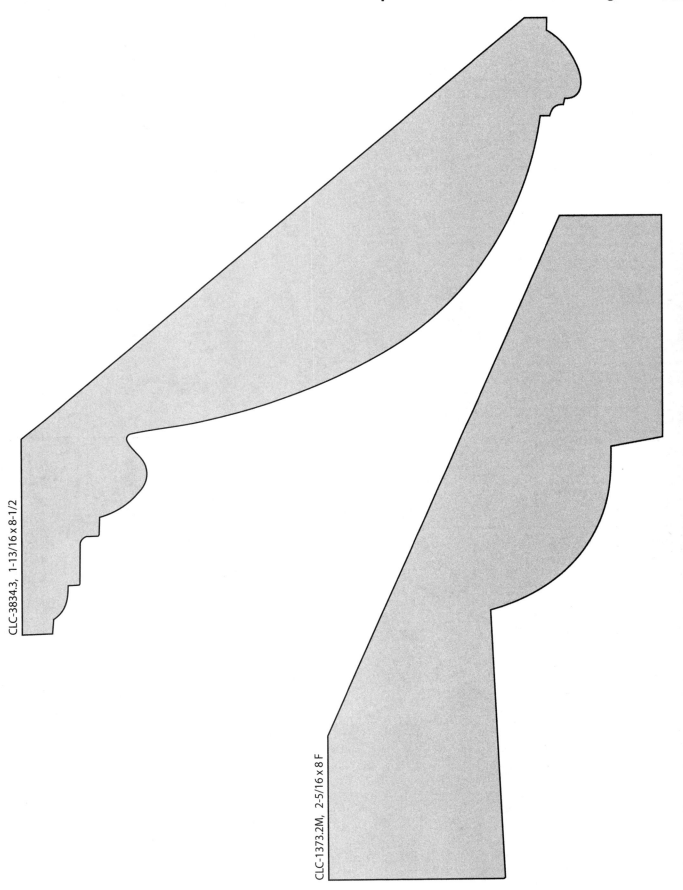

CLC-3834.3, 1-13/16 x 8-1/2

CLC-1373.2M, 2-5/16 x 8 F

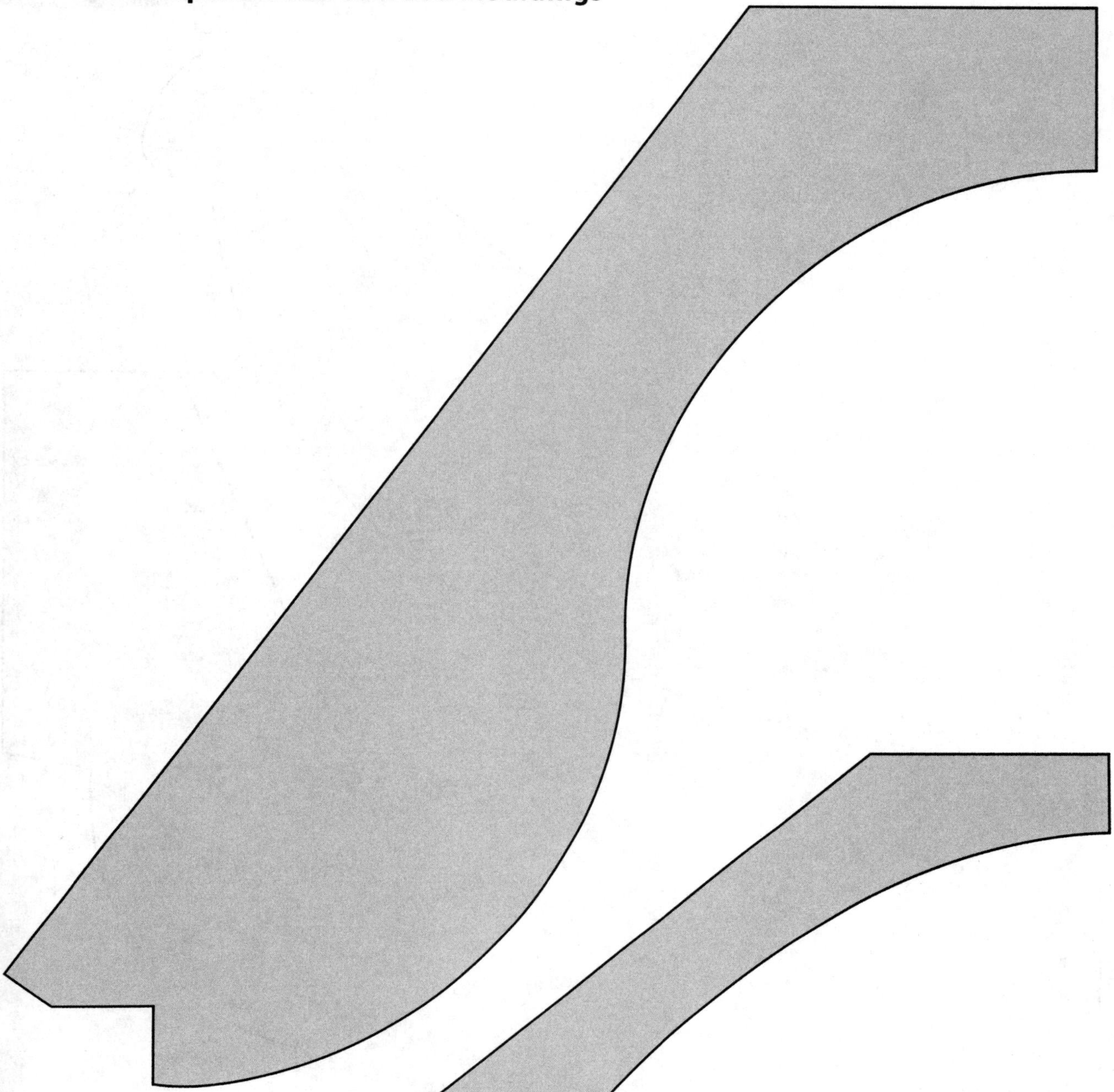

CLC-3707.4, 2-5/16 x 8-7/8

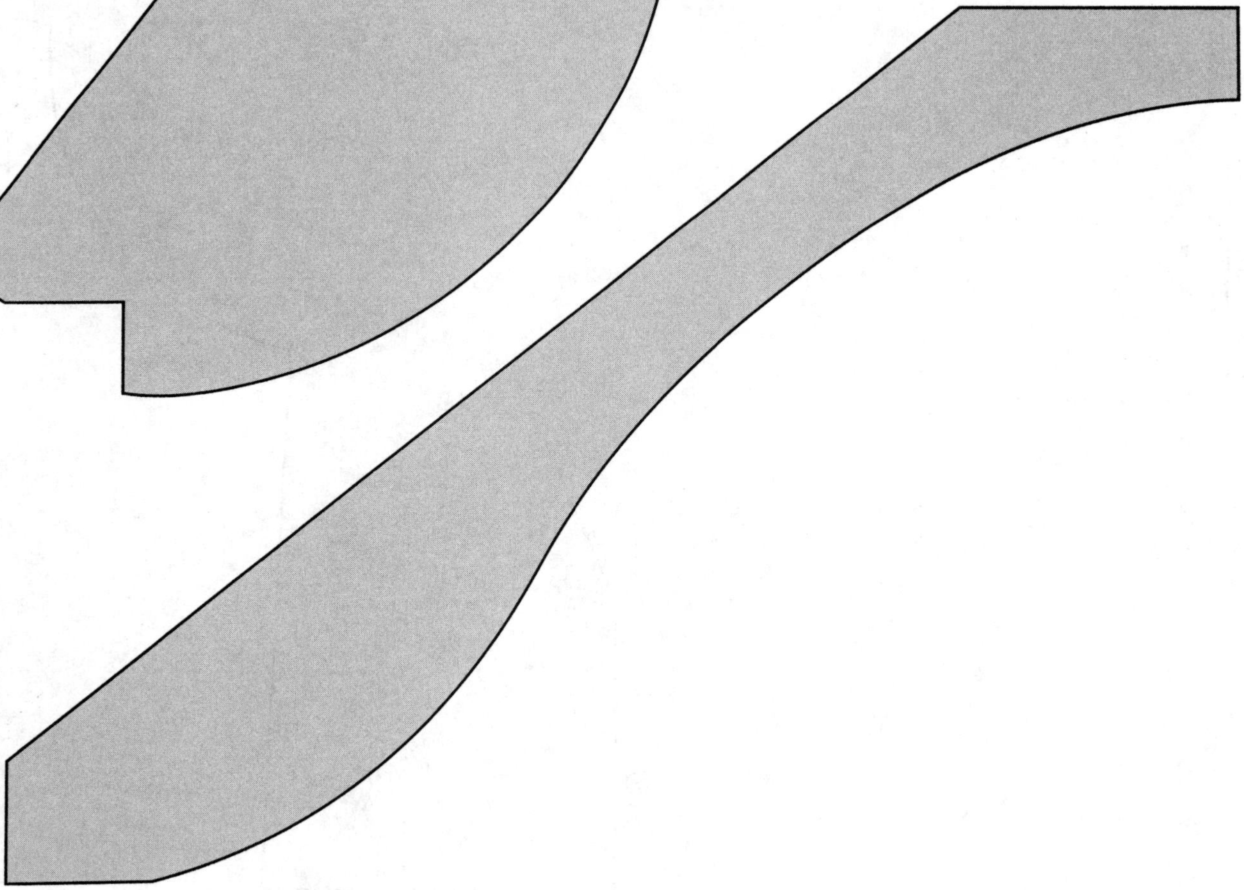

CLC-817.1, 1-5/16 x 8 F

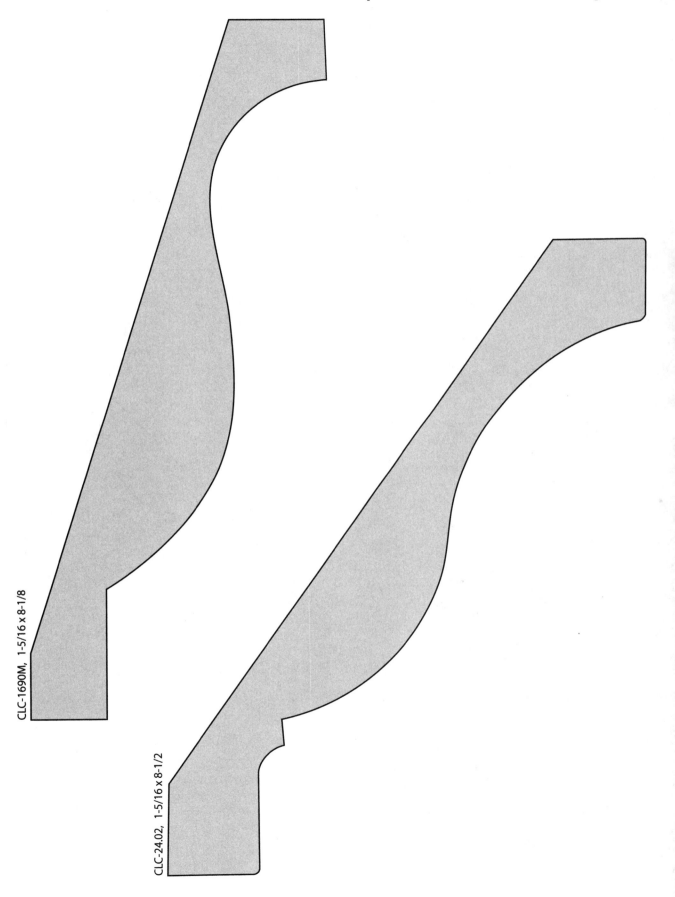

CLC-1690M, 1-5/16 x 8-1/8

CLC-24.02, 1-5/16 x 8-1/2

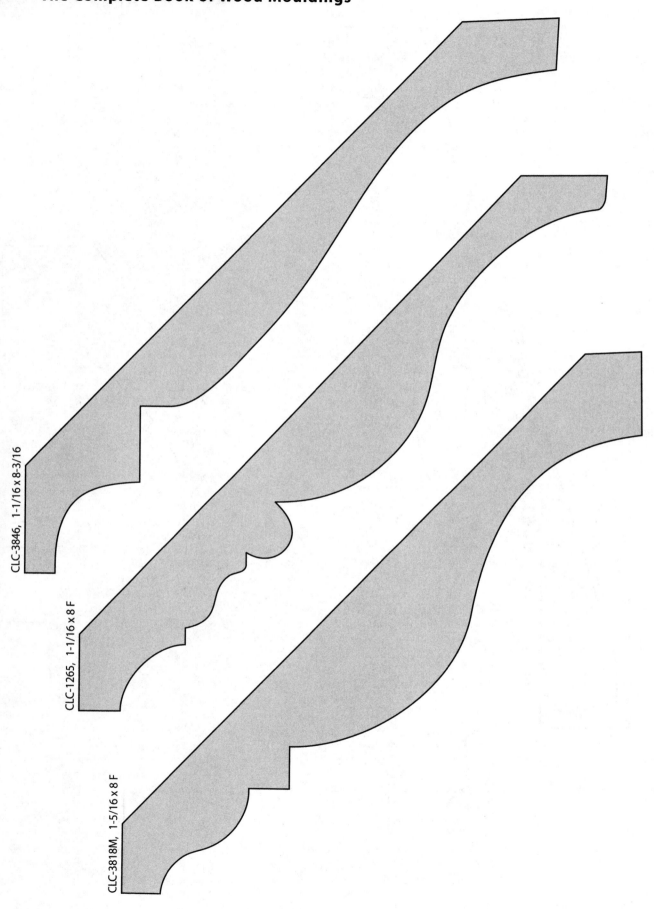

CLC-3846, 1-1/16 x 8-3/16

CLC-1265, 1-1/16 x 8 F

CLC-3818M, 1-5/16 x 8 F

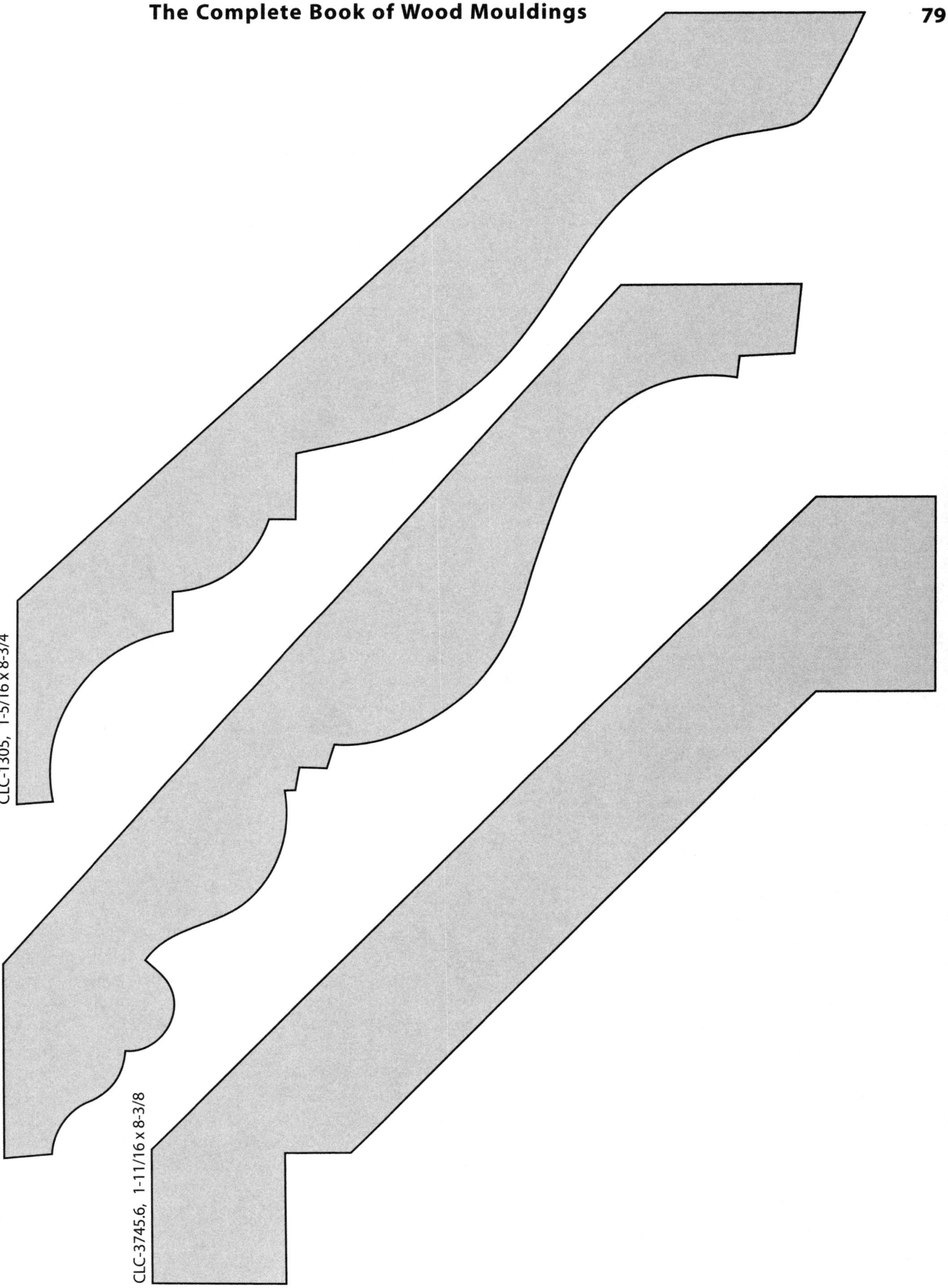

CLC-1305, 1-5/16 x 8-3/4

CLC-3860.1M, 1-5/16 x 8-15/16

CLC-3745.6, 1-11/16 x 8-3/8

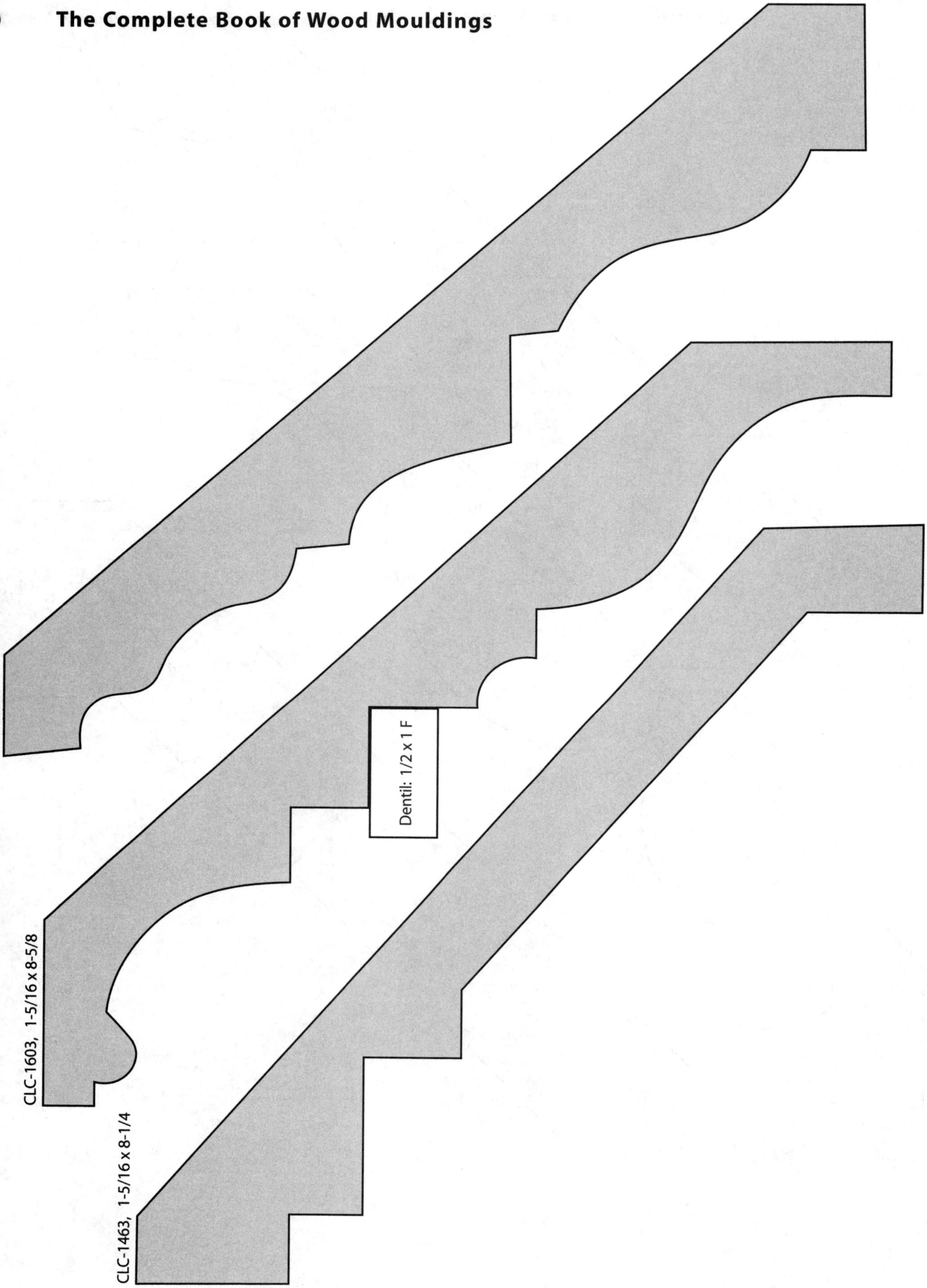

CLC-1230, 1-5/16 x 8-5/8

CLC-1603, 1-5/16 x 8-5/8

CLC-1463, 1-5/16 x 8-1/4

Dentil: 1/2 x 1 F

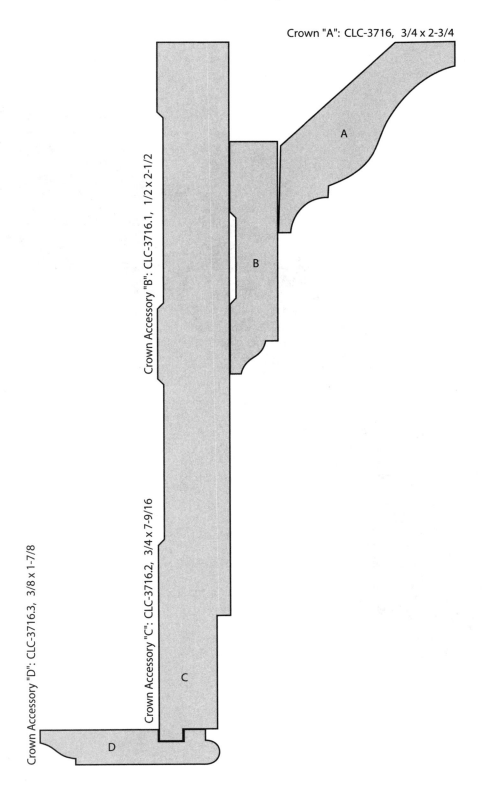

Crown "A": CLC-3716,　3/4 x 2-3/4

Crown Accessory "B": CLC-3716.1,　1/2 x 2-1/2

Crown Accessory "C": CLC-3716.2,　3/4 x 7-9/16

Crown Accessory "D": CLC-3716.3,　3/8 x 1-7/8

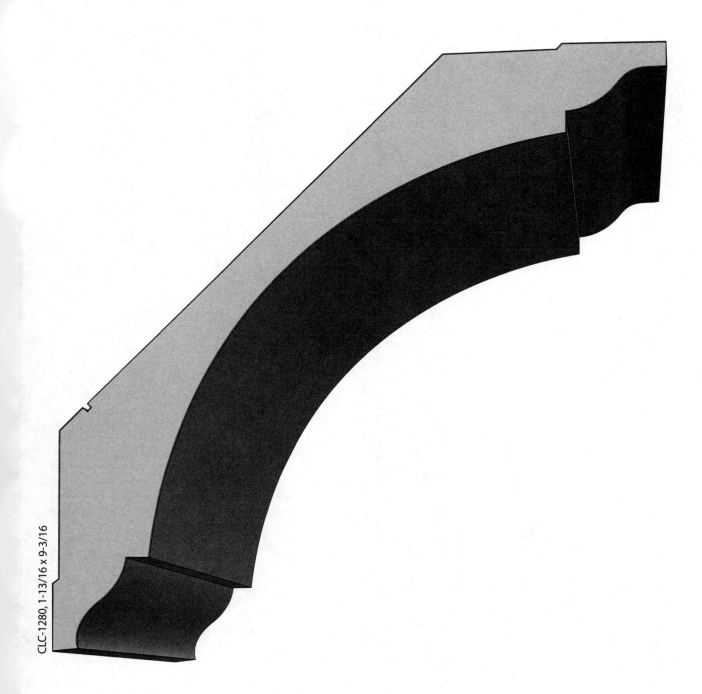

CLC-1280, 1-13/16 x 9-3/16

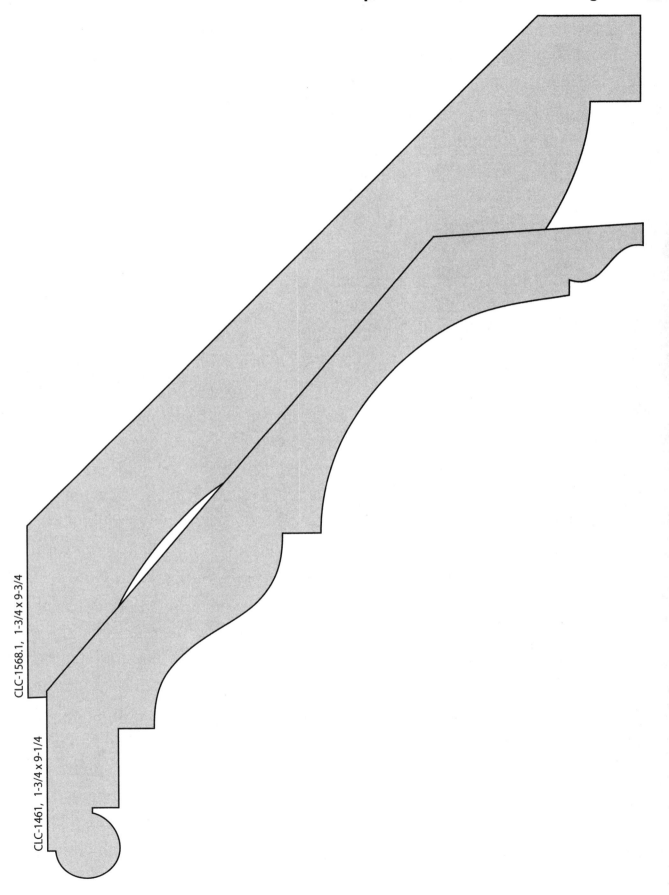

CLC-1568.1, 1-3/4 x 9-3/4

CLC-1461, 1-3/4 x 9-1/4

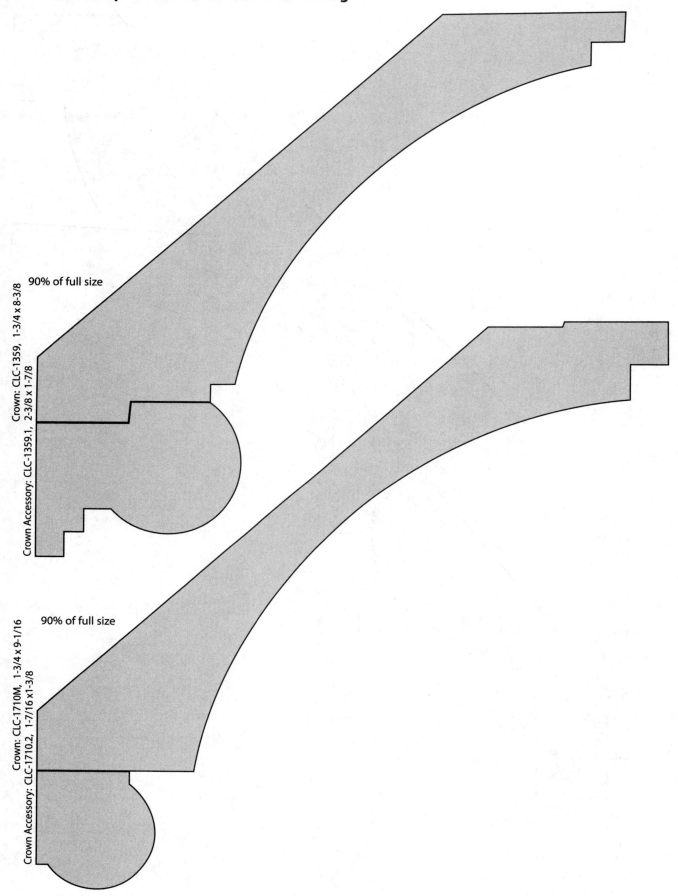

90% of full size

Crown: CLC-1359, 1-3/4 x 8-3/8

Crown Accessory: CLC-1359.1, 2-3/8 x 1-7/8

90% of full size

Crown: CLC-1710M, 1-3/4 x 9-1/16

Crown Accessory: CLC-1710.2, 1-7/16 x1-3/8

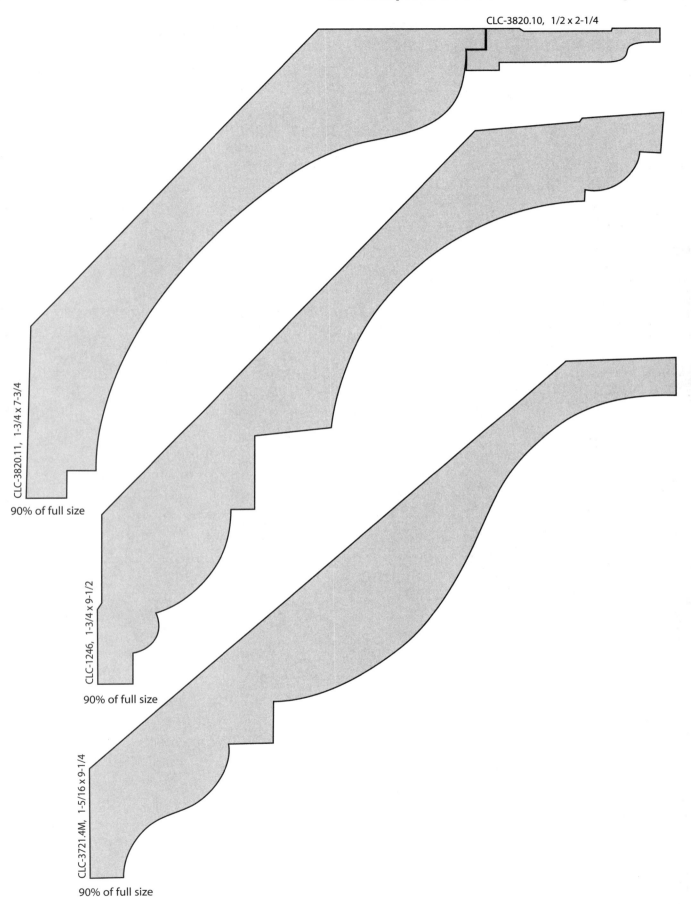

CLC-3820.10, 1/2 x 2-1/4

CLC-3820.11, 1-3/4 x 7-3/4

90% of full size

CLC-1246, 1-3/4 x 9-1/2

90% of full size

CLC-3721.4M, 1-5/16 x 9-1/4

90% of full size

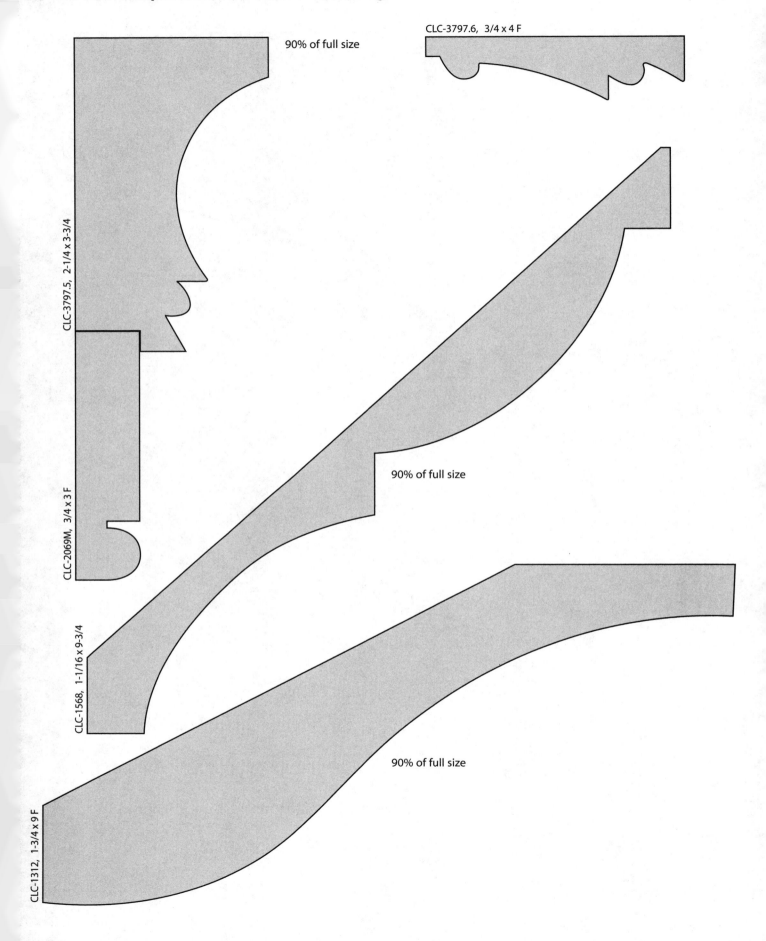

90% of full size

CLC-3797.6, 3/4 x 4 F

CLC-3797.5, 2-1/4 x 3-3/4

CLC-2069M, 3/4 x 3 F

90% of full size

CLC-1568, 1-1/16 x 9-3/4

90% of full size

CLC-1312, 1-3/4 x 9 F

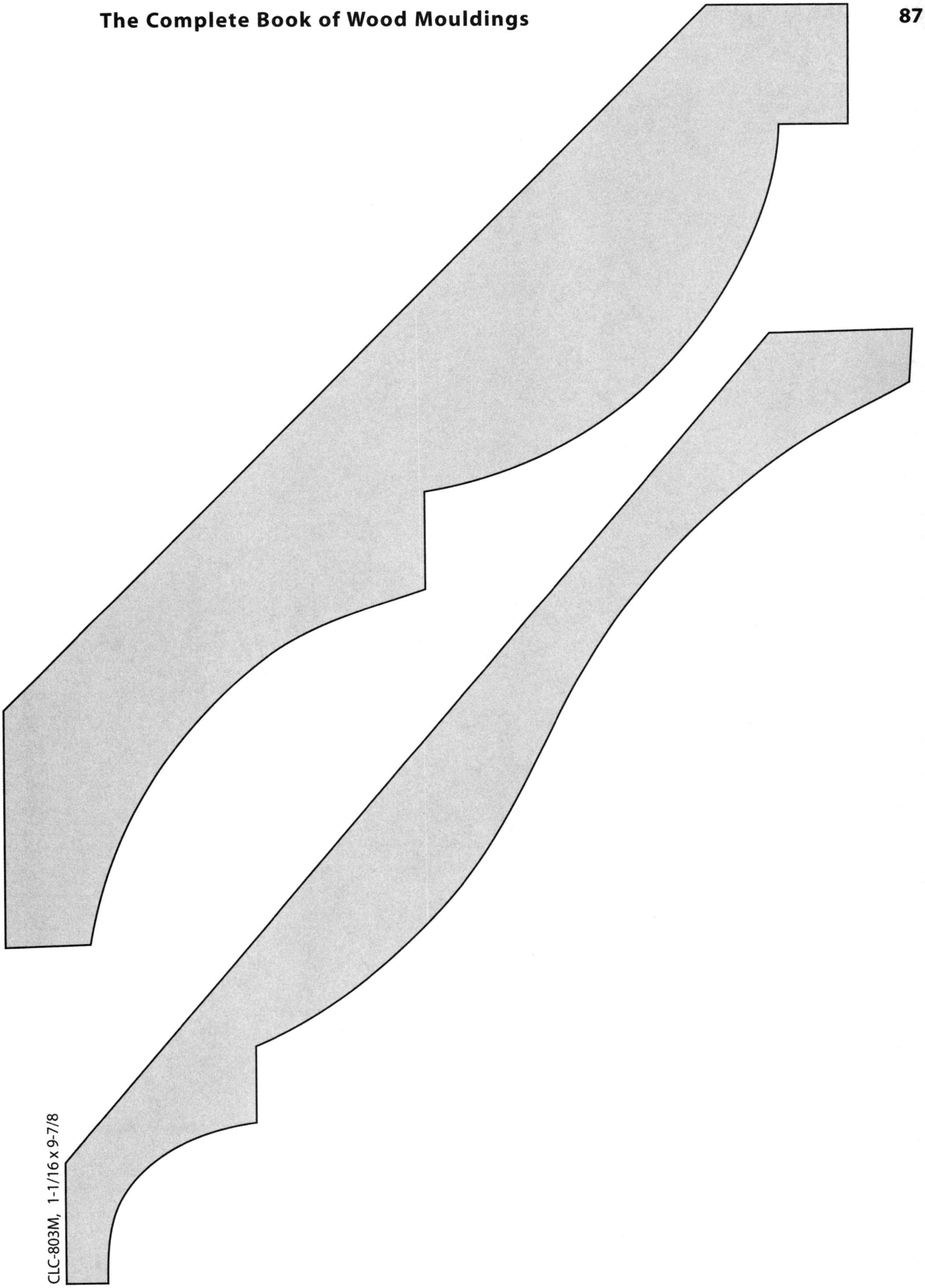

CLC-1568.1, 1-3/4 x 9-3/4

CLC-803M, 1-1/16 x 9-7/8

CLC-1369, 1-13/16 x 9-3/8

CLC-1367M, 1-3/4 x 9-7/8

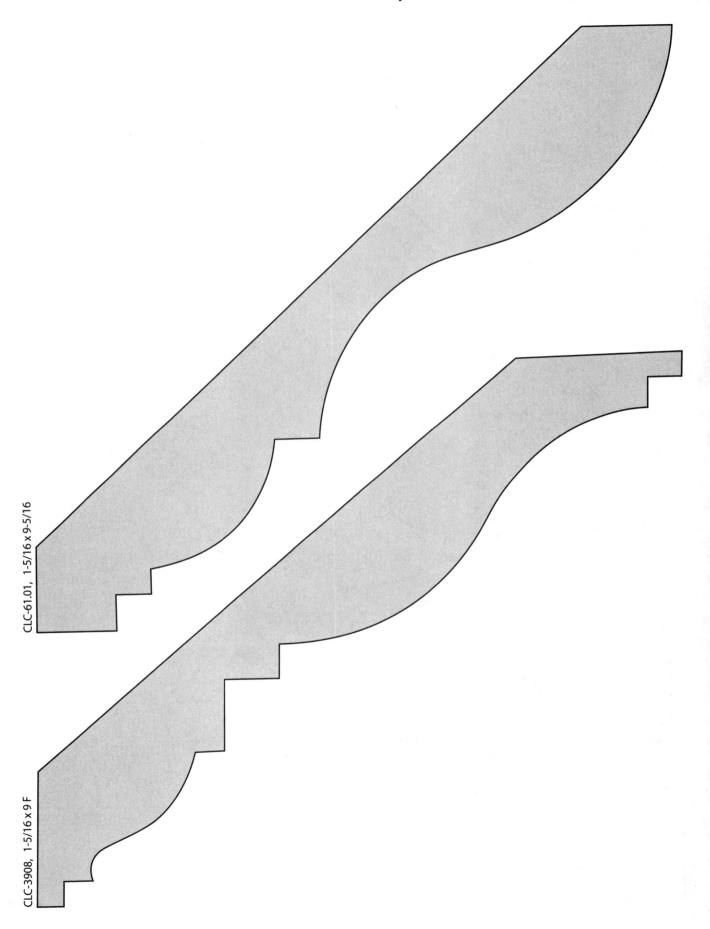

CLC-61.01, 1-5/16 x 9-5/16

CLC-3908, 1-5/16 x 9 F

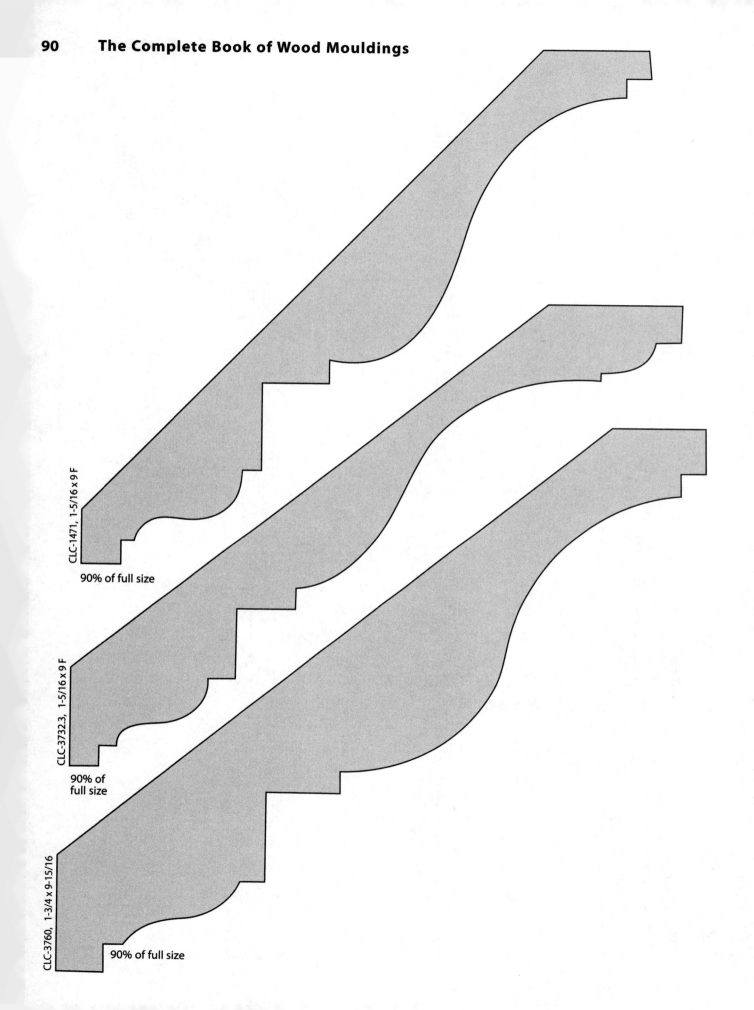

CLC-1471, 1-5/16 x 9 F

90% of full size

CLC-3732.3, 1-5/16 x 9 F

90% of
full size

CLC-3760, 1-3/4 x 9-15/16

90% of full size

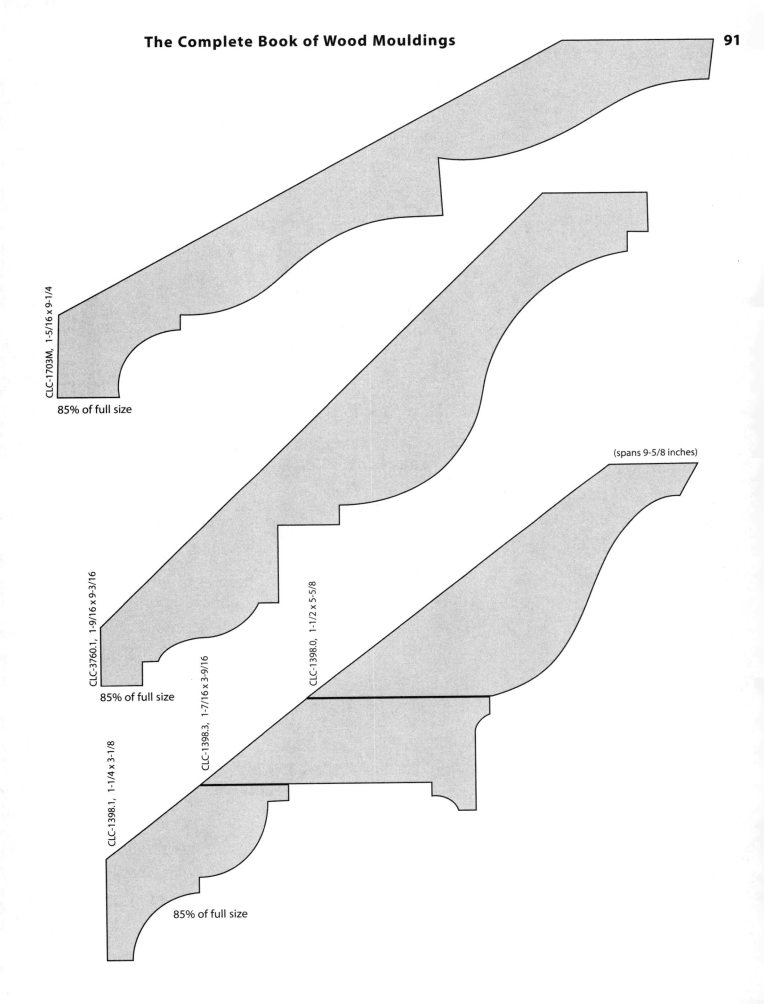

CLC-1703M, 1-5/16 x 9-1/4

85% of full size

CLC-3760.1, 1-9/16 x 9-3/16

85% of full size

(spans 9-5/8 inches)

CLC-1398.0, 1-1/2 x 5-5/8

CLC-1398.3, 1-7/16 x 3-9/16

CLC-1398.1, 1-1/4 x 3-1/8

85% of full size

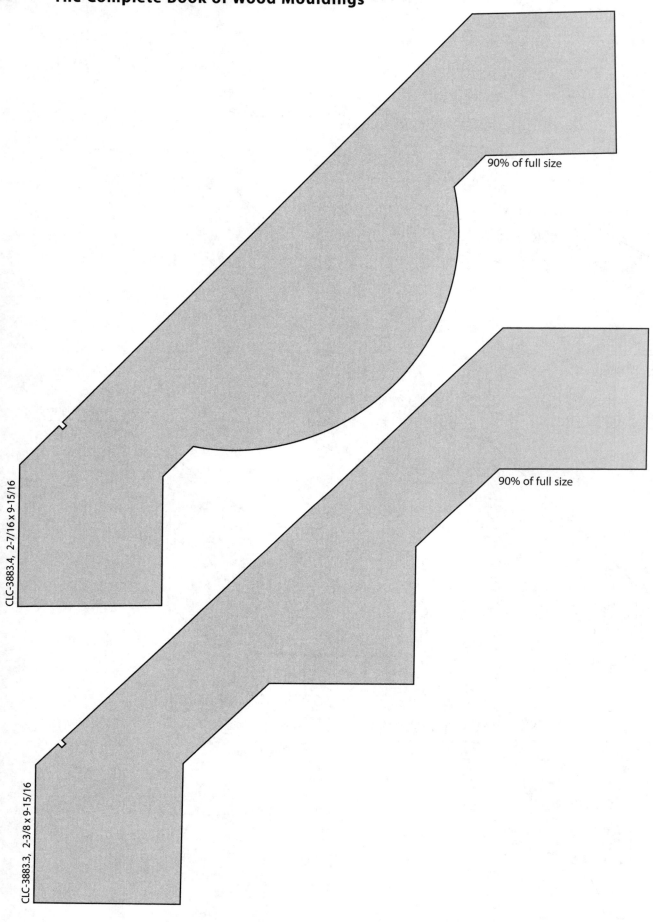

90% of full size

90% of full size

CLC-3883.4, 2-7/16 x 9-15/16

CLC-3883.3, 2-3/8 x 9-15/16

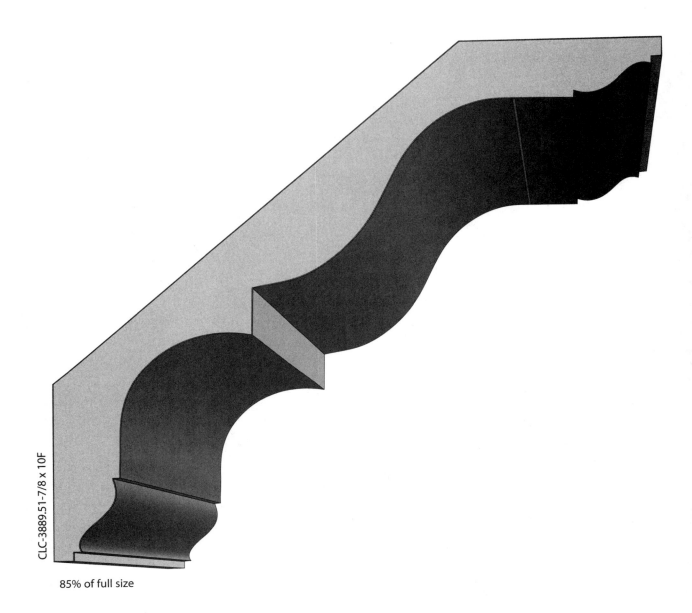

CLC-3889.51-7/8 x 10F

85% of full size

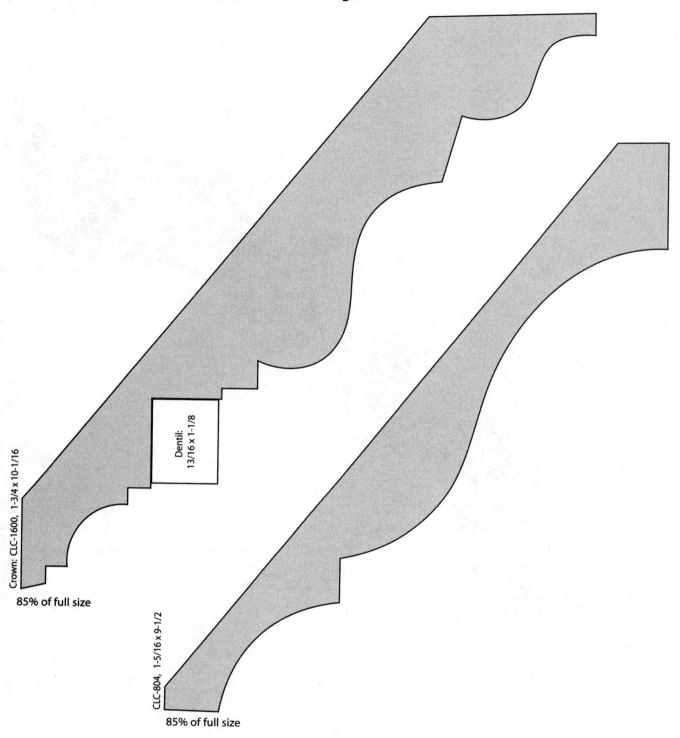

Crown: CLC-1600, 1-3/4 x 10-1/16

Dentil:
13/16 x 1-1/8

85% of full size

CLC-804, 1-5/16 x 9-1/2

85% of full size

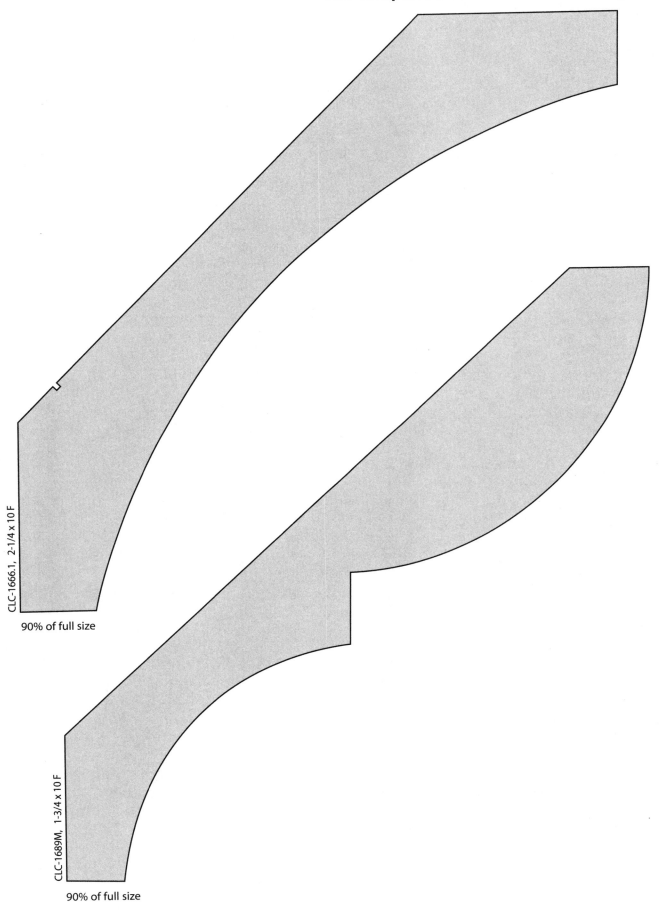

CLC-1666.1, 2-1/4 x 10 F

90% of full size

CLC-1689M, 1-3/4 x 10 F

90% of full size

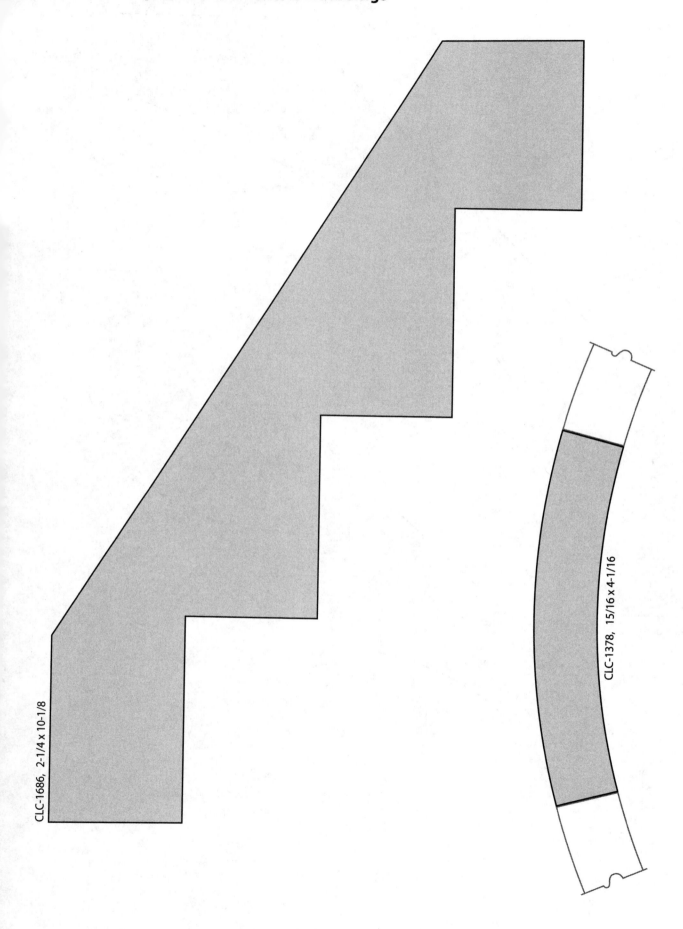

CLC-1686, 2-1/4 x 10-1/8

CLC-1378, 15/16 x 4-1/16

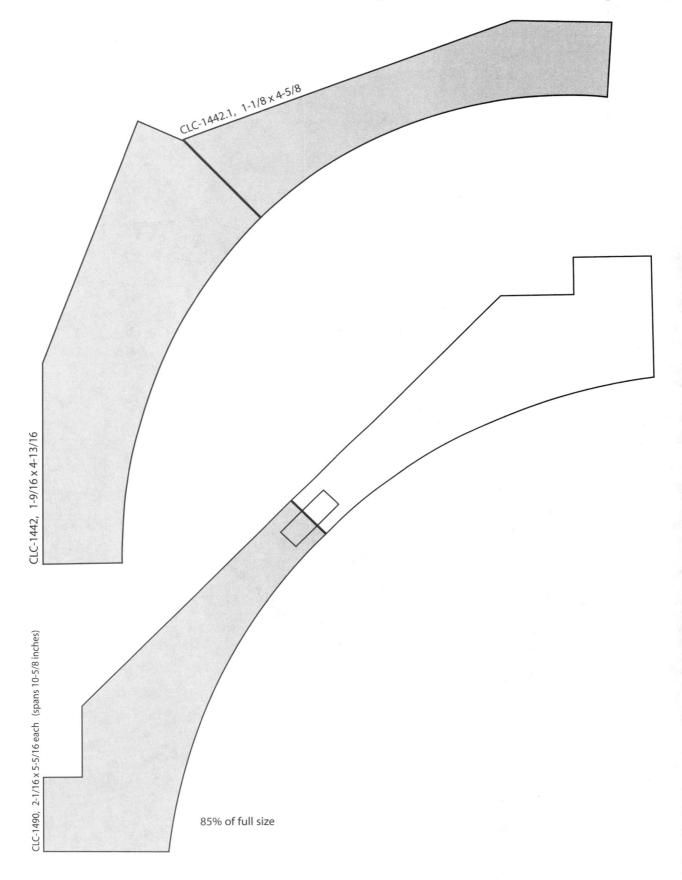

CLC-1442.1, 1-1/8 x 4-5/8

CLC-1442, 1-9/16 x 4-13/16

CLC-1490, 2-1/16 x 5-5/16 each (spans 10-5/8 inches)

85% of full size

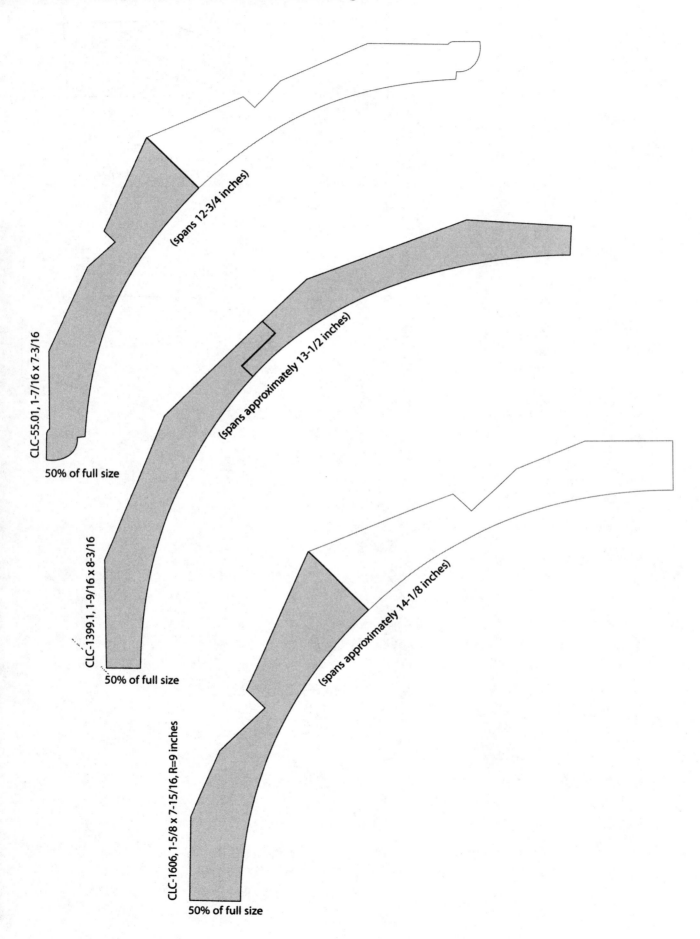

(spans 12-3/4 inches)

CLC-55.01, 1-7/16 x 7-3/16

50% of full size

(spans approximately 13-1/2 inches)

CLC-1399.1, 1-9/16 x 8-3/16

50% of full size

(spans approximately 14-1/8 inches)

CLC-1606, 1-5/8 x 7-15/16, R=9 inches

50% of full size

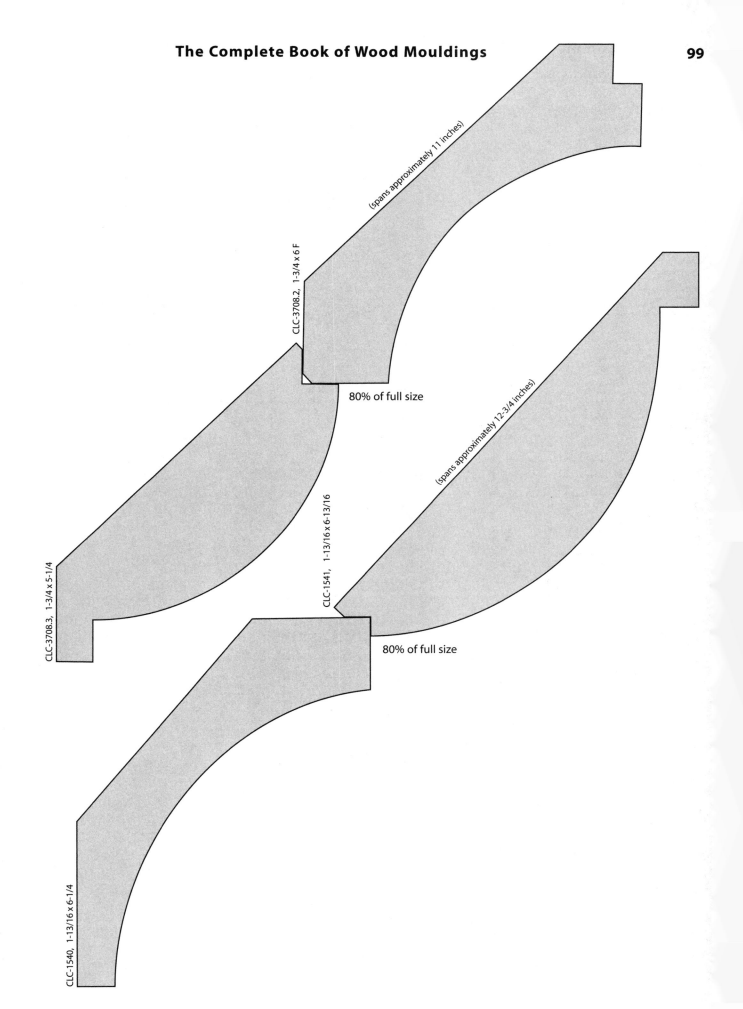

CLC-3708.2, 1-3/4 x 6 F

(spans approximately 11 inches)

80% of full size

CLC-3708.3, 1-3/4 x 5-1/4

CLC-1541, 1-13/16 x 6-13/16

(spans approximately 12-3/4 inches)

80% of full size

CLC-1540, 1-13/16 x 6-1/4

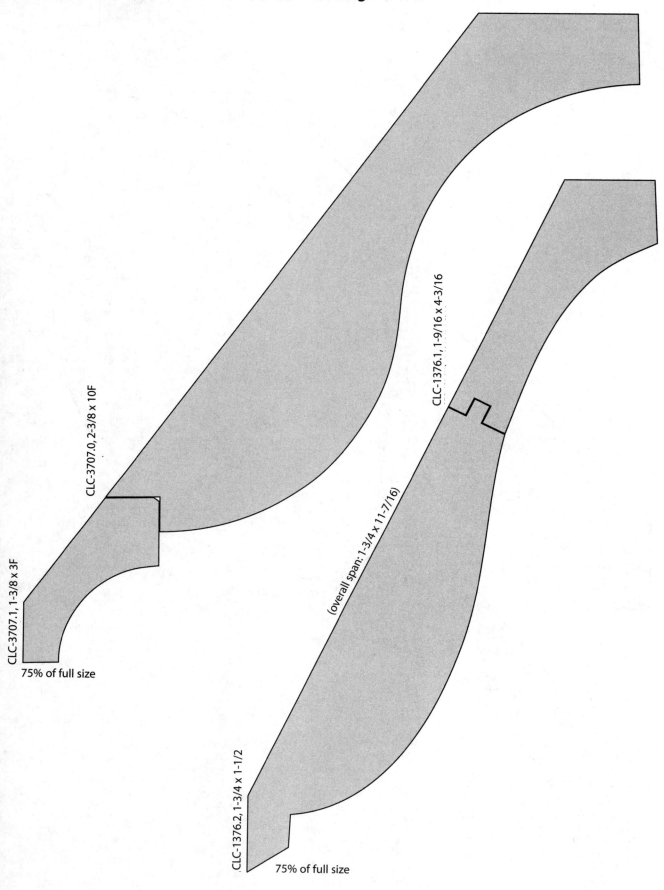

CLC-3707.0, 2-3/8 x 10F

CLC-3707.1, 1-3/8 x 3F

75% of full size

CLC-1376.1, 1-9/16 x 4-3/16

(overall span: 1-3/4 x 11-7/16)

CLC-1376.2, 1-3/4 x 1-1/2

75% of full size

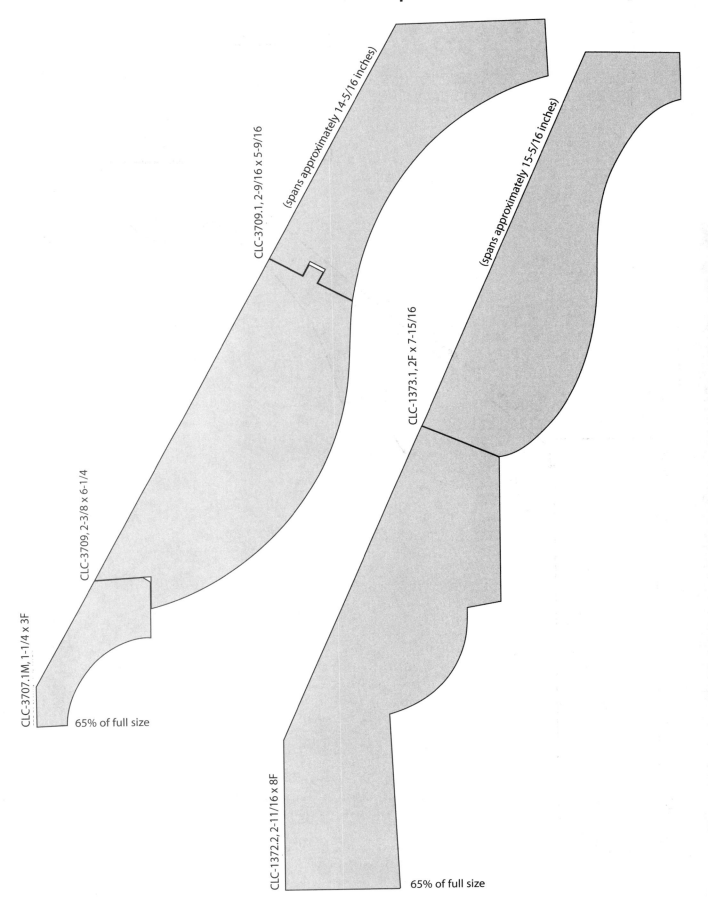

CLC-3709.1, 2-9/16 x 5-9/16

(spans approximately 14-5/16 inches)

CLC-3709, 2-3/8 x 6-1/4

CLC-3707.1M, 1-1/4 x 3F

65% of full size

CLC-1373.1, 2F x 7-15/16

(spans approximately 15-5/16 inches)

CLC-1372.2, 2-11/16 x 8F

65% of full size

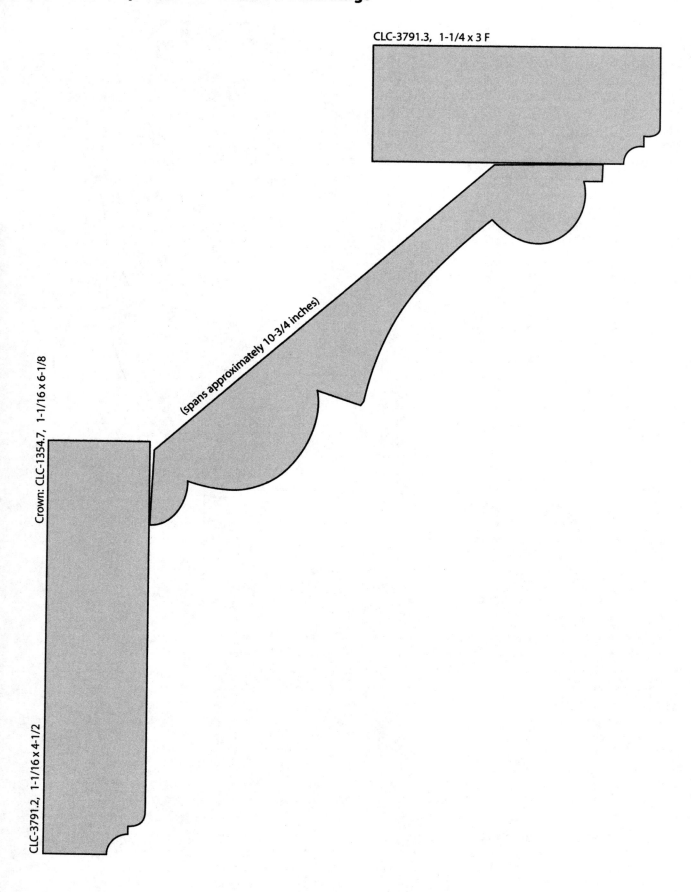

CLC-3791.3, 1-1/4 x 3 F

(spans approximately 10-3/4 inches)

Crown: CLC-1354.7, 1-1/16 x 6-1/8

CLC-3791.2, 1-1/16 x 4-1/2

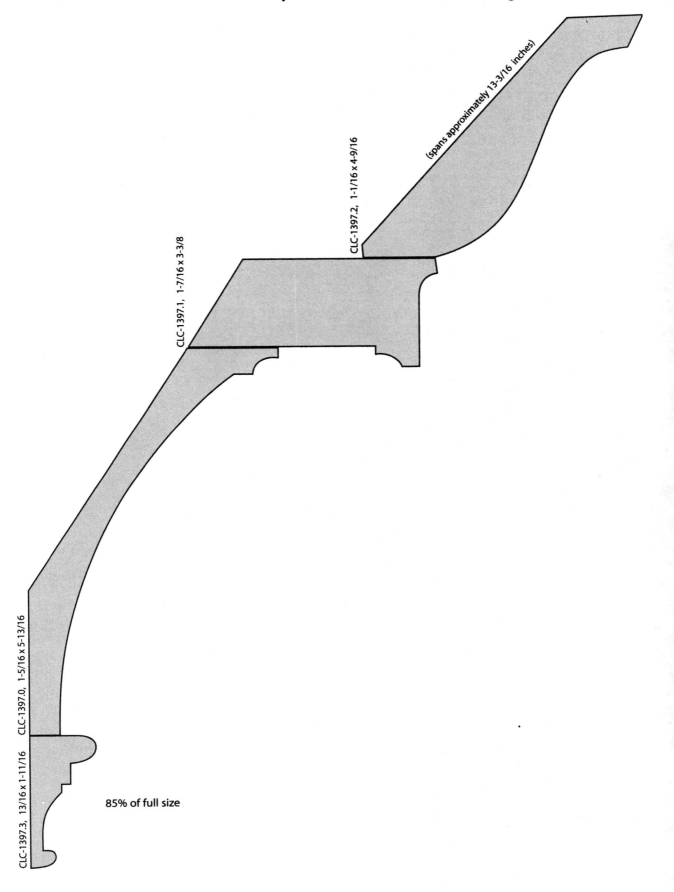

(spans approximately 13-3/16 inches)

CLC-1397.2, 1-1/16 x 4-9/16

CLC-1397.1, 1-7/16 x 3-3/8

CLC-1397.0, 1-5/16 x 5-13/16

CLC-1397.3, 13/16 x 1-11/16

85% of full size

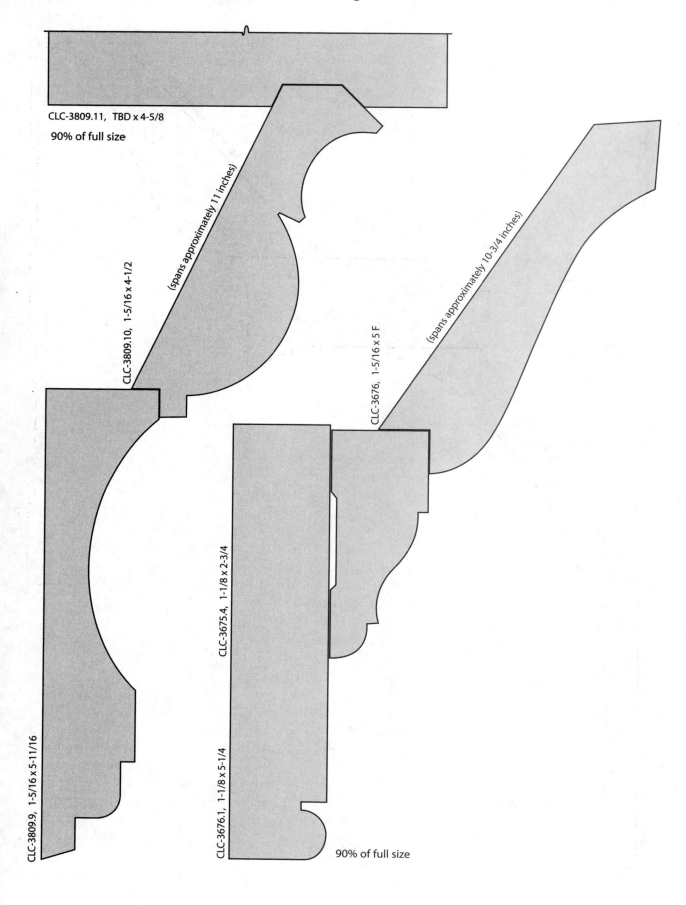

CLC-3809.11, TBD x 4-5/8

90% of full size

CLC-3809.10, 1-5/16 x 4-1/2

(spans approximately 11 inches)

CLC-3676, 1-5/16 x 5 F

(spans approximately 10-3/4 inches)

CLC-3675.4, 1-1/8 x 2-3/4

CLC-3676.1, 1-1/8 x 5-1/4

CLC-3809.9, 1-5/16 x 5-11/16

90% of full size

CLC-3830.4, 1F x 2-1/2

CLC-3830.5, 1-16 x 2-3/16

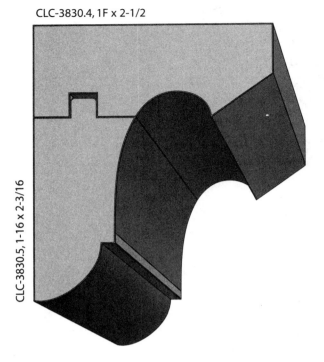

CLC-1347.1, 7/8 x 3-3/16   (spans 6-7/8 inches)

CLC-37-2.2, 1-1/16 x 3-1/4   (spans 5 inches)

CLC-1347, 1-1/16 x 4-3/4

CLC-37-2.1, 1 F x 3-3/16

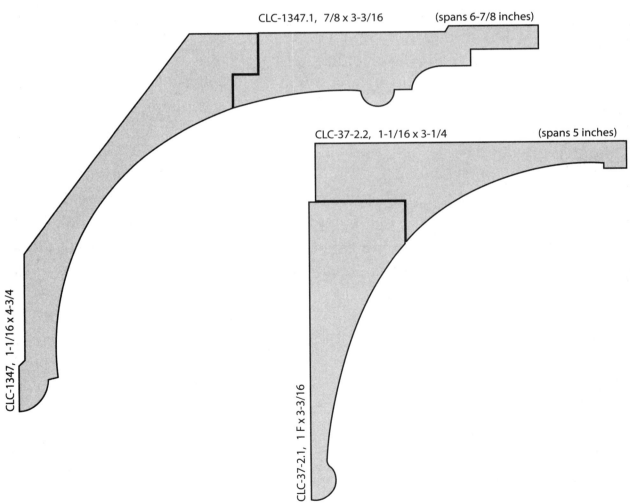

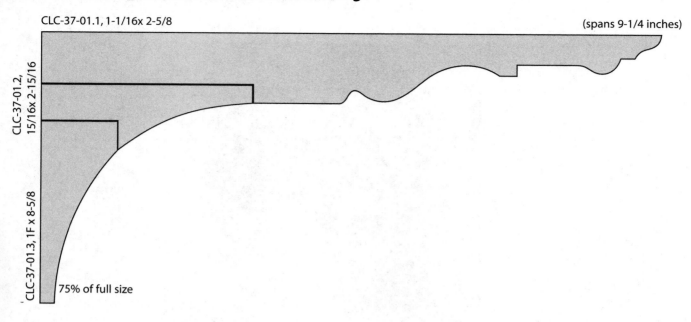

CLC-37-01.1, 1-1/16x 2-5/8

(spans 9-1/4 inches)

CLC-37-01.2, 15/16x 2-15/16

CLC-37-01.3, 1F x 8-5/8

75% of full size

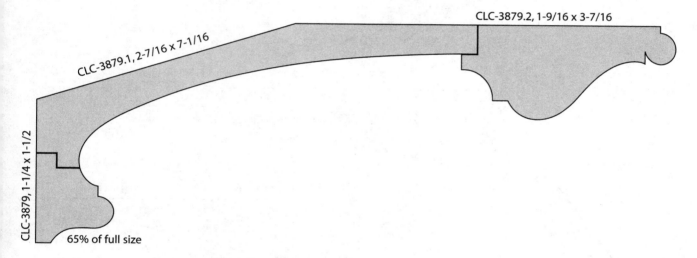

CLC-3879.2, 1-9/16 x 3-7/16

CLC-3879.1, 2-7/16 x 7-1/16

CLC-3879, 1-1/4 x 1-1/2

65% of full size

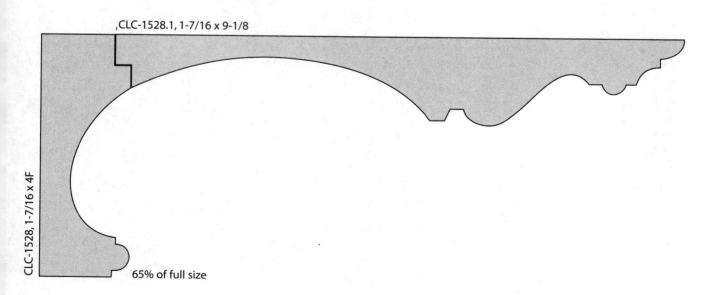

CLC-1528.1, 1-7/16 x 9-1/8

CLC-1528, 1-7/16 x 4F

65% of full size

CLC-1506, 1-1/2 x 5-7/8

CLC-1506.1, 1-3/8 x 5-15/16

CLC-1507.1, 1-3/8 x 5-1/8

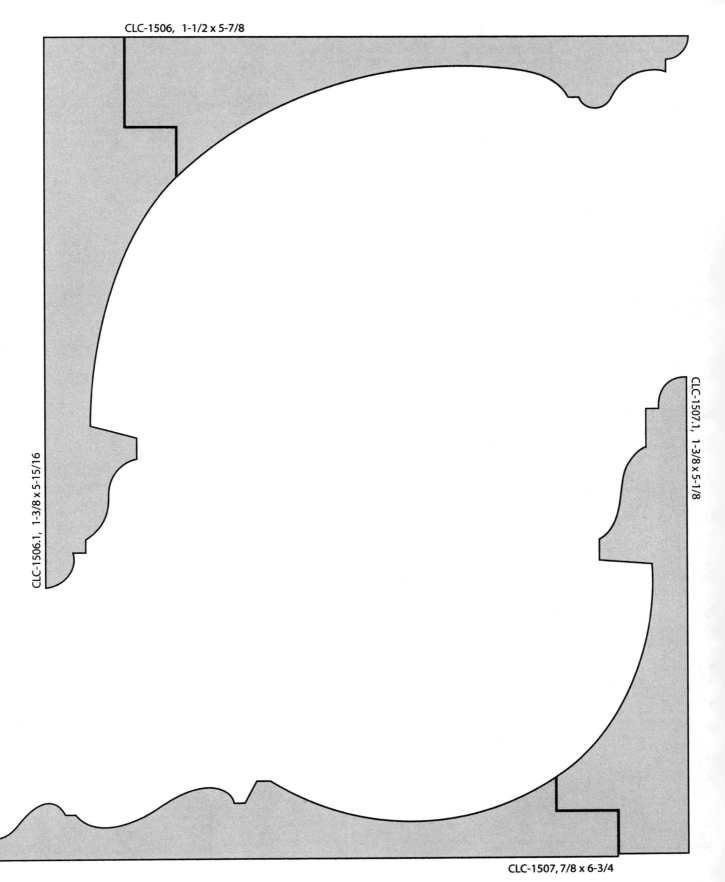

CLC-1507, 7/8 x 6-3/4

CLC-1343.1, 1-9/16 x 5-3/16

CLC-1389, 1-5/16 x 6-7/16

CLC-1343, 1-5/16 x 6 F

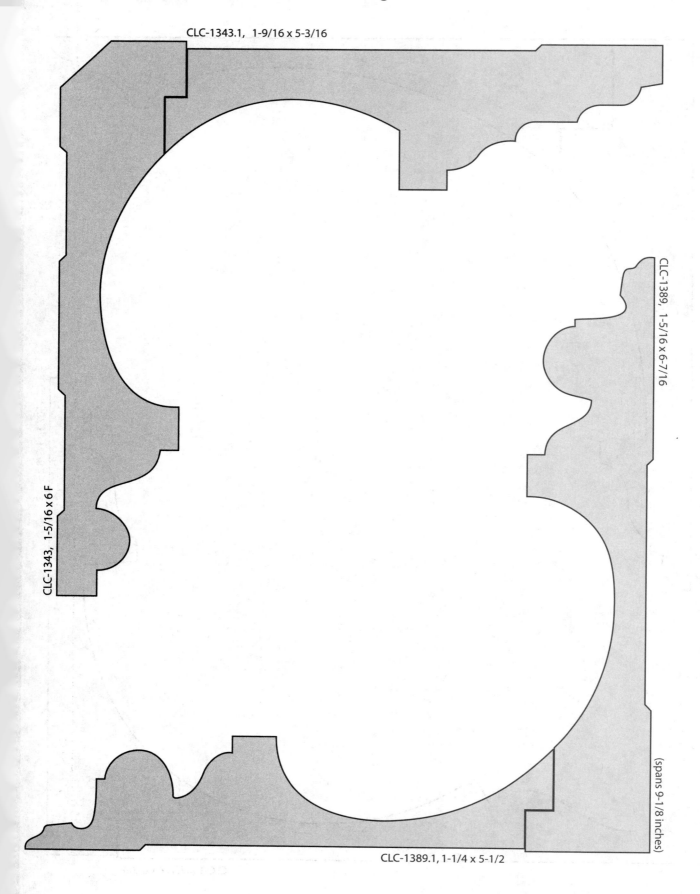

(spans 9-1/8 inches)

CLC-1389.1, 1-1/4 x 5-1/2

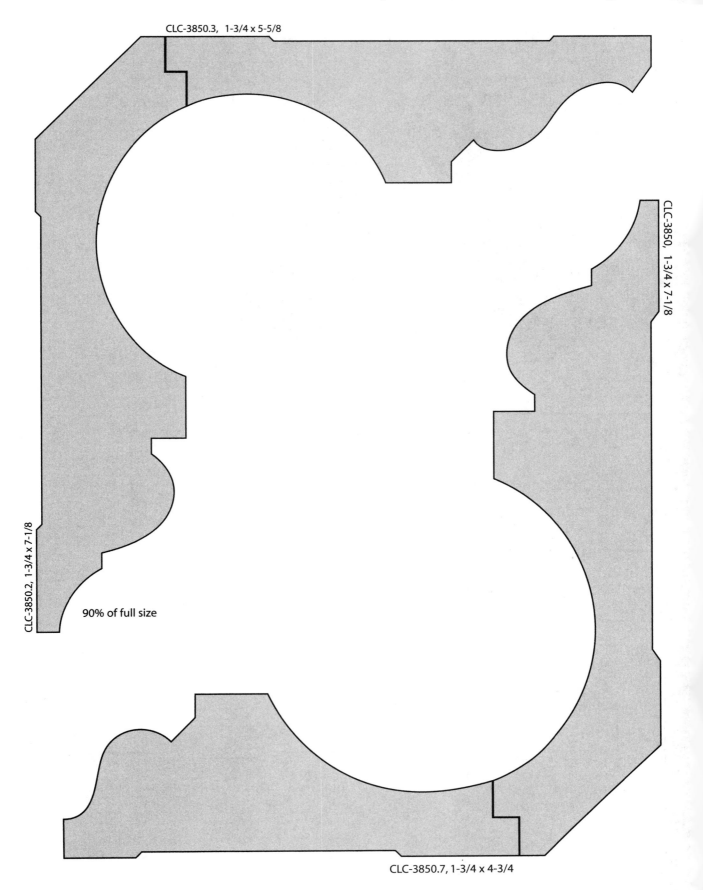

CLC-3850.3, 1-3/4 x 5-5/8

CLC-3850, 1-3/4 x 7-1/8

CLC-3850.2, 1-3/4 x 7-1/8

90% of full size

CLC-3850.7, 1-3/4 x 4-3/4

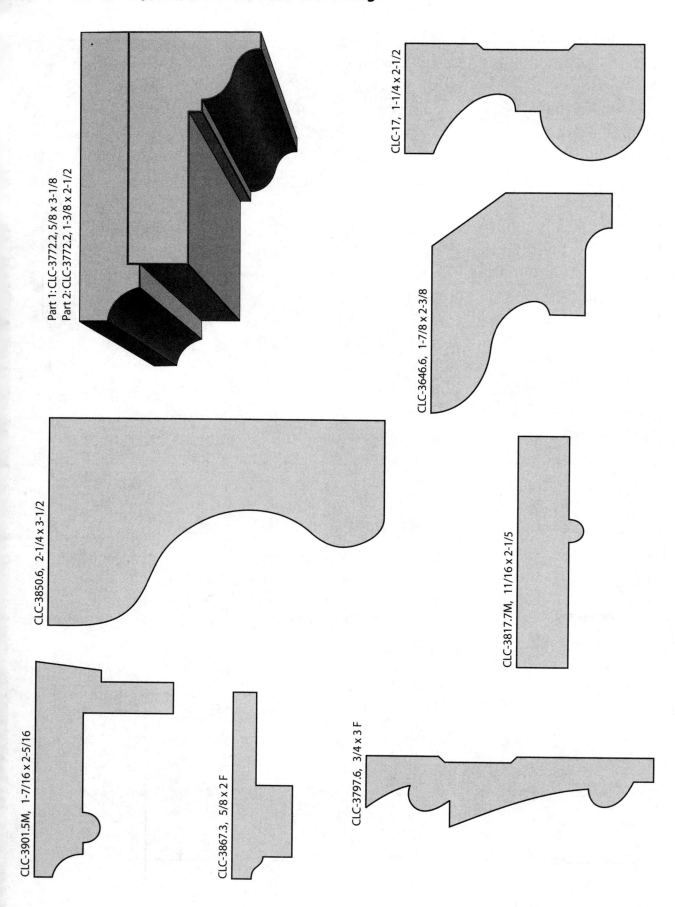

Part 1: CLC-3772.2, 5/8 x 3-1/8
Part 2: CLC-3772.2, 1-3/8 x 2-1/2

CLC-17, 1-1/4 x 2-1/2

CLC-3646.6, 1-7/8 x 2-3/8

CLC-3850.6, 2-1/4 x 3-1/2

CLC-3817.7M, 11/16 x 2-1/5

CLC-3901.5M, 1-7/16 x 2-5/16

CLC-3867.3, 5/8 x 2 F

CLC-3797.6, 3/4 x 3 F

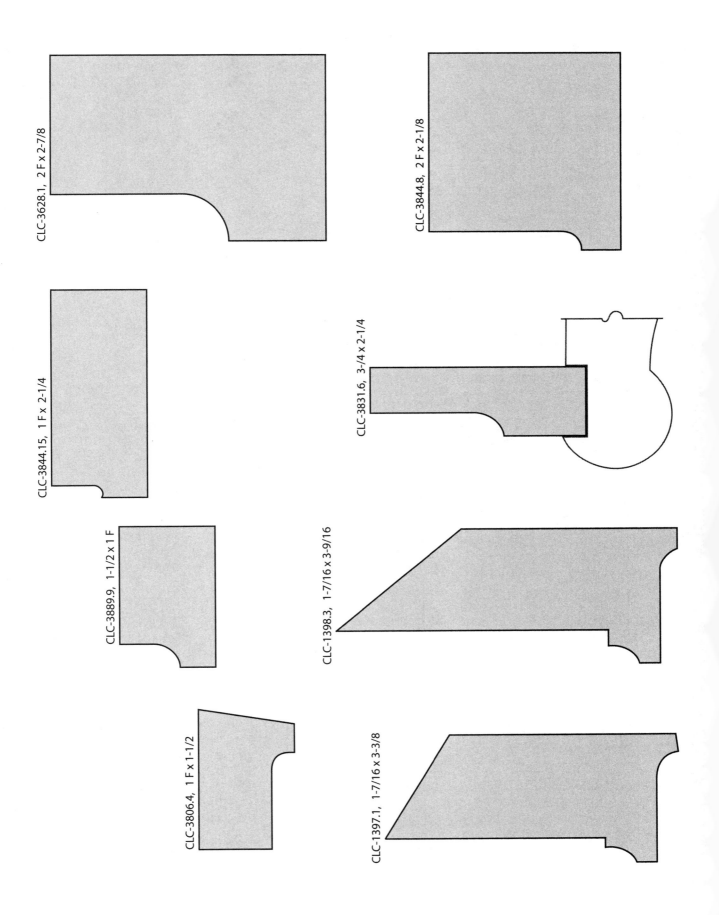

CLC-3628.1, 2 F x 2-7/8

CLC-3844.8, 2 F x 2-1/8

CLC-3844.15, 1 F x 2-1/4

CLC-3831.6, 3/4 x 2-1/4

CLC-3889.9, 1-1/2 x 1 F

CLC-1398.3, 1-7/16 x 3-9/16

CLC-3806.4, 1 F x 1-1/2

CLC-1397.1, 1-7/16 x 3-3/8

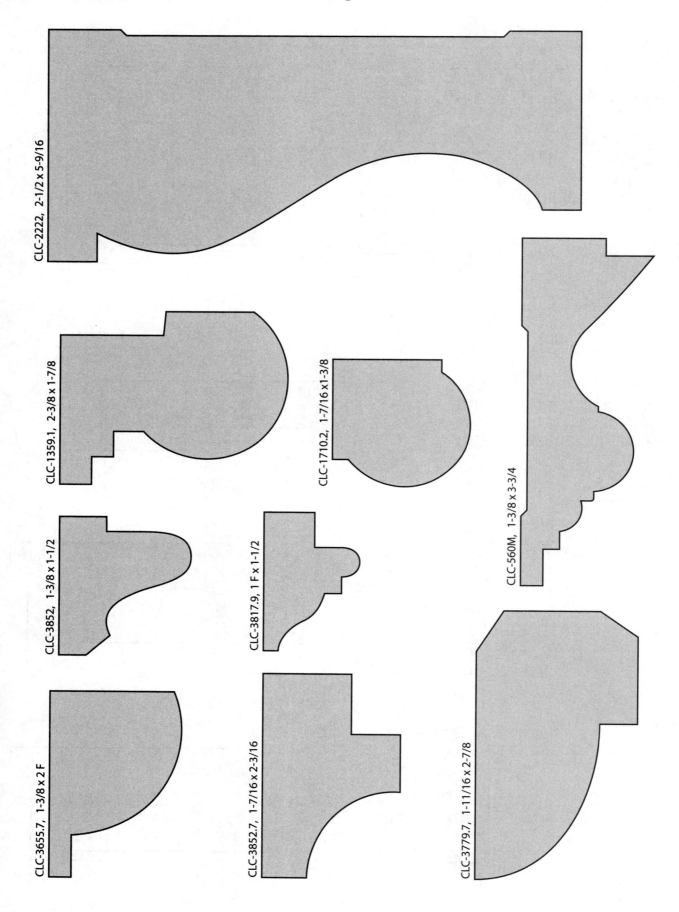

CLC-2222, 2-1/2 x 5-9/16

CLC-1359.1, 2-3/8 x 1-7/8

CLC-1710.2, 1-7/16 x1-3/8

CLC-560M, 1-3/8 x 3-3/4

CLC-3852, 1-3/8 x 1-1/2

CLC-3817.9, 1 F x 1-1/2

CLC-3655.7, 1-3/8 x 2 F

CLC-3852.7, 1-7/16 x 2-3/16

CLC-3779.7, 1-11/16 x 2-7/8

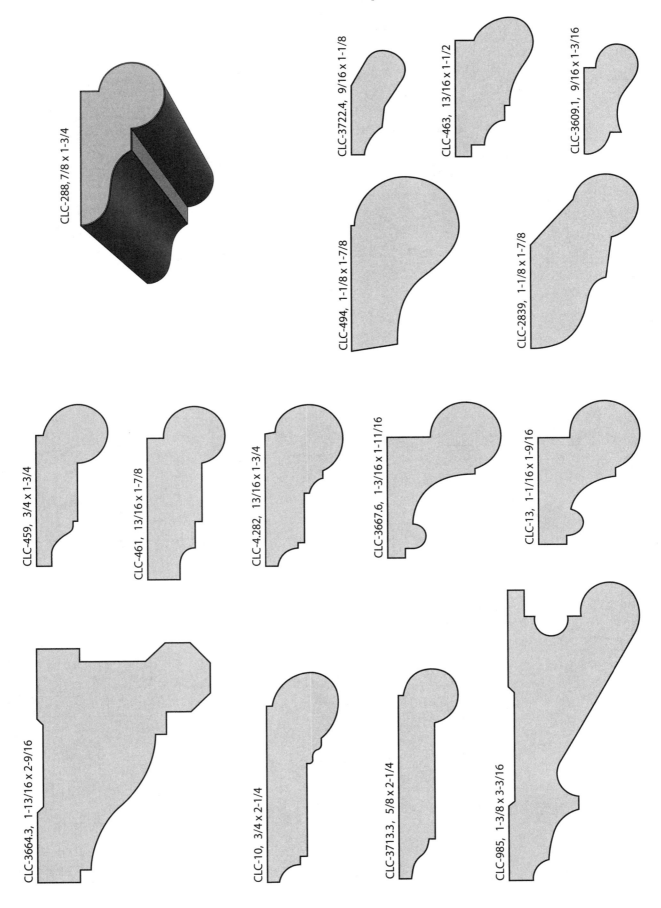

CLC-288, 7/8 x 1-3/4

CLC-3722.4, 9/16 x 1-1/8

CLC-463, 13/16 x 1-1/2

CLC-3609.1, 9/16 x 1-3/16

CLC-494, 1-1/8 x 1-7/8

CLC-2839, 1-1/8 x 1-7/8

CLC-459, 3/4 x 1-3/4

CLC-461, 13/16 x 1-7/8

CLC-4.282, 13/16 x 1-3/4

CLC-3667.6, 1-3/16 x 1-11/16

CLC-13, 1-1/16 x 1-9/16

CLC-3664.3, 1-13/16 x 2-9/16

CLC-10, 3/4 x 2-1/4

CLC-3713.3, 5/8 x 2-1/4

CLC-985, 1-3/8 x 3-3/16

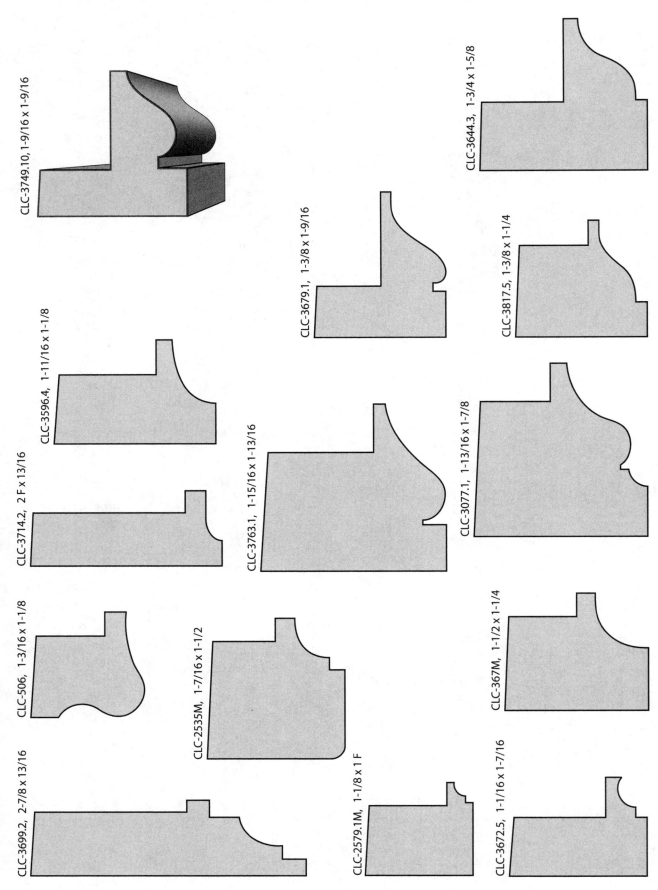

CLC-3749.10, 1-9/16 x 1-9/16

CLC-3644.3, 1-3/4 x 1-5/8

CLC-3679.1, 1-3/8 x 1-9/16

CLC-3817.5, 1-3/8 x 1-1/4

CLC-3596.4, 1-11/16 x 1-1/8

CLC-3714.2, 2 F x 13/16

CLC-3763.1, 1-15/16 x 1-13/16

CLC-3077.1, 1-13/16 x 1-7/8

CLC-506, 1-3/16 x 1-1/8

CLC-2535M, 1-7/16 x 1-1/2

CLC-367M, 1-1/2 x 1-1/4

CLC-3699.2, 2-7/8 x 13/16

CLC-2579.1M, 1-1/8 x 1 F

CLC-3672.5, 1-1/16 x 1-7/16

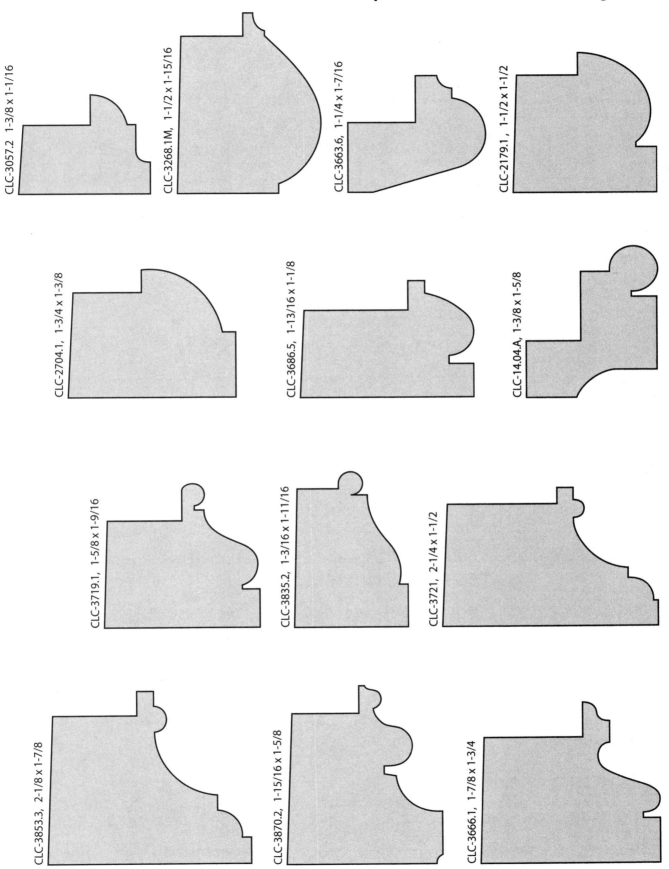

CLC-3057.2 1-3/8 x 1-1/16

CLC-3268.1M, 1-1/2 x 1-15/16

CLC-3663.6, 1-1/4 x 1-7/16

CLC-2179.1, 1-1/2 x 1-1/2

CLC-2704.1, 1-3/4 x 1-3/8

CLC-3686.5, 1-13/16 x 1-1/8

CLC-14.04.A, 1-3/8 x 1-5/8

CLC-3719.1, 1-5/8 x 1-9/16

CLC-3835.2, 1-3/16 x 1-11/16

CLC-3721, 2-1/4 x 1-1/2

CLC-3853.3, 2-1/8 x 1-7/8

CLC-3870.2, 1-15/16 x 1-5/8

CLC-3666.1, 1-7/8 x 1-3/4

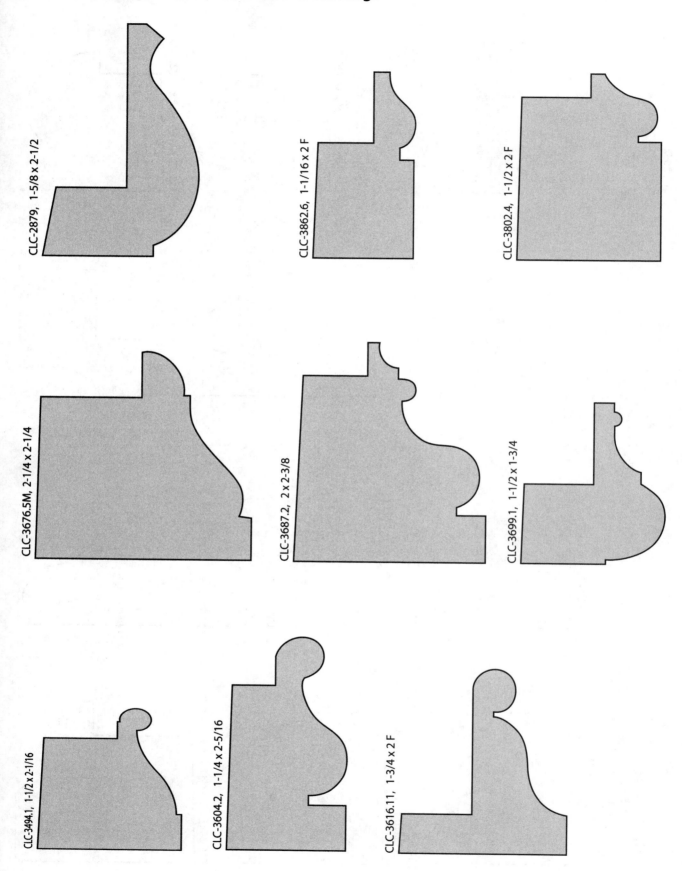

CLC-2879, 1-5/8 x 2-1/2

CLC-3862.6, 1-1/16 x 2 F

CLC-3802.4, 1-1/2 x 2 F

CLC-3676.5M, 2-1/4 x 2-1/4

CLC-3687.2, 2 x 2-3/8

CLC-3699.1, 1-1/2 x 1-3/4

CLC-3494.1, 1-1/2 x 2-1/16

CLC-3604.2, 1-1/4 x 2-5/16

CLC-3616.11, 1-3/4 x 2 F

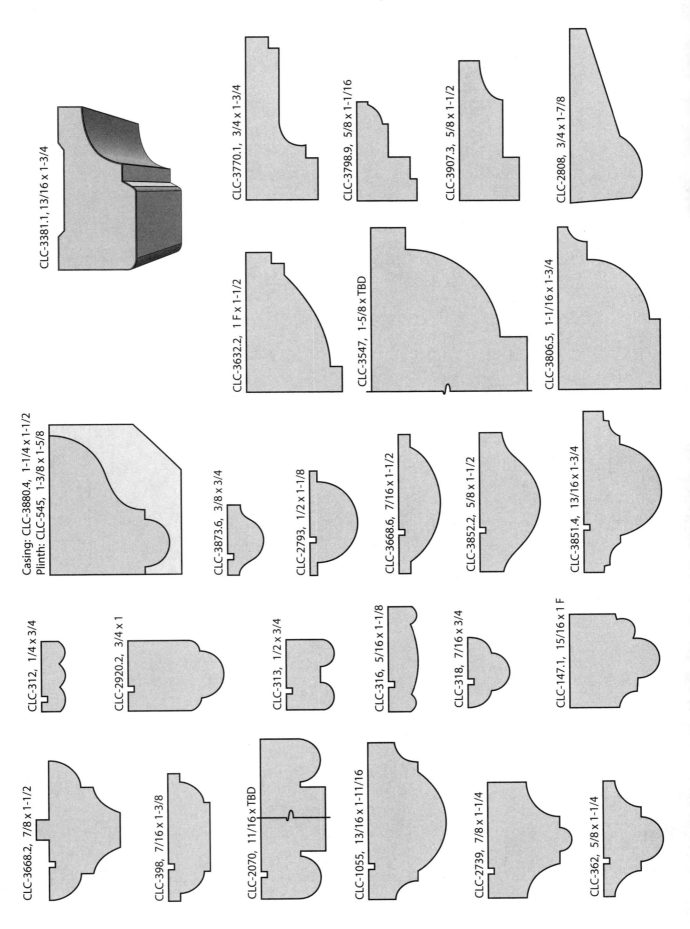

CLC-3381.1, 13/16 x 1-3/4

CLC-3770.1, 3/4 x 1-3/4

CLC-3798.9, 5/8 x 1-1/16

CLC-3907.3, 5/8 x 1-1/2

CLC-2808, 3/4 x 1-7/8

CLC-3632.2, 1 F x 1-1/2

CLC-3547, 1-5/8 x TBD

CLC-3806.5, 1-1/16 x 1-3/4

Casing: CLC-3880.4, 1-1/4 x 1-1/2
Plinth: CLC-545, 1-3/8 x 1-5/8

CLC-3873.6, 3/8 x 3/4

CLC-2793, 1/2 x 1-1/8

CLC-3668.6, 7/16 x 1-1/2

CLC-3852.2, 5/8 x 1-1/2

CLC-3851.4, 13/16 x 1-3/4

CLC-312, 1/4 x 3/4

CLC-2920.2, 3/4 x 1

CLC-313, 1/2 x 3/4

CLC-316, 5/16 x 1-1/8

CLC-318, 7/16 x 3/4

CLC-147.1, 15/16 x 1 F

CLC-3668.2, 7/8 x 1-1/2

CLC-398, 7/16 x 1-3/8

CLC-2070, 11/16 x TBD

CLC-1055, 13/16 x 1-11/16

CLC-2739, 7/8 x 1-1/4

CLC-362, 5/8 x 1-1/4

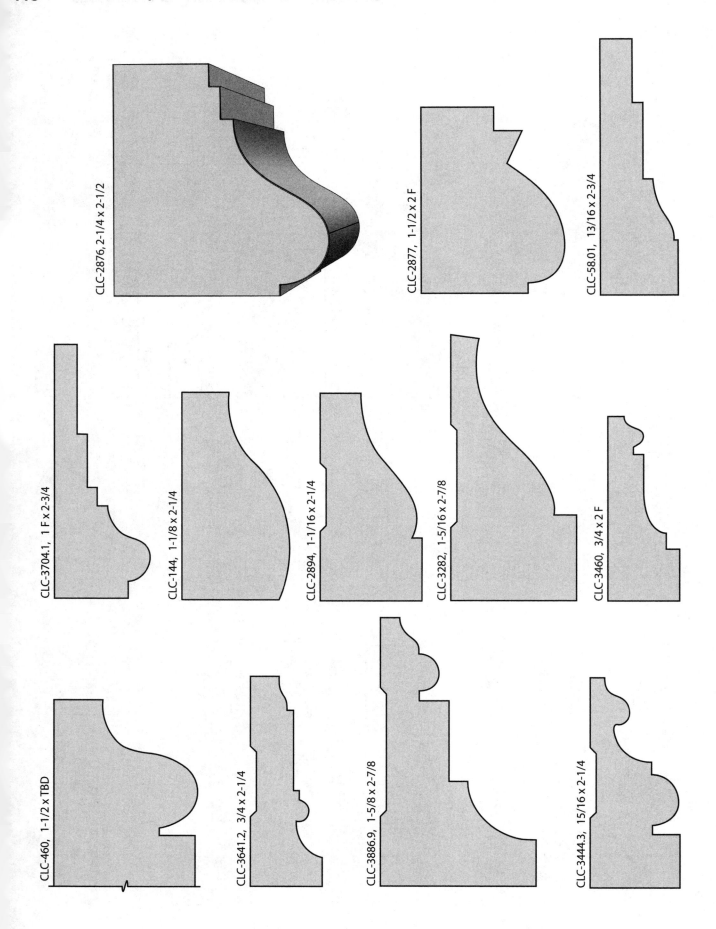

CLC-2876, 2-1/4 x 2-1/2

CLC-2877, 1-1/2 x 2 F

CLC-58.01, 13/16 x 2-3/4

CLC-3704.1, 1 F x 2-3/4

CLC-144, 1-1/8 x 2-1/4

CLC-2894, 1-1/16 x 2-1/4

CLC-3282, 1-5/16 x 2-7/8

CLC-3460, 3/4 x 2 F

CLC-460, 1-1/2 x TBD

CLC-3641.2, 3/4 x 2-1/4

CLC-3886.9, 1-5/8 x 2-7/8

CLC-3444.3, 15/16 x 2-1/4

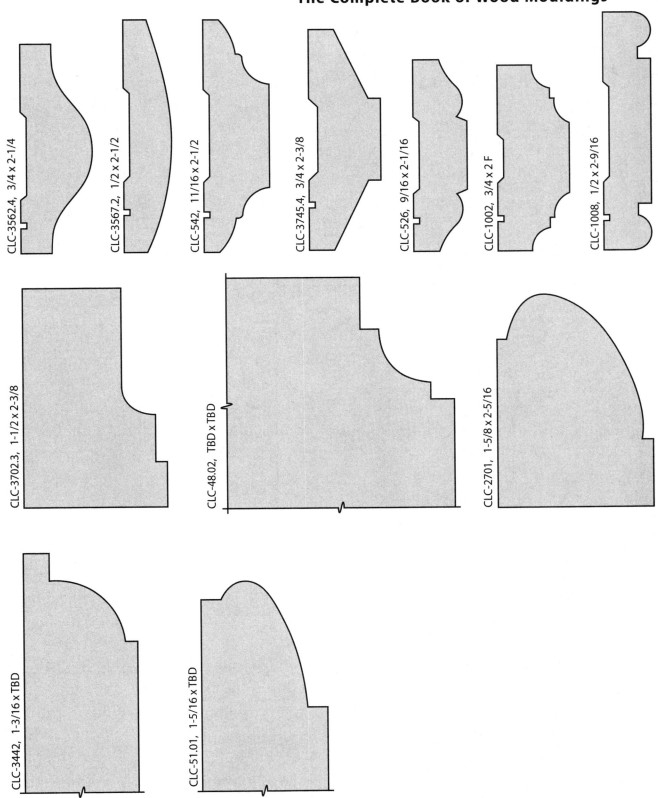

CLC-3562.4, 3/4 x 2-1/4

CLC-3567.2, 1/2 x 2-1/2

CLC-542, 11/16 x 2-1/2

CLC-3745.4, 3/4 x 2-3/8

CLC-526, 9/16 x 2-1/16

CLC-1002, 3/4 x 2 F

CLC-1008, 1/2 x 2-9/16

CLC-3702.3, 1-1/2 x 2-3/8

CLC-48.02, TBD x TBD

CLC-2701, 1-5/8 x 2-5/16

CLC-3442, 1-3/16 x TBD

CLC-51.01, 1-5/16 x TBD

CLC-3641.7, 1 F x 2-15/16

CLC-3792.3M, 1-1/16 x 2-3/8

CLC-4.125, 1-5/16 x 2-3/4

CLC-664, 1 F x 2-3/8

CLC-674, 3/4 x 2-9/16

CLC-3571.1, 13/16 x 2-1/8

CLC-3844.1, 1 F x 2-1/2

CLC-634, 3/4 x 2-1/4

CLC-653, 3/4 x 2-5/8

Casing: CLC-3817.4, 3/4 x 2-3/4
Back Band: CLC-3817.5, 1-3/8 x 1-1/4
Plinth: CLC-3817.10, 1-1/2 x 3-3/4

Casing: CLC-3590.2, 1-1/8 x 2-13/16
Plinth: CLC-3590.1, 1-3/16 x 2-13/16

CLC-3749.1, 15/16 x 2-3/8

CLC-3612-5, 7/8 x 2-3/8

CLC-752, 3/4 x 2-1/16

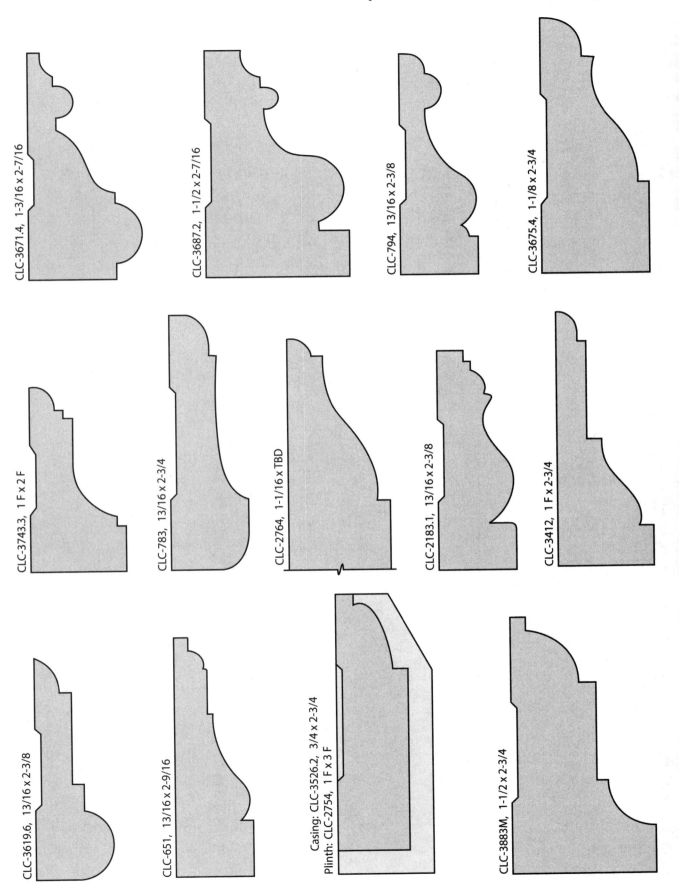

CLC-3671.4, 1-3/16 x 2-7/16

CLC-3687.2, 1-1/2 x 2-7/16

CLC-794, 13/16 x 2-3/8

CLC-3675.4, 1-1/8 x 2-3/4

CLC-3743.3, 1 F x 2 F

CLC-783, 13/16 x 2-3/4

CLC-2764, 1-1/16 x TBD

CLC-2183.1, 13/16 x 2-3/8

CLC-3412, 1 F x 2-3/4

CLC-3619.6, 13/16 x 2-3/8

CLC-651, 13/16 x 2-9/16

Casing: CLC-3526.2, 3/4 x 2-3/4
Plinth: CLC-2754, 1 F x 3 F

CLC-3883M, 1-1/2 x 2-3/4

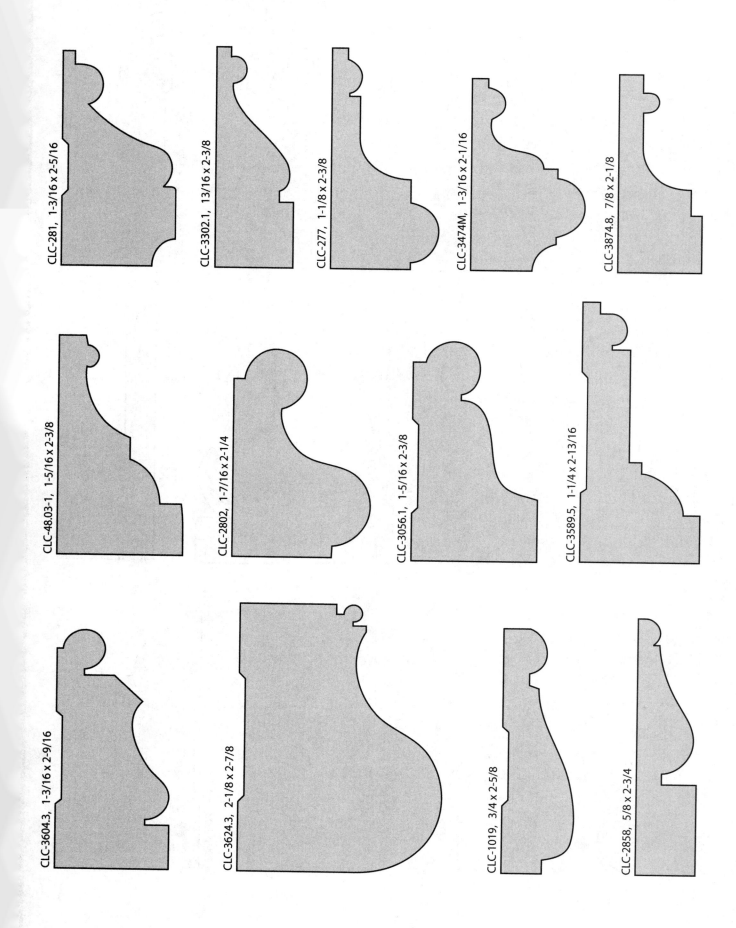

CLC-281, 1-3/16 x 2-5/16

CLC-3302.1, 13/16 x 2-3/8

CLC-277, 1-1/8 x 2-3/8

CLC-3474M, 1-3/16 x 2-1/16

CLC-3874.8, 7/8 x 2-1/8

CLC-48.03-1, 1-5/16 x 2-3/8

CLC-2802, 1-7/16 x 2-1/4

CLC-3056.1, 1-5/16 x 2-3/8

CLC-3589.5, 1-1/4 x 2-13/16

CLC-3604.3, 1-3/16 x 2-9/16

CLC-3624.3, 2-1/8 x 2-7/8

CLC-1019, 3/4 x 2-5/8

CLC-2858, 5/8 x 2-3/4

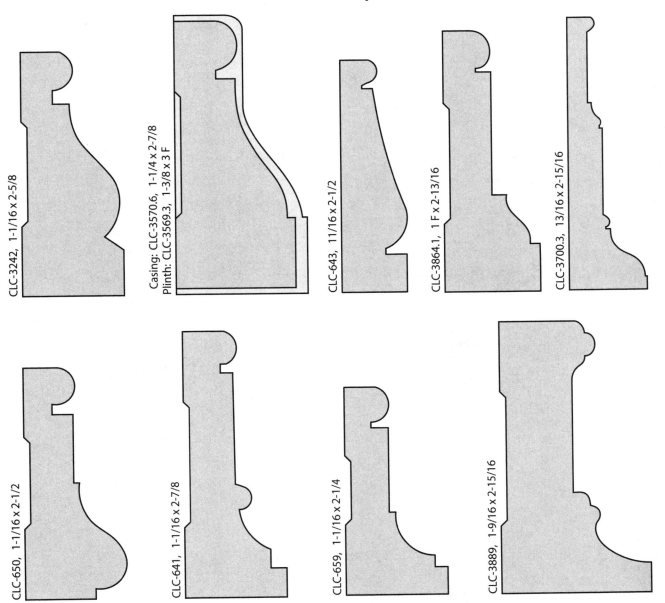

CLC-3242, 1-1/16 x 2-5/8

Casing: CLC-3570.6, 1-1/4 x 2-7/8
Plinth: CLC-3569.3, 1-3/8 x 3 F

CLC-643, 11/16 x 2-1/2

CLC-3864.1, 1 F x 2-13/16

CLC-3700.3, 13/16 x 2-15/16

CLC-650, 1-1/16 x 2-1/2

CLC-641, 1-1/16 x 2-7/8

CLC-659, 1-1/16 x 2-1/4

CLC-3889, 1-9/16 x 2-15/16

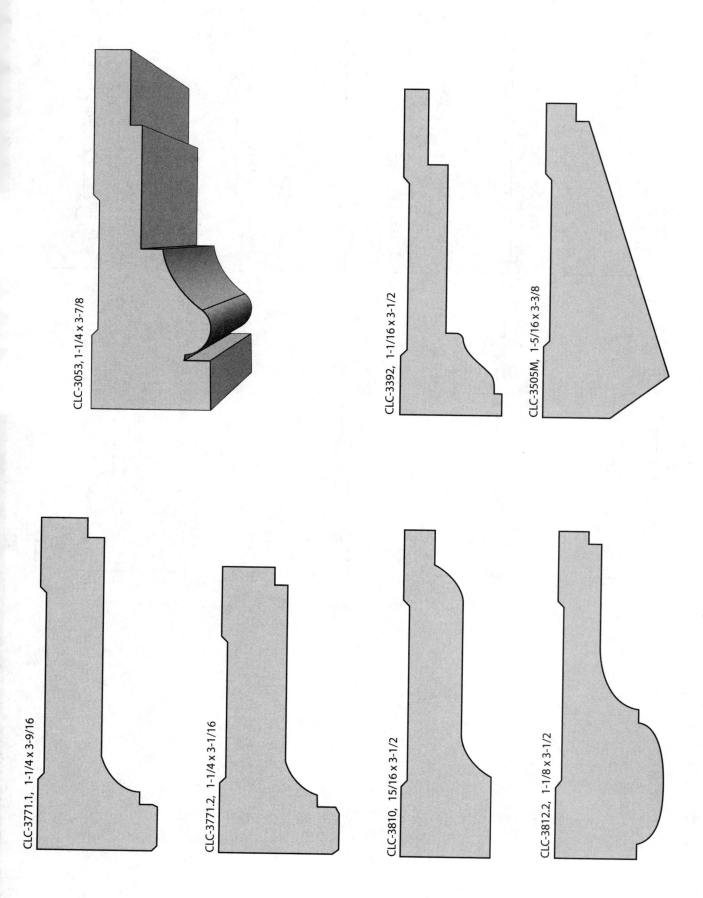

CLC-3053, 1-1/4 x 3-7/8

CLC-3392, 1-1/16 x 3-1/2

CLC-3505M, 1-5/16 x 3-3/8

CLC-3771.1, 1-1/4 x 3-9/16

CLC-3771.2, 1-1/4 x 3-1/16

CLC-3810, 15/16 x 3-1/2

CLC-3812.2, 1-1/8 x 3-1/2

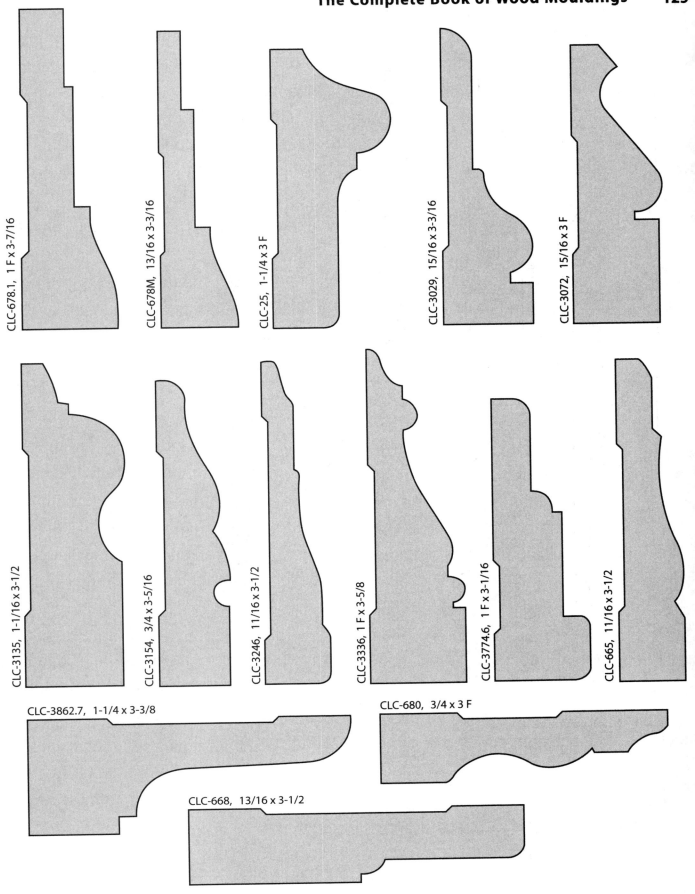

CLC-678.1, 1 F x 3-7/16

CLC-678M, 13/16 x 3-3/16

CLC-25, 1-1/4 x 3 F

CLC-3029, 15/16 x 3-3/16

CLC-3072, 15/16 x 3 F

CLC-3135, 1-1/16 x 3-1/2

CLC-3154, 3/4 x 3-5/16

CLC-3246, 11/16 x 3-1/2

CLC-3336, 1 F x 3-5/8

CLC-3774.6, 1 F x 3-1/16

CLC-665, 11/16 x 3-1/2

CLC-3862.7, 1-1/4 x 3-3/8

CLC-680, 3/4 x 3 F

CLC-668, 13/16 x 3-1/2

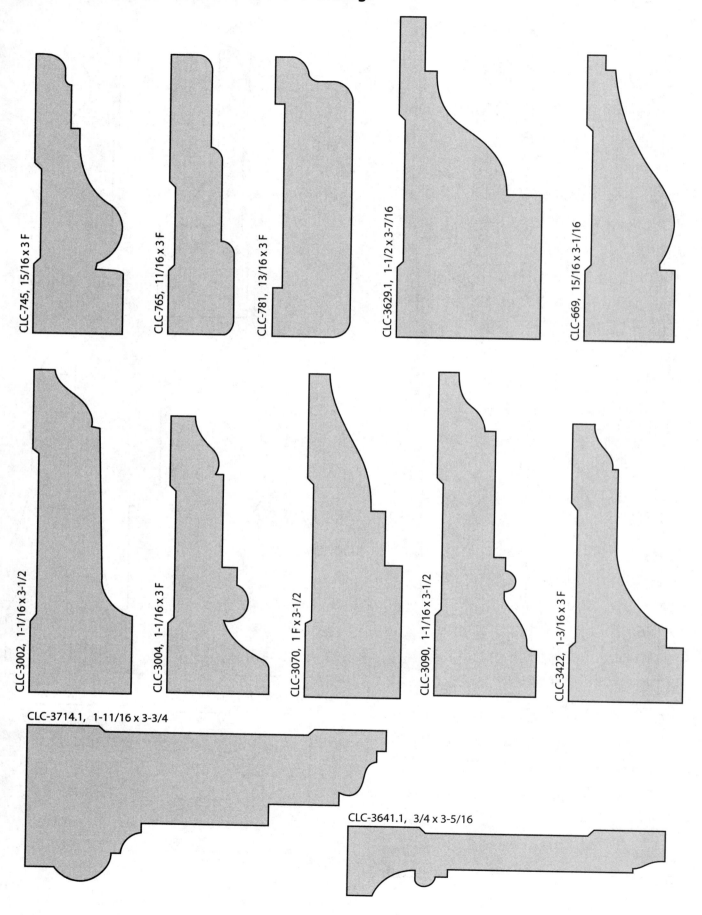

CLC-745, 15/16 x 3 F

CLC-765, 11/16 x 3 F

CLC-781, 13/16 x 3 F

CLC-3629.1, 1-1/2 x 3-7/16

CLC-669, 15/16 x 3-1/16

CLC-3002, 1-1/16 x 3-1/2

CLC-3004, 1-1/16 x 3 F

CLC-3070, 1 F x 3-1/2

CLC-3090, 1-1/16 x 3-1/2

CLC-3422, 1-3/16 x 3 F

CLC-3714.1, 1-11/16 x 3-3/4

CLC-3641.1, 3/4 x 3-5/16

CLC-3414, 13/16 x 3-1/4

CLC-619, 13/16 x 3-3/16

CLC-620, 13/16 x 3-5/16

CLC-661, 1-1/16 x 3-3/4

CLC-3120, 1-5/8 x 3-3/4

CLC-3608.3, 1-5/16 x 3-3/8

CLC-675, 13/16 x 3-3/8

CLC-3485, 13/16 x 3-5/8

CLC-3511, 1-1/4 x 3-5/8

CLC-607, 13/16 x 3-7/8

CLC-43.02, 1-1/8 x 3-1/8

CLC-559.2, 13/16 x 3-9/16

CLC-630, 1-1/16 x 3 F

Overall: 3-5/8

CLC-14.03B, 3/4 x 2-3/4

CLC-14.03A, 1-3/16 x 1-9/16

CLC-3338.1, 1-1/16 x 3-1/4

CLC-648, 3/4 x 3-1/2

CLC-3171, 1 F x 3-1/8

CLC-3277, 3/4 x 3-3/8

CLC-3615.5, 7/8 x 3-9/16

Casing: CLC-3507, 1-1/4 x 3-1/4
Plinth: CLC-79, 1-3/8 x 3-1/4

CLC-3601.4, 1-1/2 x 3-1/2

Casing: CLC-3678.1, 3/4 x 3-1/4
Plinth: CLC-3679.3, 7/8 x 3-1/2

CLC-605, 3/4 x 3-5/8

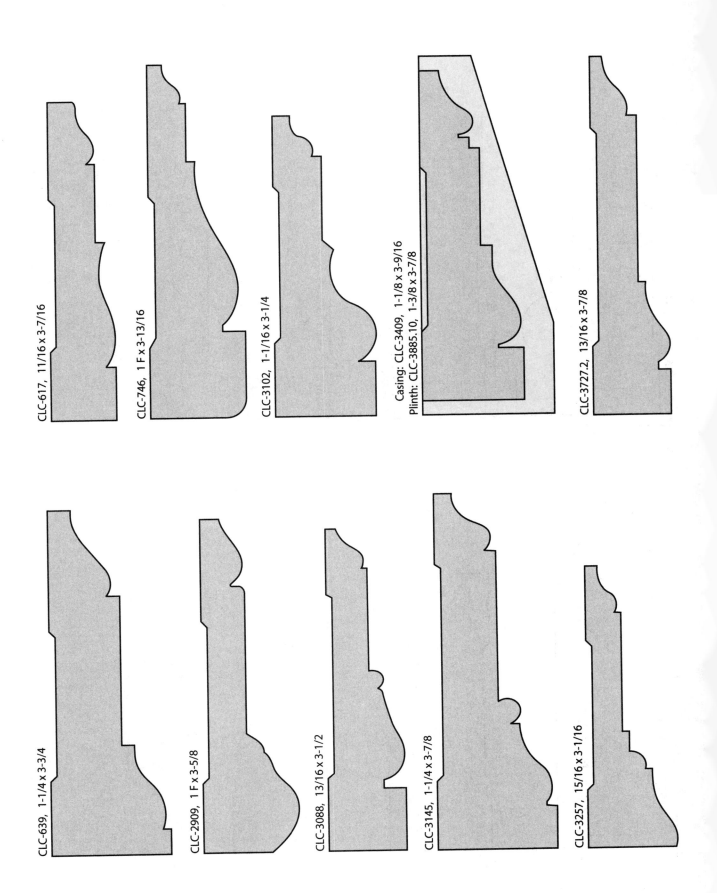

CLC-617, 11/16 x 3-7/16

CLC-746, 1 F x 3-13/16

CLC-3102, 1-1/16 x 3-1/4

Casing: CLC-3409, 1-1/8 x 3-9/16
Plinth: CLC-3885.10, 1-3/8 x 3-7/8

CLC-3727.2, 13/16 x 3-7/8

CLC-639, 1-1/4 x 3-3/4

CLC-2909, 1 F x 3-5/8

CLC-3088, 13/16 x 3-1/2

CLC-3145, 1-1/4 x 3-7/8

CLC-3257, 15/16 x 3-1/16

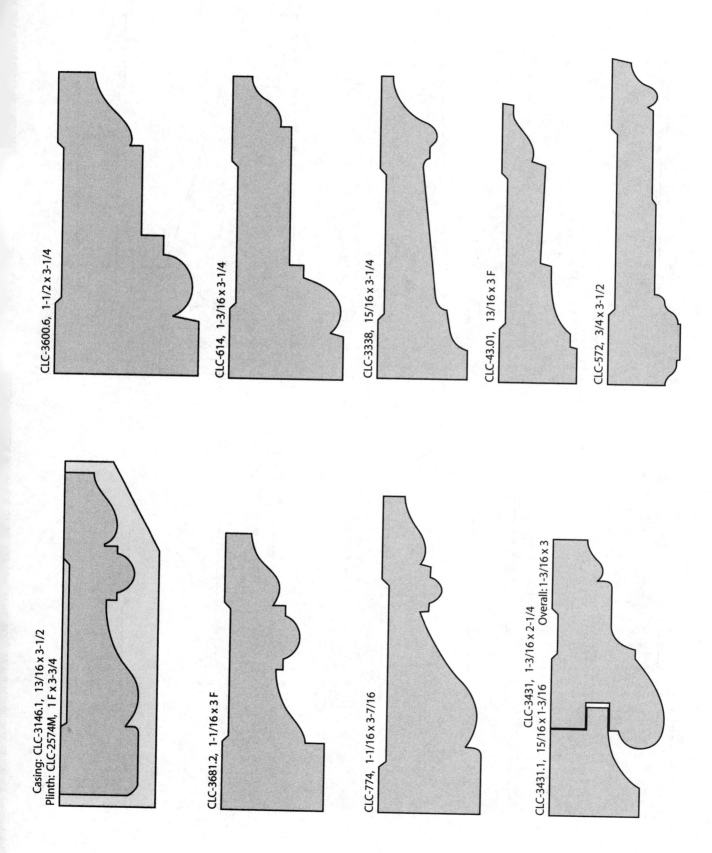

CLC-3600.6, 1-1/2 x 3-1/4

CLC-614, 1-3/16 x 3-1/4

CLC-3338, 15/16 x 3-1/4

CLC-43.01, 13/16 x 3 F

CLC-572, 3/4 x 3-1/2

Casing: CLC-3146.1, 13/16 x 3-1/2
Plinth: CLC-2574M, 1 F x 3-3/4

CLC-3681.2, 1-1/16 x 3 F

CLC-774, 1-1/16 x 3-7/16

CLC-3431, 1-3/16 x 2-1/4   Overall: 1-3/16 x 3
CLC-3431.1, 15/16 x 1-3/16

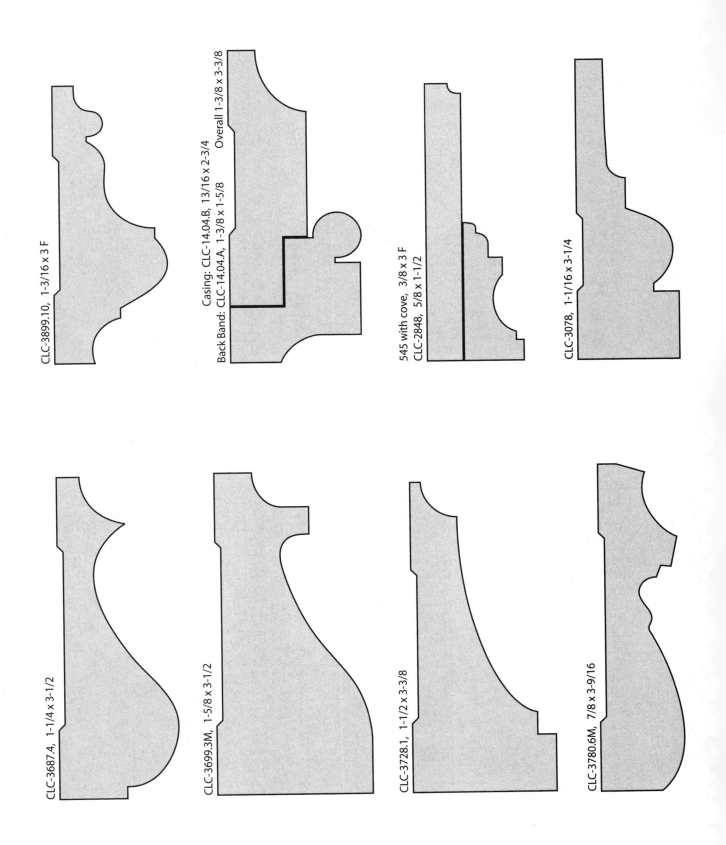

CLC-3899.10, 1-3/16 x 3 F

Casing: CLC-14.04.B, 13/16 x 2-3/4   Overall 1-3/8 x 3-3/8
Back Band: CLC-14.04.A, 1-3/8 x 1-5/8

545 with cove, 3/8 x 3 F
CLC-2848, 5/8 x 1-1/2

CLC-3078, 1-1/16 x 3-1/4

CLC-3687.4, 1-1/4 x 3-1/2

CLC-3699.3M, 1-5/8 x 3-1/2

CLC-3728.1, 1-1/2 x 3-3/8

CLC-3780.6M, 7/8 x 3-9/16

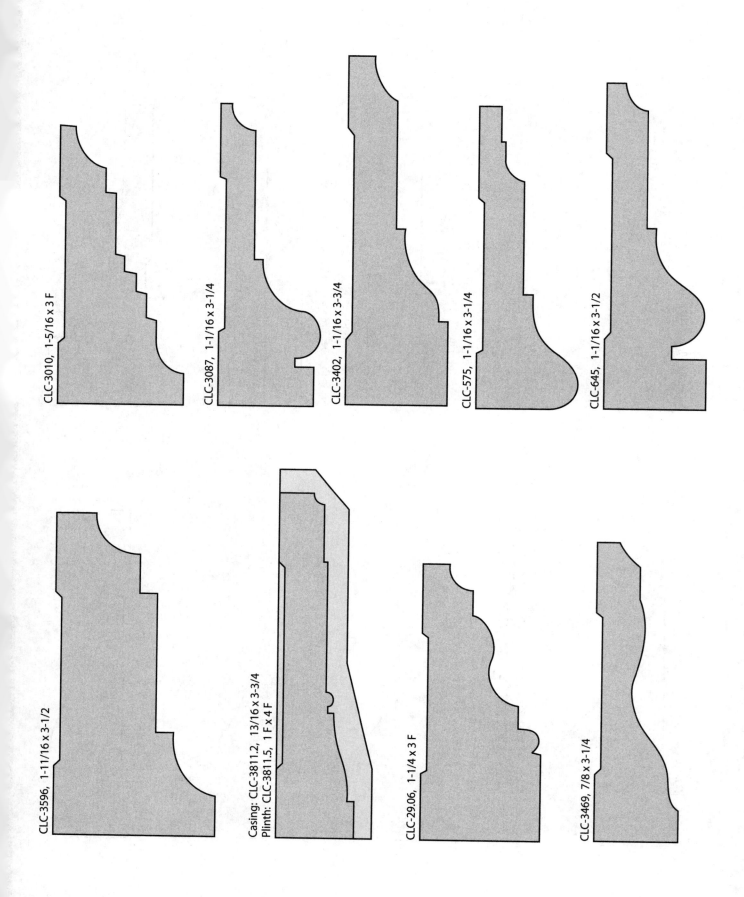

CLC-3010, 1-5/16 x 3 F

CLC-3087, 1-1/16 x 3-1/4

CLC-3402, 1-1/16 x 3-3/4

CLC-575, 1-1/16 x 3-1/4

CLC-645, 1-1/16 x 3-1/2

CLC-3596, 1-11/16 x 3-1/2

Casing: CLC-3811.2, 13/16 x 3-3/4
Plinth: CLC-3811.5,   1 F x 4 F

CLC-29.06, 1-1/4 x 3 F

CLC-3469, 7/8 x 3-1/4

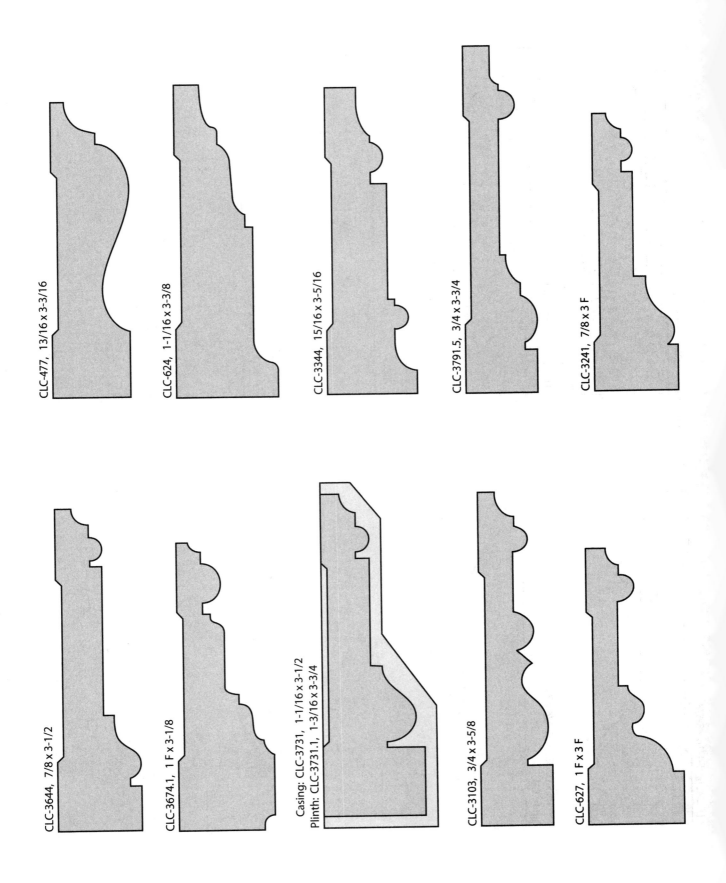

CLC-477, 13/16 x 3-3/16

CLC-624, 1-1/16 x 3-3/8

CLC-3344, 15/16 x 3-5/16

CLC-3791.5, 3/4 x 3-3/4

CLC-3241, 7/8 x 3 F

CLC-3644, 7/8 x 3-1/2

CLC-3674.1, 1 F x 3-1/8

Casing: CLC-3731, 1-1/16 x 3-1/2
Plinth: CLC-3731.1, 1-3/16 x 3-3/4

CLC-3103, 3/4 x 3-5/8

CLC-627, 1 F x 3 F

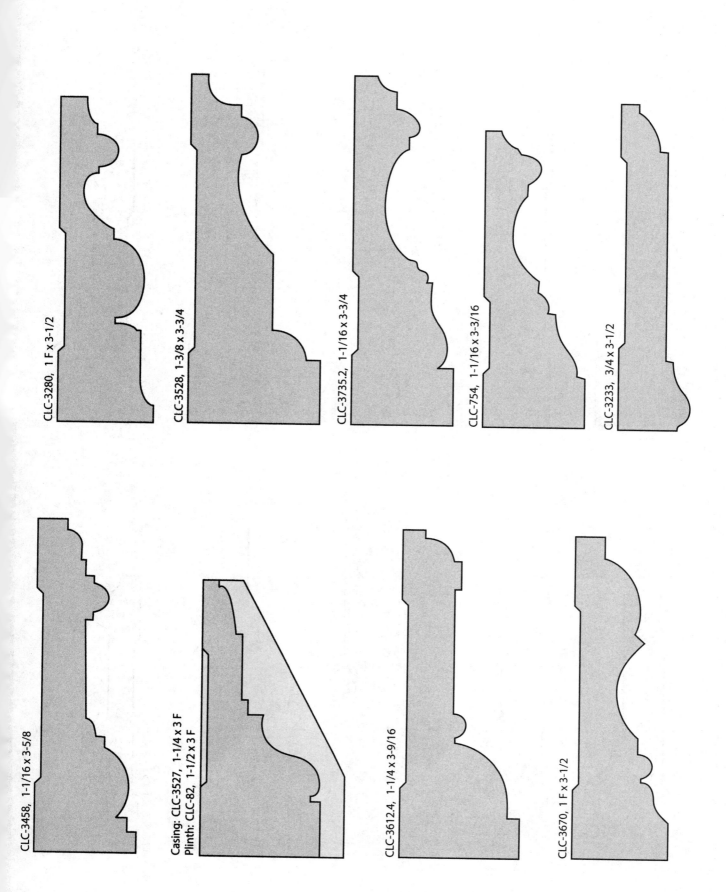

CLC-3280, 1 F x 3-1/2

CLC-3528, 1-3/8 x 3-3/4

CLC-3735.2, 1-1/16 x 3-3/4

CLC-754, 1-1/16 x 3-3/16

CLC-3233, 3/4 x 3-1/2

CLC-3458, 1-1/16 x 3-5/8

Casing: CLC-3527, 1-1/4 x 3 F
Plinth: CLC-82, 1-1/2 x 3 F

CLC-3612.4, 1-1/4 x 3-9/16

CLC-3670, 1 F x 3-1/2

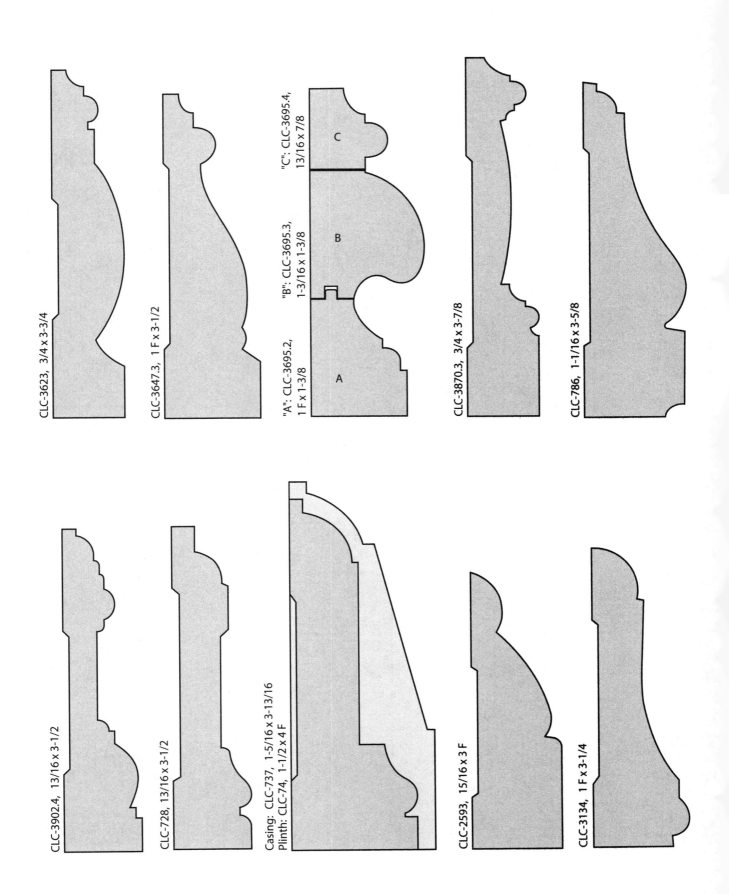

CLC-3623, 3/4 x 3-3/4

CLC-3647.3, 1 F x 3-1/2

"A": CLC-3695.2, 1 F x 1-3/8

"B": CLC-3695.3, 1-3/16 x 1-3/8

"C": CLC-3695.4, 13/16 x 7/8

CLC-3870.3, 3/4 x 3-7/8

CLC-786, 1-1/16 x 3-5/8

CLC-3902.4, 13/16 x 3-1/2

CLC-728, 13/16 x 3-1/2

Casing: CLC-737, 1-5/16 x 3-13/16
Plinth: CLC-74, 1-1/2 x 4 F

CLC-2593, 15/16 x 3 F

CLC-3134, 1 F x 3-1/4

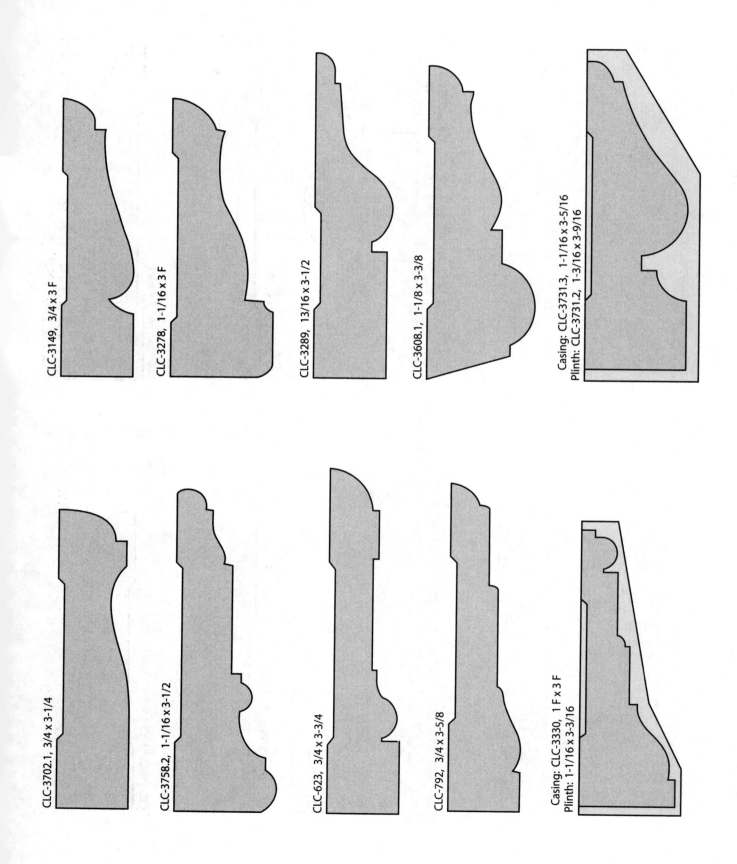

CLC-3149, 3/4 x 3 F

CLC-3278, 1-1/16 x 3 F

CLC-3289, 13/16 x 3-1/2

CLC-3608.1, 1-1/8 x 3-3/8

Casing: CLC-3731.3, 1-1/16 x 3-5/16
Plinth: CLC-3731.2, 1-3/16 x 3-9/16

CLC-3702.1, 3/4 x 3-1/4

CLC-3758.2, 1-1/16 x 3-1/2

CLC-623, 3/4 x 3-3/4

CLC-792, 3/4 x 3-5/8

Casing: CLC-3330, 1 F x 3 F
Plinth: 1-1/16 x 3-3/16

CLC-3432, 15/16 x 3-1/2

CLC-3465, 1-5/16 x 3-1/4

CLC-3627.5, 1-1/16 x 3-7/16

CLC-615, 1-1/16 x 3-1/2

CLC-3667.5, 1-3/16 x 3-1/8

CLC-658, 1 F x 3-1/8

CLC-771, 1 F x 3-5/16

CLC-9.06, 1-1/16 x 3-1/16

CLC-3247, 1-1/16 x 3-1/4

CLC-3295, 1-1/4 x 3-3/4

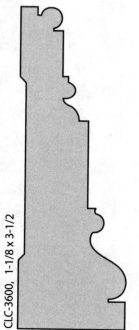

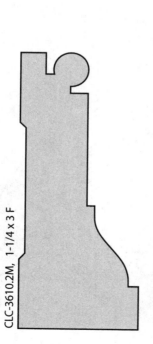

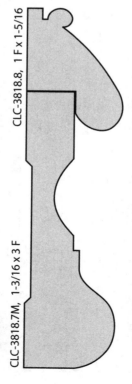

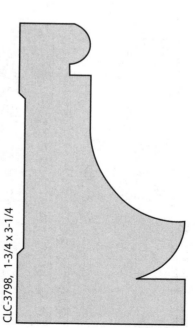

CLC-3672.4, 1-1/8 x 3 F

CLC-3494, 13/16 x 3 F

Casing: CLC-3561, 1-1/4 x 3 F
Plinth: CLC-3879.4, 1-3/8 x 3-1/4

Casing: CLC-3672.2, 1 F x 3-13/16
Back Band: CLC-3672.5, 1-1/16 x 1-7/16
Plinth: CLC-3672, 1-3/4 x 4-13/16

CLC-3600, 1-1/8 x 3-1/2

CLC-3610.2M, 1-1/4 x 3 F

CLC-3818.8, 1 F x 1-5/16
CLC-3818.7M, 1-3/16 x 3 F

CLC-3798, 1-3/4 x 3-1/4

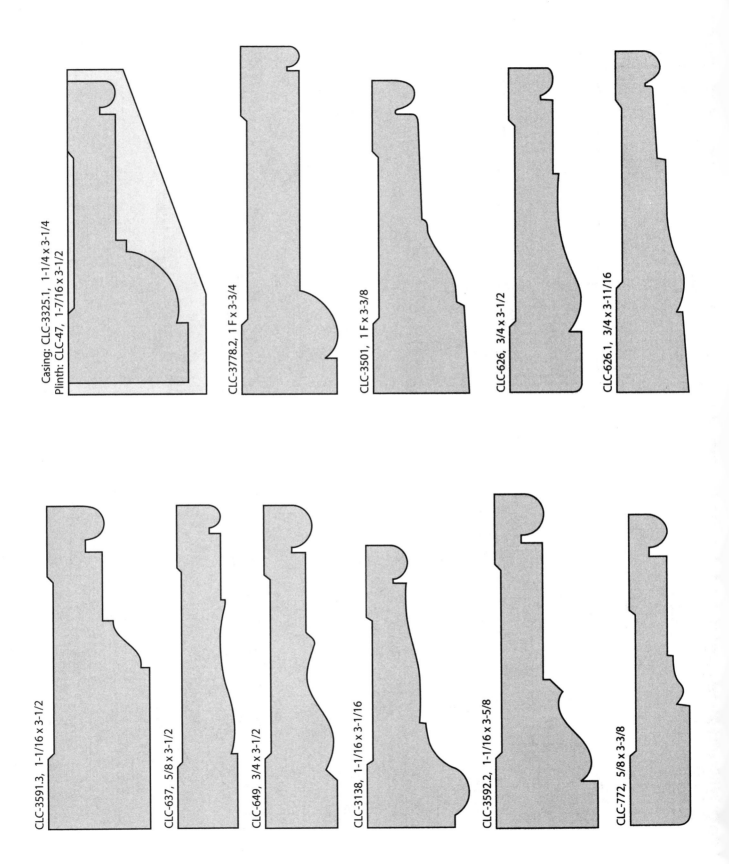

Casing: CLC-3325.1, 1-1/4 x 3-1/4
Plinth: CLC-47, 1-7/16 x 3-1/2

CLC-3778.2, 1 F x 3-3/4

CLC-3501, 1 F x 3-3/8

CLC-626, 3/4 x 3-1/2

CLC-626.1, 3/4 x 3-11/16

CLC-3591.3, 1-1/16 x 3-1/2

CLC-637, 5/8 x 3-1/2

CLC-649, 3/4 x 3-1/2

CLC-3138, 1-1/16 x 3-1/16

CLC-3592.2, 1-1/16 x 3-5/8

CLC-772, 5/8 x 3-3/8

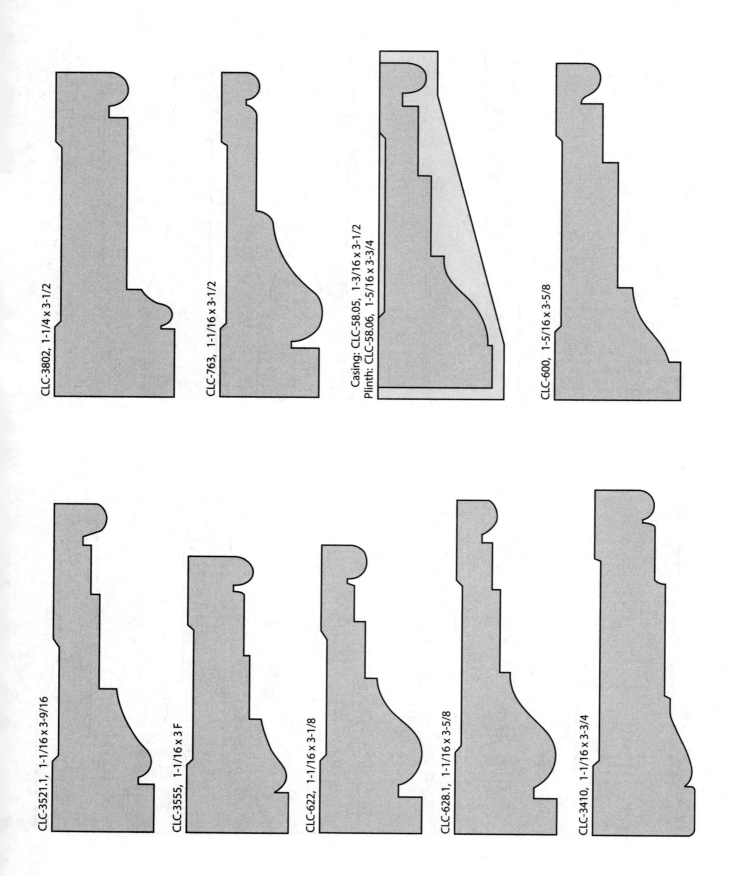

CLC-3802, 1-1/4 x 3-1/2

CLC-763, 1-1/16 x 3-1/2

Casing: CLC-58.05, 1-3/16 x 3-1/2
Plinth: CLC-58.06, 1-5/16 x 3-3/4

CLC-600, 1-5/16 x 3-5/8

CLC-3521.1, 1-1/16 x 3-9/16

CLC-3555, 1-1/16 x 3 F

CLC-622, 1-1/16 x 3-1/8

CLC-628.1, 1-1/16 x 3-5/8

CLC-3410, 1-1/16 x 3-3/4

CLC-777, 1-1/16 x 3-1/2

CLC-3471, 1-1/16 x 3-9/16

CLC-751, 1-1/16 x 3-1/3

CLC-3301.3, 1-1/16 x 3-1/2

CLC-3571.3, 1-3/4 x 3-1/2

CLC-3545.2, 1-1/16 x 3-3/4

CLC-3858.5, 3/4 x 3-1/4

CLC-3001, 13/16 x 3 F

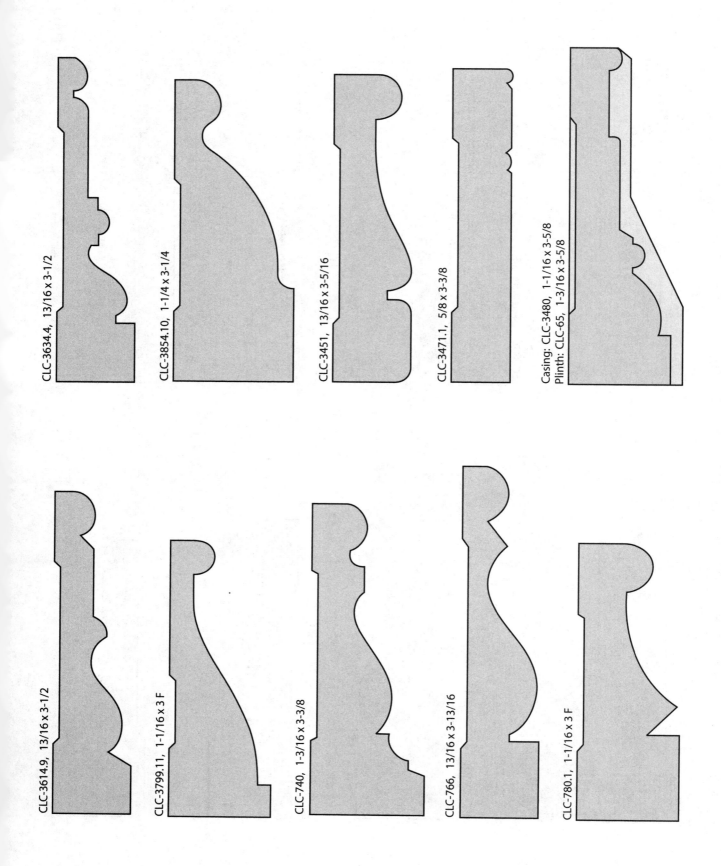

CLC-3634.4, 13/16 x 3-1/2

CLC-3854.10, 1-1/4 x 3-1/4

CLC-3451, 13/16 x 3-5/16

CLC-3471.1, 5/8 x 3-3/8

Casing: CLC-3480, 1-1/16 x 3-5/8
Plinth: CLC-65, 1-3/16 x 3-5/8

CLC-3614.9, 13/16 x 3-1/2

CLC-3799.11, 1-1/16 x 3 F

CLC-740, 1-3/16 x 3-3/8

CLC-766, 13/16 x 3-13/16

CLC-780.1, 1-1/16 x 3 F

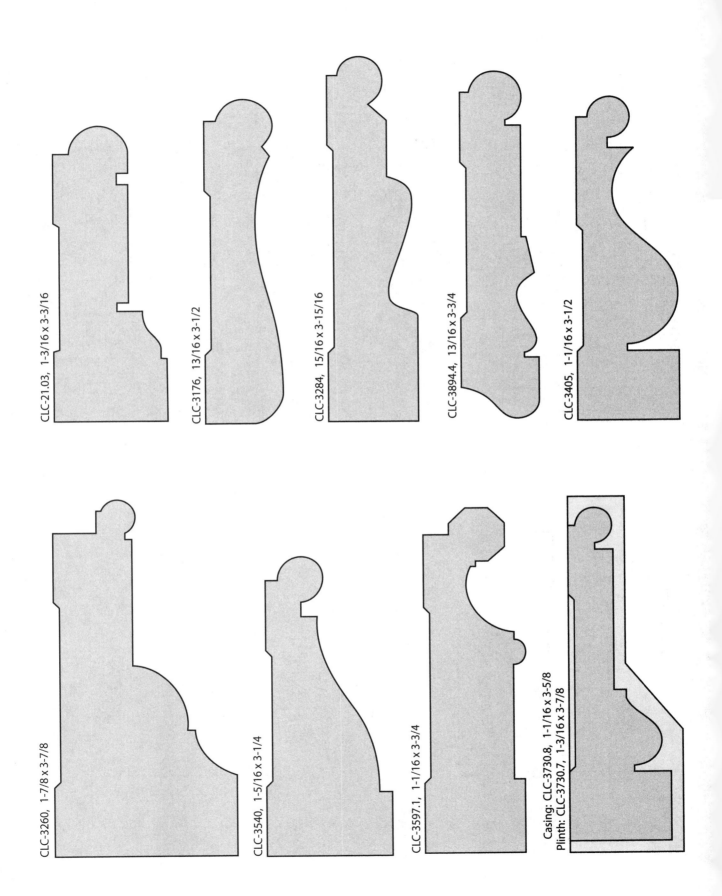

CLC-21.03, 1-3/16 x 3-3/16

CLC-3176, 13/16 x 3-1/2

CLC-3284, 15/16 x 3-15/16

CLC-3894.4, 13/16 x 3-3/4

CLC-3405, 1-1/16 x 3-1/2

CLC-3260, 1-7/8 x 3-7/8

CLC-3540, 1-5/16 x 3-1/4

CLC-3597.1, 1-1/16 x 3-3/4

Casing: CLC-3730.8, 1-1/16 x 3-5/8
Plinth: CLC-3730.7, 1-3/16 x 3-7/8

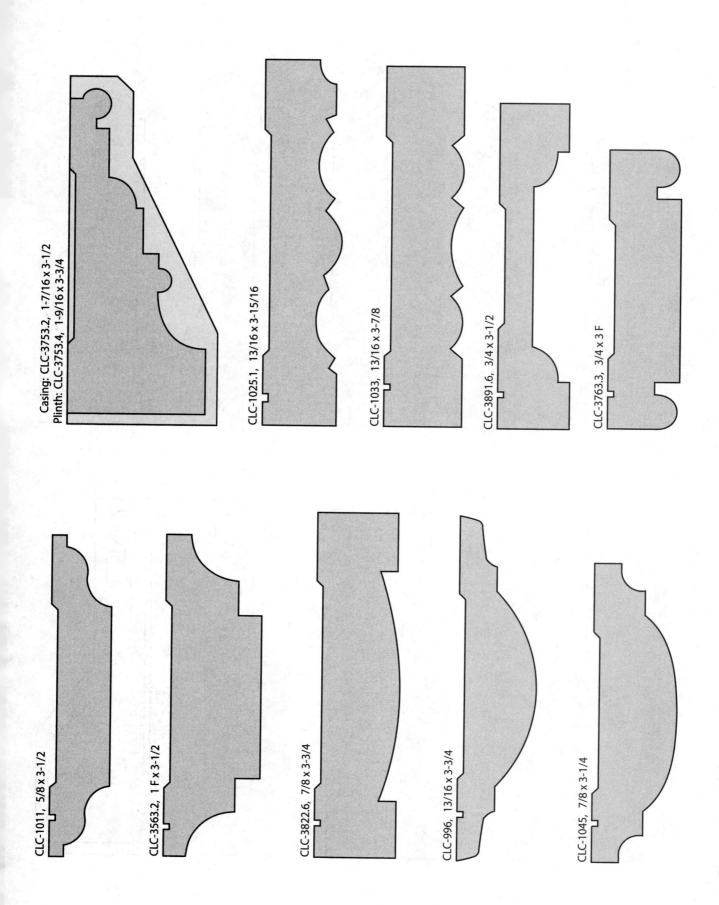

Casing: CLC-3753.2, 1-7/16 x 3-1/2
Plinth: CLC-3753.4, 1-9/16 x 3-3/4

CLC-1025.1, 13/16 x 3-15/16

CLC-1033, 13/16 x 3-7/8

CLC-3891.6, 3/4 x 3-1/2

CLC-3763.3, 3/4 x 3 F

CLC-1011, 5/8 x 3-1/2

CLC-3563.2, 1 F x 3-1/2

CLC-3822.6, 7/8 x 3-3/4

CLC-996, 13/16 x 3-3/4

CLC-1045, 7/8 x 3-1/4

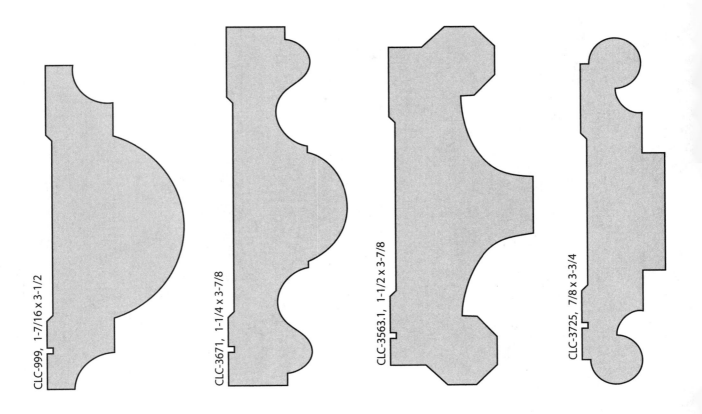

CLC-999, 1-7/16 x 3-1/2

CLC-3671, 1-1/4 x 3-7/8

CLC-3563.1, 1-1/2 x 3-7/8

CLC-3725, 7/8 x 3-3/4

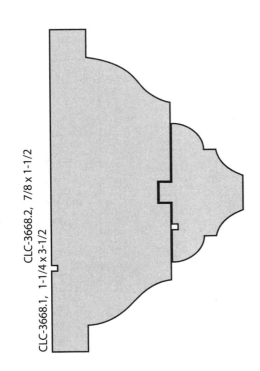

CLC-3668.2, 7/8 x 1-1/2

CLC-3668.1, 1-1/4 x 3-1/2

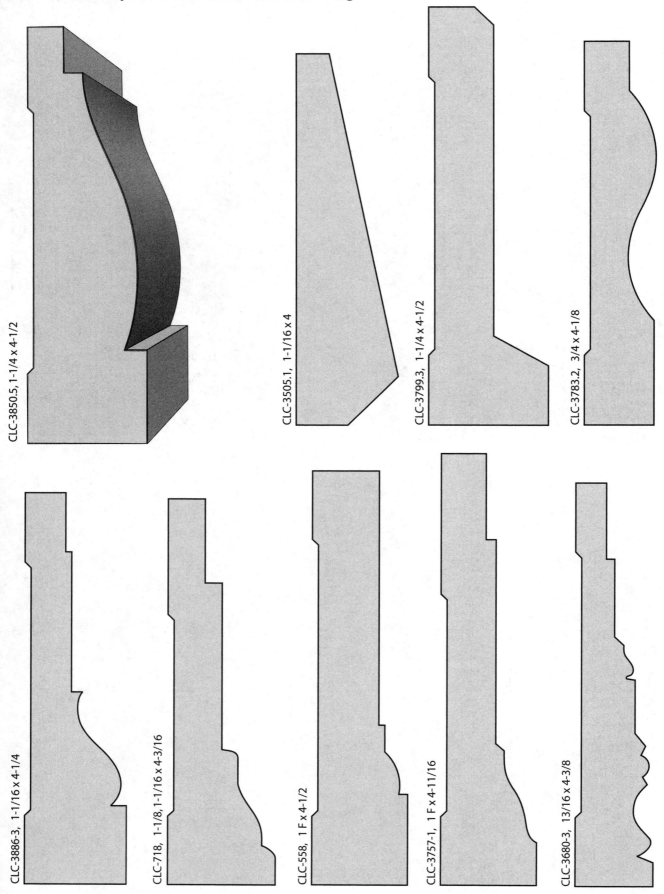

CLC-3850.5, 1-1/4 x 4-1/2

CLC-3505.1, 1-1/16 x 4

CLC-3799.3, 1-1/4 x 4-1/2

CLC-3783.2, 3/4 x 4-1/8

CLC-3886-3, 1-1/16 x 4-1/4

CLC-718, 1-1/8, 1-1/16 x 4-3/16

CLC-558, 1 F x 4-1/2

CLC-3757-1, 1 F x 4-11/16

CLC-3680-3, 13/16 x 4-3/8

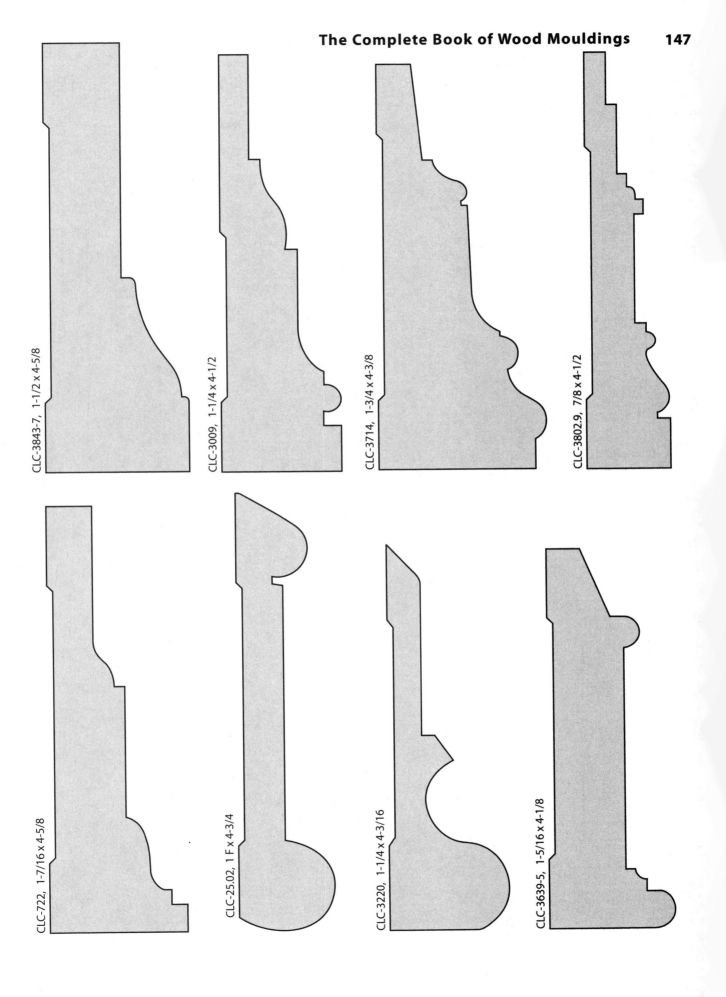

CLC-3843-7, 1-1/2 x 4-5/8

CLC-3009, 1-1/4 x 4-1/2

CLC-3714, 1-3/4 x 4-3/8

CLC-3802.9, 7/8 x 4-1/2

CLC-722, 1-7/16 x 4-5/8

CLC-25.02, 1 F x 4-3/4

CLC-3220, 1-1/4 x 4-3/16

CLC-3639-5, 1-5/16 x 4-1/8

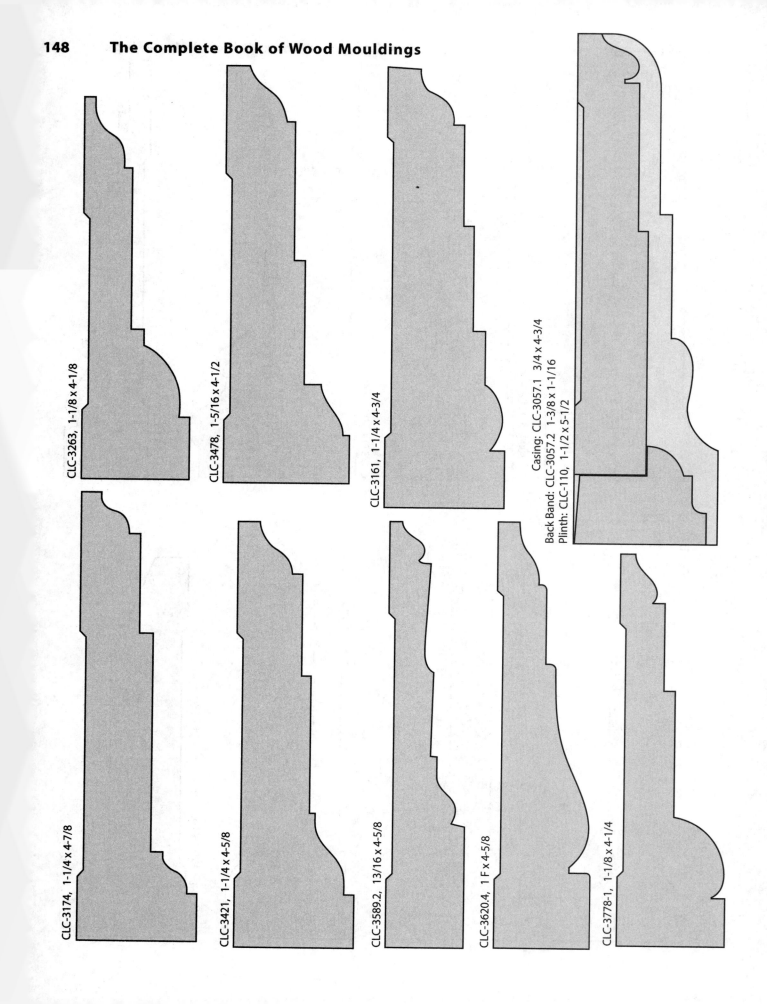

CLC-3263, 1-1/8 x 4-1/8

CLC-3478, 1-5/16 x 4-1/2

CLC-3161, 1-1/4 x 4-3/4

Casing: CLC-3057.1   3/4 x 4-3/4
Back Band: CLC-3057.2   1-3/8 x 1-1/16
Plinth: CLC-110,   1-1/2 x 5-1/2

CLC-3174, 1-1/4 x 4-7/8

CLC-3421, 1-1/4 x 4-5/8

CLC-3589.2, 13/16 x 4-5/8

CLC-3620.4, 1 F x 4-5/8

CLC-3778-1, 1-1/8 x 4-1/4

Casing: CLC-3582.1, 1-3/8 x 4-5/8
Plinth: CLC-3582.2, 1-9/16 x 5-1/8

Casing: CLC-3679, 11/16 x 3-11/16
Back Band: CLC-3679.1, 1-3/8 x 1-9/16
Plinth: CLC-3679.2, 1-9/16 x 4-1/2

CLC-3701.3, 3/4 x 4-3/8

CLC-3864.12, 1-1/8 x 4-1/2

CLC-753, 1 F x 4-1/2

CLC-770, 3/4 x 4-1/2

CLC-245, 11/16 x 4-5/8

CLC-3441, 1-1/16 x 4-1/4

Casing: CLC-3801.1, 1-1/4 x 4-7/16
Plinth: CLC-3758.11M, 1-7/16 x 4-9/16

CLC-3381, 13/16 x 4 F
CLC-3381.1, 13/16 x 1-3/4
CLC-3381.2, 11/16 x 1 F

CLC-3857.8, 1-3/8 x 4-3/4

CLC-3685.7, 1-3/16 x 4-1/8

CLC-3896.2, 1-1/16 x 4-9/16

CLC-28.7, 13/16 x 4 F

CLC-3357, 1 F x 4 F

CLC-559, 1-1/8 x 4-9/16

CLC-557, 1-5/16 x 4-1/2

CLC-719, 1-1/16 x 4-5/8

Casing: CLC-3899.4, 1-1/2 x 4-3/16
Plinth: CLC-3899-9, 1-11/16 x 4-9/16

CLC-3836.2, 1-3/4 x 4-5/8

CLC-3018, 13/16 x 4-1/16

CLC-3021, 1-1/16 x 4-7/16

CLC-3239, 1-3/4 x 4-1/4

CLC-3799.2, 1-1/2 x 4-1/2

CLC-3884.2, 1-1/2 x 4-1/4

CLC-756, 1-1/16 x 4-1/8

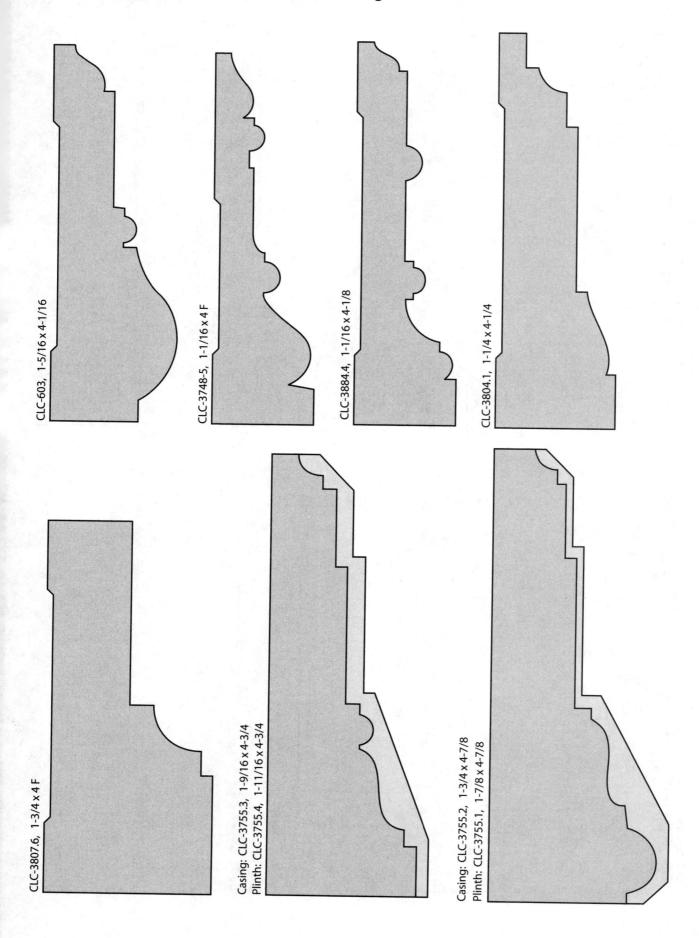

CLC-603, 1-5/16 x 4-1/16

CLC-3748-5, 1-1/16 x 4 F

CLC-3884.4, 1-1/16 x 4-1/8

CLC-3804.1, 1-1/4 x 4-1/4

CLC-3807.6, 1-3/4 x 4 F

Casing: CLC-3755.3, 1-9/16 x 4-3/4
Plinth: CLC-3755.4, 1-11/16 x 4-3/4

Casing: CLC-3755.2, 1-3/4 x 4-7/8
Plinth: CLC-3755.1, 1-7/8 x 4-7/8

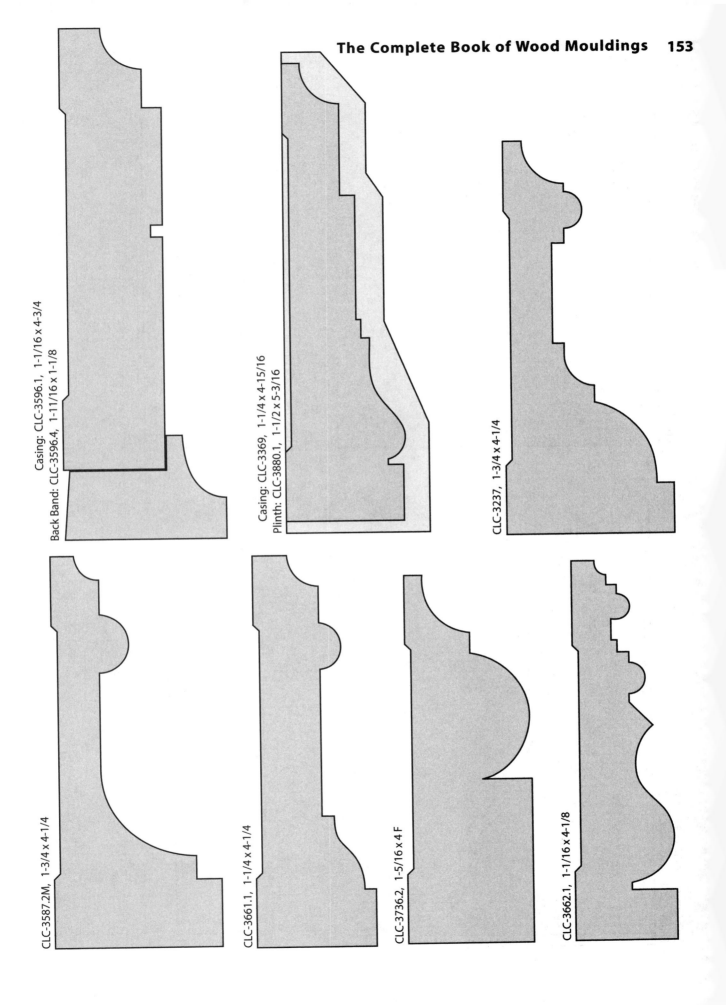

Casing: CLC-3596.1, 1-1/16 x 4-3/4
Back Band: CLC-3596.4, 1-11/16 x 1-1/8

Casing: CLC-3369, 1-1/4 x 4-15/16
Plinth: CLC-3880.1, 1-1/2 x 5-3/16

CLC-3237, 1-3/4 x 4-1/4

CLC-3587.2M, 1-3/4 x 4-1/4

CLC-3661.1, 1-1/4 x 4-1/4

CLC-3736.2, 1-5/16 x 4 F

CLC-3662.1, 1-1/16 x 4-1/8

CLC-3736.1M   1-3/4 x 3-7/8

CLC-3082, 1-5/16 x 4 F

CLC-3240, 1-1/4 x 4 F

Casing: CLC-3720.11, 1-1/16 x 4-1/2
Plinth: CLC-70M, 1-1/4 x 4-7/8

Casing: CLC-3337.1, 2 F x 4-15/16
Plinth: CLC-3885.3, 2-1/8 x 5-1/4

CLC-791, 1-1/8 x 4-11/16

CLC-3793.3, 1 F x 4-9/16

CLC-3740.5, 1-1/16 x 4-3/16

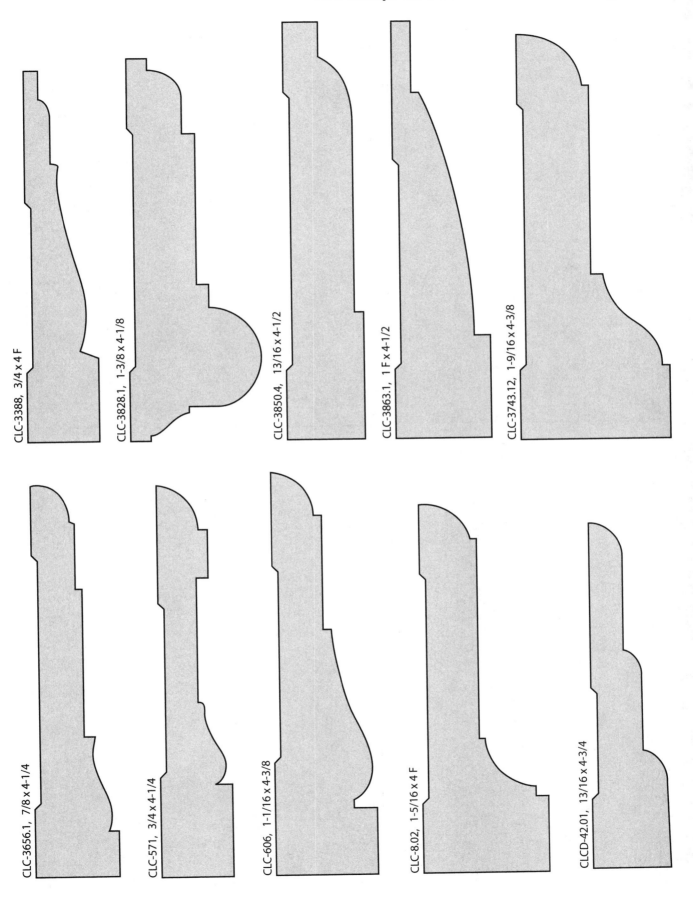

CLC-3388, 3/4 x 4 F

CLC-3828.1, 1-3/8 x 4-1/8

CLC-3850.4, 13/16 x 4-1/2

CLC-3863.1, 1 F x 4-1/2

CLC-3743.12, 1-9/16 x 4-3/8

CLC-3656.1, 7/8 x 4-1/4

CLC-571, 3/4 x 4-1/4

CLC-606, 1-1/16 x 4-3/8

CLC-8.02, 1-5/16 x 4 F

CLCD-42.01, 13/16 x 4-3/4

CLC-3000, 1-1/4 x 4 F

CLC-3008, 13/16 x 4-3/8

CLC-3552, 1-1/16 x 4-1/8

Casing: CLC-3808, 1-1/16 x 4-1/2

CLC-2520, 3/4 x 4-7/8

CLC-757, 1-1/16 x 4-3/8

Casing: CLC-3500, 13/16 x 4-1/2
Plinth: CLC-23M, 1 F x 4-3/4

CLC-3766.2, 1-1/16 x 4-1/2

CLC-18.01, 15/16 x 4 F

CLC-23.0, 1-3/16 x 4-9/16

Casing: CLC-3559.1, 13/16 x 4-1/4

Base Cap: CLC-3559.2, 3/4 x 7/8

Casing: CLC-3638.3, 1-1/16 x 4-5/8
Plinth: CLC-3638.2, 1-1/4 x 5 F

CLC-3812.3, 1-3/8 x 4-3/4

CLC-3752.2, 1-1/16 x 4 F

CLC-51.11, 1-11/16 x 4-13/16

CLC-3839.6, 1-1/2 x 4-1/4

CLC-3754, 1-1/4 x 4-3/8

CLC-8.01, 1-5/16 x 4 F

CLC-3807.4, 1-1/2 x 4-1/4

CLC-3804.2, 1-3/8 x 4-1/16

CLC-3621.2, 13/16 x 4-1/2

CLC-555, 7/8 x 4-3/4

CLC-562, 1-1/4 x 4-5/8

CLC-3864.4, 1-3/8 x 4-1/4

Casing: CLC-3301, 1-1/16 x 4-1/2
Plinth: CLC-3900.5, 1-1/4 x 4-3/4

Casing: CLC-3645.3, 3/4 x 3-1/4
Back Band: CLC-3645.5M, 1-11/16 x 1-15/16
Plinth: CLC-3645.1, 1-13/16 x 4-1/4

CLC-3266M, 1-1/16 x 4-1/16

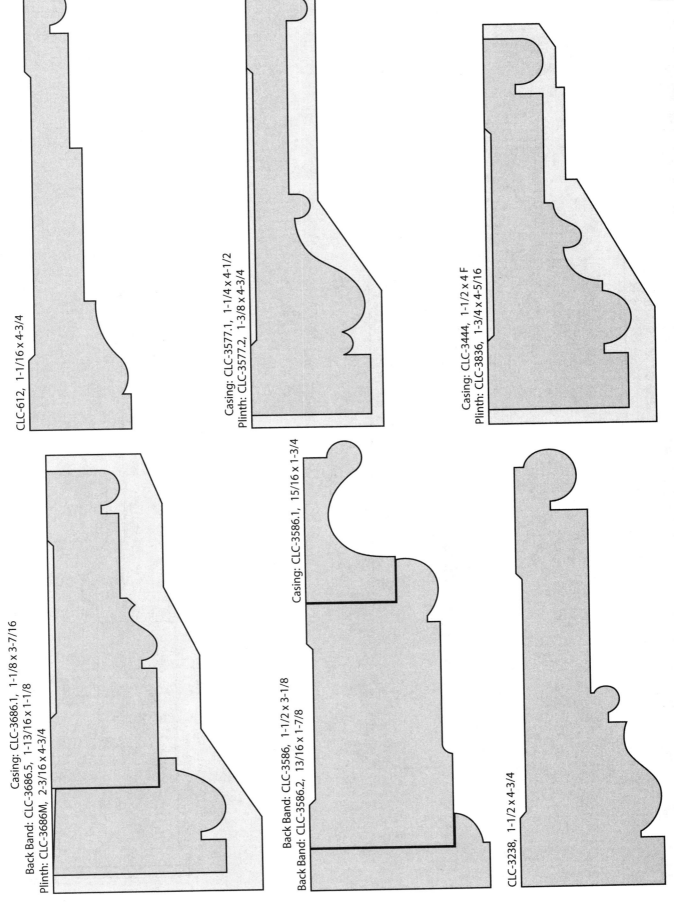

159

CLC-612, 1-1/16 x 4-3/4

Casing: CLC-3577.1, 1-1/4 x 4-1/2
Plinth: CLC-3577.2, 1-3/8 x 4-3/4

Casing: CLC-3444, 1-1/2 x 4 F
Plinth: CLC-3836, 1-3/4 x 4-5/16

Casing: CLC-3686.1, 1-1/8 x 3-7/16
Back Band: CLC-3686.5, 1-13/16 x 1-1/8
Plinth: CLC-3686M, 2-3/16 x 4-3/4

Casing: CLC-3586.1, 15/16 x 1-3/4
Back Band: CLC-3586, 1-1/2 x 3-1/8
Back Band: CLC-3586.2, 13/16 x 1-7/8

CLC-3238, 1-1/2 x 4-3/4

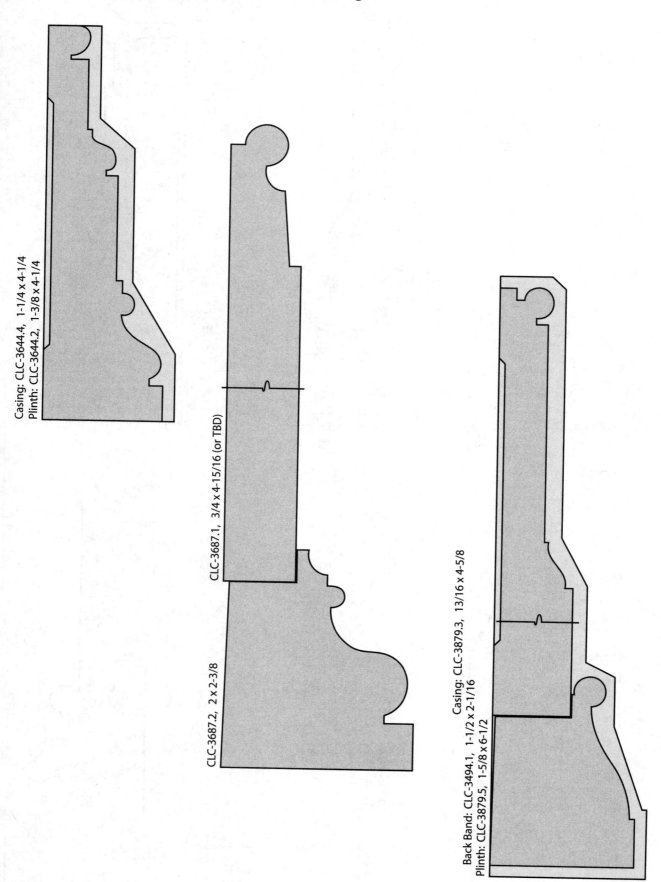

Casing: CLC-3644.4, 1-1/4 x 4-1/4
Plinth: CLC-3644.2, 1-3/8 x 4-1/4

CLC-3687.1, 3/4 x 4-15/16 (or TBD)

CLC-3687.2, 2 x 2-3/8

Casing: CLC-3879.3, 13/16 x 4-5/8

Back Band: CLC-3494.1, 1-1/2 x 2-1/16
Plinth: CLC-3879.5, 1-5/8 x 6-1/2

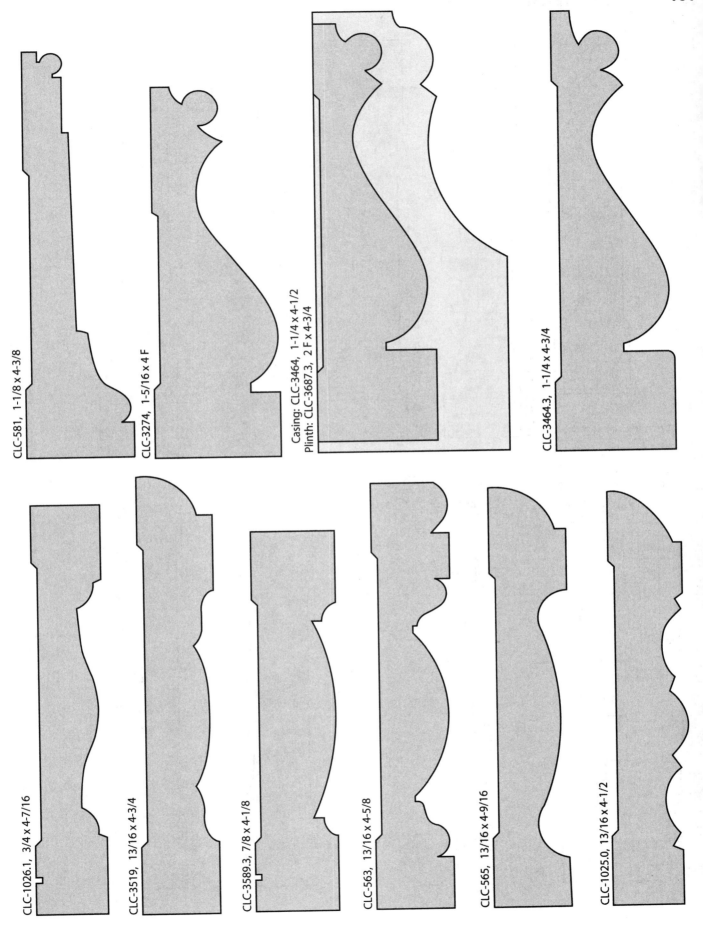

161

CLC-581, 1-1/8 x 4-3/8

CLC-3274, 1-5/16 x 4 F

Casing: CLC-3464, 1-1/4 x 4-1/2
Plinth: CLC-3687.3, 2 F x 4-3/4

CLC-3464.3, 1-1/4 x 4-3/4

CLC-1026.1, 3/4 x 4-7/16

CLC-3519, 13/16 x 4-3/4

CLC-3589.3, 7/8 x 4-1/8

CLC-563, 13/16 x 4-5/8

CLC-565, 13/16 x 4-9/16

CLC-1025.0, 13/16 x 4-1/2

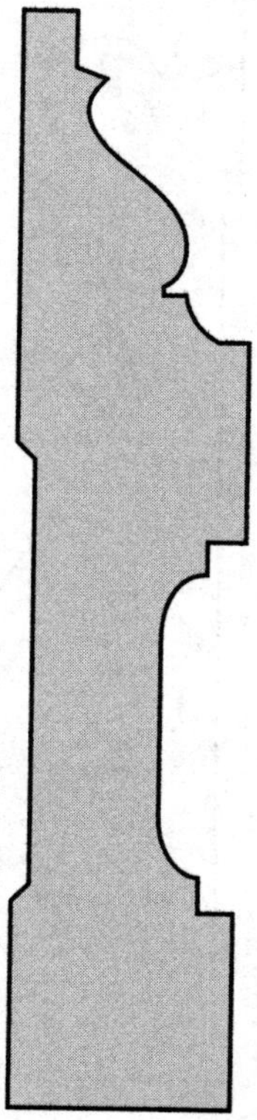

CLC-3751.4, 13/16 x 4 F

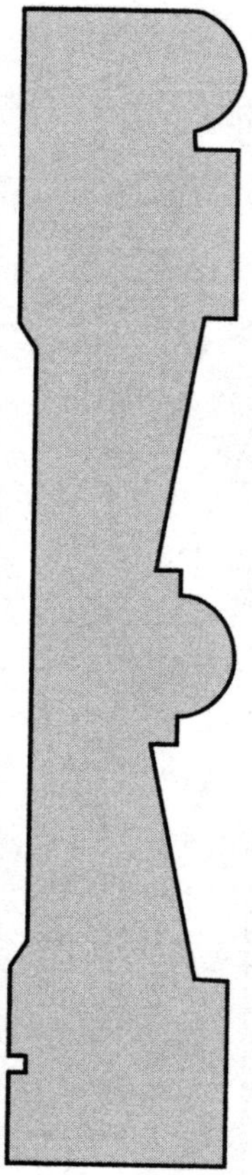

CLC-3520, 13/16 x 4-3/8

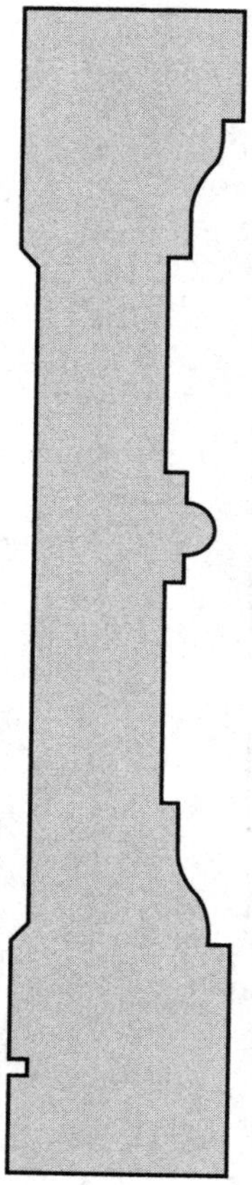

CLC-51.09, 13/16 x 4-7/16

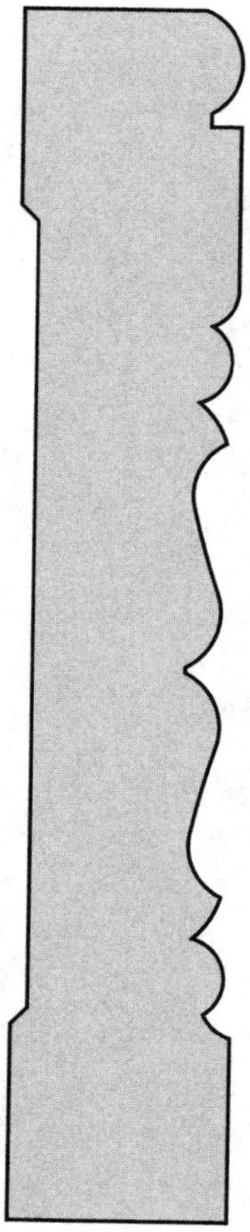

CLC-953, 13/16 x 4-5/8

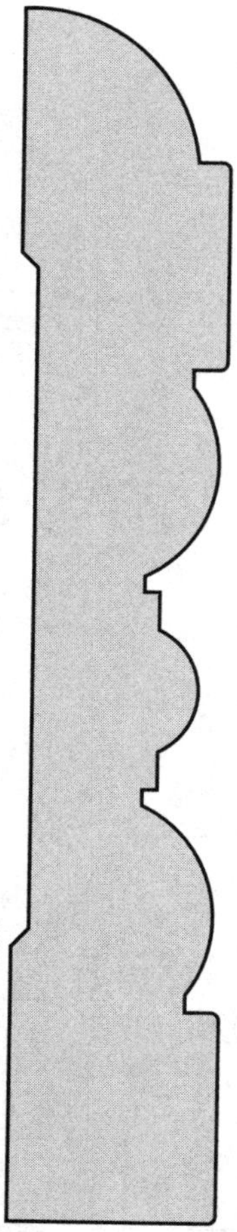

CLC-951, 13/16 x 4-7/8

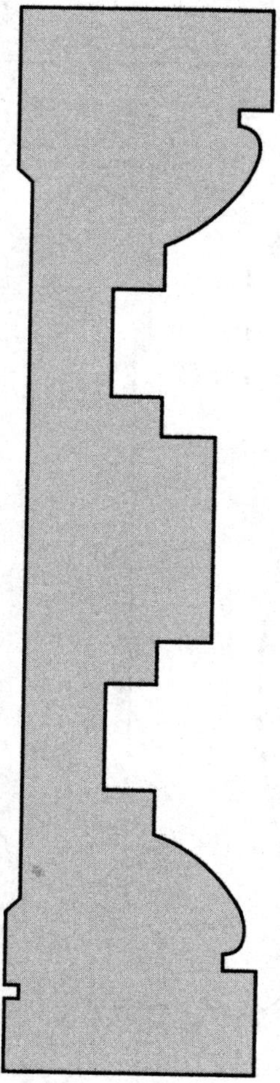

CLC-3804, 1-1/8 x 4-15/16

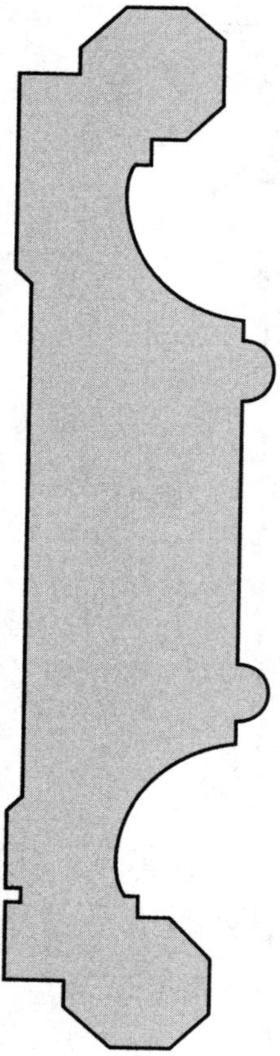

CLC-3668.5, 1-1/16 x 4-7/16

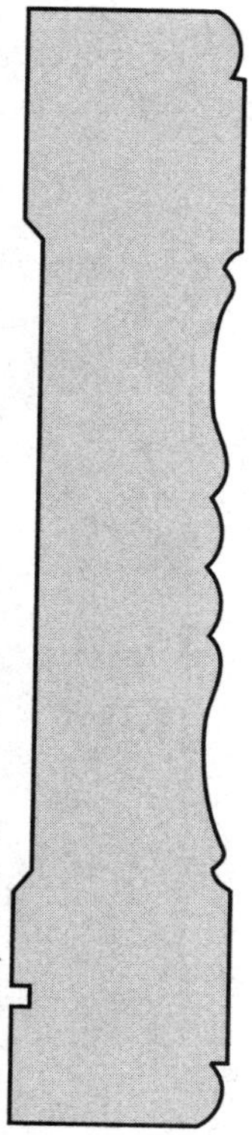

CLC-1030.1, 3/4 x 4 F

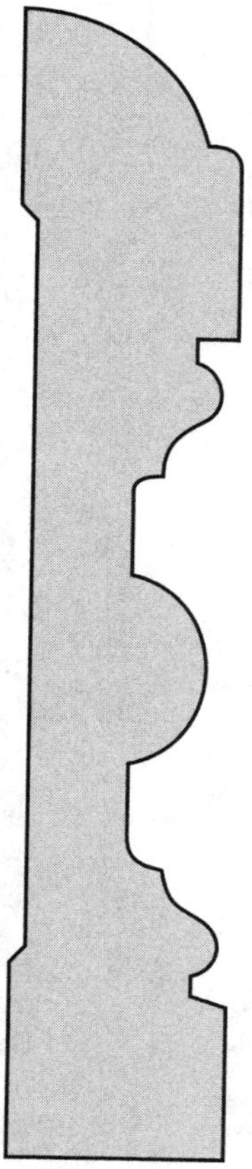

CLC-3867.6, 13/16 x 4-7/16

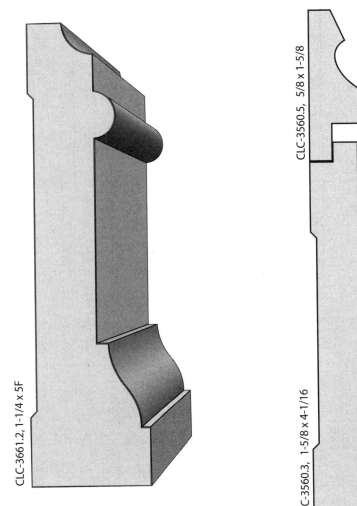

CLC-3661.2, 1-1/4 x 5F

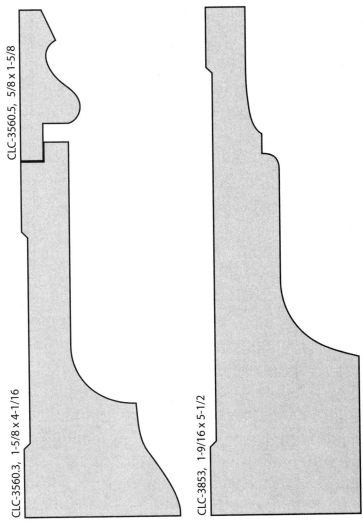

CLC-3560.5, 5/8 x 1-5/8

CLC-3560.3, 1-5/8 x 4-1/16

CLC-3853, 1-9/16 x 5-1/2

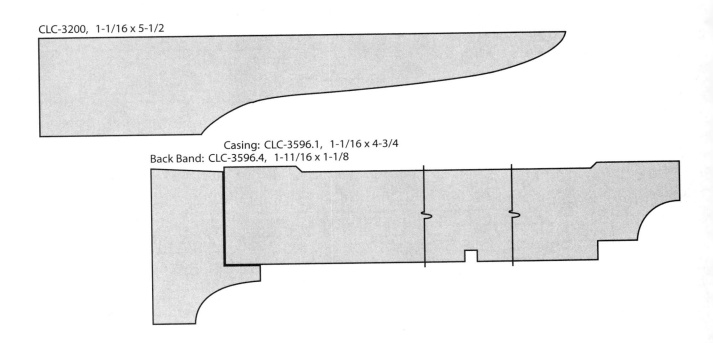

CLC-3200, 1-1/16 x 5-1/2

Casing: CLC-3596.1, 1-1/16 x 4-3/4
Back Band: CLC-3596.4, 1-11/16 x 1-1/8

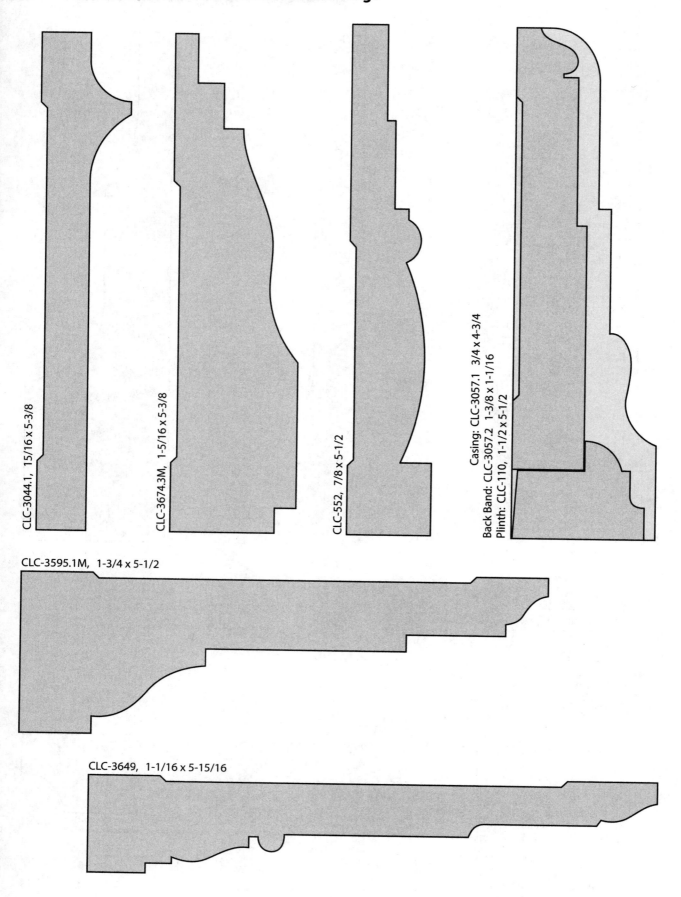

CLC-3044.1, 15/16 x 5-3/8

CLC-3674.3M, 1-5/16 x 5-3/8

CLC-552, 7/8 x 5-1/2

Casing: CLC-3057.1 3/4 x 4-3/4
Back Band: CLC-3057.2 1-3/8 x 1-1/16
Plinth: CLC-110, 1-1/2 x 5-1/2

CLC-3595.1M, 1-3/4 x 5-1/2

CLC-3649, 1-1/16 x 5-15/16

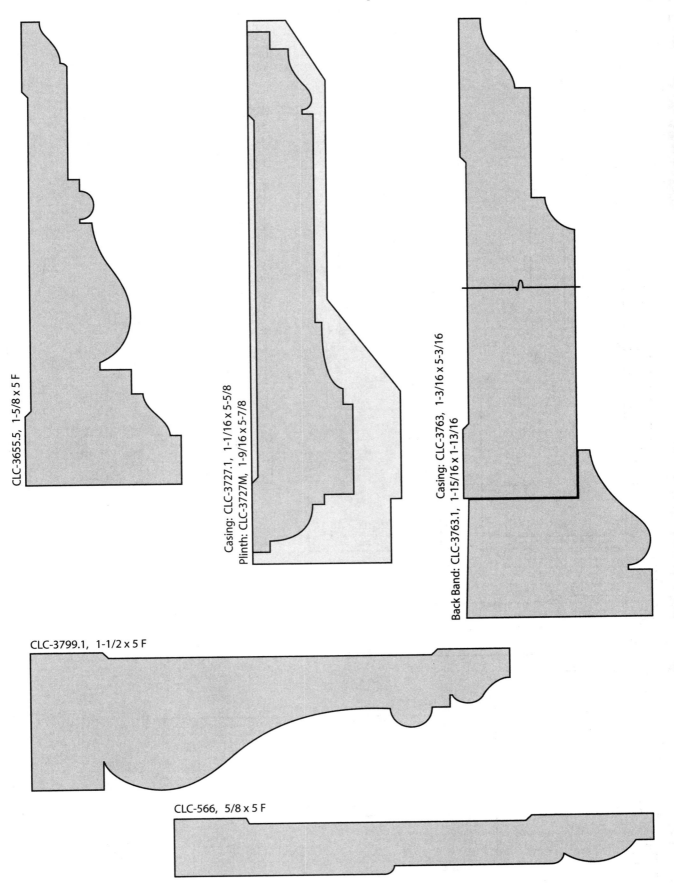

CLC-3655.5, 1-5/8 x 5 F

Casing: CLC-3727.1, 1-1/16 x 5-5/8
Plinth: CLC-3727M, 1-9/16 x 5-7/8

Casing: CLC-3763, 1-3/16 x 5-3/16

Back Band: CLC-3763.1, 1-15/16 x 1-13/16

CLC-3799.1, 1-1/2 x 5 F

CLC-566, 5/8 x 5 F

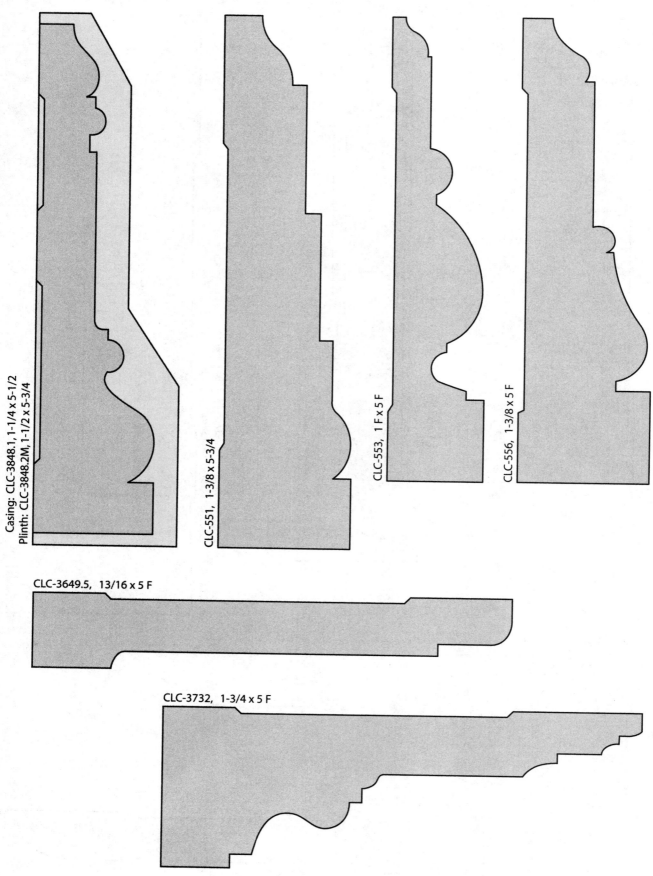

Casing: CLC-3848.1, 1-1/4 x 5-1/2
Plinth: CLC-3848.2M, 1-1/2 x 5-3/4

CLC-551, 1-3/8 x 5-3/4

CLC-553, 1 F x 5 F

CLC-556, 1-3/8 x 5 F

CLC-3649.5, 13/16 x 5 F

CLC-3732, 1-3/4 x 5 F

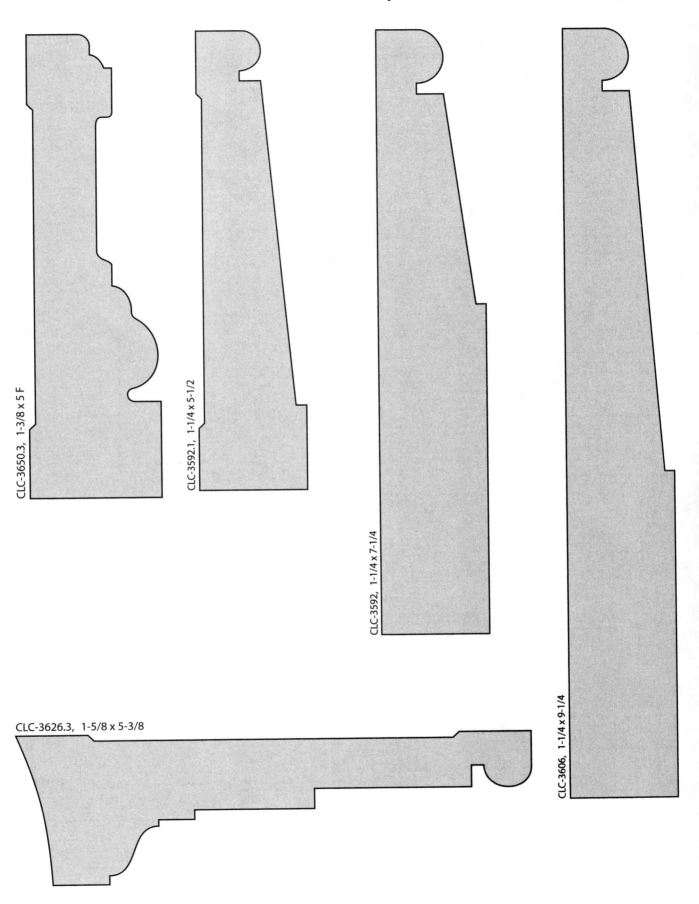

CLC-3650.3, 1-3/8 x 5 F

CLC-3592.1, 1-1/4 x 5-1/2

CLC-3592, 1-1/4 x 7-1/4

CLC-3626.3, 1-5/8 x 5-3/8

CLC-3606, 1-1/4 x 9-1/4

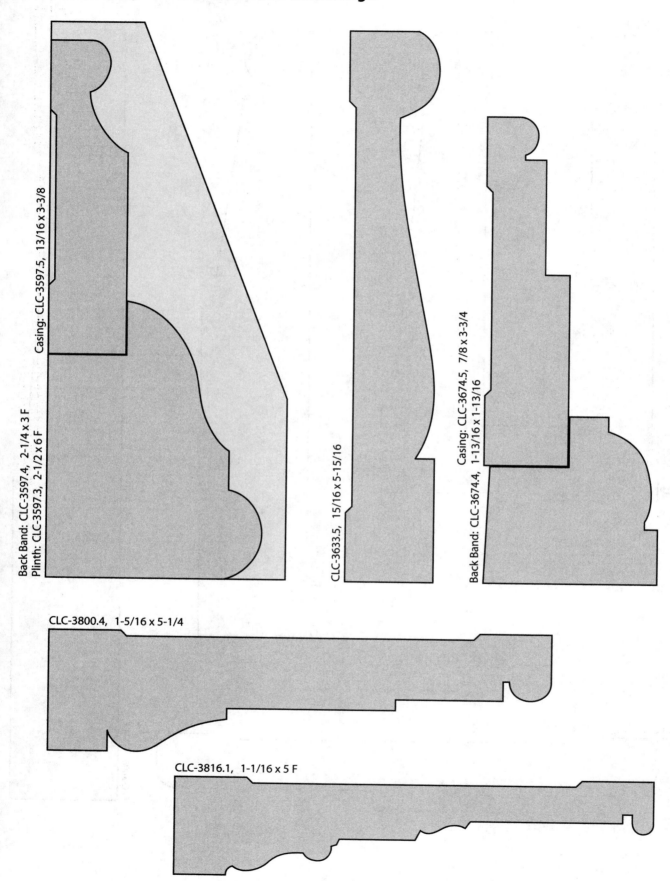

Casing: CLC-3597.5, 13/16 x 3-3/8

Back Band: CLC-3597.4, 2-1/4 x 3 F
Plinth: CLC-3597.3, 2-1/2 x 6 F

CLC-3633.5, 15/16 x 5-15/16

Casing: CLC-3674.5, 7/8 x 3-3/4

Back Band: CLC-3674.4, 1-13/16 x 1-13/16

CLC-3800.4, 1-5/16 x 5-1/4

CLC-3816.1, 1-1/16 x 5 F

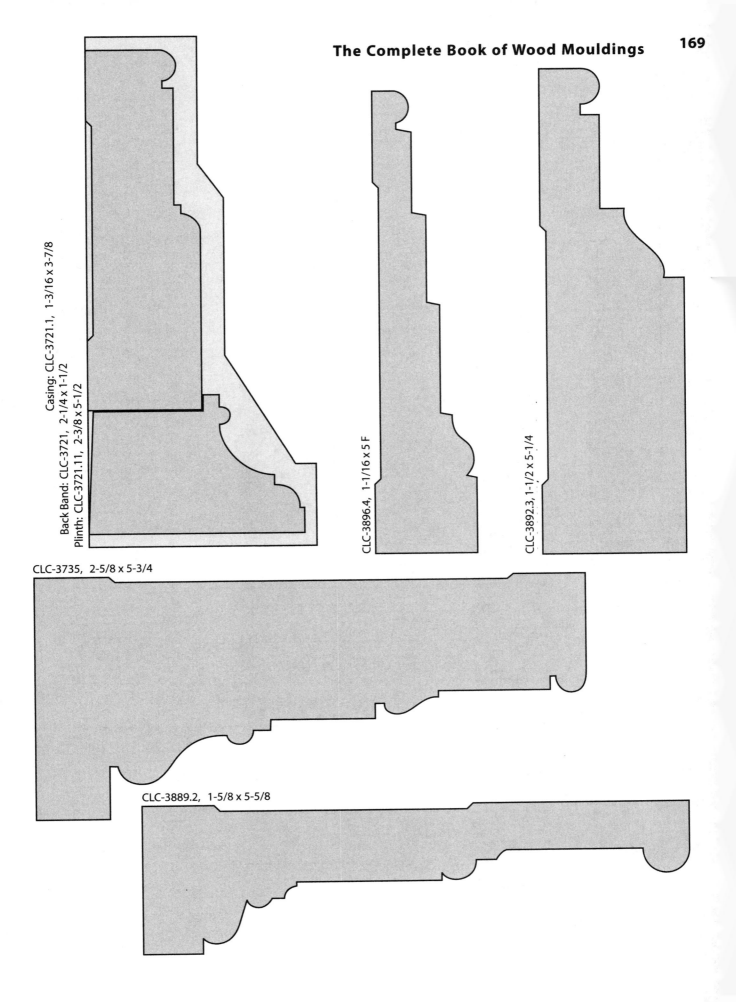

Casing: CLC-3721.1, 1-3/16 x 3-7/8

Back Band: CLC-3721, 2-1/4 x 1-1/2
Plinth: CLC-3721.11, 2-3/8 x 5-1/2

CLC-3896.4, 1-1/16 x 5 F

CLC-3892.3, 1-1/2 x 5-1/4

CLC-3735, 2-5/8 x 5-3/4

CLC-3889.2, 1-5/8 x 5-5/8

CLC-550, 13/16 x 5-1/2

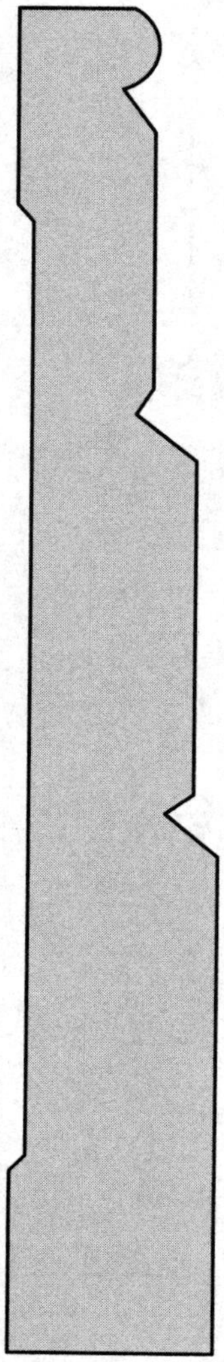

Casing: CLC-3604.1, 1/2 x 3-1/4

Back Band: CLC-3604.2, 1-1/4 x 2-5/16

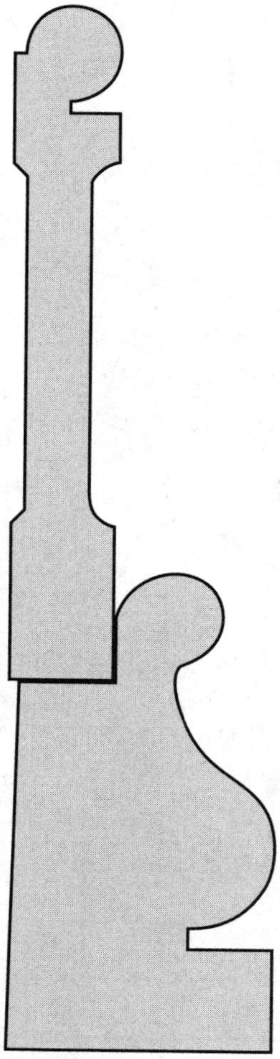

CLC-3682, 1-3/8 x 5 F

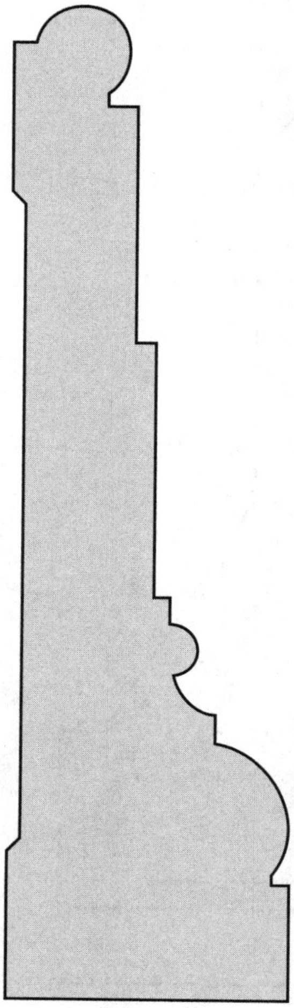

CLC-3607.3, 1-1/16 x 5-3/4

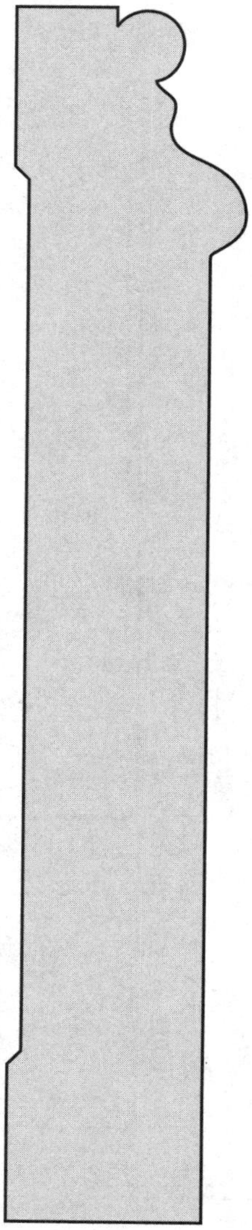

CLC-3612.3, 1/2 x 5-1/4 (or TBD)

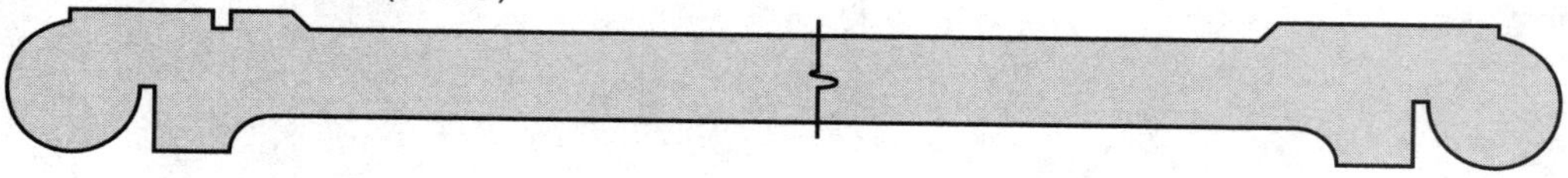

CLC-3612, 1/2 x 6 F (or TBD)

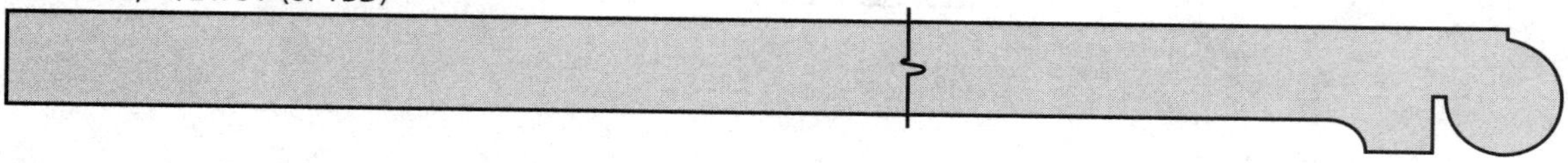

CLC-3832.2, 1-5/16 x 5 F

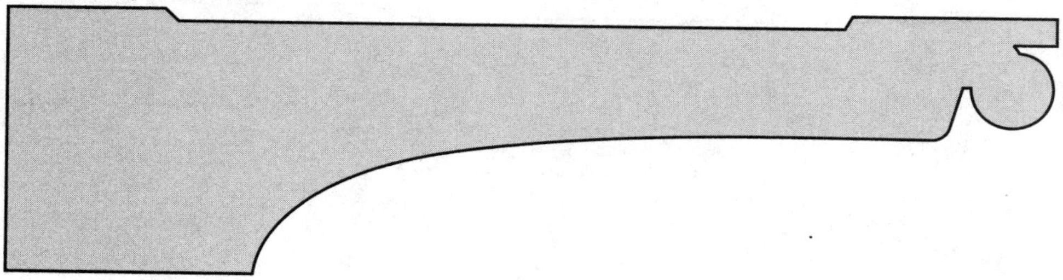

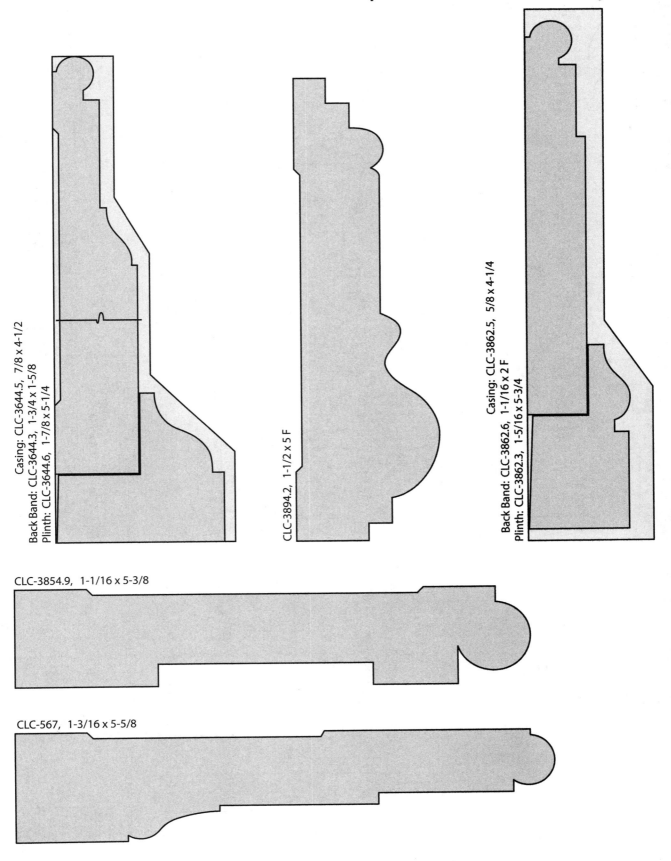

Casing: CLC-3644.5, 7/8 x 4-1/2
Back Band: CLC-3644.3, 1-3/4 x 1-5/8
Plinth: CLC-3644.6, 1-7/8 x 5-1/4

CLC-3894.2, 1-1/2 x 5 F

Casing: CLC-3862.5, 5/8 x 4-1/4
Back Band: CLC-3862.6, 1-1/16 x 2 F
Plinth: CLC-3862.3, 1-5/16 x 5-3/4

CLC-3854.9, 1-1/16 x 5-3/8

CLC-567, 1-3/16 x 5-5/8

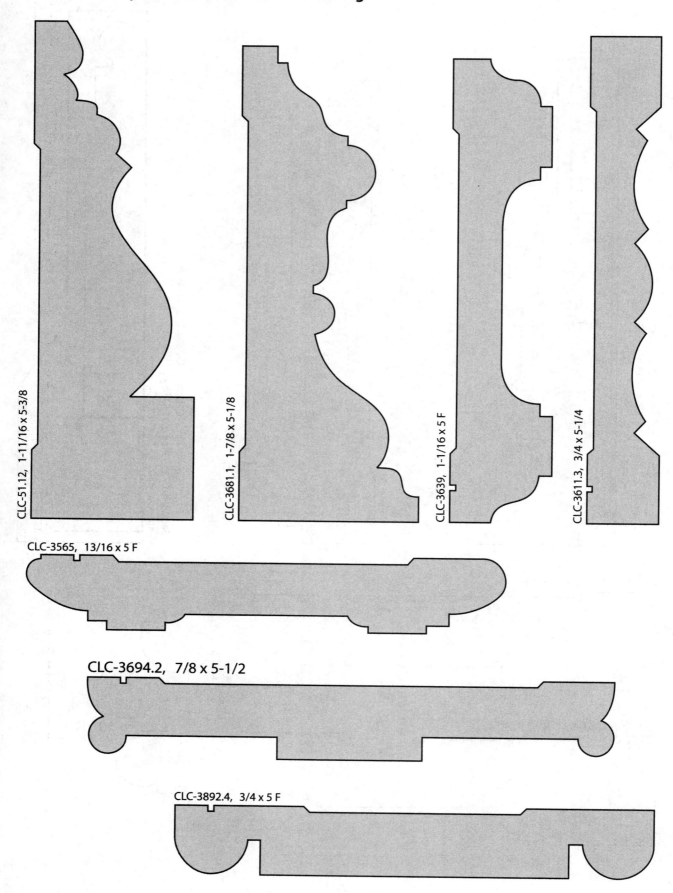

CLC-51.12, 1-11/16 x 5-3/8

CLC-3681.1, 1-7/8 x 5-1/8

CLC-3639, 1-1/16 x 5 F

CLC-3611.3, 3/4 x 5-1/4

CLC-3565, 13/16 x 5 F

CLC-3694.2, 7/8 x 5-1/2

CLC-3892.4, 3/4 x 5 F

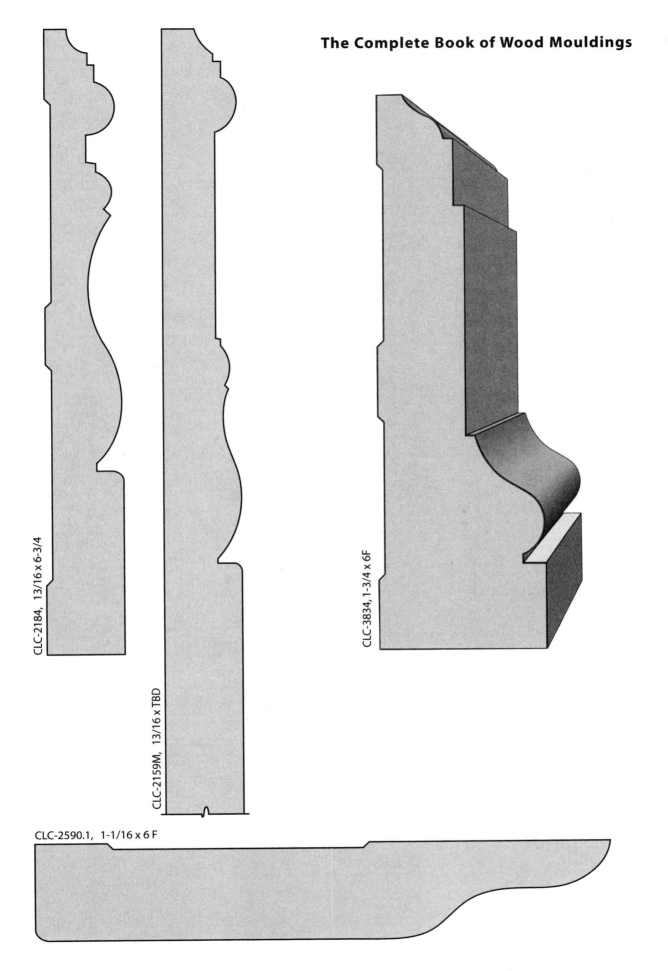

CLC-2184, 13/16 x 6-3/4

CLC-2159M, 13/16 x TBD

CLC-3834, 1-3/4 x 6F

CLC-2590.1, 1-1/16 x 6 F

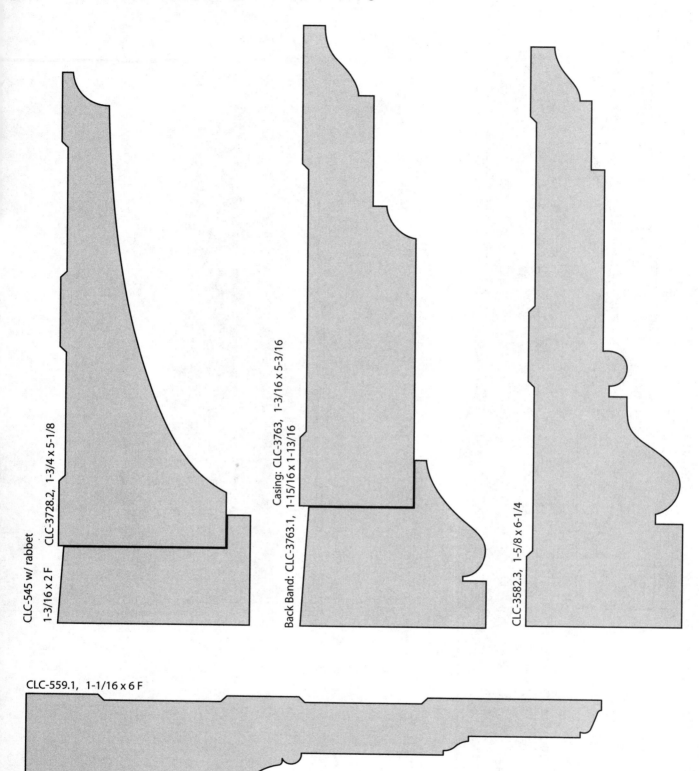

CLC-545 w/ rabbet

CLC-3728.2, 1-3/4 x 5-1/8

1-3/16 x 2 F

Casing: CLC-3763, 1-3/16 x 5-3/16

Back Band: CLC-3763.1, 1-15/16 x 1-13/16

CLC-3582.3, 1-5/8 x 6-1/4

CLC-559.1, 1-1/16 x 6 F

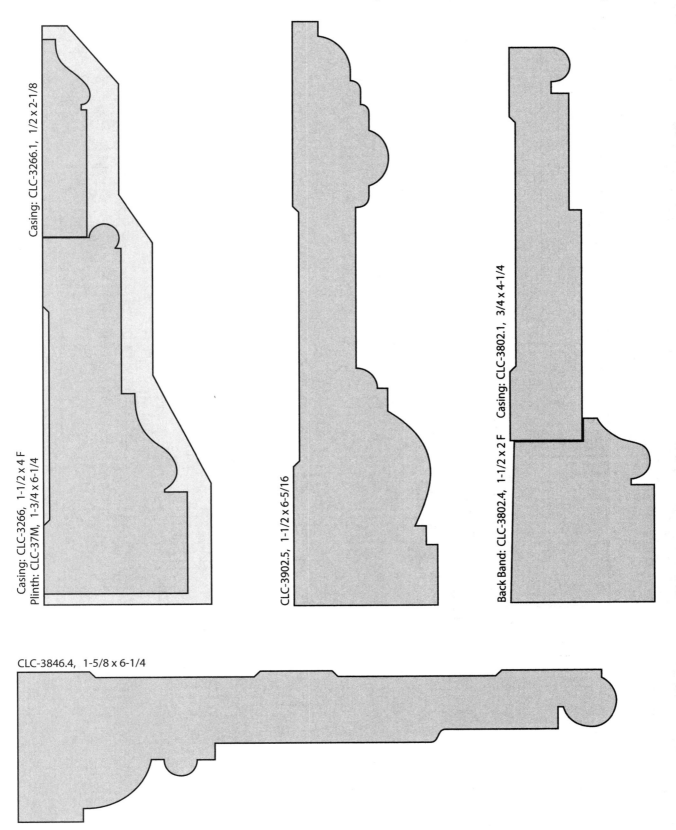

Casing: CLC-3266.1, 1/2 x 2-1/8

Casing: CLC-3266, 1-1/2 x 4 F
Plinth: CLC-37M, 1-3/4 x 6-1/4

CLC-3902.5, 1-1/2 x 6-5/16

Casing: CLC-3802.1, 3/4 x 4-1/4

Back Band: CLC-3802.4, 1-1/2 x 2 F

CLC-3846.4, 1-5/8 x 6-1/4

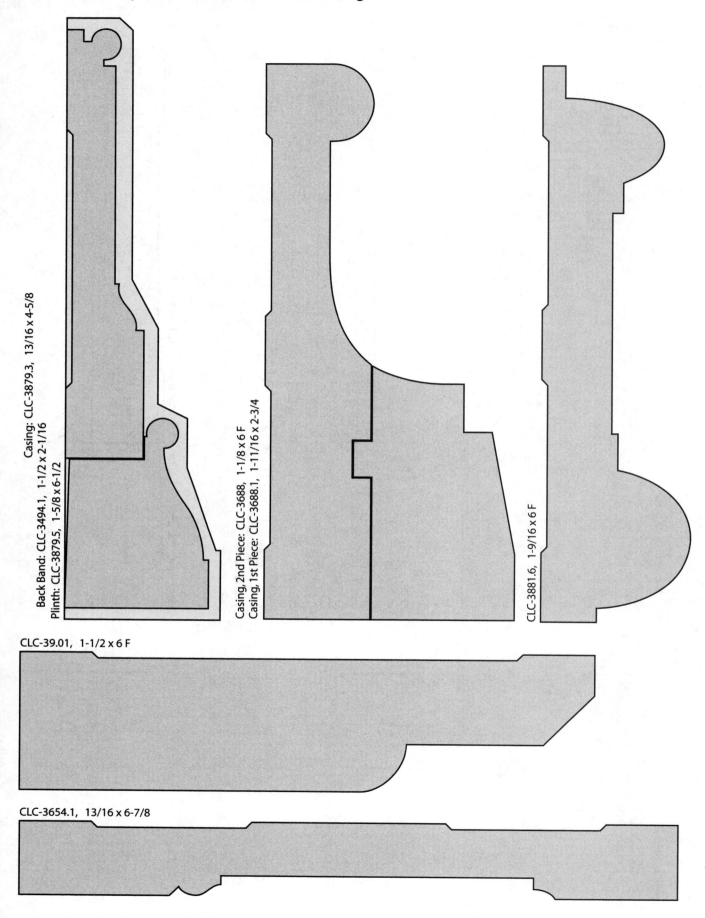

Casing: CLC-3879.3, 13/16 x 4-5/8

Back Band: CLC-3494.1, 1-1/2 x 2-1/16

Plinth: CLC-3879.5, 1-5/8 x 6-1/2

Casing, 2nd Piece: CLC-3688, 1-1/8 x 6 F
Casing, 1st Piece: CLC-3688.1, 1-11/16 x 2-3/4

CLC-3881.6, 1-9/16 x 6 F

CLC-39.01, 1-1/2 x 6 F

CLC-3654.1, 13/16 x 6-7/8

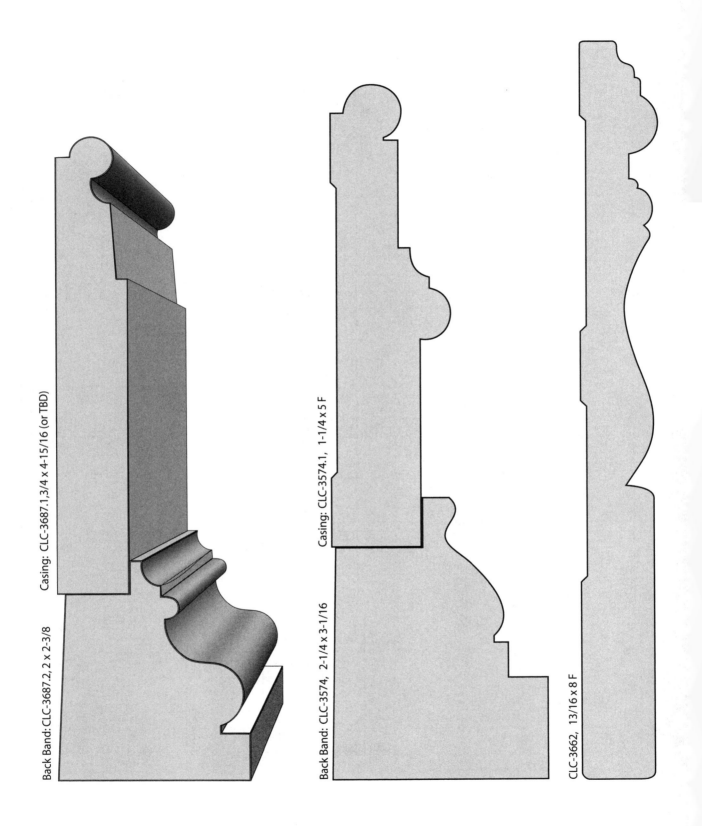

Casing: CLC-3687.1,3/4 x 4-15/16 (or TBD)

Back Band: CLC-3687.2, 2 x 2-3/8

Casing: CLC-3574.1, 1-1/4 x 5 F

Back Band: CLC-3574, 2-1/4 x 3-1/16

CLC-3662, 13/16 x 8 F

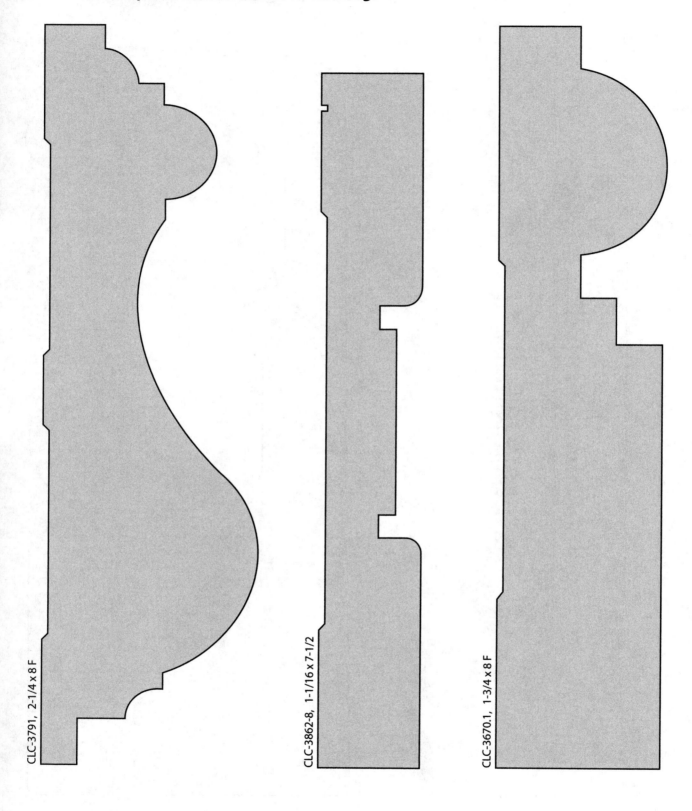

CLC-3791, 2-1/4 x 8 F

CLC-3862-8, 1-1/16 x 7-1/2

CLC-3670.1, 1-3/4 x 8 F

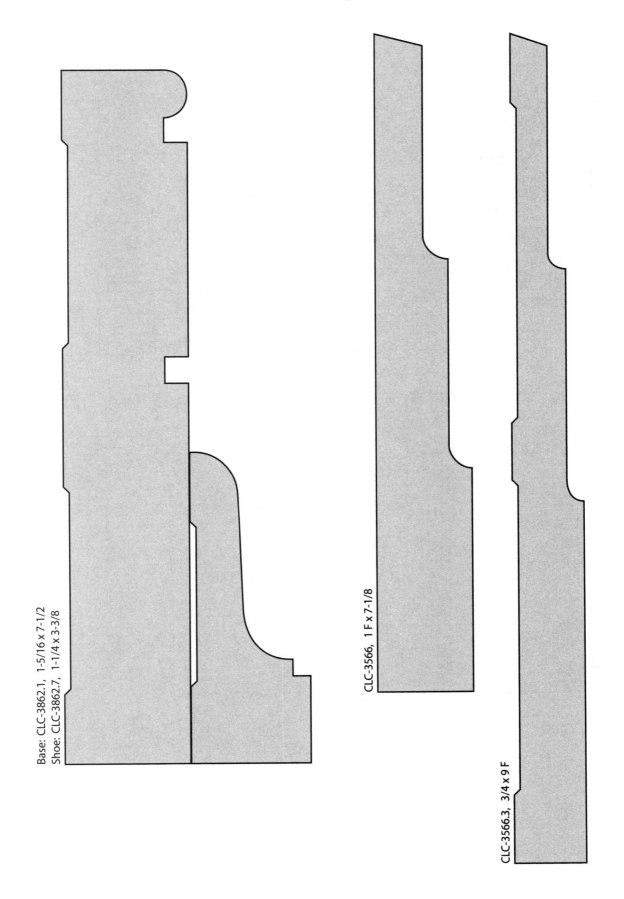

Base: CLC-3862.1, 1-5/16 x 7-1/2
Shoe: CLC-3862.7, 1-1/4 x 3-3/8

CLC-3566, 1 F x 7-1/8

CLC-3566.3, 3/4 x 9 F

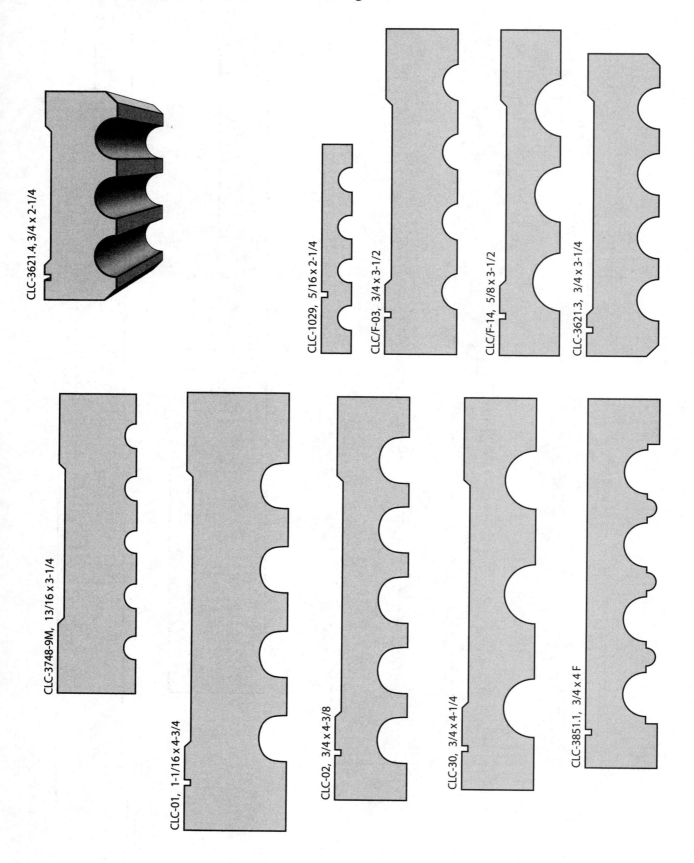

CLC-3621.4, 3/4 x 2-1/4

CLC-1029, 5/16 x 2-1/4

CLC/F-03, 3/4 x 3-1/2

CLC/F-14, 5/8 x 3-1/2

CLC-3621.3, 3/4 x 3-1/4

CLC-3748-9M, 13/16 x 3-1/4

CLC-01, 1-1/16 x 4-3/4

CLC-02, 3/4 x 4-3/8

CLC-30, 3/4 x 4-1/4

CLC-3851.1, 3/4 x 4 F

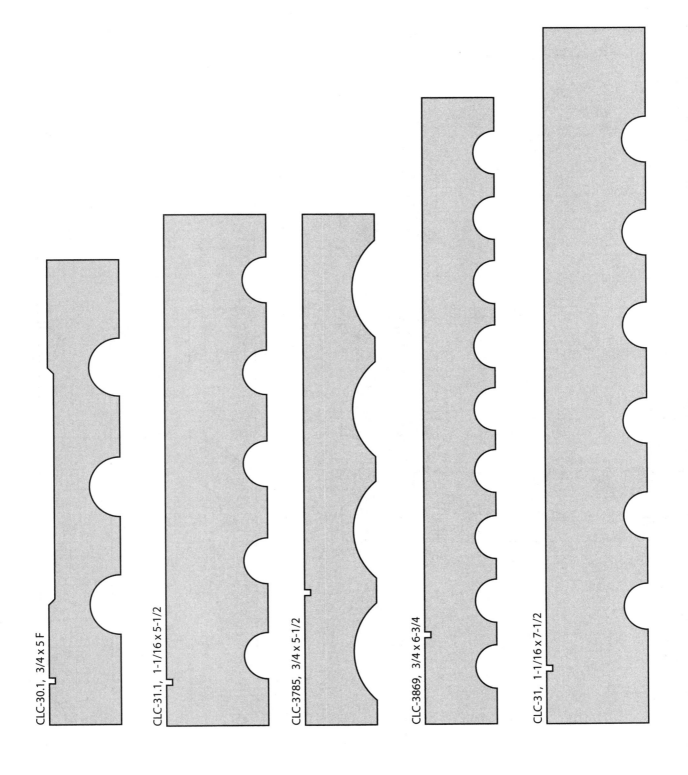

CLC-30.1, 3/4 x 5 F

CLC-31.1, 1-1/16 x 5-1/2

CLC-3785, 3/4 x 5-1/2

CLC-3869, 3/4 x 6-3/4

CLC-31, 1-1/16 x 7-1/2

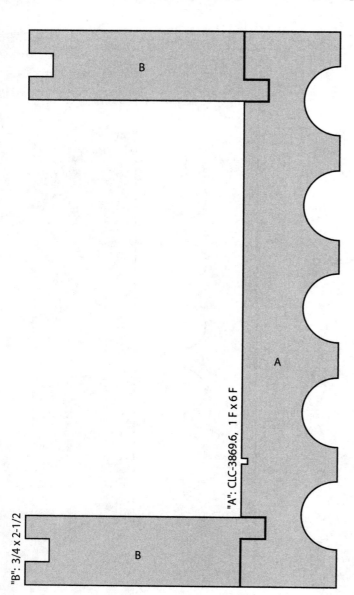

"A": CLC-3869.6, 1 F x 6 F

"B": 3/4 x 2-1/2

A

B

B

CLC-29, 3/4 x 9-7/8

CLC-32F, 3/4 x 9F

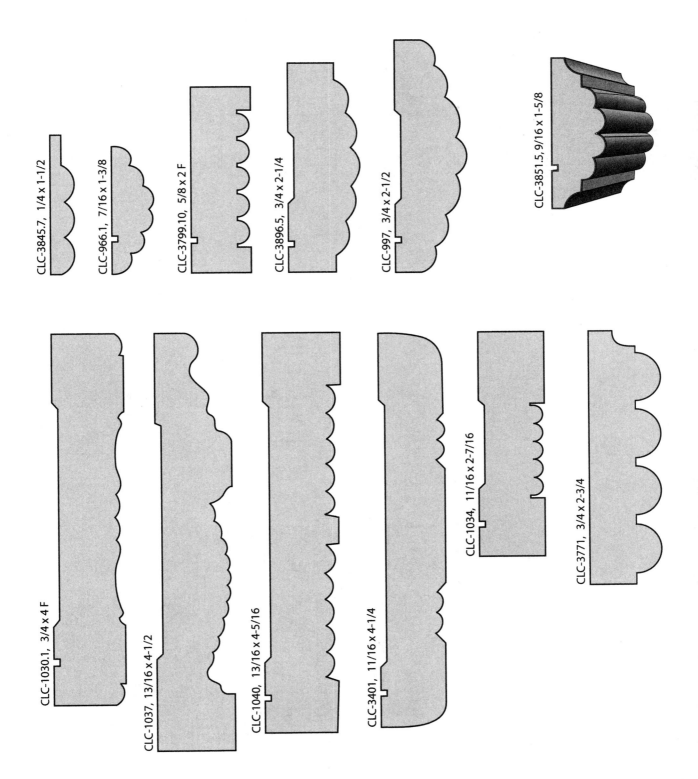

CLC-3845.7, 1/4 x 1-1/2

CLC-966.1, 7/16 x 1-3/8

CLC-3799.10, 5/8 x 2 F

CLC-3896.5, 3/4 x 2-1/4

CLC-997, 3/4 x 2-1/2

CLC-3851.5, 9/16 x 1-5/8

CLC-1030.1, 3/4 x 4 F

CLC-1037, 13/16 x 4-1/2

CLC-1040, 13/16 x 4-5/16

CLC-3401, 11/16 x 4-1/4

CLC-1034, 11/16 x 2-7/16

CLC-3771, 3/4 x 2-3/4

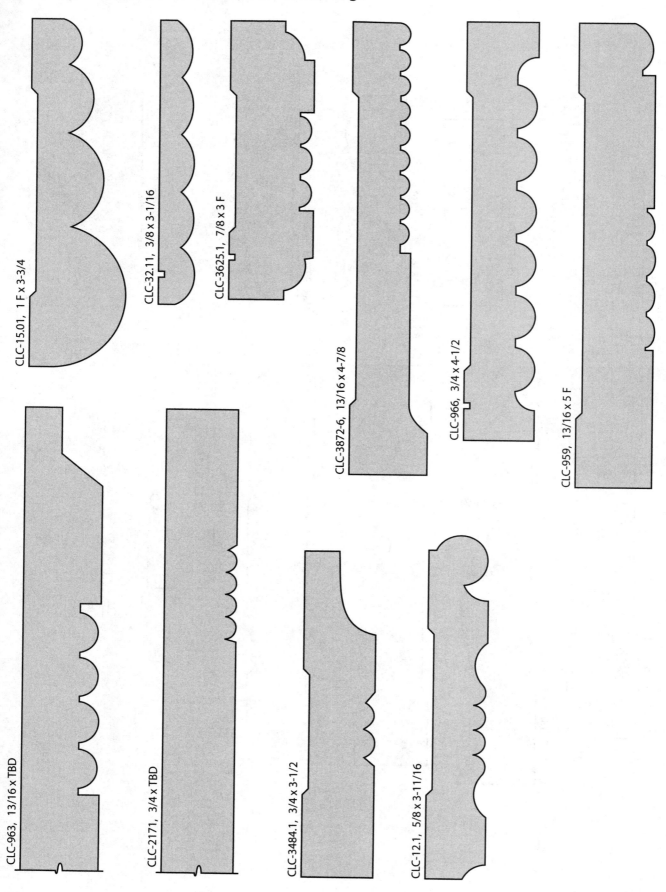

CLC-15.01, 1 F x 3-3/4

CLC-32.11, 3/8 x 3-1/16

CLC-3625.1, 7/8 x 3 F

CLC-3872-6, 13/16 x 4-7/8

CLC-966, 3/4 x 4-1/2

CLC-959, 13/16 x 5 F

CLC-963, 13/16 x TBD

CLC-2171, 3/4 x TBD

CLC-3484.1, 3/4 x 3-1/2

CLC-12.1, 5/8 x 3-11/16

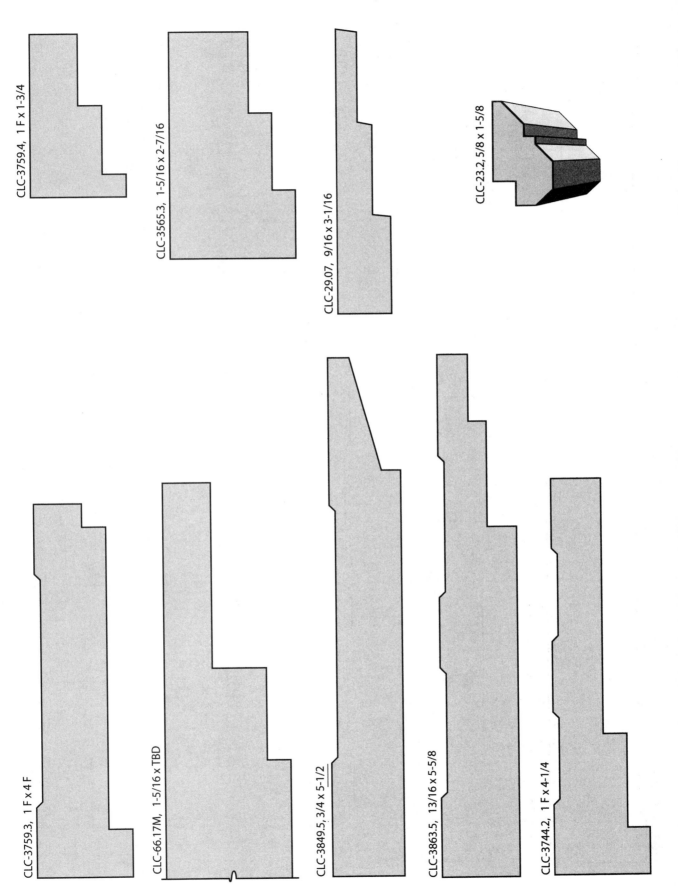

CLC-3759.4, 1 F x 1-3/4

CLC-3565.3, 1-5/16 x 2-7/16

CLC-29.07, 9/16 x 3-1/16

CLC-23.2, 5/8 x 1-5/8

CLC-3759.3, 1 F x 4 F

CLC-66.17M, 1-5/16 x TBD

CLC-3849.5, 3/4 x 5-1/2

CLC-3863.5, 13/16 x 5-5/8

CLC-3744.2, 1 F x 4-1/4

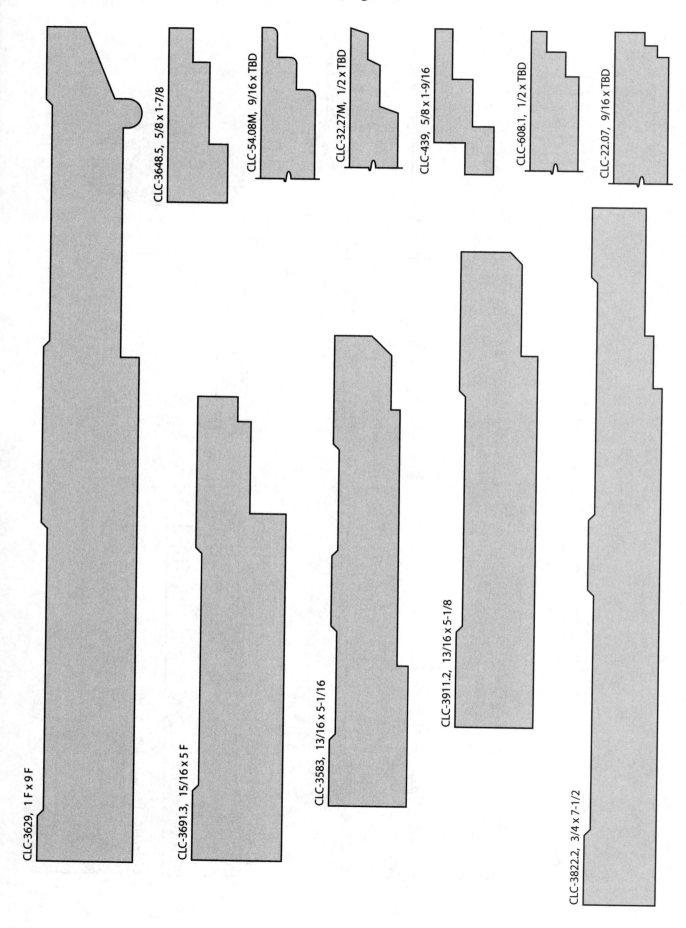

CLC-3629, 1 F x 9 F

CLC-3648.5, 5/8 x 1-7/8

CLC-54.08M, 9/16 x TBD

CLC-32.27M, 1/2 x TBD

CLC-439, 5/8 x 1-9/16

CLC-608.1, 1/2 x TBD

CLC-22.07, 9/16 x TBD

CLC-3691.3, 15/16 x 5 F

CLC-3583, 13/16 x 5-1/16

CLC-3911.2, 13/16 x 5-1/8

CLC-3822.2, 3/4 x 7-1/2

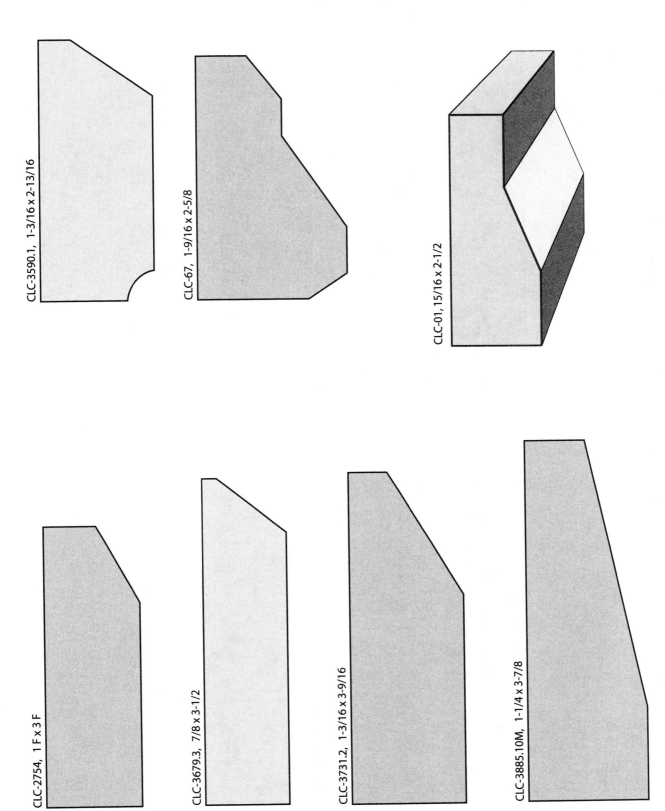

CLC-3590.1, 1-3/16 x 2-13/16

CLC-67, 1-9/16 x 2-5/8

CLC-01, 15/16 x 2-1/2

CLC-2754, 1 F x 3 F

CLC-3679.3, 7/8 x 3-1/2

CLC-3731.2, 1-3/16 x 3-9/16

CLC-3885.10M, 1-1/4 x 3-7/8

PLINTH 2" & 3"

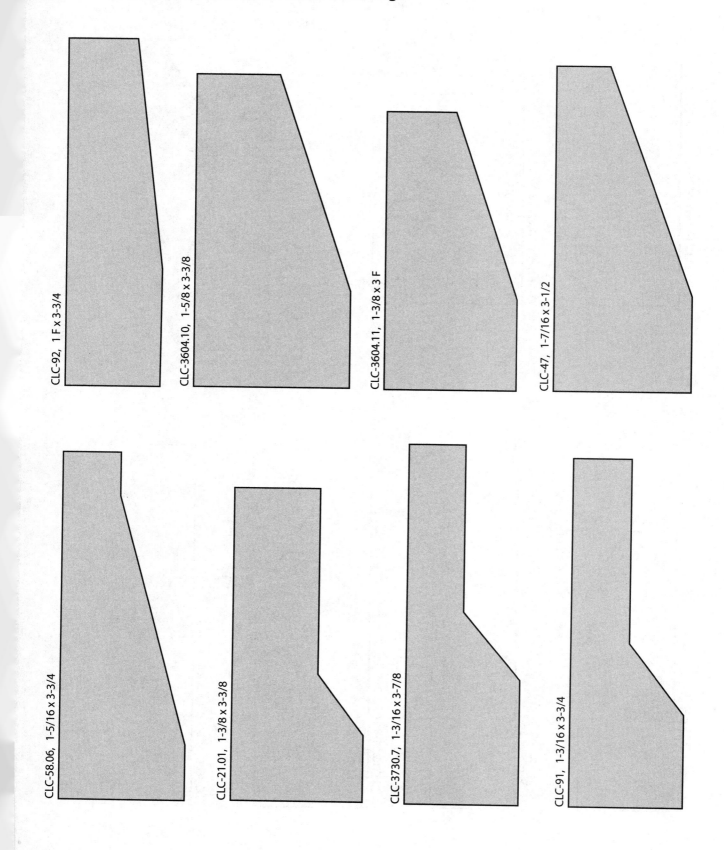

CLC-92, 1 F x 3-3/4

CLC-3604.10, 1-5/8 x 3-3/8

CLC-3604.11, 1-3/8 x 3 F

CLC-47, 1-7/16 x 3-1/2

CLC-58.06, 1-5/16 x 3-3/4

CLC-21.01, 1-3/8 x 3-3/8

CLC-3730.7, 1-3/16 x 3-7/8

CLC-91, 1-3/16 x 3-3/4

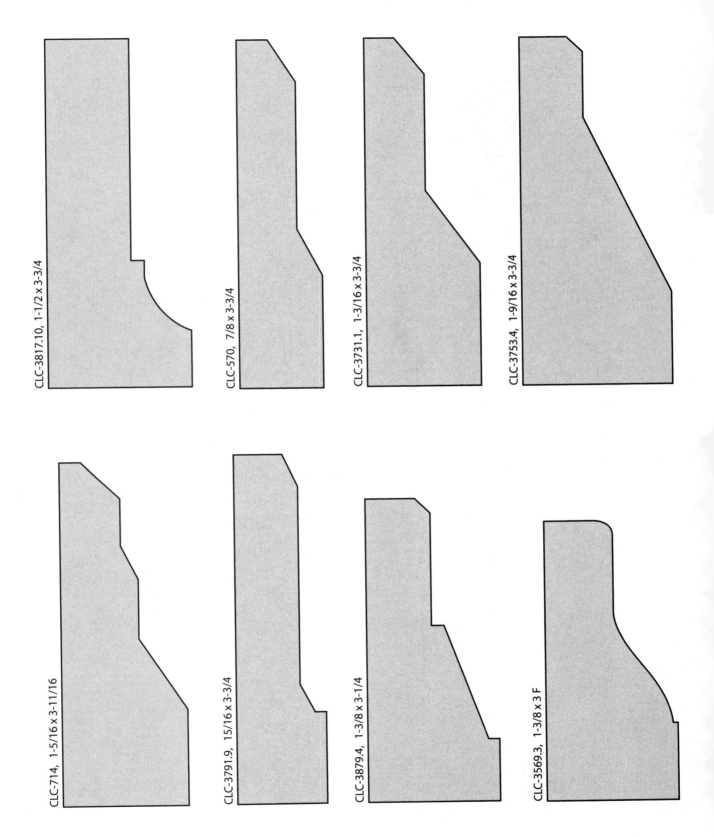

CLC-3817.10, 1-1/2 x 3-3/4

CLC-570, 7/8 x 3-3/4

CLC-3731.1, 1-3/16 x 3-3/4

CLC-3753.4, 1-9/16 x 3-3/4

CLC-714, 1-5/16 x 3-11/16

CLC-3791.9, 15/16 x 3-3/4

CLC-3879.4, 1-3/8 x 3-1/4

CLC-3569.3, 1-3/8 x 3 F

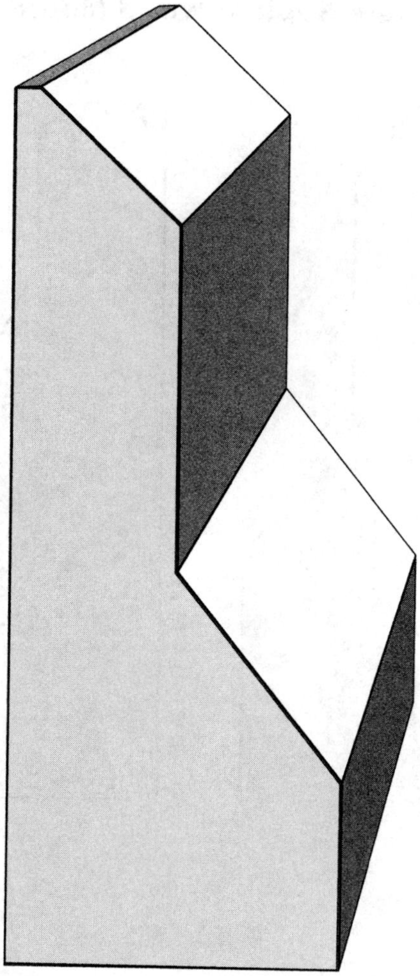

CLC-36M, 1-3/4 x 4-3/4

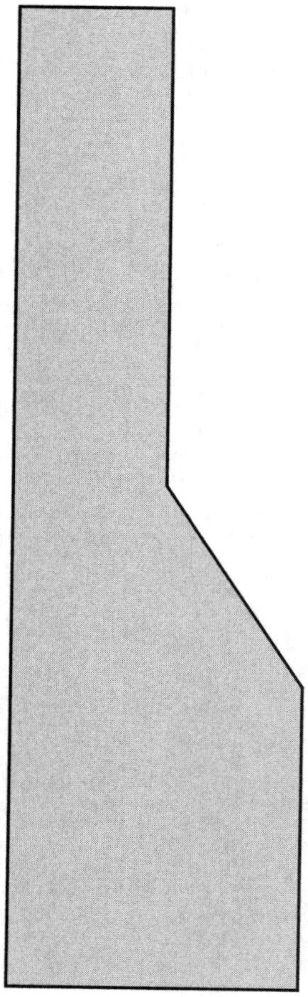

CLC-3577.2, 1-3/8 x 4-3/4

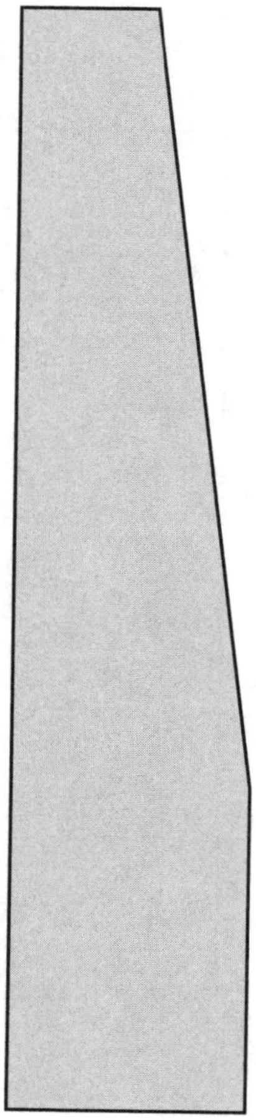

CLC-23M, 1 F x 4-3/4

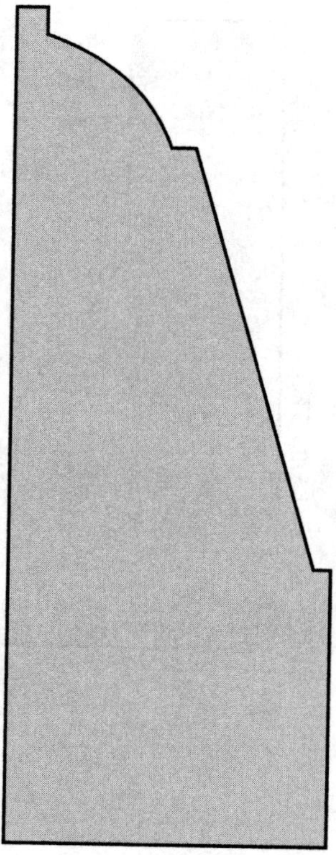

CLC-74, 1-1/2 x 4 F

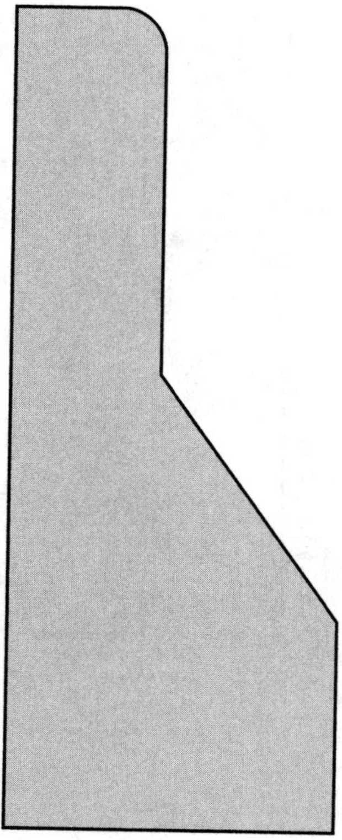

CLC-3376.4, 1-9/16 x 4 F

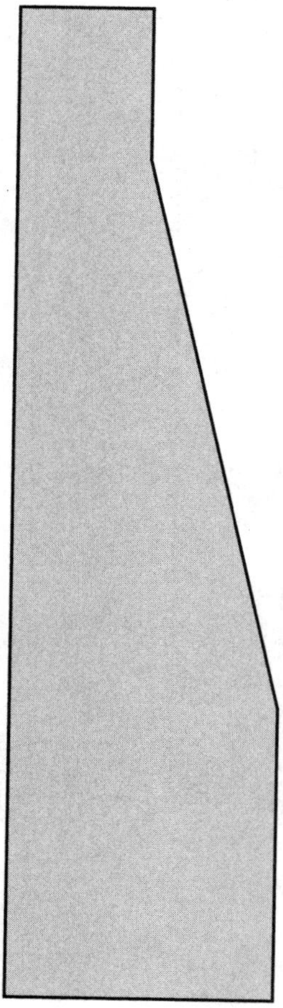

CLC-3900.5, 1-1/4 x 4-3/4

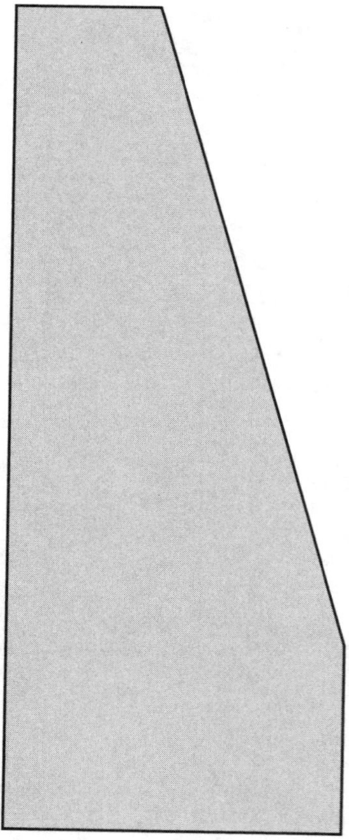

CLC-3885.9, 1-3/4 x 4-3/8

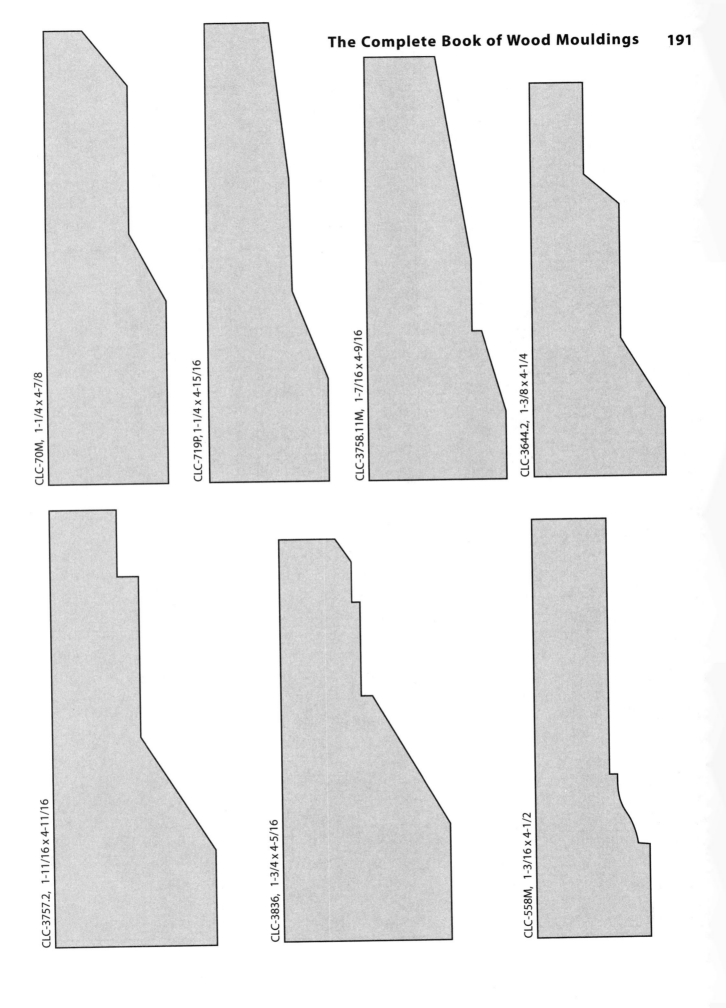

CLC-70M, 1-1/4 x 4-7/8

CLC-719P, 1-1/4 x 4-15/16

CLC-3758.11M, 1-7/16 x 4-9/16

CLC-3644.2, 1-3/8 x 4-1/4

CLC-3757.2, 1-11/16 x 4-11/16

CLC-3836, 1-3/4 x 4-5/16

CLC-558M, 1-3/16 x 4-1/2

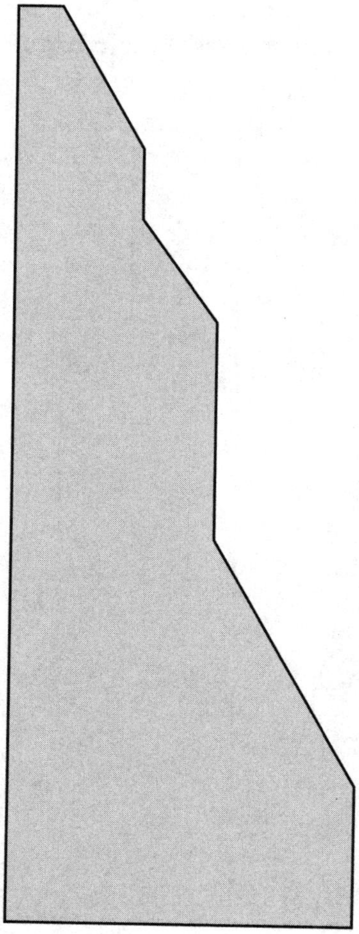

CLC-32P, 1-13/16 x 4-15/16

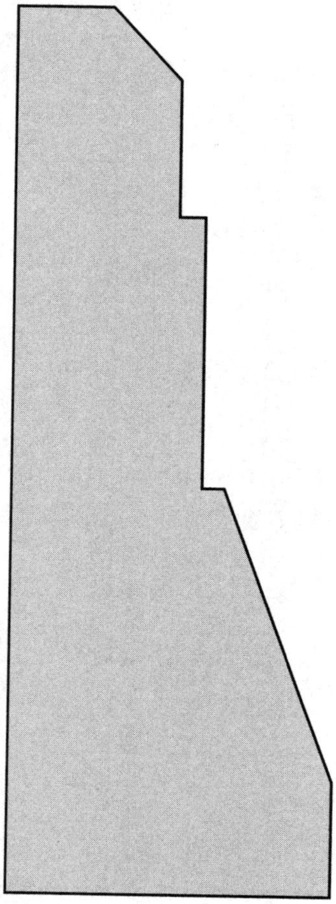

CLC-3755.4, 1-11/16 x 4-3/4

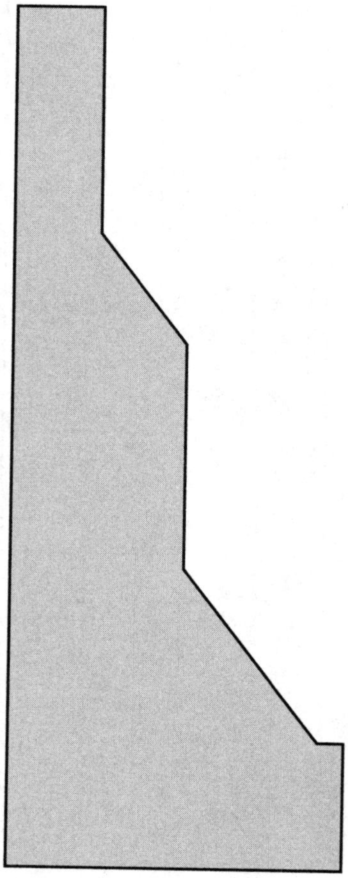

CLC-3768, 1-3/4 x 4-5/8

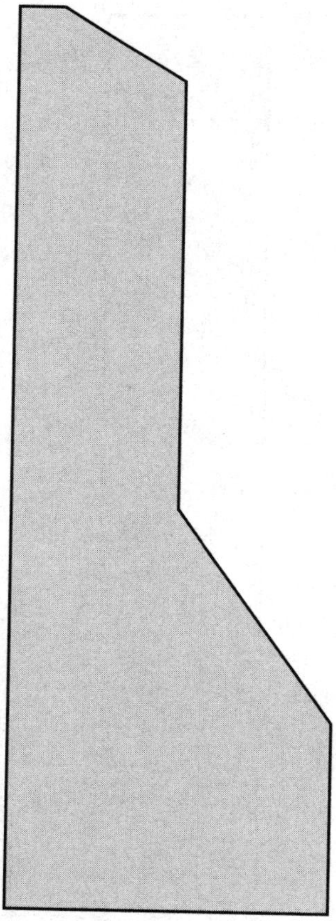

CLC-3679.2, 1-9/16 x 4-1/2

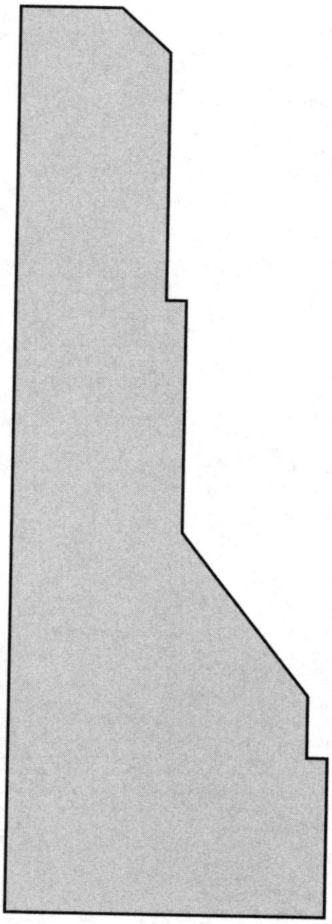

CLC-3704.13, 1-5/8 x 4-3/4

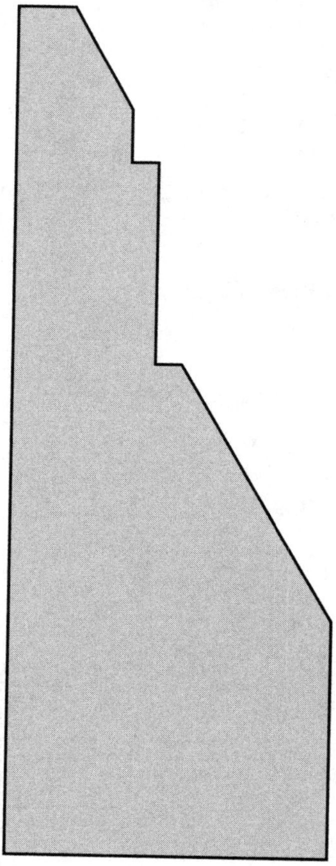

CLC-3899.9, 1-11/16 x 4-9/16

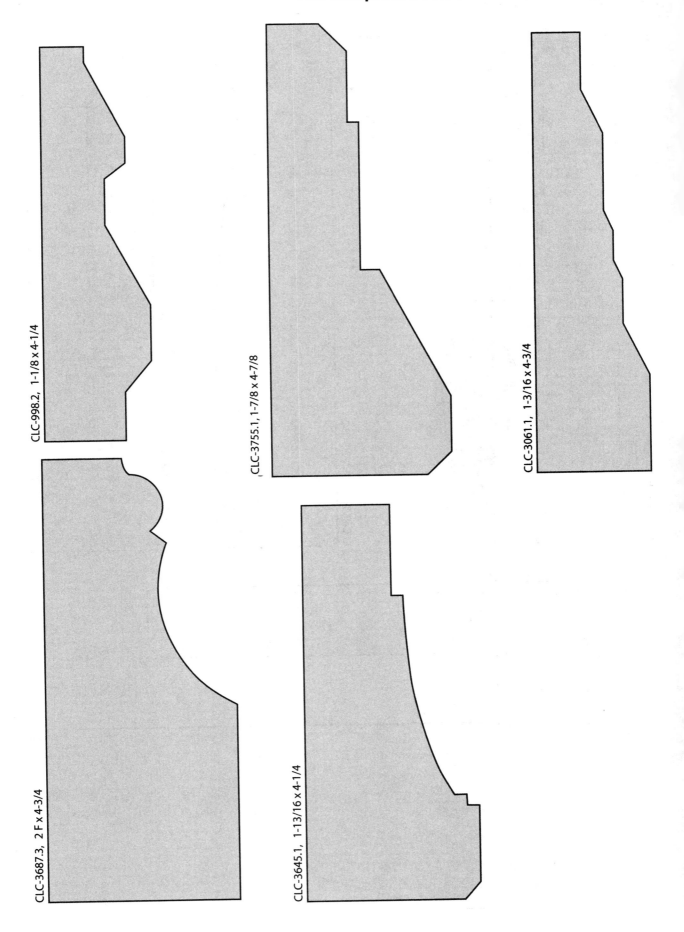

CLC-998.2, 1-1/8 x 4-1/4

CLC-3687.3, 2 F x 4-3/4

CLC-3755.1, 1-7/8 x 4-7/8

CLC-3645.1, 1-13/16 x 4-1/4

CLC-3061.1, 1-3/16 x 4-3/4

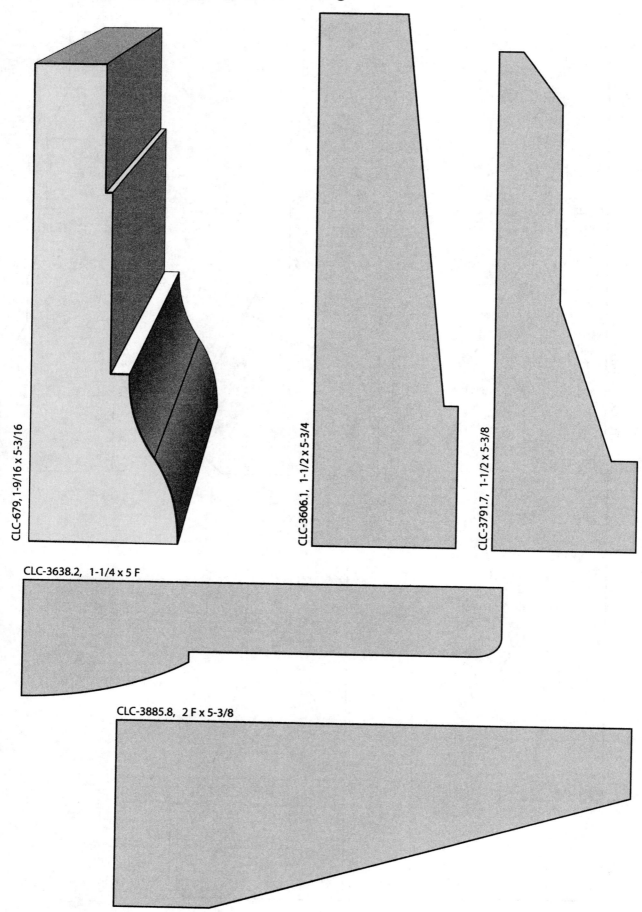

CLC-679, 1-9/16 x 5-3/16

CLC-3606.1, 1-1/2 x 5-3/4

CLC-3791.7, 1-1/2 x 5-3/8

CLC-3638.2, 1-1/4 x 5 F

CLC-3885.8, 2 F x 5-3/8

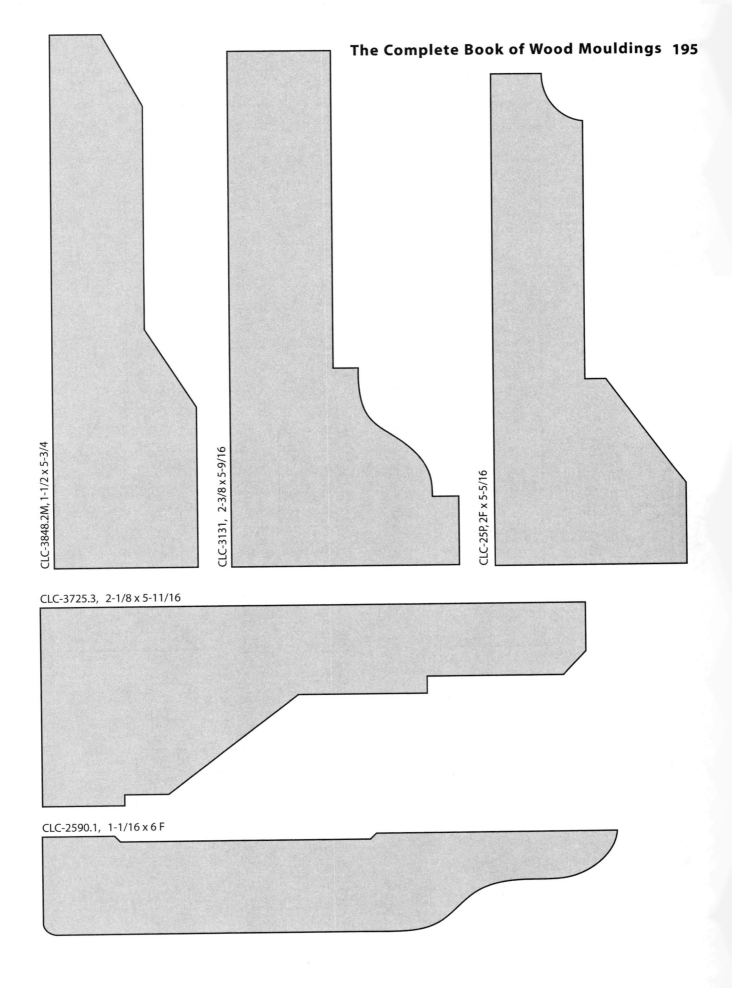

CLC-3848.2M, 1-1/2 x 5-3/4

CLC-3131, 2-3/8 x 5-9/16

CLC-25P, 2F x 5-5/16

CLC-3725.3, 2-1/8 x 5-11/16

CLC-2590.1, 1-1/16 x 6 F

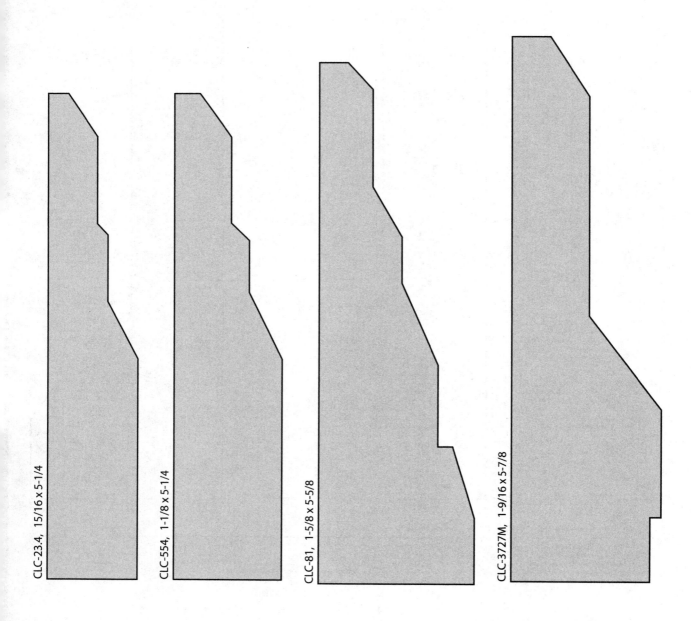

CLC-23.4, 15/16 x 5-1/4

CLC-554, 1-1/8 x 5-1/4

CLC-81, 1-5/8 x 5-5/8

CLC-3727M, 1-9/16 x 5-7/8

CLC-3902.3, 2 F x 5-3/4

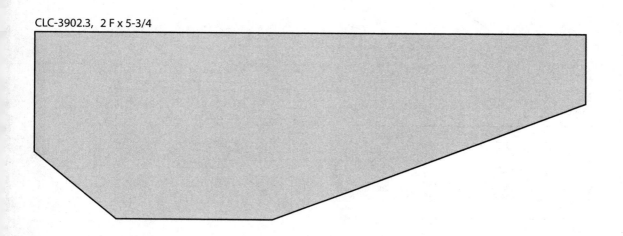

CLC-37M, 1-3/4 x 6-1/4

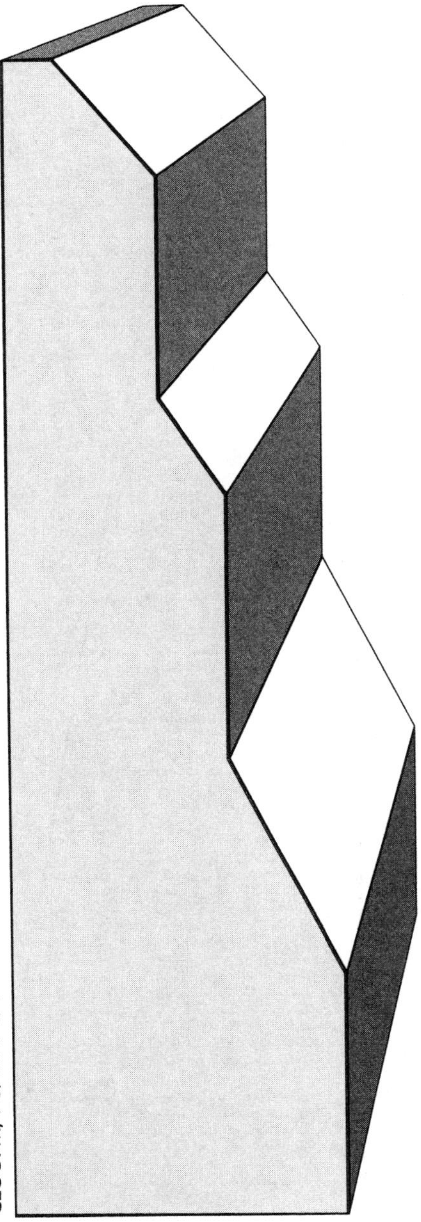

Plinth: CLC-3879-5, 1-5/8 x 6-1/2

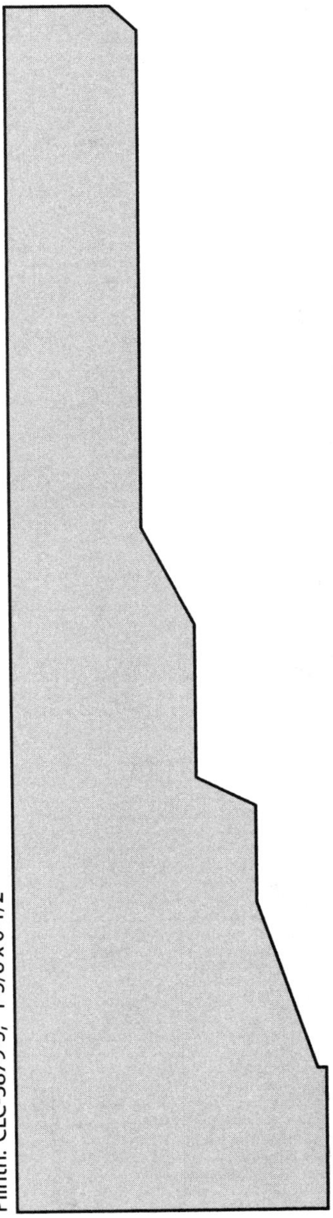

CLC-3894.3, 1-5/8 x 5-5/8

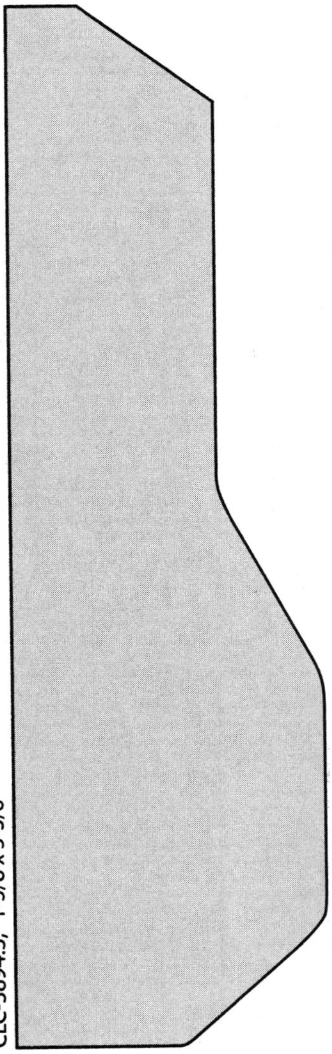

CLC-3597.3, 2-1/2 x 6 F

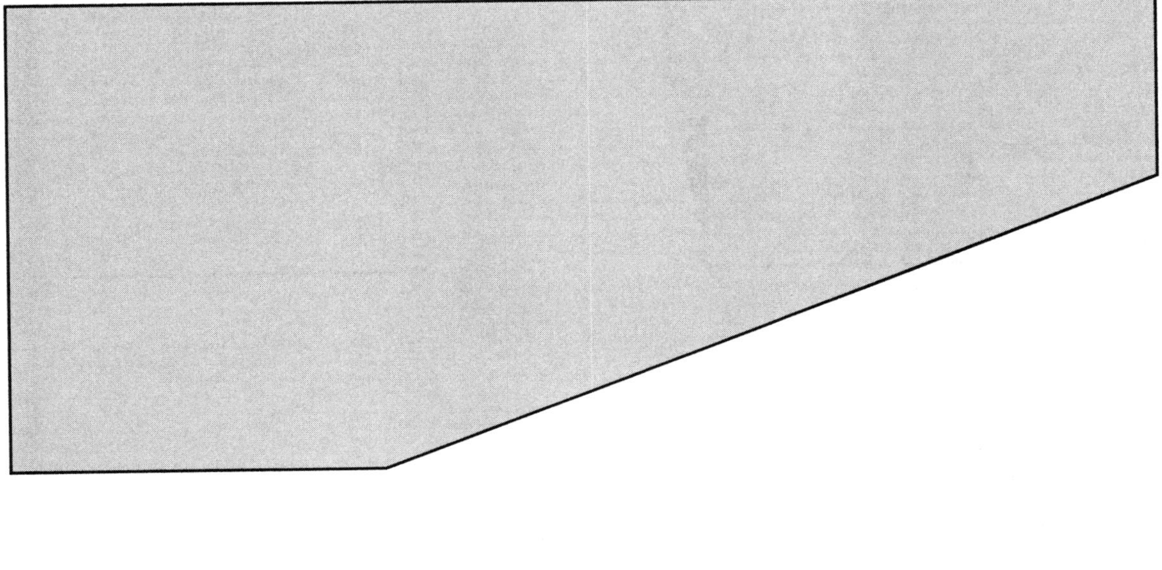

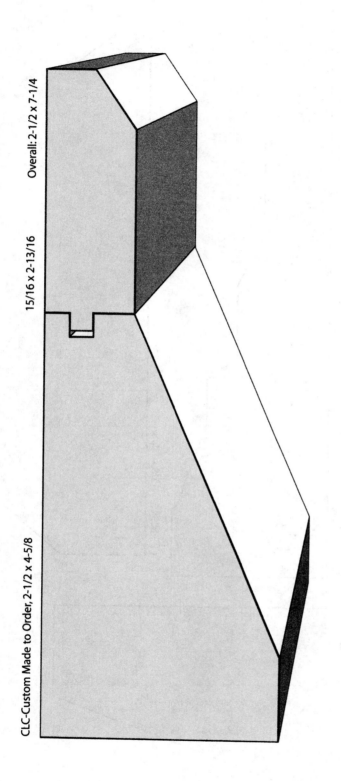

Overall: 2-1/2 x 7-1/4

15/16 x 2-13/16

CLC–Custom Made to Order, 2-1/2 x 4-5/8

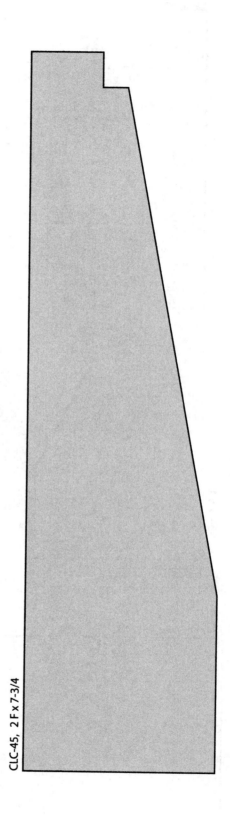

CLC-45, 2 F x 7-3/4

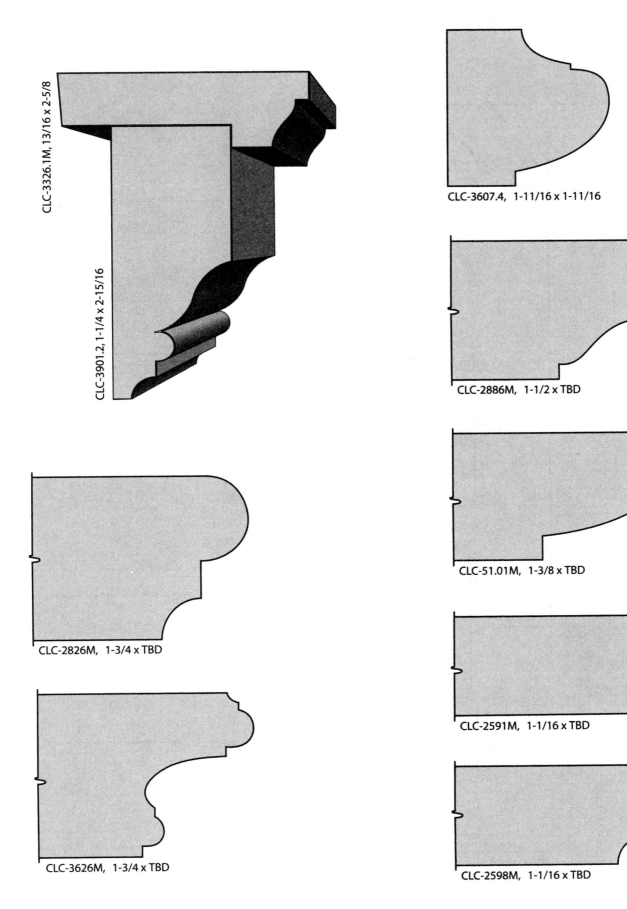

CLC-3326.1M, 13/16 x 2-5/8

CLC-3901.2, 1-1/4 x 2-15/16

CLC-3607.4, 1-11/16 x 1-11/16

CLC-2886M, 1-1/2 x TBD

CLC-51.01M, 1-3/8 x TBD

CLC-2591M, 1-1/16 x TBD

CLC-2826M, 1-3/4 x TBD

CLC-3626M, 1-3/4 x TBD

CLC-2598M, 1-1/16 x TBD

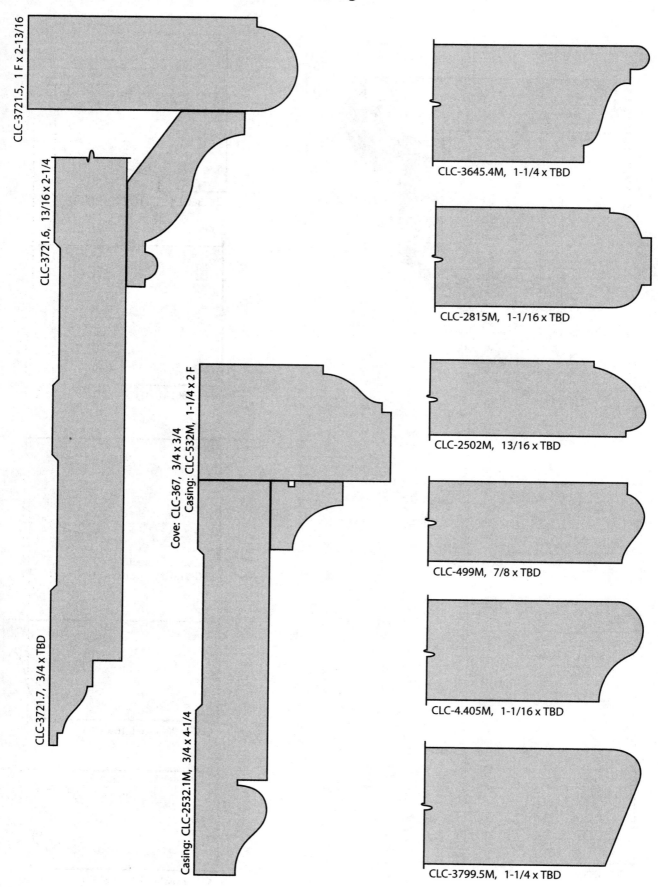

CLC-3721.5, 1 F x 2-13/16

CLC-3721.6, 13/16 x 2-1/4

CLC-3721.7, 3/4 x TBD

Cove: CLC-367, 3/4 x 3/4
Casing: CLC-532M, 1-1/4 x 2 F

Casing: CLC-2532.1M, 3/4 x 4-1/4

CLC-3645.4M, 1-1/4 x TBD

CLC-2815M, 1-1/16 x TBD

CLC-2502M, 13/16 x TBD

CLC-499M, 7/8 x TBD

CLC-4.405M, 1-1/16 x TBD

CLC-3799.5M, 1-1/4 x TBD

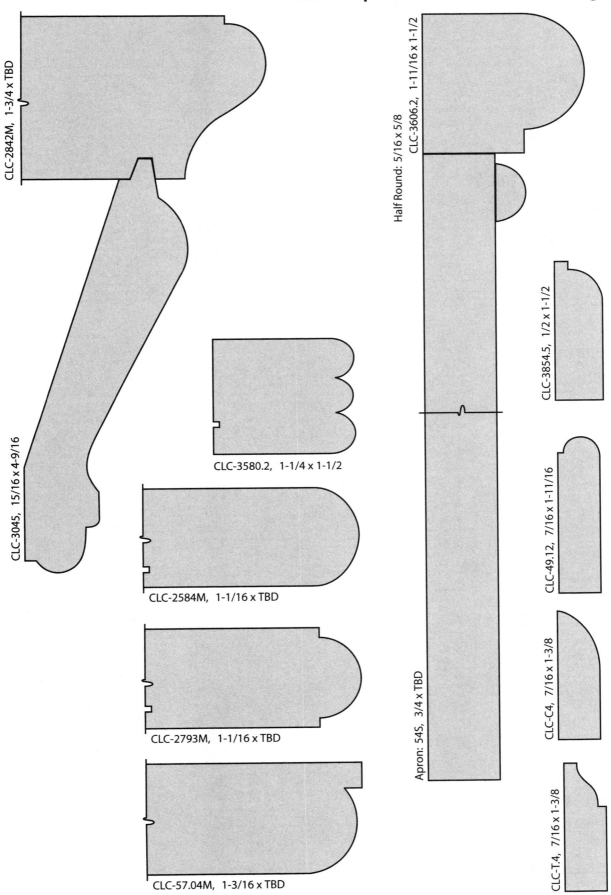

CLC-2842M, 1-3/4 x TBD

CLC-3045, 15/16 x 4-9/16

CLC-3580.2, 1-1/4 x 1-1/2

CLC-2584M, 1-1/16 x TBD

CLC-2793M, 1-1/16 x TBD

CLC-57.04M, 1-3/16 x TBD

Half Round: 5/16 x 5/8

CLC-3606.2, 1-11/16 x 1-1/2

Apron: 54S, 3/4 x TBD

CLC-3854.5, 1/2 x 1-1/2

CLC-49.12, 7/16 x 1-11/16

CLC-C4, 7/16 x 1-3/8

CLC-T.4, 7/16 x 1-3/8

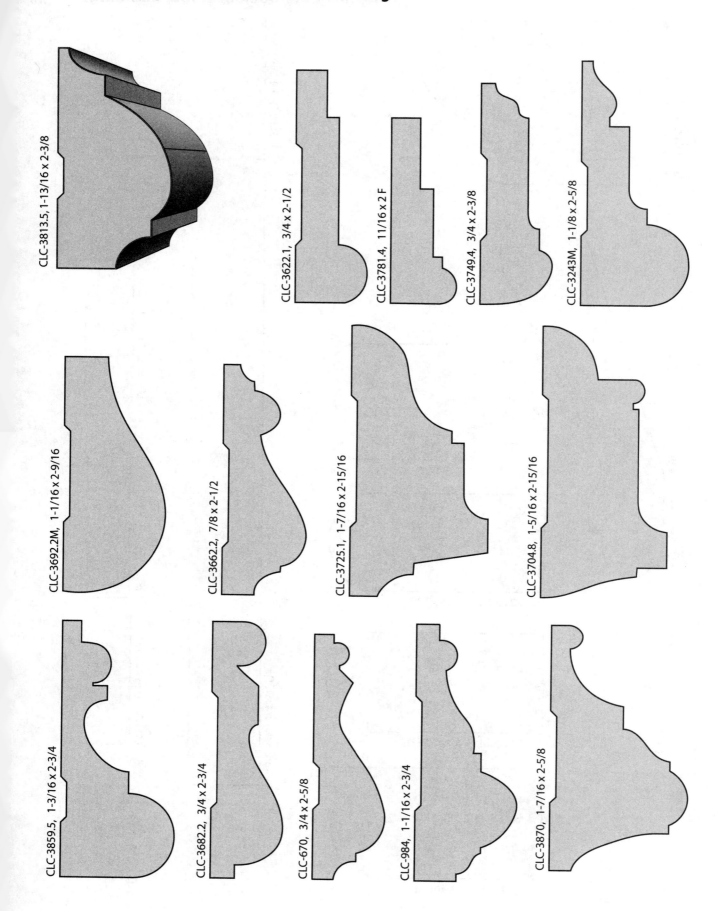

CLC-3813.5, 1-13/16 x 2-3/8

CLC-3622.1, 3/4 x 2-1/2

CLC-3781.4, 11/16 x 2 F

CLC-3749.4, 3/4 x 2-3/8

CLC-3243M, 1-1/8 x 2-5/8

CLC-3692.2M, 1-1/16 x 2-9/16

CLC-3662.2, 7/8 x 2-1/2

CLC-3725.1, 1-7/16 x 2-15/16

CLC-3704.8, 1-5/16 x 2-15/16

CLC-3859.5, 1-3/16 x 2-3/4

CLC-3682.2, 3/4 x 2-3/4

CLC-670, 3/4 x 2-5/8

CLC-984, 1-1/16 x 2-3/4

CLC-3870, 1-7/16 x 2-5/8

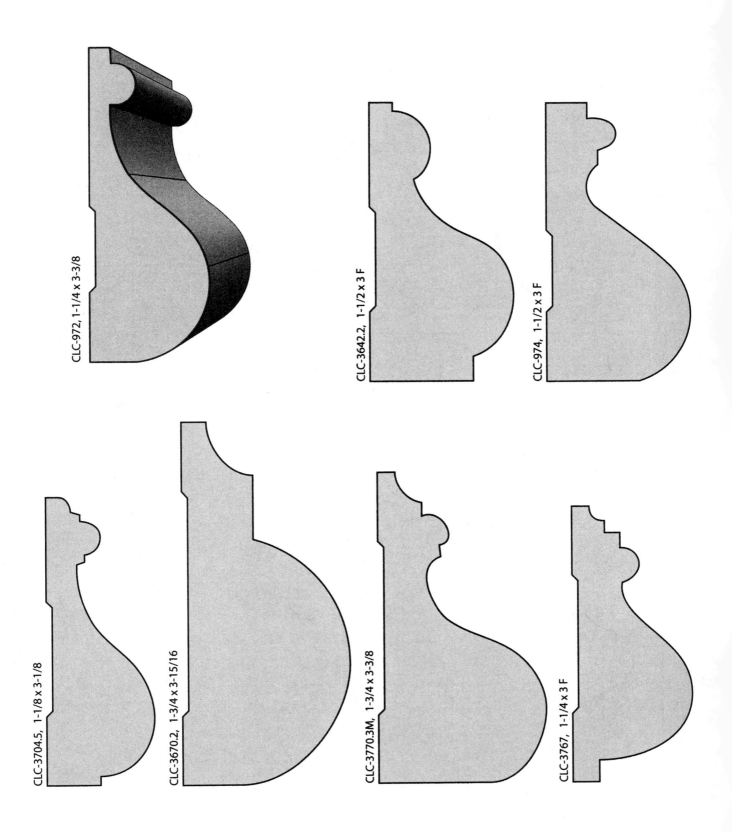

CLC-972, 1-1/4 x 3-3/8

CLC-3642.2, 1-1/2 x 3 F

CLC-974, 1-1/2 x 3 F

CLC-3704.5, 1-1/8 x 3-1/8

CLC-3670.2, 1-3/4 x 3-15/16

CLC-3770.3M, 1-3/4 x 3-3/8

CLC-3767, 1-1/4 x 3 F

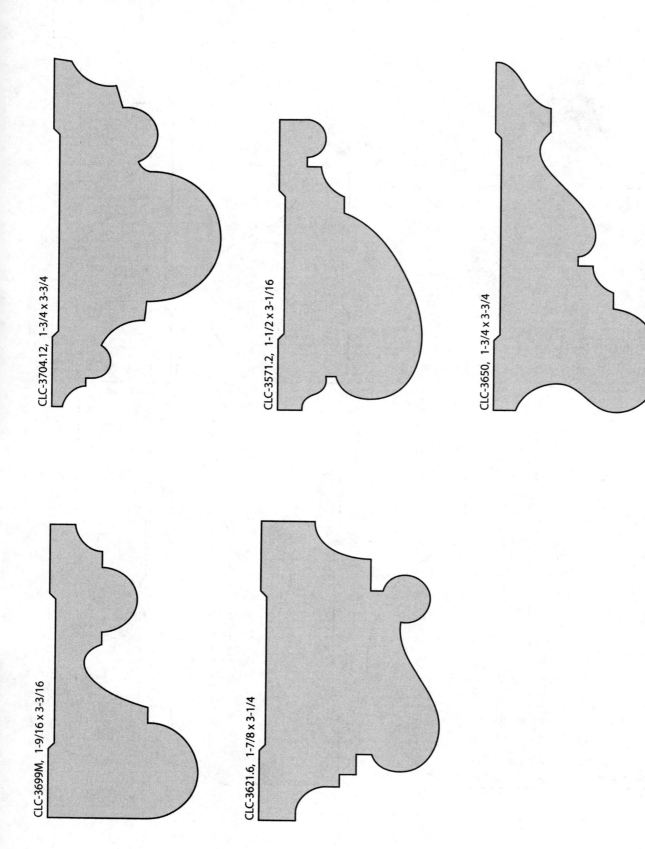

CLC-3704.12, 1-3/4 x 3-3/4

CLC-3571.2, 1-1/2 x 3-1/16

CLC-3650, 1-3/4 x 3-3/4

CLC-3699M, 1-9/16 x 3-3/16

CLC-3621.6, 1-7/8 x 3-1/4

CLC-3740.15, 1-3/8 x 3F

CLC-3614.4, 1-1/4 x 3 F

CLC-3780.4, 1-7/8 x 3-3/4

CLC-3543, 13/16 x 3-7/16

CLC-3688.3, 1-1/2 x 3-5/8

CLC-3805.2, 1-11/16 x 3-1/2

CLC-3765.4, 1-5/16 x 3-3/8

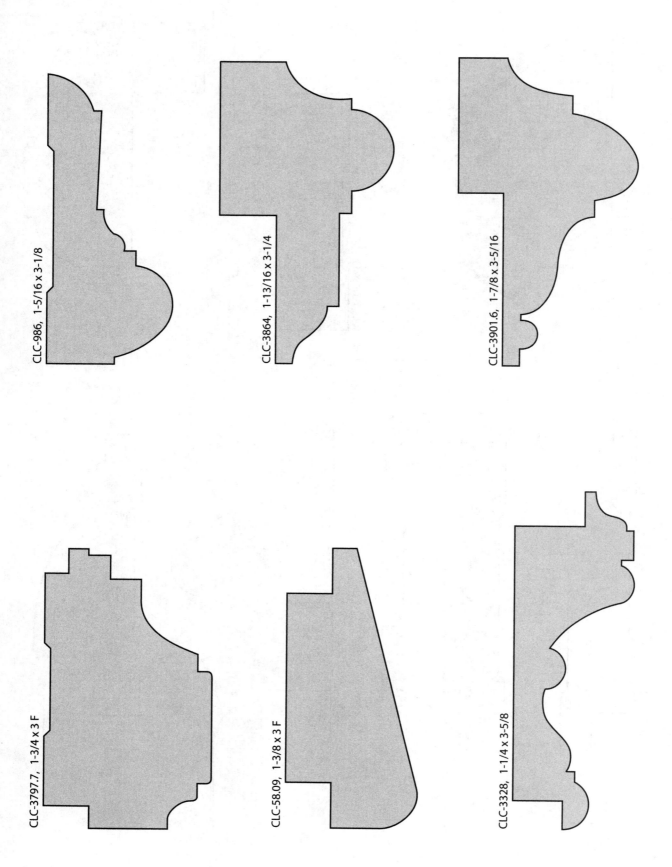

CLC-986, 1-5/16 x 3-1/8

CLC-3864, 1-13/16 x 3-1/4

CLC-3901.6, 1-7/8 x 3-5/16

CLC-3797.7, 1-3/4 x 3 F

CLC-58.09, 1-3/8 x 3 F

CLC-3328, 1-1/4 x 3-5/8

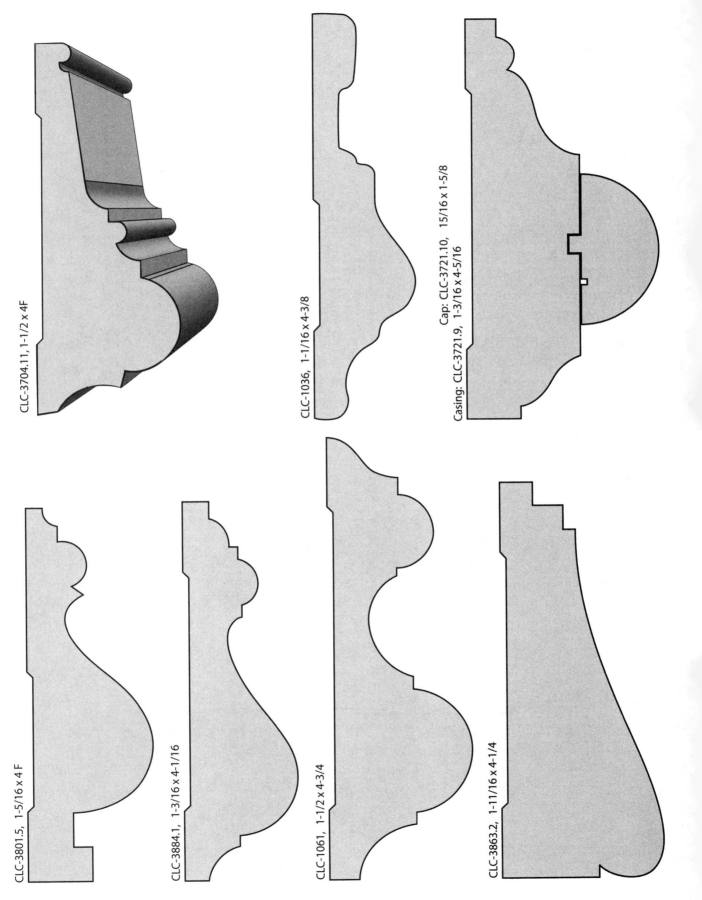

CLC-3704.11, 1-1/2 x 4F

CLC-1036, 1-1/16 x 4-3/8

Cap: CLC-3721.10, 15/16 x 1-5/8

Casing: CLC-3721.9, 1-3/16 x 4-5/16

CLC-3801.5, 1-5/16 x 4 F

CLC-3884.1, 1-3/16 x 4-1/16

CLC-1061, 1-1/2 x 4-3/4

CLC-3863.2, 1-11/16 x 4-1/4

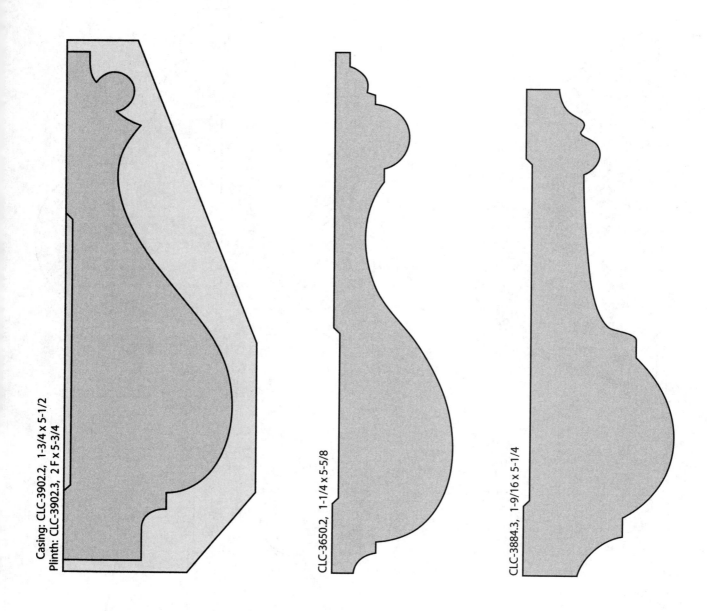

Casing: CLC-3902.2, 1-3/4 x 5-1/2
Plinth: CLC-3902.3, 2 F x 5-3/4

CLC-3650.2, 1-1/4 x 5-5/8

CLC-3884.3, 1-9/16 x 5-1/4

CLC-3812.4, 1-7/16 x 5-1/4

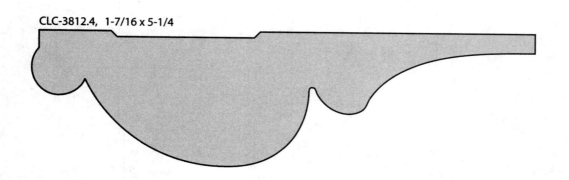

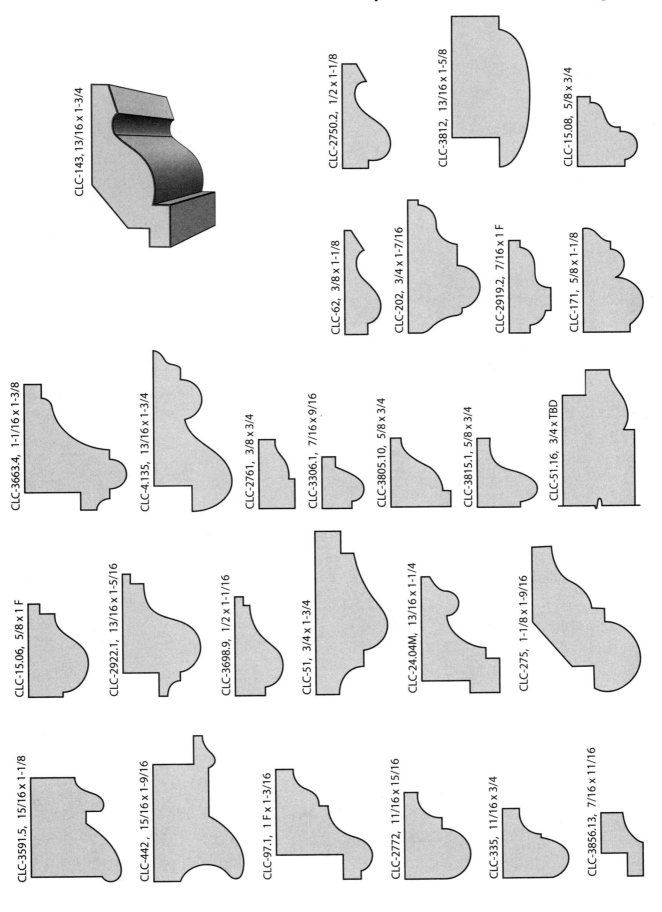

CLC-143, 13/16 x 1-3/4

CLC-2750.2, 1/2 x 1-1/8

CLC-3812, 13/16 x 1-5/8

CLC-15.08, 5/8 x 3/4

CLC-62, 3/8 x 1-1/8

CLC-202, 3/4 x 1-7/16

CLC-2919.2, 7/16 x 1 F

CLC-171, 5/8 x 1-1/8

CLC-3663.4, 1-1/16 x 1-3/8

CLC-4.135, 13/16 x 1-3/4

CLC-2761, 3/8 x 3/4

CLC-3306.1, 7/16 x 9/16

CLC-3805.10, 5/8 x 3/4

CLC-3815.1, 5/8 x 3/4

CLC-51.16, 3/4 x TBD

CLC-15.06, 5/8 x 1 F

CLC-2922.1, 13/16 x 1-5/16

CLC-3698.9, 1/2 x 1-1/16

CLC-51, 3/4 x 1-3/4

CLC-24.04M, 13/16 x 1-1/4

CLC-275, 1-1/8 x 1-9/16

CLC-3591.5, 15/16 x 1-1/8

CLC-442, 15/16 x 1-9/16

CLC-97.1, 1 F x 1-3/16

CLC-2772, 11/16 x 15/16

CLC-335, 11/16 x 3/4

CLC-3856.13, 7/16 x 11/16

CLC-3793.9, 7/16 x 1-1/4

CLC-205, 3/4 x 15/16

CLC-49.11, 5/8 x 7/8

CLC-3890.3, 1 F x 1 F

CLC-3718.2, 7/8 x 1-3/4

CLC-3748.7, 13/16 x 1-1/2

CLC-3587, 11/16 x 1-3/4

CLC-3784.5, 9/16 x 1-1/2

CLC-3865.3, 1/2 x 1-7/16

CLC-3758.5, 11/16 x 7/8

CLC-1032.1, 9/16 x 1-13/16

CLC-3867.5, 5/8 x 1

CLC-115, 9/16 x 1-1/4

CLC-3576.6M, 1 F x 1-7/16

CLC-71, 13/16 x 1-7/8

CLC-3632.1, 1-1/8 x 1-13/16

CLC-3859.8, 13/16 x 1-1/2

CLC-13A, 7/16 x 7/8

CLC-3580.4, 1/2 x 1-1/8

CLC-3701.4, 11/16 x 1-1/2

CLC-377.1, 7/16 x 1 F

CLC-166, 3/4 x 1-7/8

CLC-4.271, 3/8 x 1-7/16

CLC-4.272, 9/16 x 1-3/4

CLC-136, 5/16 x 13/16

CLCD-25.13, 13/16 x 1-1/4

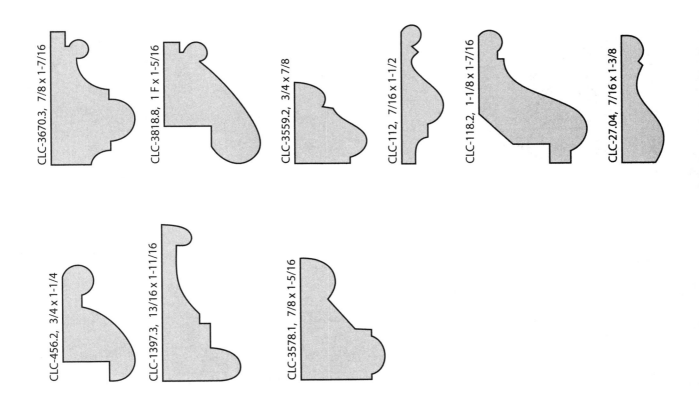

CLC-3670.3, 7/8 x 1-7/16

CLC-3818.8, 1 F x 1-5/16

CLC-3559.2, 3/4 x 7/8

CLC-112, 7/16 x 1-1/2

CLC-118.2, 1-1/8 x 1-7/16

CLC-27.04, 7/16 x 1-3/8

CLC-456.2, 3/4 x 1-1/4

CLC-1397.3, 13/16 x 1-11/16

CLC-3578.1, 7/8 x 1-5/16

PANEL HIP

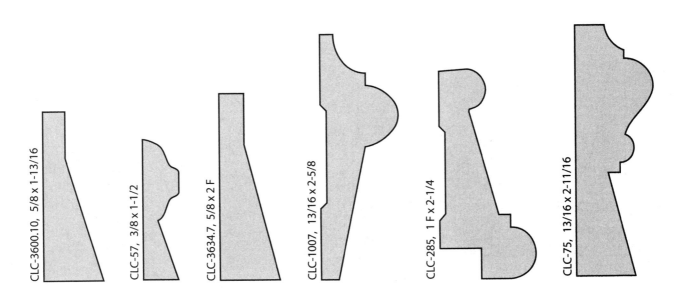

CLC-3600.10, 5/8 x 1-13/16

CLC-57, 3/8 x 1-1/2

CLC-3634.7, 5/8 x 2 F

CLC-1007, 13/16 x 2-5/8

CLC-285, 1 F x 2-1/4

CLC-75, 13/16 x 2-11/16

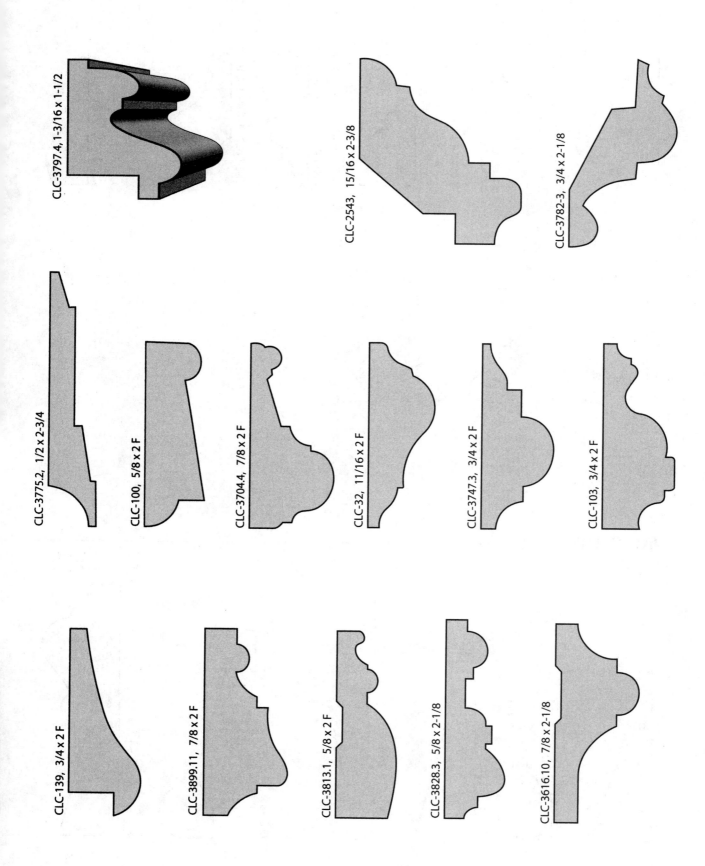

CLC-3797.4, 1-3/16 x 1-1/2

CLC-2543, 15/16 x 2-3/8

CLC-3782-3, 3/4 x 2-1/8

CLC-3775.2, 1/2 x 2-3/4

CLC-100, 5/8 x 2 F

CLC-3704.4, 7/8 x 2 F

CLC-32, 11/16 x 2 F

CLC-3747.3, 3/4 x 2 F

CLC-103, 3/4 x 2 F

CLC-139, 3/4 x 2 F

CLC-3899.11, 7/8 x 2 F

CLC-3813.1, 5/8 x 2 F

CLC-3828.3, 5/8 x 2-1/8

CLC-3616.10, 7/8 x 2-1/8

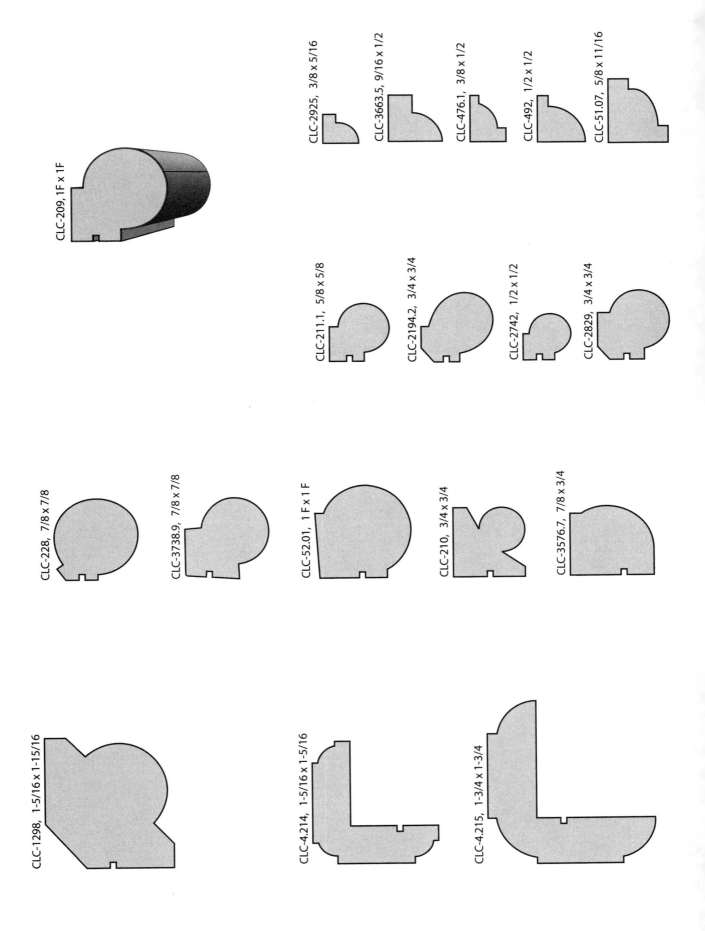

CLC-209, 1F x 1F

CLC-2925, 3/8 x 5/16

CLC-3663.5, 9/16 x 1/2

CLC-476.1, 3/8 x 1/2

CLC-492, 1/2 x 1/2

CLC-51.07, 5/8 x 11/16

CLC-211.1, 5/8 x 5/8

CLC-2194.2, 3/4 x 3/4

CLC-2742, 1/2 x 1/2

CLC-2829, 3/4 x 3/4

CLC-228, 7/8 x 7/8

CLC-3738.9, 7/8 x 7/8

CLC-52.01, 1F x 1F

CLC-210, 3/4 x 3/4

CLC-3576.7, 7/8 x 3/4

CLC-1298, 1-5/16 x 1-15/16

CLC-4.214, 1-5/16 x 1-5/16

CLC-4.215, 1-3/4 x 1-3/4

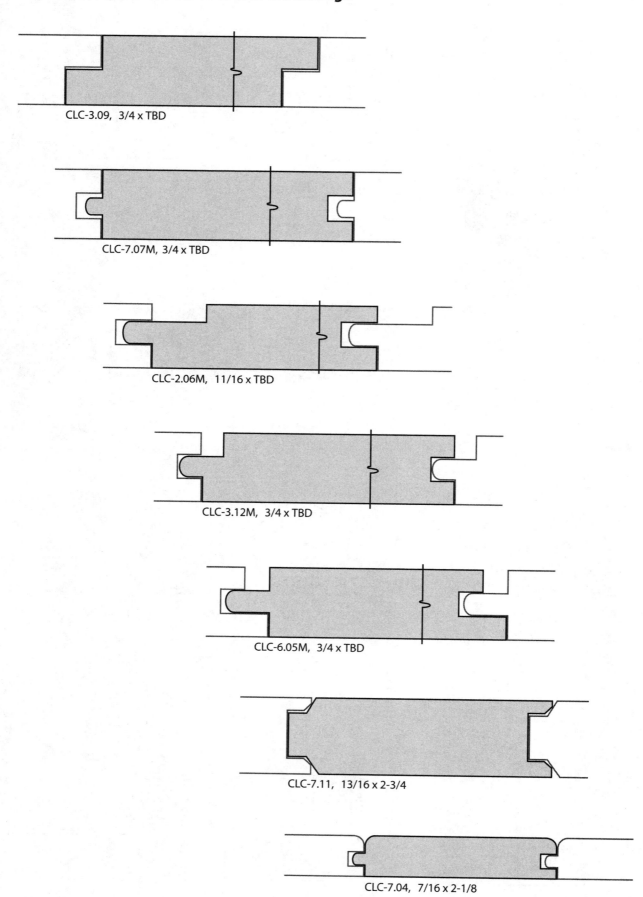

CLC-3.09, 3/4 x TBD

CLC-7.07M, 3/4 x TBD

CLC-2.06M, 11/16 x TBD

CLC-3.12M, 3/4 x TBD

CLC-6.05M, 3/4 x TBD

CLC-7.11, 13/16 x 2-3/4

CLC-7.04, 7/16 x 2-1/8

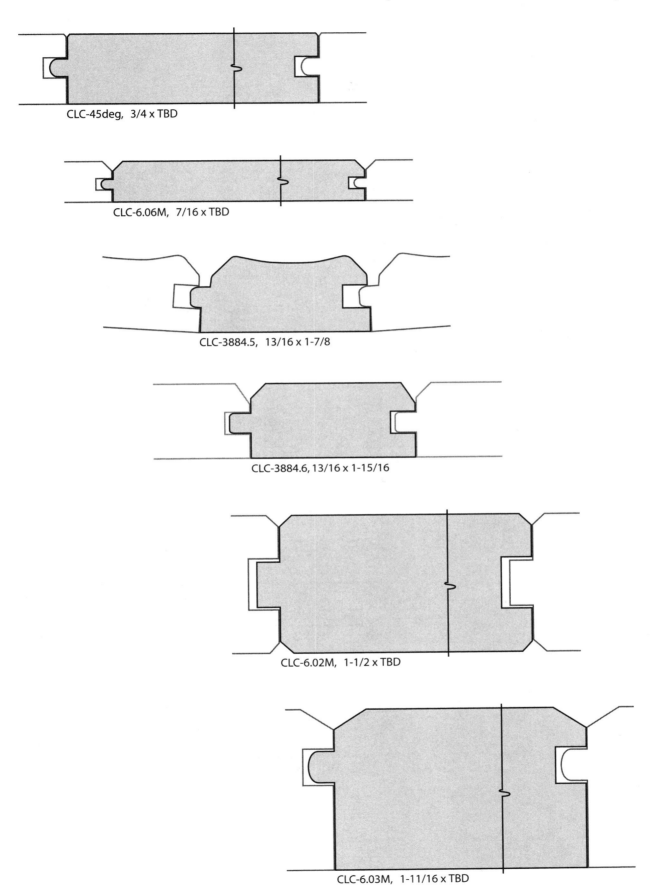

CLC-45deg, 3/4 x TBD

CLC-6.06M, 7/16 x TBD

CLC-3884.5, 13/16 x 1-7/8

CLC-3884.6, 13/16 x 1-15/16

CLC-6.02M, 1-1/2 x TBD

CLC-6.03M, 1-11/16 x TBD

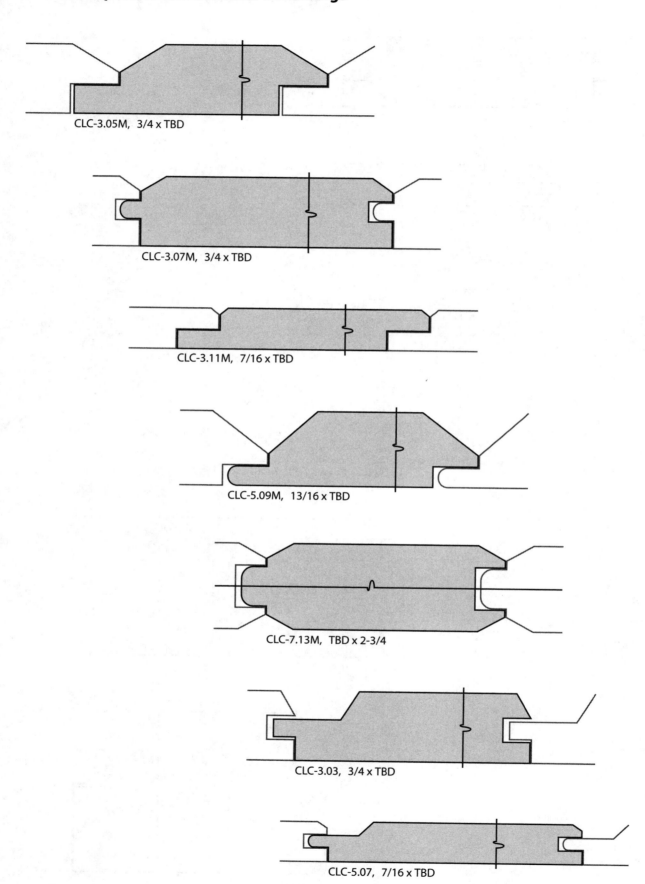

CLC-3.05M, 3/4 x TBD

CLC-3.07M, 3/4 x TBD

CLC-3.11M, 7/16 x TBD

CLC-5.09M, 13/16 x TBD

CLC-7.13M, TBD x 2-3/4

CLC-3.03, 3/4 x TBD

CLC-5.07, 7/16 x TBD

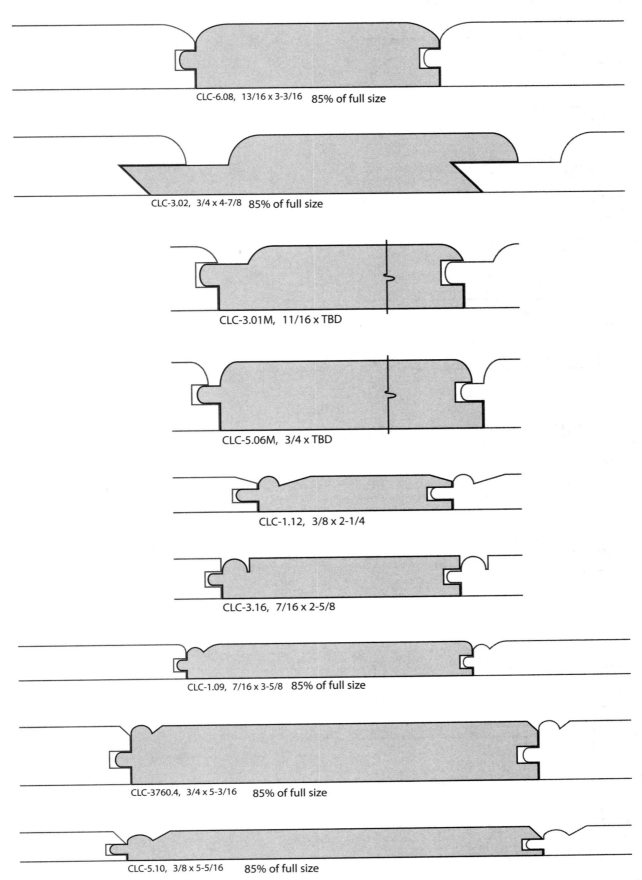

CLC-6.08, 13/16 x 3-3/16 85% of full size

CLC-3.02, 3/4 x 4-7/8 85% of full size

CLC-3.01M, 11/16 x TBD

CLC-5.06M, 3/4 x TBD

CLC-1.12, 3/8 x 2-1/4

CLC-3.16, 7/16 x 2-5/8

CLC-1.09, 7/16 x 3-5/8 85% of full size

CLC-3760.4, 3/4 x 5-3/16 85% of full size

CLC-5.10, 3/8 x 5-5/16 85% of full size

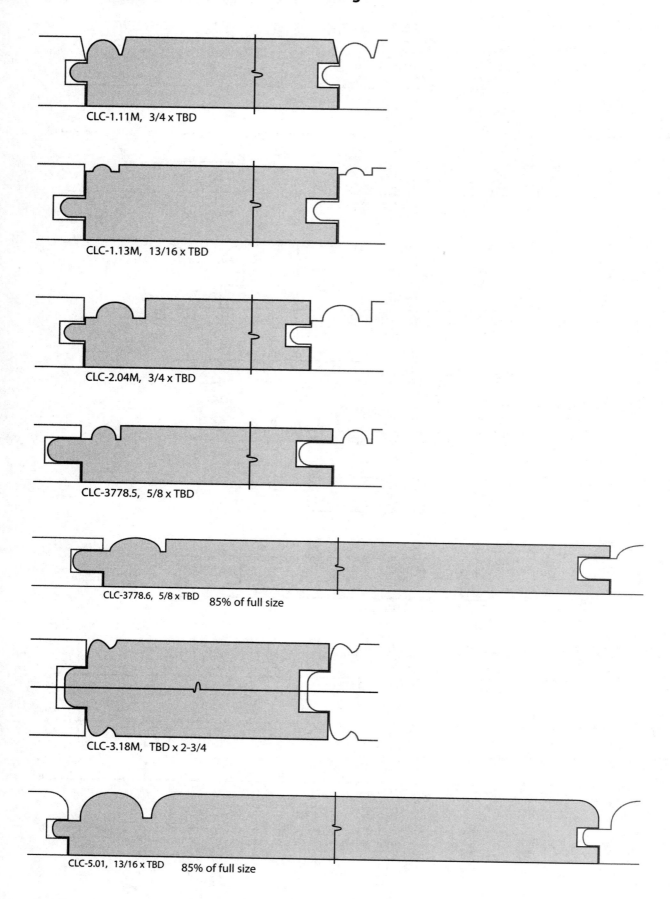

CLC-1.11M, 3/4 x TBD

CLC-1.13M, 13/16 x TBD

CLC-2.04M, 3/4 x TBD

CLC-3778.5, 5/8 x TBD

CLC-3778.6, 5/8 x TBD   85% of full size

CLC-3.18M, TBD x 2-3/4

CLC-5.01, 13/16 x TBD   85% of full size

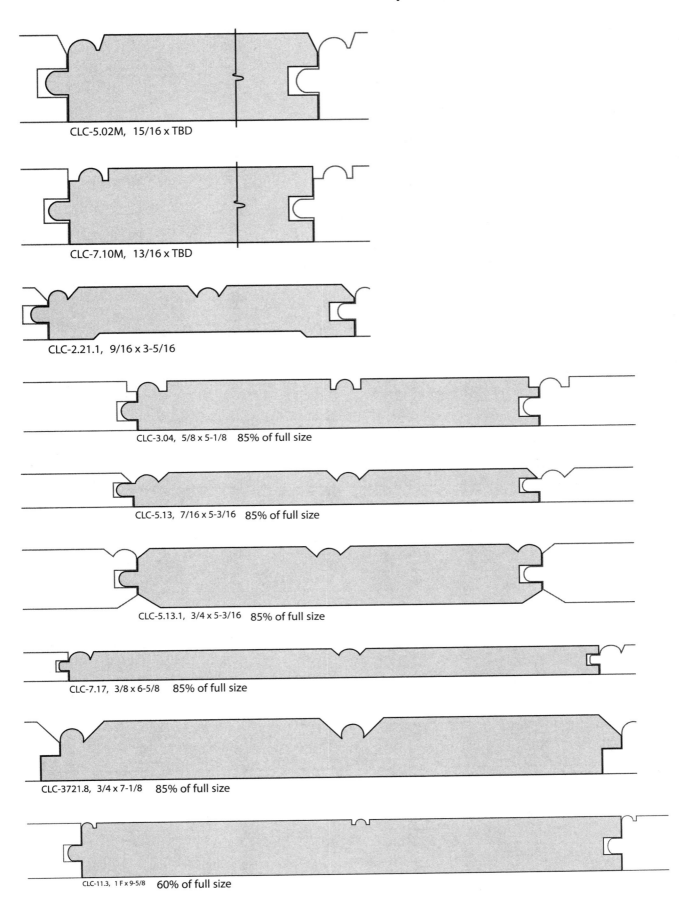

CLC-5.02M, 15/16 x TBD

CLC-7.10M, 13/16 x TBD

CLC-2.21.1, 9/16 x 3-5/16

CLC-3.04, 5/8 x 5-1/8   85% of full size

CLC-5.13, 7/16 x 5-3/16   85% of full size

CLC-5.13.1, 3/4 x 5-3/16   85% of full size

CLC-7.17, 3/8 x 6-5/8   85% of full size

CLC-3721.8, 3/4 x 7-1/8   85% of full size

CLC-11.3, 1 F x 9-5/8   60% of full size

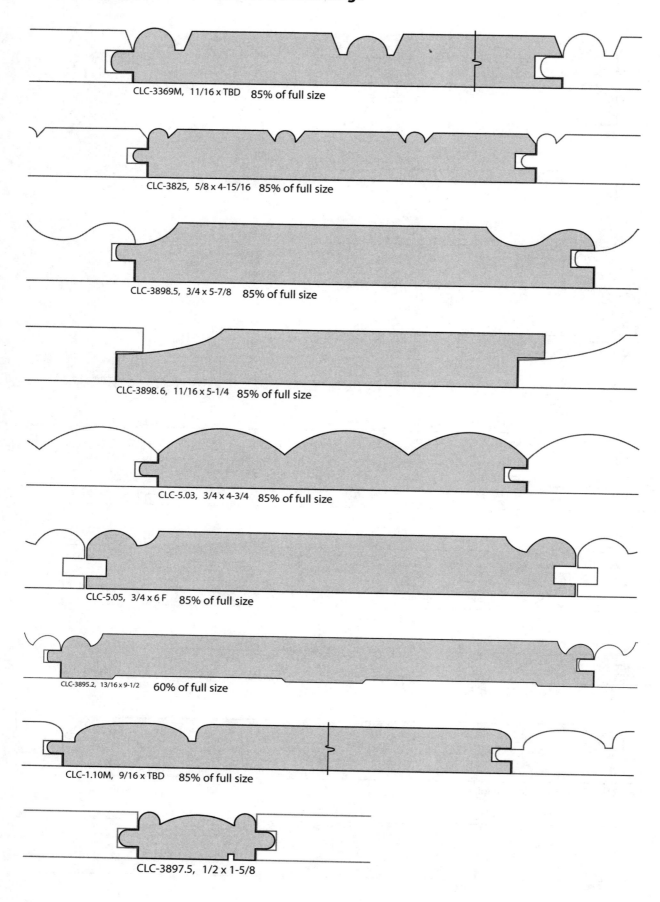

CLC-3369M, 11/16 x TBD   85% of full size

CLC-3825, 5/8 x 4-15/16   85% of full size

CLC-3898.5, 3/4 x 5-7/8   85% of full size

CLC-3898.6, 11/16 x 5-1/4   85% of full size

CLC-5.03, 3/4 x 4-3/4   85% of full size

CLC-5.05, 3/4 x 6 F   85% of full size

CLC-3895.2, 13/16 x 9-1/2   60% of full size

CLC-1.10M, 9/16 x TBD   85% of full size

CLC-3897.5, 1/2 x 1-5/8

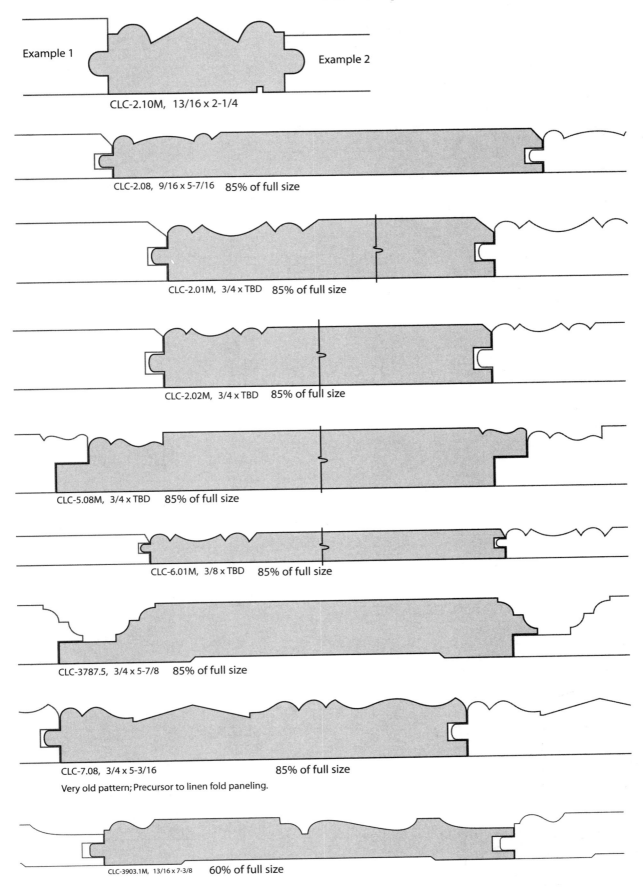

Example 1

Example 2

CLC-2.10M, 13/16 x 2-1/4

CLC-2.08, 9/16 x 5-7/16   85% of full size

CLC-2.01M, 3/4 x TBD   85% of full size

CLC-2.02M, 3/4 x TBD   85% of full size

CLC-5.08M, 3/4 x TBD   85% of full size

CLC-6.01M, 3/8 x TBD   85% of full size

CLC-3787.5, 3/4 x 5-7/8   85% of full size

CLC-7.08, 3/4 x 5-3/16   85% of full size

Very old pattern; Precursor to linen fold paneling.

CLC-3903.1M, 13/16 x 7-3/8   60% of full size

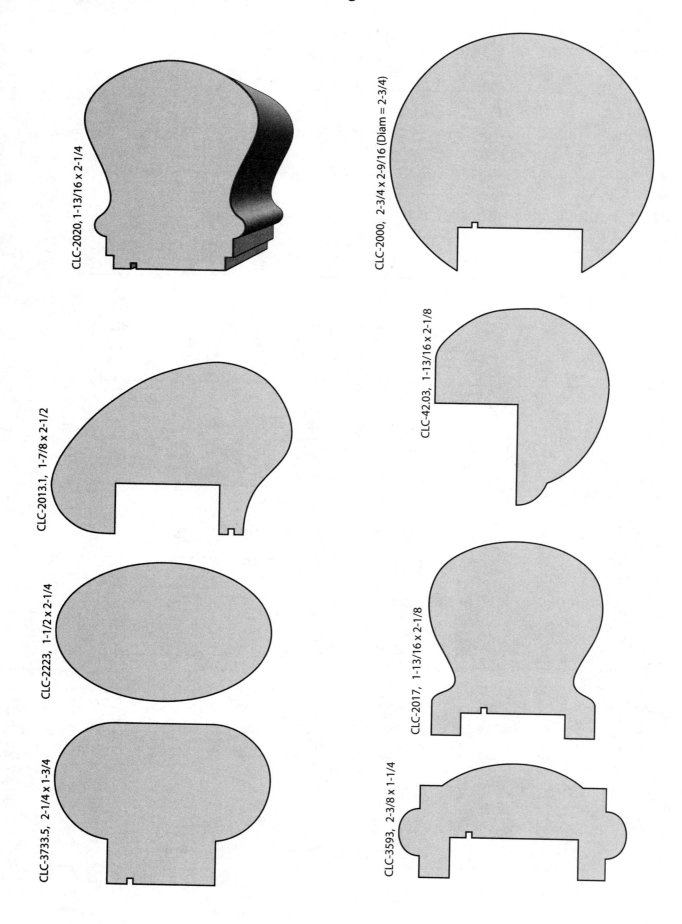

CLC-2020, 1-13/16 x 2-1/4

CLC-2000, 2-3/4 x 2-9/16 (Diam = 2-3/4)

CLC-2013.1, 1-7/8 x 2-1/2

CLC-42.03, 1-13/16 x 2-1/8

CLC-2223, 1-1/2 x 2-1/4

CLC-2017, 1-13/16 x 2-1/8

CLC-3733.5, 2-1/4 x 1-3/4

CLC-3593, 2-3/8 x 1-1/4

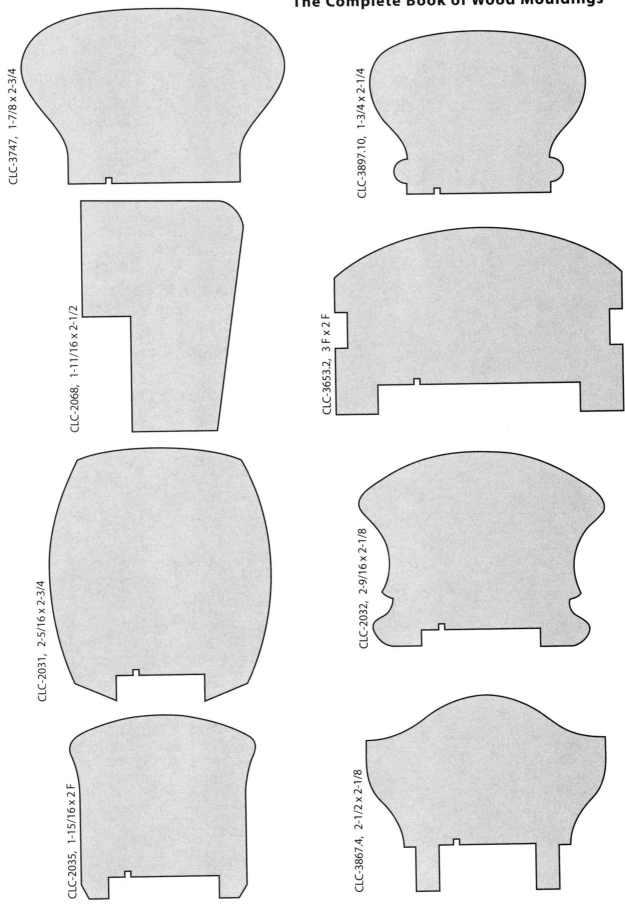

CLC-3747, 1-7/8 x 2-3/4

CLC-3897.10, 1-3/4 x 2-1/4

CLC-2068, 1-11/16 x 2-1/2

CLC-3653.2, 3 F x 2 F

CLC-2031, 2-5/16 x 2-3/4

CLC-2032, 2-9/16 x 2-1/8

CLC-2035, 1-15/16 x 2 F

CLC-3867.4, 2-1/2 x 2-1/8

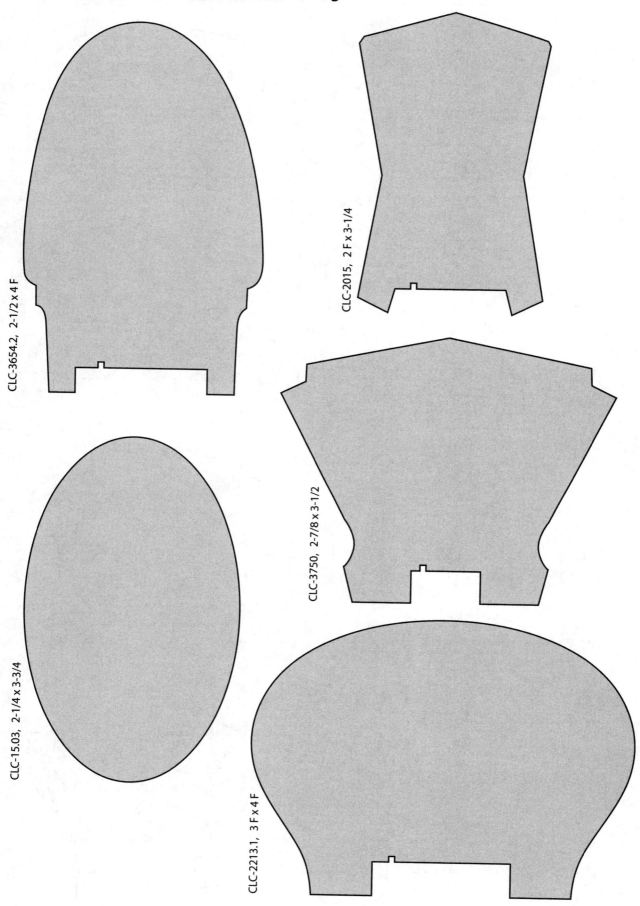

CLC-3654.2, 2-1/2 x 4 F

CLC-2015, 2 F x 3-1/4

CLC-3750, 2-7/8 x 3-1/2

CLC-15.03, 2-1/4 x 3-3/4

CLC-2213.1, 3 F x 4 F

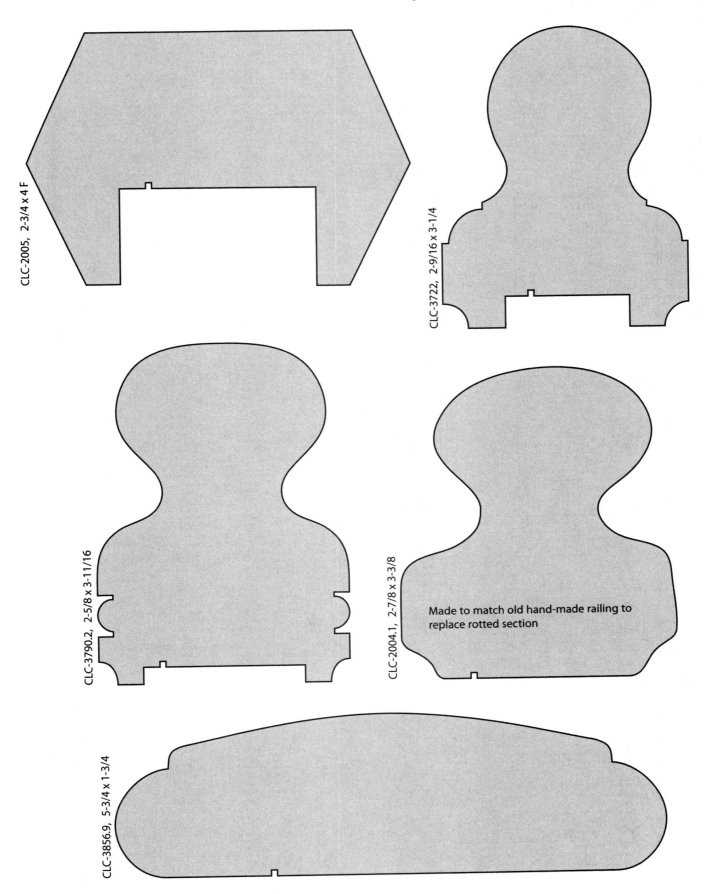

CLC-2005, 2-3/4 x 4 F

CLC-3722, 2-9/16 x 3-1/4

CLC-3790.2, 2-5/8 x 3-11/16

CLC-2004.1, 2-7/8 x 3-3/8

Made to match old hand-made railing to replace rotted section

CLC-3856.9, 5-3/4 x 1-3/4

CLC-3637.4, 1-1/2 x 5-1/2

CLC-3659, 1-9/16 x 5-3/8

CLC-3814, 1-9/16 x 5 F

CLC-2019, 2-15/16 x 3-5/8

CLC-2022, 3-1/16 x 3-5/8

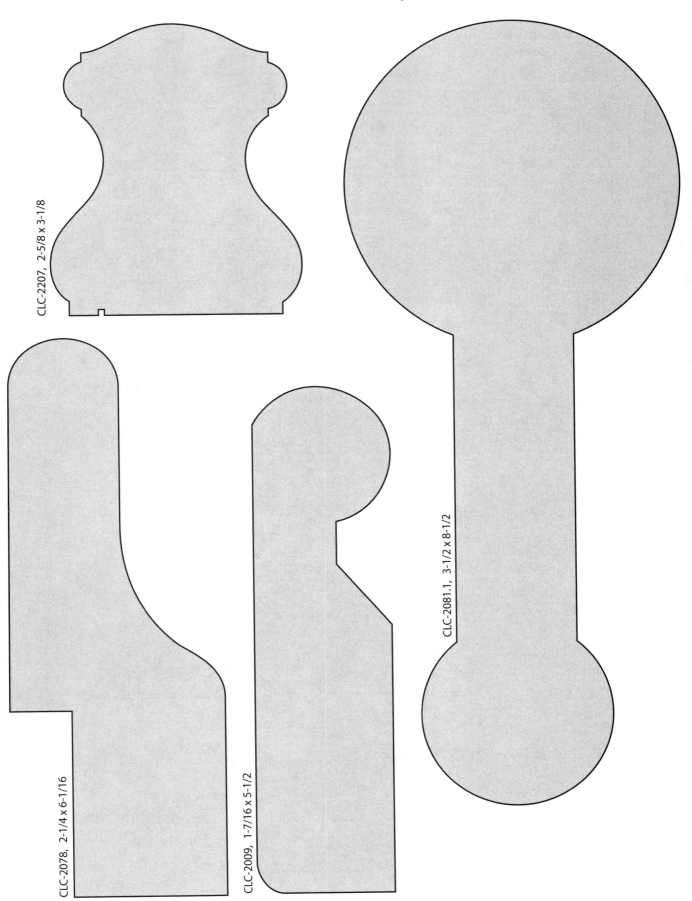

CLC-2207, 2-5/8 x 3-1/8

CLC-2078, 2-1/4 x 6-1/16

CLC-2009, 1-7/16 x 5-1/2

CLC-2081.1, 3-1/2 x 8-1/2

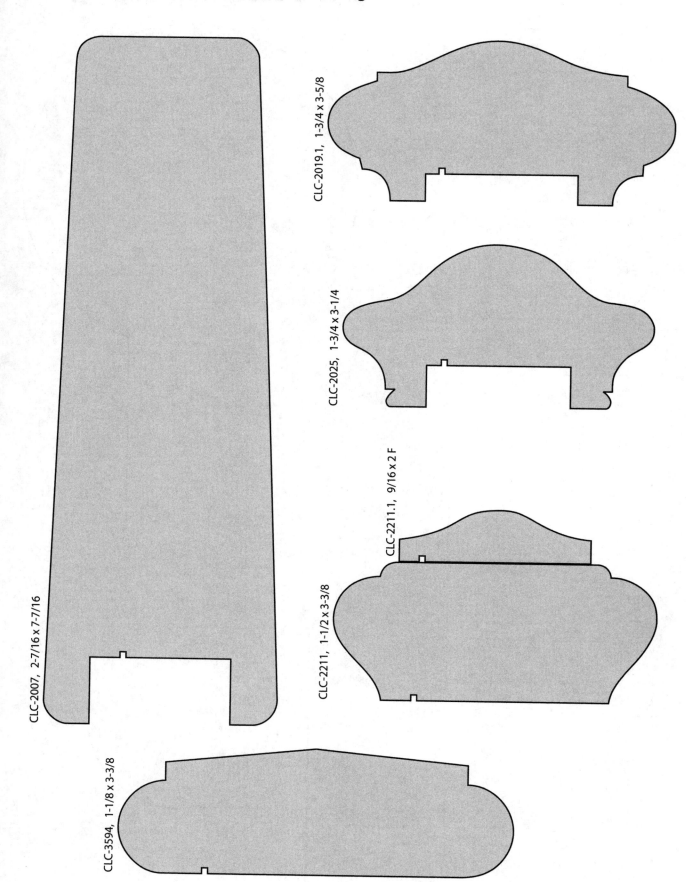

CLC-2019.1, 1-3/4 x 3-5/8

CLC-2025, 1-3/4 x 3-1/4

CLC-2211.1, 9/16 x 2 F

CLC-2211, 1-1/2 x 3-3/8

CLC-2007, 2-7/16 x 7-7/16

CLC-3594, 1-1/8 x 3-3/8

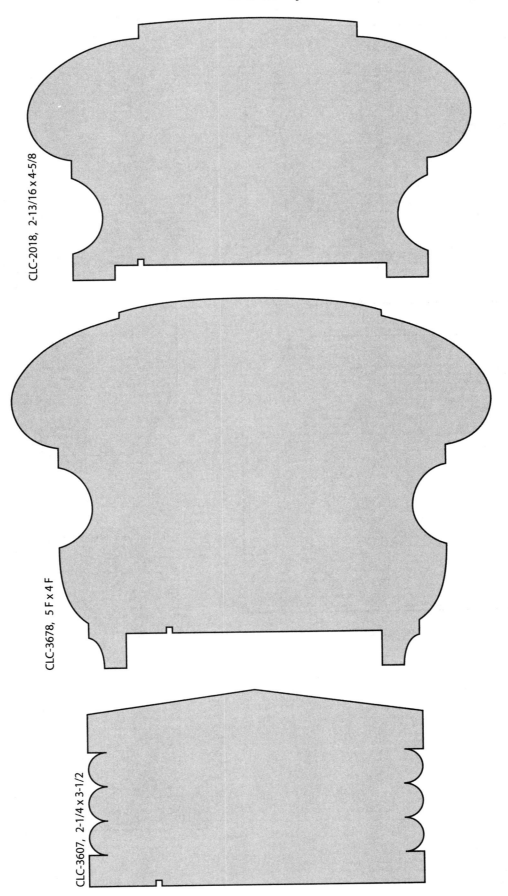

CLC-2018, 2-13/16 x 4-5/8

CLC-3678, 5 F x 4 F

CLC-3607, 2-1/4 x 3-1/2

CLC-2094.1, 3 F x 3 F   (Top Cap or Top Rail)

CLC-2094, 3 F x 3-1/2   (Bottom or Top Rail)

CLC-3682.4, 3-1/4 x 3-1/4

CLC-3682.3, 2-15/16 x 3-3/16

CLC-3870.8, 2 F x 7 F

CLC-3855.1, 3-3/8 x 3-7/16

CLC-3855, 3-3/8 x 4-5/8

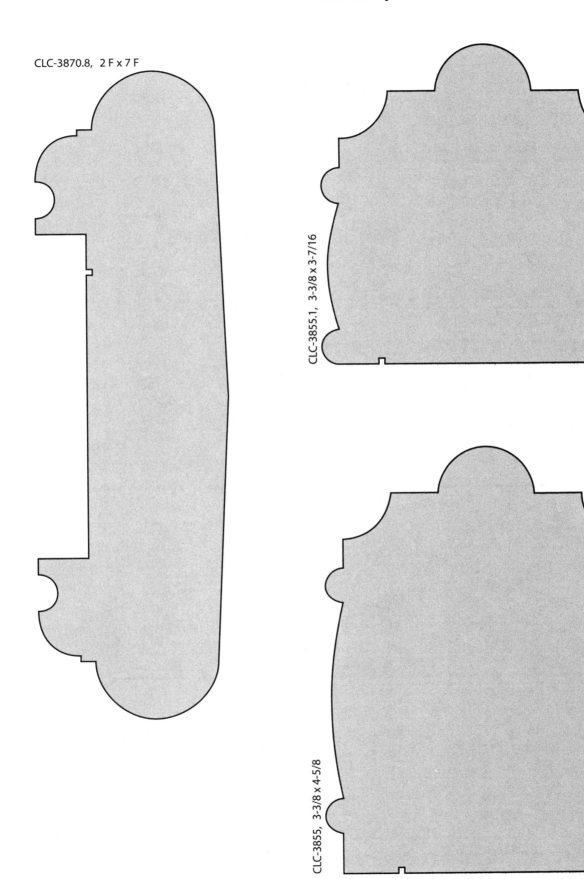

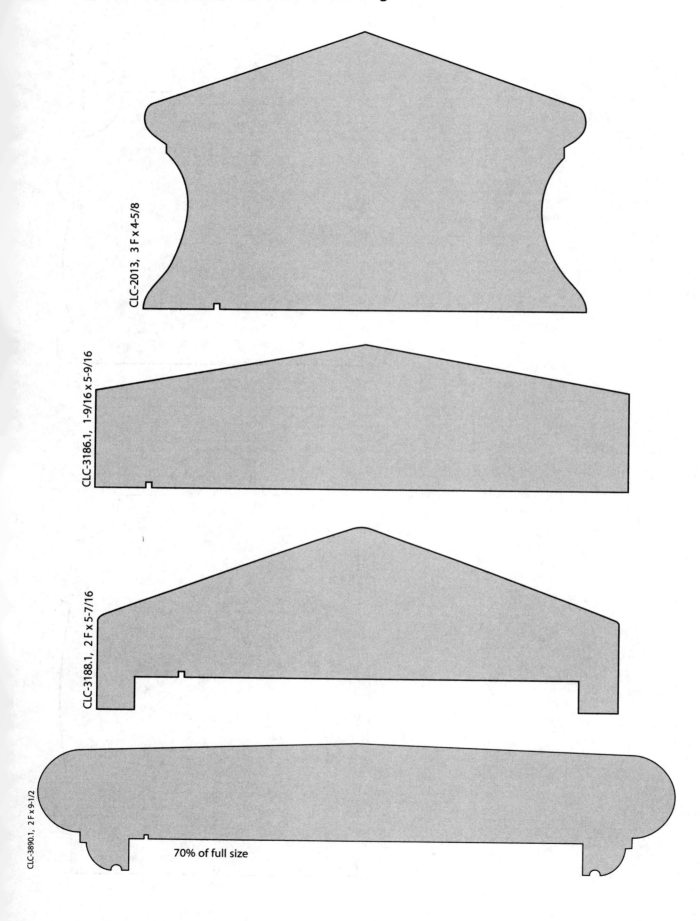

CLC-2013, 3 F x 4-5/8

CLC-3186.1, 1-9/16 x 5-9/16

CLC-3188.1, 2 F x 5-7/16

CLC-3890.1, 2 F x 9-1/2

70% of full size

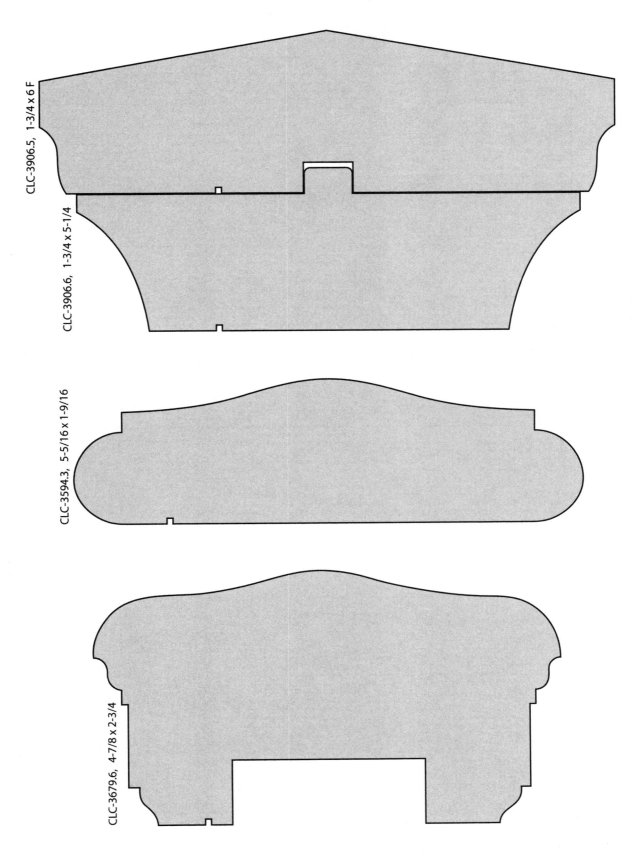

CLC-3906.5, 1-3/4 x 6 F

CLC-3906.6, 1-3/4 x 5-1/4

CLC-3594.3, 5-5/16 x 1-9/16

CLC-3679.6, 4-7/8 x 2-3/4

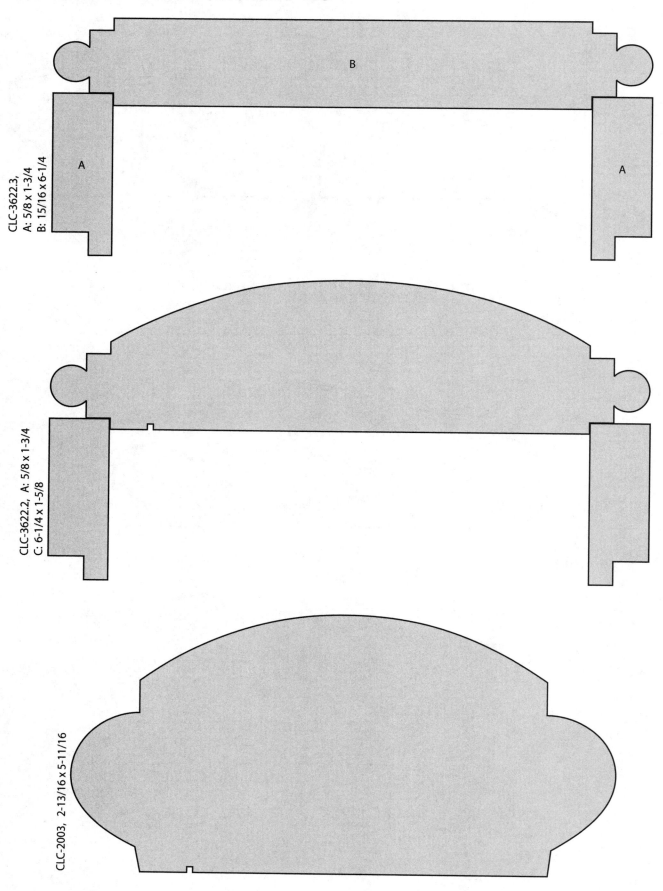

CLC-3622.3,
A: 5/8 x 1-3/4
B: 15/16 x 6-1/4

CLC-3622.2, A: 5/8 x 1-3/4
C: 6-1/4 x 1-5/8

CLC-2003, 2-13/16 x 5-11/16

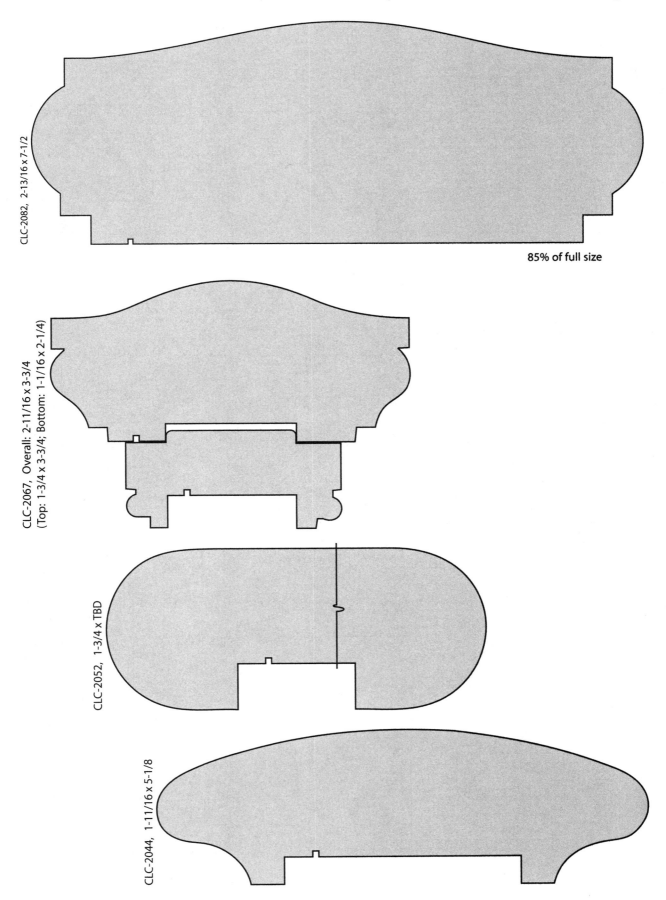

CLC-2082, 2-13/16 x 7-1/2

85% of full size

CLC-2067, Overall: 2-11/16 x 3-3/4
(Top: 1-3/4 x 3-3/4; Bottom: 1-1/16 x 2-1/4)

CLC-2052, 1-3/4 x TBD

CLC-2044, 1-11/16 x 5-1/8

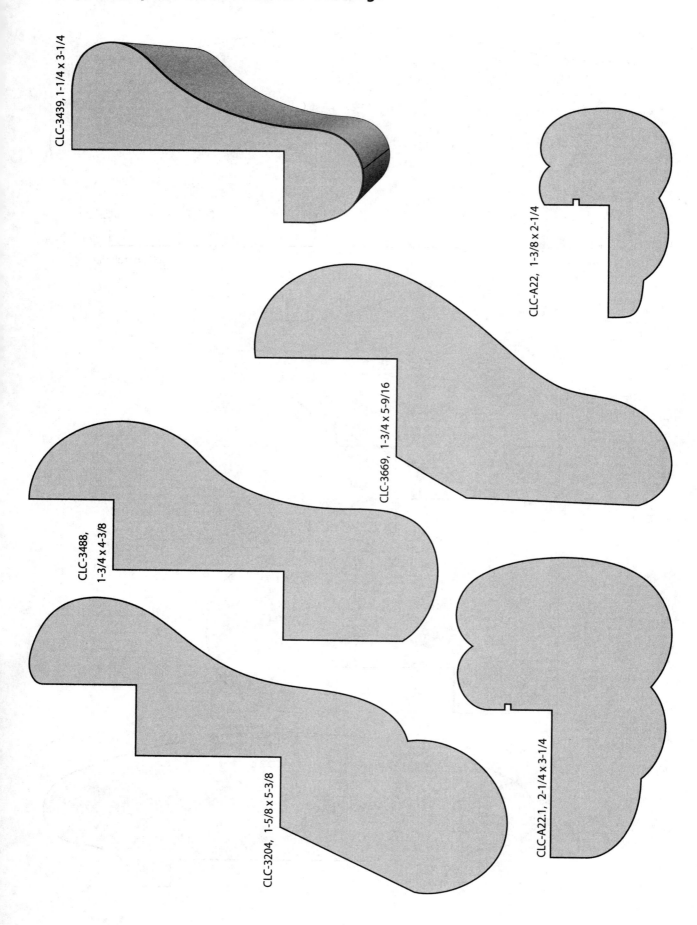

CLC-3439, 1-1/4 x 3-1/4

CLC-A22, 1-3/8 x 2-1/4

CLC-3669, 1-3/4 x 5-9/16

CLC-3488,
1-3/4 x 4-3/8

CLC-3204, 1-5/8 x 5-3/8

CLC-A22.1, 2-1/4 x 3-1/4

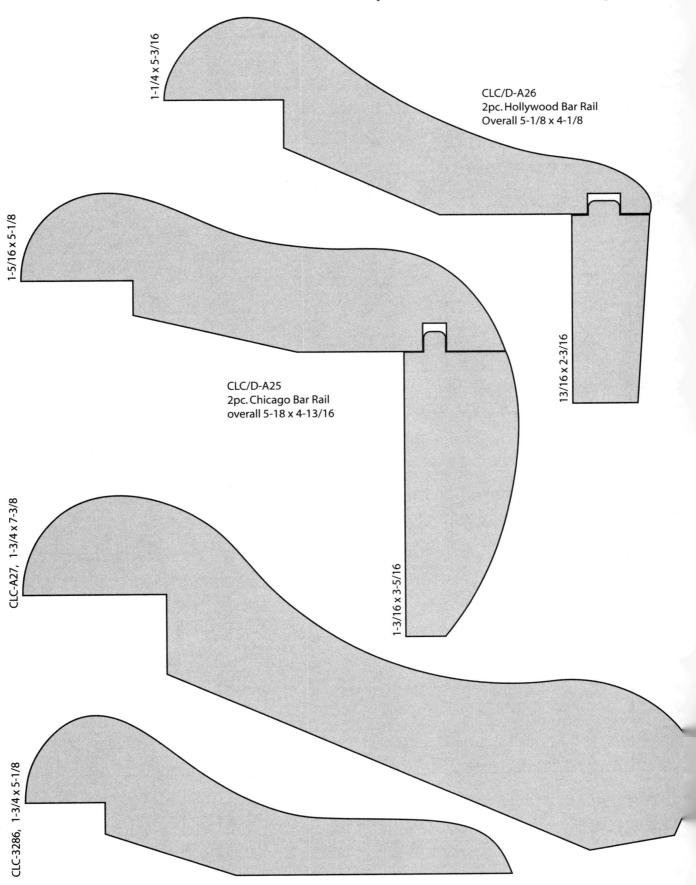

1-1/4 x 5-3/16

CLC/D-A26
2pc. Hollywood Bar Rail
Overall 5-1/8 x 4-1/8

13/16 x 2-3/16

1-5/16 x 5-1/8

CLC/D-A25
2pc. Chicago Bar Rail
overall 5-18 x 4-13/16

1-3/16 x 3-5/16

CLC-A27, 1-3/4 x 7-3/8

CLC-3286, 1-3/4 x 5-1/8

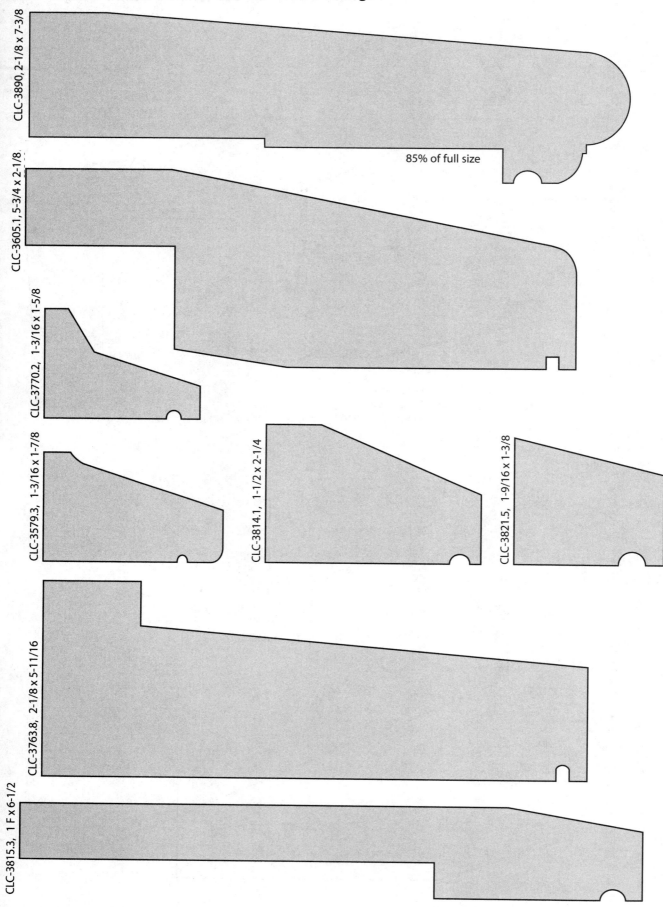

CLC-3890, 2-1/8 x 7-3/8

85% of full size

CLC-3605.1, 5-3/4 x 2-1/8

CLC-3770.2, 1-3/16 x 1-5/8

CLC-3579.3, 1-3/16 x 1-7/8

CLC-3814.1, 1-1/2 x 2-1/4

CLC-3821.5, 1-9/16 x 1-3/8

CLC-3763.8, 2-1/8 x 5-11/16

CLC-3815.3, 1 F x 6-1/2

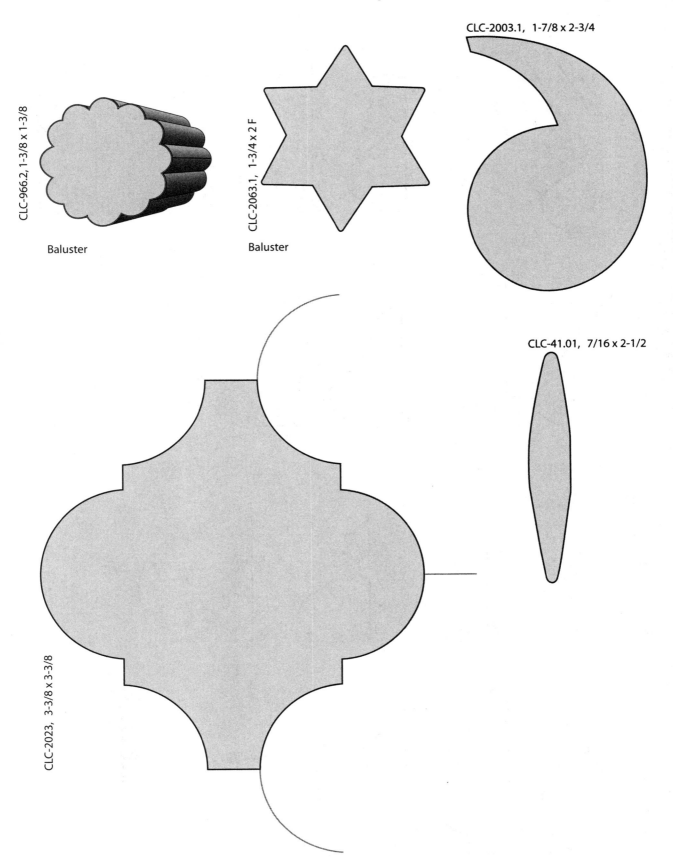

CLC-966.2, 1-3/8 x 1-3/8

Baluster

CLC-2063.1, 1-3/4 x 2 F

Baluster

CLC-2003.1, 1-7/8 x 2-3/4

CLC-41.01, 7/16 x 2-1/2

CLC-2023, 3-3/8 x 3-3/8

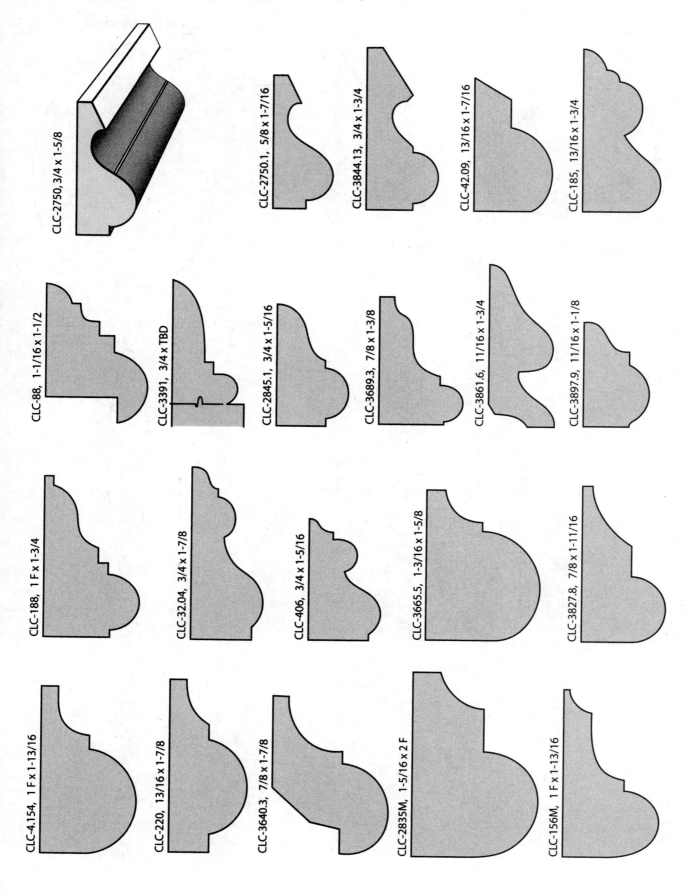

CLC-2750, 3/4 x 1-5/8

CLC-2750.1, 5/8 x 1-7/16

CLC-3844.13, 3/4 x 1-3/4

CLC-42.09, 13/16 x 1-7/16

CLC-185, 13/16 x 1-3/4

CLC-88, 1-1/16 x 1-1/2

CLC-3391, 3/4 x TBD

CLC-2845.1, 3/4 x 1-5/16

CLC-3689.3, 7/8 x 1-3/8

CLC-3861.6, 11/16 x 1-3/4

CLC-3897.9, 11/16 x 1-1/8

CLC-188, 1 F x 1-3/4

CLC-32.04, 3/4 x 1-7/8

CLC-406, 3/4 x 1-5/16

CLC-3665.5, 1-3/16 x 1-5/8

CLC-3827.8, 7/8 x 1-11/16

CLC-4.154, 1 F x 1-13/16

CLC-220, 13/16 x 1-7/8

CLC-3640.3, 7/8 x 1-7/8

CLC-2835M, 1-5/16 x 2 F

CLC-156M, 1 F x 1-13/16

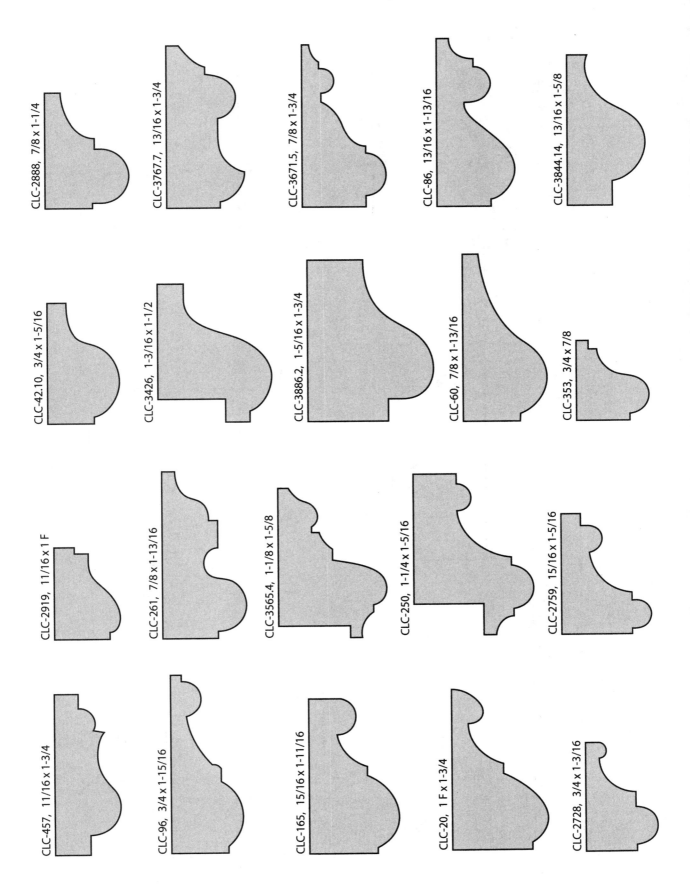

CLC-2888, 7/8 x 1-1/4

CLC-3767.7, 13/16 x 1-3/4

CLC-3671.5, 7/8 x 1-3/4

CLC-86, 13/16 x 1-13/16

CLC-3844.14, 13/16 x 1-5/8

CLC-42.10, 3/4 x 1-5/16

CLC-3426, 1-3/16 x 1-1/2

CLC-3886.2, 1-5/16 x 1-3/4

CLC-60, 7/8 x 1-13/16

CLC-353, 3/4 x 7/8

CLC-2919, 11/16 x 1 F

CLC-261, 7/8 x 1-13/16

CLC-3565.4, 1-1/8 x 1-5/8

CLC-250, 1-1/4 x 1-5/16

CLC-2759, 15/16 x 1-5/16

CLC-457, 11/16 x 1-3/4

CLC-96, 3/4 x 1-15/16

CLC-165, 15/16 x 1-11/16

CLC-20, 1 F x 1-3/4

CLC-2728, 3/4 x 1-3/16

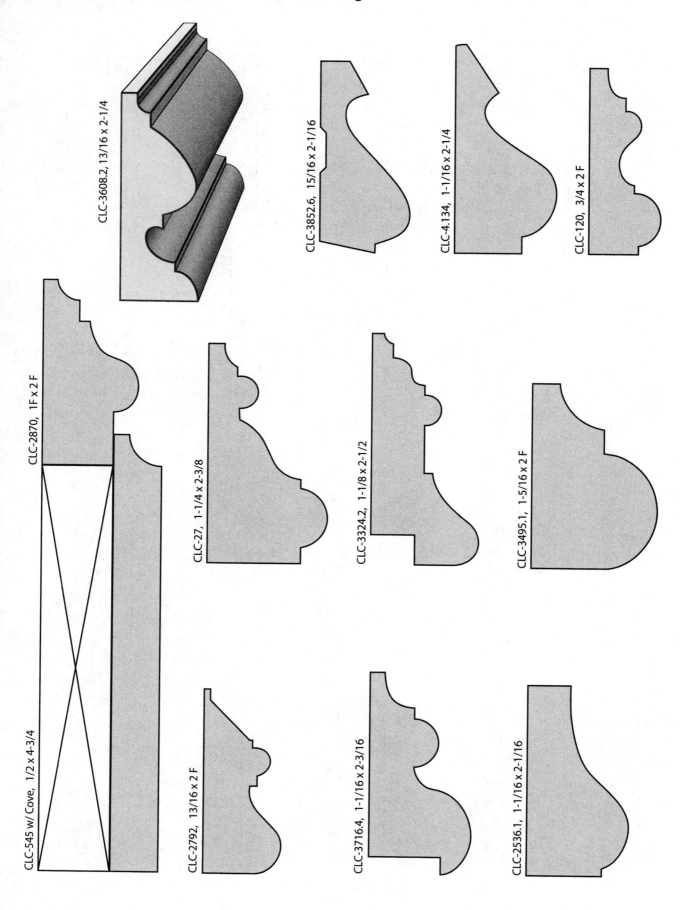

CLC-3608.2, 13/16 x 2-1/4

CLC-3852.6, 15/16 x 2-1/16

CLC-4.134, 1-1/16 x 2-1/4

CLC-120, 3/4 x 2 F

CLC-2870, 1 F x 2 F

CLC-27, 1-1/4 x 2-3/8

CLC-3324.2, 1-1/8 x 2-1/2

CLC-3495.1, 1-5/16 x 2 F

CLC-545 w/ Cove, 1/2 x 4-3/4

CLC-2792, 13/16 x 2 F

CLC-3716.4, 1-1/16 x 2-3/16

CLC-2536.1, 1-1/16 x 2-1/16

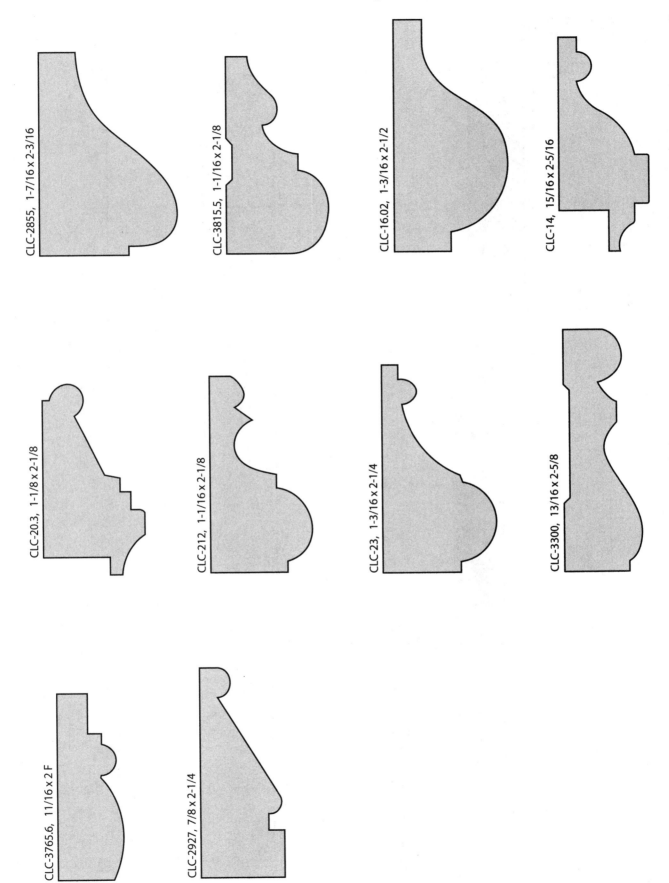

CLC-2855, 1-7/16 x 2-3/16

CLC-3815.5, 1-1/16 x 2-1/8

CLC-16.02, 1-3/16 x 2-1/2

CLC-14, 15/16 x 2-5/16

CLC-20.3, 1-1/8 x 2-1/8

CLC-212, 1-1/16 x 2-1/8

CLC-23, 1-3/16 x 2-1/4

CLC-3300, 13/16 x 2-5/8

CLC-3765.6, 11/16 x 2 F

CLC-2927, 7/8 x 2-1/4

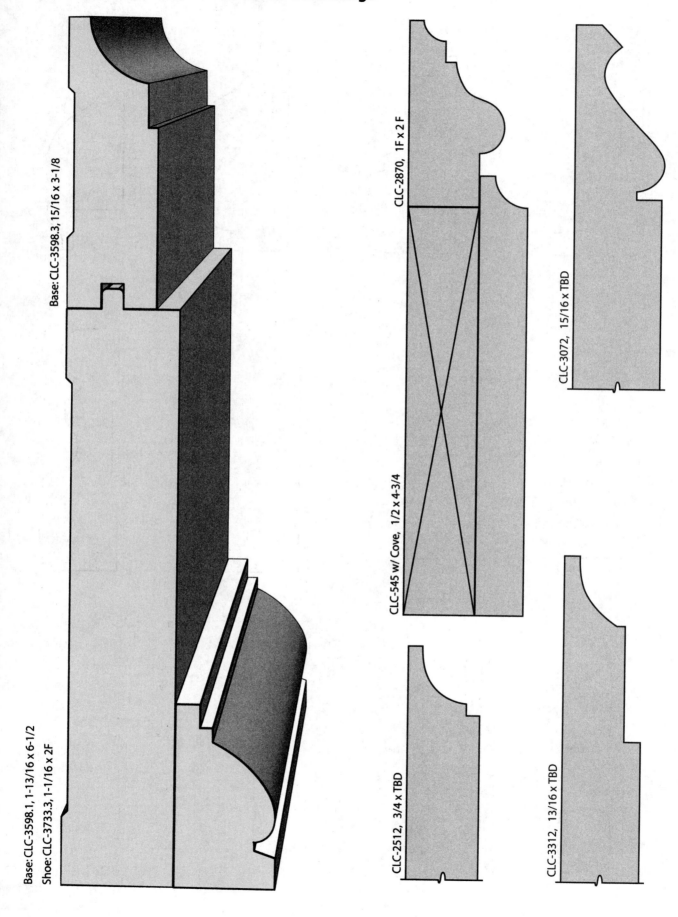

Base: CLC-3598.3, 15/16 x 3-1/8

Base: CLC-3598.1, 1-13/16 x 6-1/2

Shoe: CLC-3733.3, 1-1/16 x 2F

CLC-2870, 1F x 2 F

CLC-3072, 15/16 x TBD

CLC-545 w/ Cove, 1/2 x 4-3/4

CLC-2512, 3/4 x TBD

CLC-3312, 13/16 x TBD

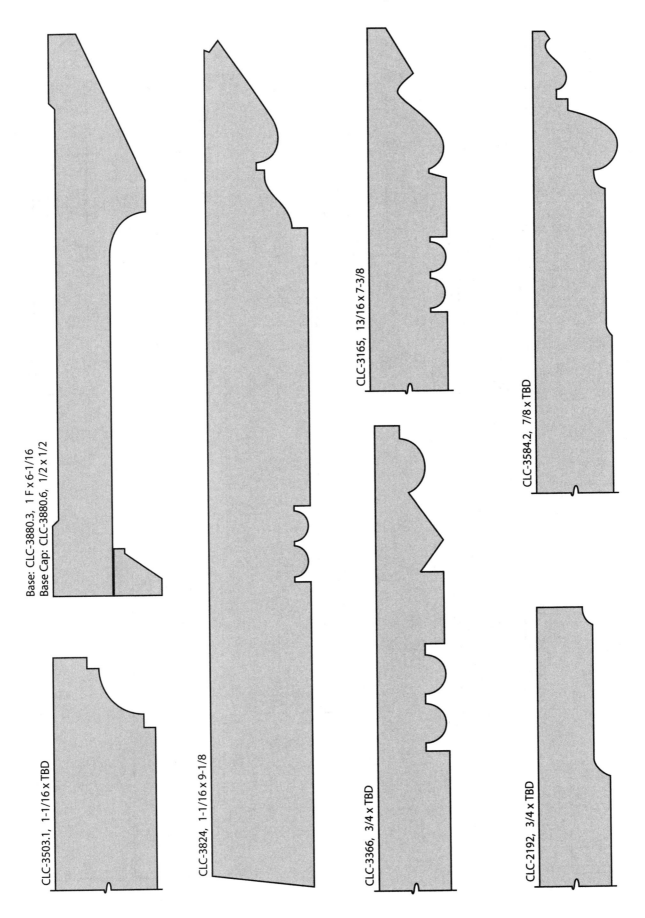

Base: CLC-3880.3, 1 F x 6-1/16
Base Cap: CLC-3880.6, 1/2 x 1/2

CLC-3165, 13/16 x 7-3/8

CLC-3584.2, 7/8 x TBD

CLC-3503.1, 1-1/16 x TBD

CLC-3824, 1-1/16 x 9-1/8

CLC-3366, 3/4 x TBD

CLC-2192, 3/4 x TBD

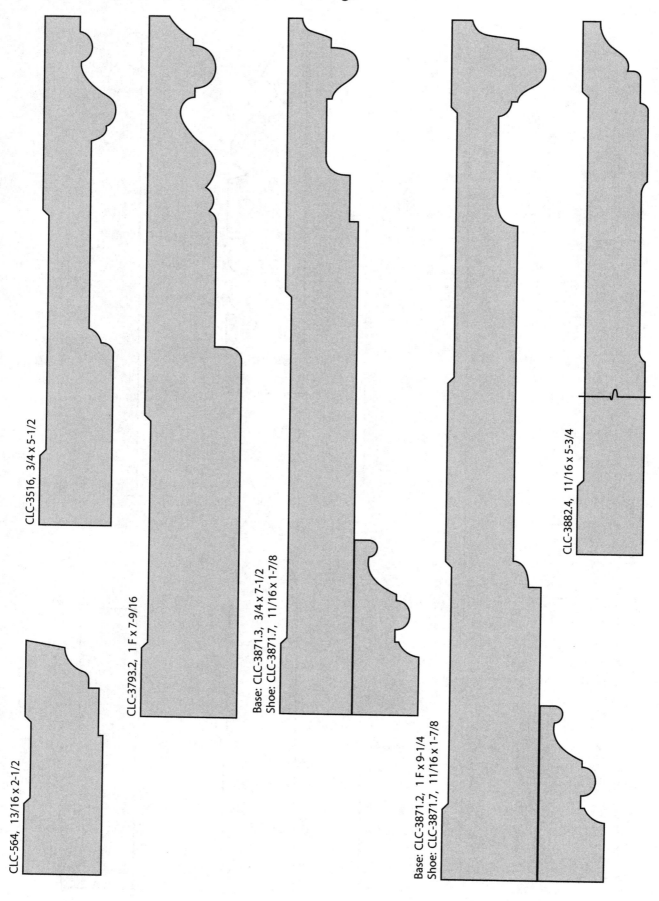

CLC-3516, 3/4 x 5-1/2

CLC-3793.2, 1 F x 7-9/16

Base: CLC-3871.3, 3/4 x 7-1/2
Shoe: CLC-3871.7, 11/16 x 1-7/8

Base: CLC-3871.2, 1 F x 9-1/4
Shoe: CLC-3871.7, 11/16 x 1-7/8

CLC-564, 13/16 x 2-1/2

CLC-3882.4, 11/16 x 5-3/4

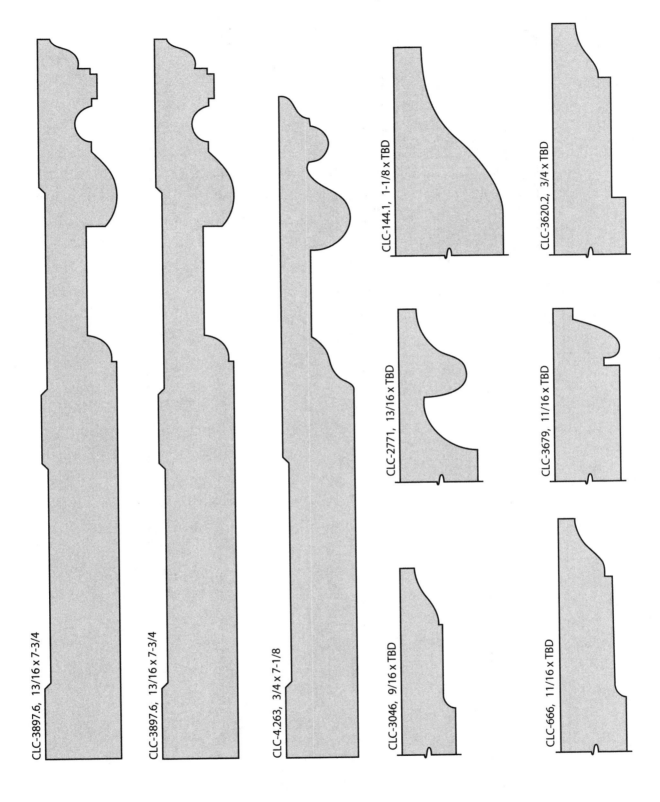

CLC-3897.6, 13/16 x 7-3/4

CLC-3897.6, 13/16 x 7-3/4

CLC-4.263, 3/4 x 7-1/8

CLC-144.1, 1-1/8 x TBD

CLC-2771, 13/16 x TBD

CLC-3046, 9/16 x TBD

CLC-3620.2, 3/4 x TBD

CLC-3679, 11/16 x TBD

CLC-666, 11/16 x TBD

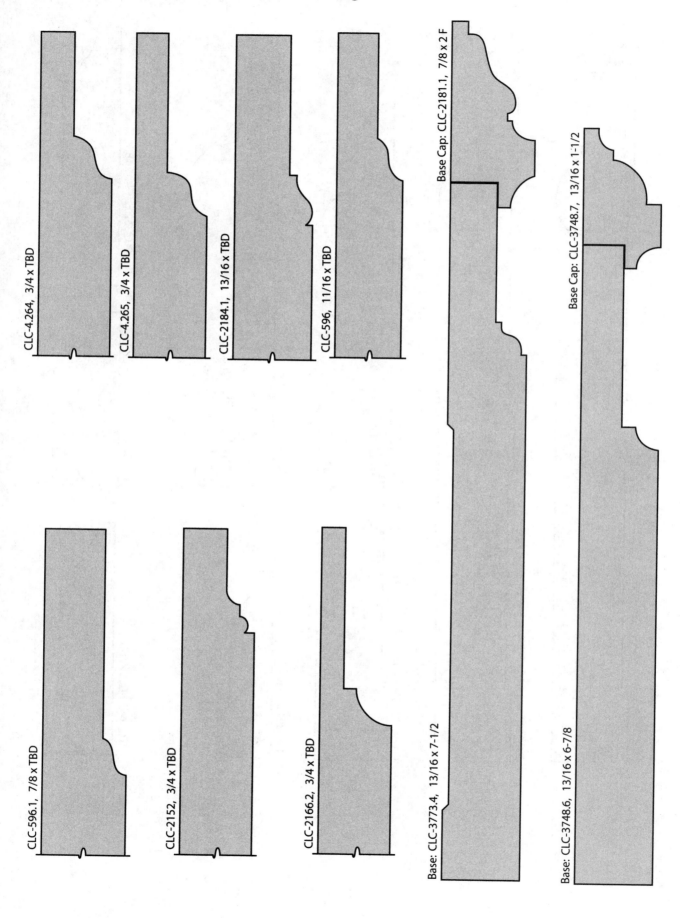

CLC-4.264, 3/4 x TBD

CLC-4.265, 3/4 x TBD

CLC-2184.1, 13/16 x TBD

CLC-596, 11/16 x TBD

Base Cap: CLC-2181.1, 7/8 x 2 F

Base Cap: CLC-3748.7, 13/16 x 1-1/2

CLC-596.1, 7/8 x TBD

CLC-2152, 3/4 x TBD

CLC-2166.2, 3/4 x TBD

Base: CLC-3773.4, 13/16 x 7-1/2

Base: CLC-3748.6, 13/16 x 6-7/8

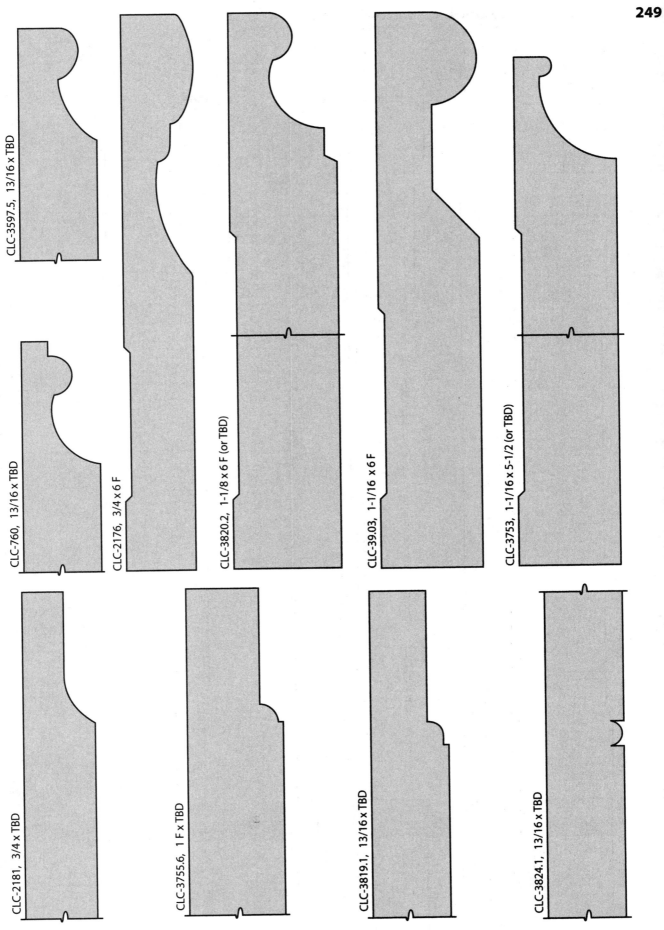

249

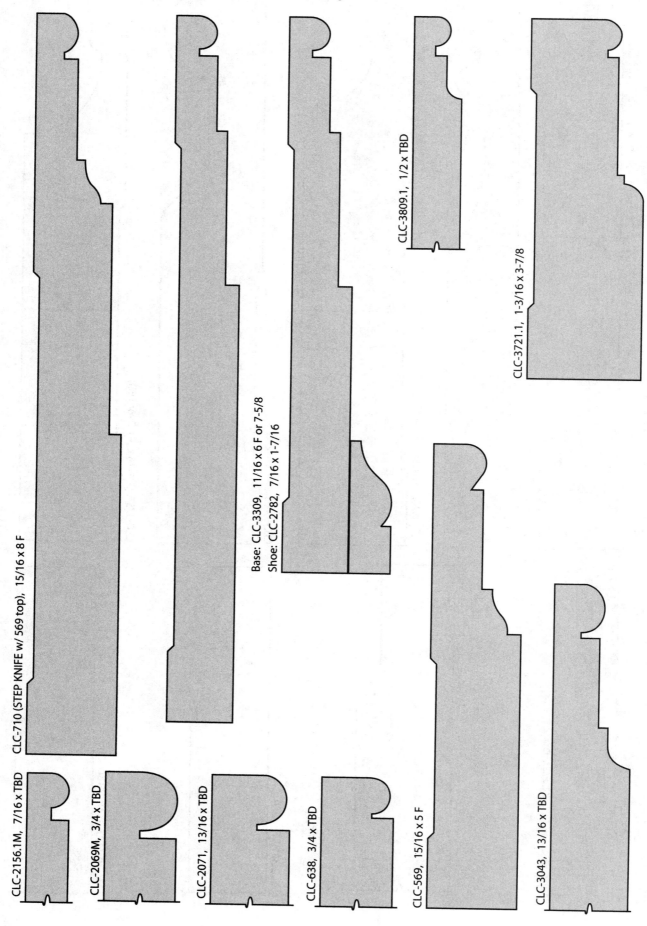

CLC-710 (STEP KNIFE w/ 569 top), 15/16 x 8 F

Base: CLC-3309, 11/16 x 6 F or 7-5/8
Shoe: CLC-2782, 7/16 x 1-7/16

CLC-3809.1, 1/2 x TBD

CLC-3721.1, 1-3/16 x 3-7/8

CLC-2156.1M, 7/16 x TBD

CLC-2069M, 3/4 x TBD

CLC-2071, 13/16 x TBD

CLC-638, 3/4 x TBD

CLC-569, 15/16 x 5 F

CLC-3043, 13/16 x TBD

Base: CLC-3765.5, 3/4 x 7-1/2
Shoe: CLC-3765.8, 3/8 x 1-1/8

CLC-3764.5, 1-1/16 x 9-3/4

CLC-2203, 3/4 x TBD

CLC-287, 13/16 x TBD

CLC-3600.2, 7/8 x TBD

CLC-50.11, 3/4 x TBD

CLC-3617.8, 13/16 x TBD

CLC-3595.5, 11/16 x TBD

CLC-3508, 3/4 x TBD

CLC-3429, 3/4 x TBD

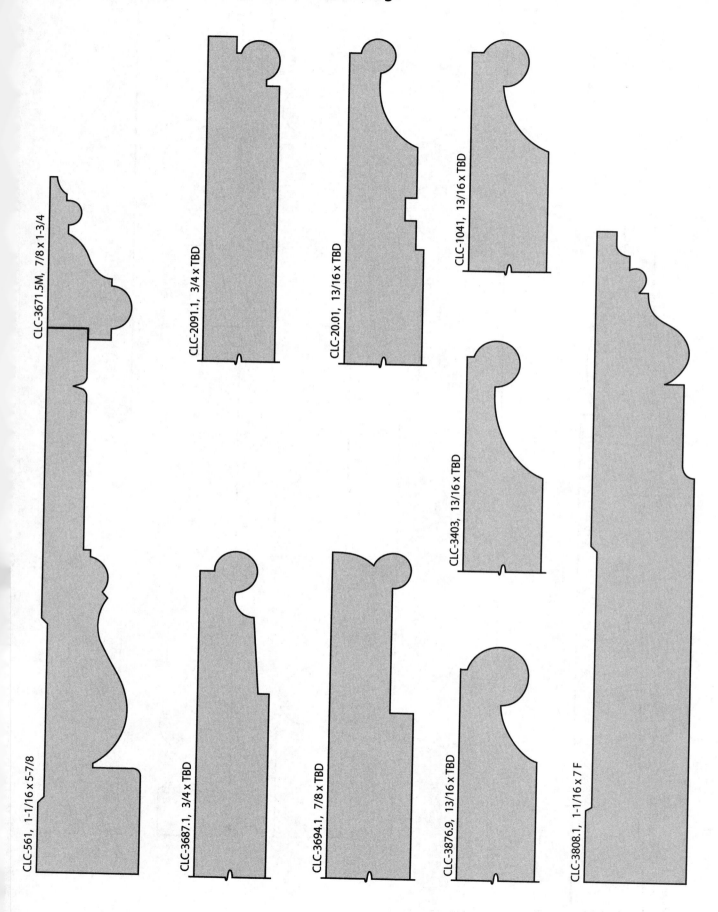

CLC-3671.5M, 7/8 x 1-3/4

CLC-2091.1, 3/4 x TBD

CLC-20.01, 13/16 x TBD

CLC-1041, 13/16 x TBD

CLC-561, 1-1/16 x 5-7/8

CLC-3687.1, 3/4 x TBD

CLC-3694.1, 7/8 x TBD

CLC-3403, 13/16 x TBD

CLC-3876.9, 13/16 x TBD

CLC-3808.1, 1-1/16 x 7 F

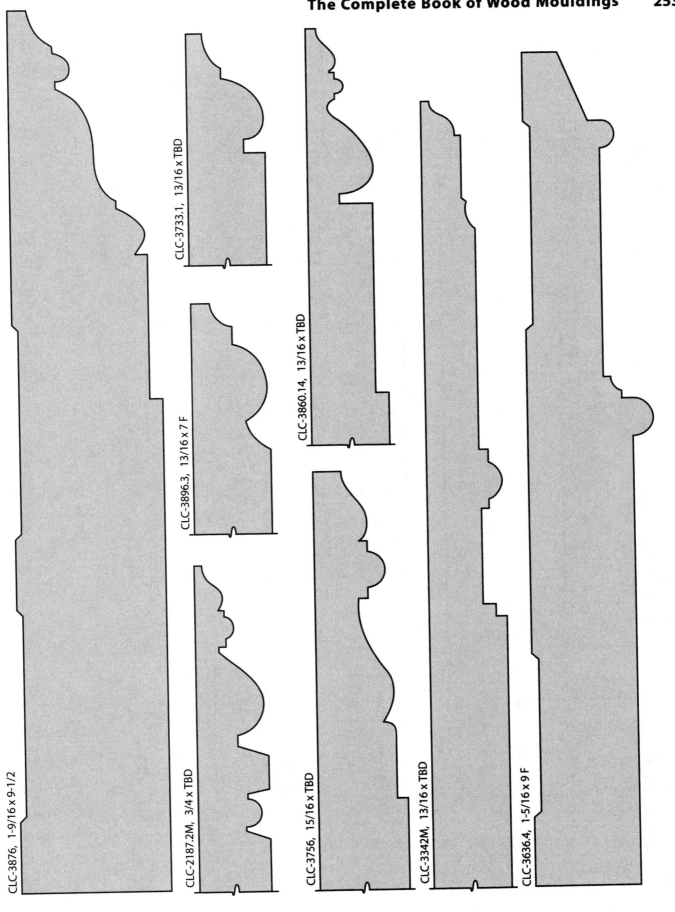

CLC-3876, 1-9/16 x 9-1/2

CLC-3733.1, 13/16 x TBD

CLC-3896.3, 13/16 x 7 F

CLC-2187.2M, 3/4 x TBD

CLC-3860.14, 13/16 x TBD

CLC-3756, 15/16 x TBD

CLC-3342M, 13/16 x TBD

CLC-3636.4, 1-5/16 x 9 F

CLC-3324.2, 1-1/8 x 2-1/2

CLC-3324.1, 3/4 x TBD

Back Band: CLC-3324, 1-1/4 x TBD
Shoe: CLC-477.1, 3/4 x 1 F

CLC-2155M, 3/4 x TBD

CLC-3693.1, 1-1/16 x 6 F

CLC-3358, 7/8 x 6 F

CLC-3734, 3/4 x 6 F (or TBD)

CLC-3876.10, 13/16 x 1-3/4

CLC-3636.2, 13/16 x TBD

CLC-373, 13/16 x TBD

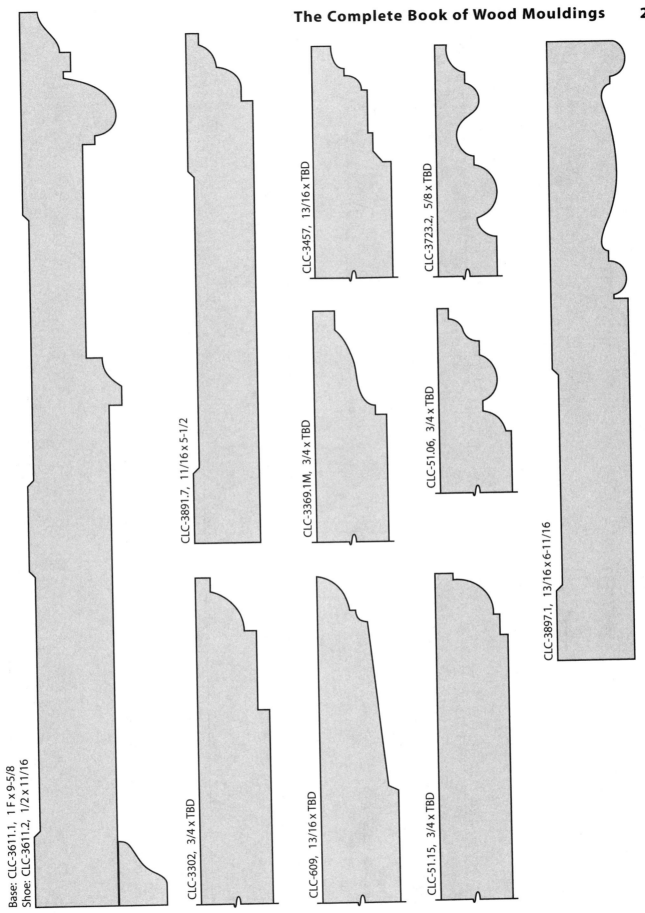

Base: CLC-3611.1, 1 F x 9-5/8
Shoe: CLC-3611.2, 1/2 x 11/16

CLC-3891.7, 11/16 x 5-1/2

CLC-3302, 3/4 x TBD

CLC-3457, 13/16 x TBD

CLC-3369.1M, 3/4 x TBD

CLC-609, 13/16 x TBD

CLC-3723.2, 5/8 x TBD

CLC-51.06, 3/4 x TBD

CLC-51.15, 3/4 x TBD

CLC-3897.1, 13/16 x 6-11/16

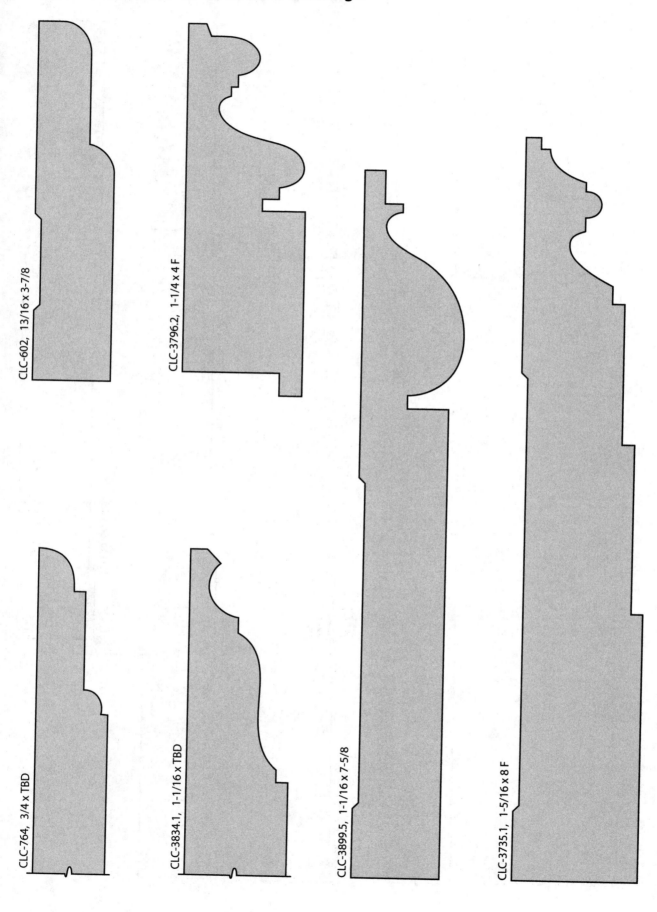

CLC-602, 13/16 x 3-7/8

CLC-3796.2, 1-1/4 x 4 F

CLC-764, 3/4 x TBD

CLC-3834.1, 1-1/16 x TBD

CLC-3899.5, 1-1/16 x 7-5/8

CLC-3735.1, 1-5/16 x 8 F

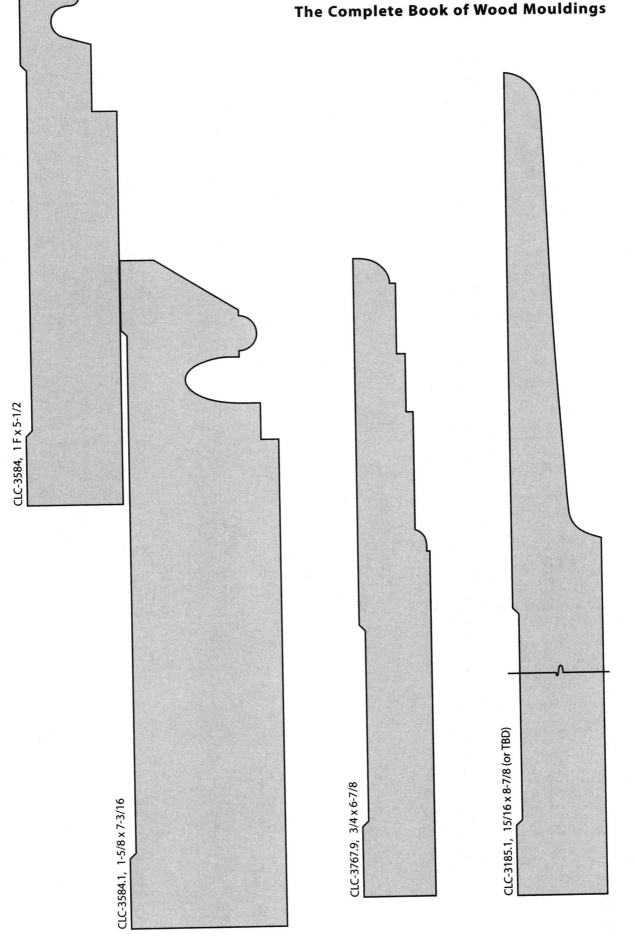

CLC-3584, 1 F x 5-1/2

CLC-3584.1, 1-5/8 x 7-3/16

CLC-3767.9, 3/4 x 6-7/8

CLC-3185.1, 15/16 x 8-7/8 (or TBD)

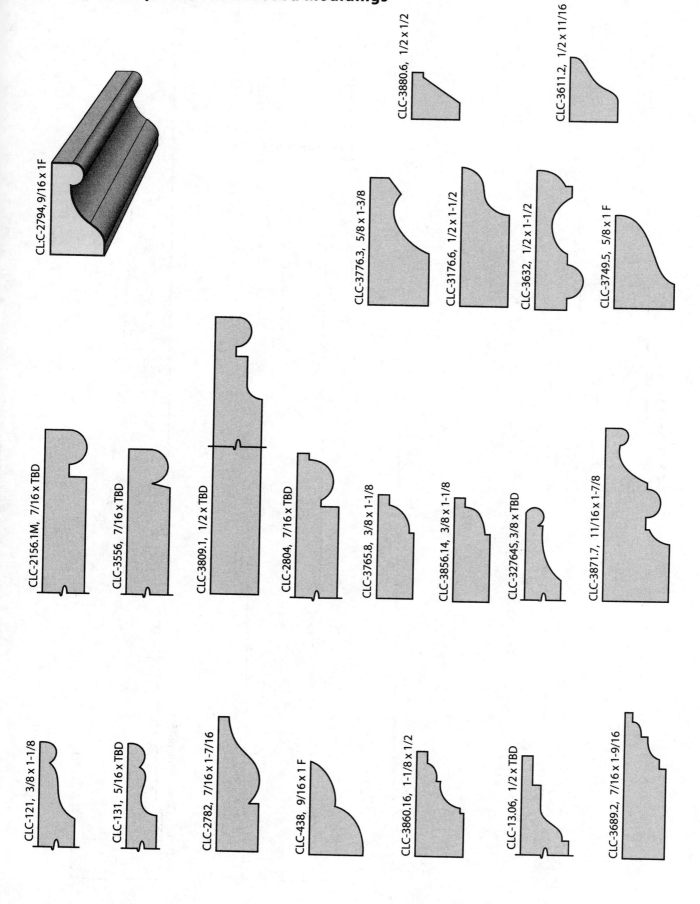

CLC-3880.6, 1/2 x 1/2

CLC-3611.2, 1/2 x 11/16

CL:C-2794, 9/16 x 1F

CLC-3776.3, 5/8 x 1-3/8

CLC-3176.6, 1/2 x 1-1/2

CLC-3632, 1/2 x 1-1/2

CLC-3749.5, 5/8 x 1 F

CLC-2156.1M, 7/16 x TBD

CLC-3556, 7/16 x TBD

CLC-3809.1, 1/2 x TBD

CLC-2804, 7/16 x TBD

CLC-3765.8, 3/8 x 1-1/8

CLC-3856.14, 3/8 x 1-1/8

CLC-327645, 3/8 x TBD

CLC-3871.7, 11/16 x 1-7/8

CLC-121, 3/8 x 1-1/8

CLC-131, 5/16 x TBD

CLC-2782, 7/16 x 1-7/16

CLC-438, 9/16 x 1F

CLC-3860.16, 1-1/8 x 1/2

CLC-13.06, 1/2 x TBD

CLC-3689.2, 7/16 x 1-9/16